This Will Happen Again and It Did

A Comparison of FBI Investigations of JFK Assassination & Trump Coup

GW00777642

By

Richard V. Roth

Dedication

This book is dedicated to the Special Agents of the Federal Bureau of Investigation who

work hard and perform their duties regardless of politics.

Acknowledgment

I would like to acknowledge former FBI Special Agent Zach Shelton for his contribution to the writing of this book. Zach had a highly successful career in the FBI, particularly with his assignment in the Chicago Field office, where he worked on high-level Organized Crime cases.

After retiring from the Bureau, Zach began a private investigation business. Zach also began an interest in the Assassination of President John F. Kennedy. He worked for several years on the case and interviewed several major "players," such as FBI Special Agent James Sibert and James Files.

Zach and I have worked on several cases together, including the investigation into child abuse by members of the Catholic Church.

I would also like to acknowledge Michael Corvin, the Amazon team leader who was instrumental in publishing this book. Michael was very enthusiastic about being assigned to the team and advised that he has a great interest in law enforcement. His knowledge helped him to quickly grasp the multiple details of the subject matter.

About The Author

Richard V. "Dick" Roth is a former Special Agent of the Federal Bureau of Investigation.

He began his career in the Buffalo, New York, Field Office in 1980. He was transferred to Hartford Ct. Resident Agency in the New Haven, Ct. Field Office in 1982. He was then transferred to the New York, New York Field Office in 1983. Mr. Roth was assigned to criminal cases in each Field Office. Mr. Roth received several letters of commendation from the Director.

Mr. Roth began his law enforcement career in 1973 as a Revenue Agent of the Internal Revenue Service. He then worked as an Investigative Accountant for the New York State Organized Crime Task Force from 1977 to 1980. Mr. Roth graduated from the State University of New York at Albany in 1973 with a B.S. in Public Accounting. He is a retired Certified Public Accountant (retired status.) Mr. Roth also graduated from Fordham University with a master's degree in Business Administration.

After his career with the F.B.I, Mr. Roth operated a Forensic Accounting business in 1980. His assignments included monitoring unions allegedly controlled by Organized Crime figures, monitoring construction sites for compliance with contracts, bank frauds and embezzlements, monitoring banks for compliance with anti-money laundering statutes, investment frauds, and background checks.

Mr. Roth has a son who is an officer in the United States Navy assigned to Nuclear Powered Submarines.

Table of Contents

Prologue

Emily Compagno blasts Robert Mueller following Clinton bombshell: His team should be 'extremely embarrassed.'

Former Clinton campaign manager Robby Mook testified Friday that Hillary Clinton approved of leaking Trump-Russia allegations to the media.

Emily Compagno: Robert Mueller should be embarrassed

'Outnumbered' co-host Emily Compagno argues it is 'absolutely unacceptable' that Robert Mueller's report didn't include that Hillary Clinton approved the leak of Trump-Russia allegations to the media.

Emily Compagno sounded off on special counsel Robert Mueller following the bombshell testimony from former Clinton campaign manager Robby Mook. The "Outnumbered" co-host said Monday it is "absolutely unacceptable" that Mueller's report didn't mention Hillary Clinton approved of leaking the Trump-Russia allegations to the media, given the extensive resources for Mueller's investigation.

EMILY COMPAGNO: *They used 19 special prosecutors and more than 40 FBI agents. We footed that entire bill. They produced three separate reports that basically said, 'well, we can't prove a connection between Trump and Russia, but we can't disprove it.' All it would have taken is five minutes spent in a room with this guy who could have said, 'yes, actually, it was greenlit by Hillary Clinton. Actually, yes. There was not one modicum of truth to this.'*

And instead, this really important person is the one who approved of and spearheaded it being leaked to the media. And listen, if I was one of the attorneys on Mueller's team, I would not only be extremely embarrassed right now, but I would have a lot of questions. Because either they did know, and it didn't make it into the report, or they didn't know. And either of those answers is absolutely unacceptable.

SPECIAL AGENT ROTH AND EMILY COMPAGNO FOX NEWS - Great minds think alike.

The entire theme of this book is how easily and quickly the Clinton Collusion scam could have been stopped. All it took was one interview.

SPECIAL AGENT AND ROTH:

Let's jump right into the "meat" of this book

Section 1

Part One

Predicate Hillary Trump Russian Collusion Case

I'm convinced of it': Hillary Clinton believes Trump's campaign team colluded with Russia to influence the election

Secretary Clinton contested the election of Donald Trump as President on the grounds that the Government of Russia had interfered with the 2016 United States Presidential Election. Secretary Clinton announced unequivocally that "she was certain that Russia had meddled in the Presidential Election."

'There certainly was communication, and there certainly was an understanding of some sort,' the Democratic presidential candidate said in the interview. "Because there's no doubt in my mind that Putin wanted me to lose and wanted Trump to win, and there's no doubt in my mind that there is a tangle of financial relationships between Trump and his operation with Russian money."

Clinton said she believed Trump's team communicated with the Russian government and had 'an understanding of some sort.'

Secretary Clinton was also under investigation by the Department of Justice and the Federal Bureau of Investigation for violations of security requirements that her official State Department emails be properly protected

This book is based on the findings of James Comey, Director of the Federal Bureau of Investigation, and Secretary Clinton's announcements which were provided to the United States citizens by the media, both television and newspaper, and the subsequent publishing of the information by almost all the media outlets. Numerous Democratic members of Congress also made statements identical to Secretary Clinton.

Hillary Clinton says 2020 candidates need to watch for Russian interference in the election.

By Amanda Golden

Published 9:24 pm EDT, Sat, April 27, 2019

Secretary Clinton continuing to repeat her statement regarding Russian interference as late as April 27, 2019.

(CNN) —

Hillary Clinton reiterated warnings for Democratic candidates ahead of 2020 to be wary of interference in the election, following up on an editorial she wrote in the Washington Post earlier this week.

"We know that there is going to be continuing interference in line with what the Mueller report concluded about sweeping and systemic interference," Clinton said Saturday evening during "An Evening with The Clintons" event in Washington, DC. "We know it happened, and what we are hearing is that it is going to happen again."

Clinton, the 2016 Democratic nominee for president, advised the 2020 candidates to keep their eyes focused.

"You could work your heart out, you could get the nomination, and there would still be factors that would undermine a legitimate election," she said.

Clinton also commented on how Russian interference came in many forms, often through social media, but included deep fakes, bots, and trolls.

"I don't know how we combat that," she said, noting that people didn't know how effective it was in 2016.

SPECIAL AGENT ROTH- IT SHOULD BE NOTED THAT THE ALLEGATIONS MADE BY CLINTON OCCURRED DURING THE OBAMA ADMINISTRATION. WHY DID NOT OBAMA AND THE FBI STOP RUSSIAN INTERFERENCE?

CLINTON RUSSIA TRUMP COLLUSION

- **Hillary Clinton says she is convinced Donald Trump's campaign team colluded with Russia to meddle in the 2016 election**

- **She believes Trump's team communicated with Russia and that they had some sort of understanding**

- **Clinton said there was no doubt that Putin wanted her to lose the election**

- **She spoke out ahead of the Tuesday release of her new memoir What Happened**

By Emily Crane for Dailymail.com

PUBLISHED: 00:29 EST, September 12, 2017, | **UPDATED:** 04:52 EST, September 12, 2017

Hillary Clinton says she is 'convinced' **Donald Trump's** campaign team colluded with **Russia** to meddle in the 2016 election.

In an interview with **USA Today**, Clinton said she believes Trump's aides communicated with the Russian government and had 'an understanding of some sort.'

'I'm convinced of it,' Clinton said when asked directly if she thought there was collusion by Trump associates.

Hillary Clinton said she is 'convinced' Donald Trump's campaign team colluded with Russia to meddle in the 2016 election

'I happen to believe in the rule of law and believe in evidence, so I'm not going to go off and make all kinds of outrageous claims. But if you look at what we've learned since (the election), it's pretty troubling.'

SPECIAL AGENT ROTH is CONVINCED THAT THERE WAS NO COLLUSION BETWEEN

TRUMP AND RUSSIA... SO IS ROBERT MUELLER AND THE SENATE INTELLIGENCE COMMITTEE.

IN FACT, MANY PEOPLE ARE CONVINCED THAT HILLARY CLINTON MADE UP THE ENTIRE TRUMP-RUSSIA COLLUSION STORY.

ROBBY MOOK, CLINTON CAMPAIGN Manager

TESTIFIED AT SUSSMAN TRIAL QUOTE, the defense called Clinton's 2106 campaign manager, Robby Mook, who promptly and surprisingly testified that Hillary Clinton approved the strategy to take to the media the same false information about a Trump/Russia "hotline" that Sussmann wanted the FBI to investigate.

She has been opening up about her campaign trail experiences and her loss to Trump ahead of the release of her new memoir What Happened.

'There certainly was communication, and there certainly was an understanding of some sort,' the Democratic presidential candidate said in the interview.

'Because there's no doubt in my mind that Putin wanted me to lose and wanted Trump to win. And there's no doubt in my mind that there is a tangle of financial relationships between Trump and his operation with Russian money.

Clinton said she believed Trump's team communicated with the Russian government and had 'an understanding of some sort.' Clinton said there was no doubt that Vladimir Putin wanted her to lose the election

'And there's no doubt in my mind that the Trump campaign and other associates have worked really hard to hide their connections with Russians.'

In the interview, Clinton said she accepted the shortcomings of her campaign but doubled down on blaming some people for her loss, including then-FBI director James Comey and Russian President Vladimir Putin.

Clinton Purchases House For Secret Service

Hillary Clinton reveals that she bought a $1.6million property next door to her home just three months before the election for Secret Service to live in after she won the presidency

Hillary Clinton revealed in her first sit-down interview since her election loss last November that she purchased a home for Secret Service agents

The Democratic hopeful paid $1.6million for the property next door to the home she shared with her husband Bill in August 2016

Three months later, she lost the election to President Donald Trump

She told Jane Pauley that she was still happy with her purchase and wrote her new memoir 'What Happened' at the dining room table in the home

The Democratic hopeful told Jane Pauley during an appearance on CBS Sunday Morning over the weekend that she plunked down the money to purchase her neighbor's home back in August 2016 to make the transition easier come that November.

'I know something about what it takes to move a president, and I thought I was going to win,' explained Hillary.

Clinton's Reaction To Comey

She writes in her memoir that Comey 'shivved' her by releasing a trove of emails just 11 days before the election.

'My first instinct was that my campaign should hit back hard and explain to the public that Comey had badly overstepped his bounds,' she said.

'My team raised concerns with that kind of confrontational approach. In the end, we decided it would be better to just let it go and try to move on. Looking back, that was a mistake.'

She lost just three months after she bought the property.

Logistics Of Mrs. Clinton's Charges

SPECIAL AGENT ROTH- A conspiracy of this magnitude would take a minimum of 25 people on the Trump team and a minimum of 25 people **on the Russian team to execute. One of the first steps the FBI takes in prepasring for a major case is to estimate how many agents the FBI needs to work on this case. Did the FBI make such as estimate?**

BREITBART

Hillary Clinton Screaming Obscenities and Throwing Objects in Election Night Meltdown

DANIEL J. FLYNN

The mystery of Hillary Clinton, the milk-carton missing on election night, appears solved.

A Tuesday of catharsis for Donald Trump voters turned into an evening of rage for Hillary Clinton. The Democratic presidential nominee, anticipating the postelection reaction of many of her supporters, began shouting profanities, banging tables, and turning objects not nailed down into projectiles.

"Sources have told *The American Spectator* that on Tuesday night, after Hillary realized she had lost, she went into a rage," R. Emmett Tyrrell reports. "Secret Service officers told at least one source that she began yelling, screaming obscenities, and pounding furniture. She picked up objects and threw them at the attendants and staff. She was in an uncontrollable rage."

The appearance of campaign chairman John Podesta at Manhattan's Javitz Center, and the dematerialization of his heretofore ubiquitous charge, perplexed in the first hours of Wednesday.

"They're still counting votes, and every vote should count," Podesta declared to a sad and stunned hall. "Several states are too close to call, so we're not going to have anything more to say tonight."

As Podesta recalcitrantly refused to recognize reality early Wednesday morning, Hillary Clinton called Donald Trump to offer congratulations. The juxtaposition of the campaign chairman publicly vowing to fight around the time the candidate privately conceded the election left observers scratching their heads.

Tyrrell's reporting indicates that Mrs. Clinton's mental state made it impossible for her to address her supporters on election night as custom requests. So, instead, Podesta gave a rah-rah speech on a boo-hoo night to cover for the absence of the first woman president, her fireworks, and her victory speech shout-outs to the mothers of the Black Lives Matter martyrs.

"She is not done yet," Podesta claimed. Tyrrell's reporting indicates that, indeed, Clinton remained far from done.

"Her aides could not allow her to come out in public," he writes. "It would take her hours to calm down. So, Podesta went out and gave his aimless speech. I wish we could report on Bill's whereabouts, but we cannot."

Bill appeared the following day at Hillary's belated concession speech wearing a purple tie but, thankfully, no purple marks on his face, suggesting experience dictated avoidance the previous evening.

"People say they're amazed Bill's marriage survived," Tyrrell noted to Breitbart. "I'm amazed Bill survived his marriage."

Tyrrell's reporting remains a thorn in the side of the Clintons more than two decades after the *American Spectator* published its Trooper gate stories detailing Bill Clinton's escapades as told by his Arkansas security detail, stories that first referenced Paula Jones and pushed the president on the road to impeachment. Nearly 19 years after Hillary Clinton imagined a "vast, right-wing conspiracy" out to get her husband, the cabal's charter member again relies on the accounts of the Clintons' long-suffering security to unmask the public faces worn by the power couple now out of power.

"In the '90s, we published several pieces that documented her throwing lamps and books," Tyrrell tells Breitbart. "This happened pretty often. She has such a foul mouth that the Arkansas state troopers learned a thing or two from her. She has a foul mouth and a good throwing arm."

SPECIAL AGENT ROTH- Losing a Presidential Election is a very tough life event for anybody to take. Especially if the candidates think that there was election fraud, Hillary Clinton vented her disappointment. Isn't Donald Trump entitled to vent his disappointment?

Attorney General DOJ Guidelines re: FBI

SPECIAL AGENT ROTH- the FBI is extremely regulated By various

Department of Justice Guidelines and its own Guidelines. One of the most important guidelines is to communicate with the Department of Justice.

a. The conduct of investigations and other activities authorized by these Guidelines may present choices between the use of different investigative methods that are each operationally sound and effective but that are more or less intrusive, considering such factors as the effect on privacy and civil liberties of individuals and potential damage to reputation. The least intrusive method feasible is to be used in such situations. It is recognized. However, the choice of methods is a matter of judgment. The FBI shall not hesitate to use any lawful method consistent with these

Guidelines, even if intrusive, where the degree of intrusiveness is warranted in light of the seriousness of a criminal or national security threat or the strength of the information indicating its existence, or in light of the importance of foreign intelligence sought to the United States' interests. This point is to be particularly observed in investigations relating to terrorism.

b. United States persons shall be dealt with openly and consensually to the extent practicable when collecting foreign intelligence that does not concern criminal activities or threats to national security.

c. Respect for Legal Rights

PREDICTION OF INVESTIGATION AND SUPERVISORY APPROVAL

Subpart B of this Part authorizes a second level of investigative activity, predicated investigations. The purposes or objectives of predicated investigations are essentially the same as those of assessments, but predication, as provided in these Guidelines, is needed- generally, allegations, reports, facts, or circumstances indicative of possible criminal or national security threatening activity or the potential for acquiring information responsive to foreign intelligence requirements -and supervisory approval must be obtained, to initiate predicated investigations.

Corresponding to the stronger predication and approval requirements, all lawful methods may be used in predicated investigations. A classified directive provides further specifications concerning circumstances supporting certain predicated investigations.

Predicated investigations that concern federal crimes or threats to national security are subdivided into preliminary investigations and full investigations. Preliminary investigations may be initiated on the basis of any allegation or information indicative of possible criminal or national security-threatening activity, but more substantial factual predication is required for full investigations. While time limits are set for the completion of preliminary investigations, full investigations may be pursued without preset limits on their duration.

CIRCUMSTANCES WARRANTING INVESTIGATION

A predicated investigation may be initiated on the basis of any of the following circumstances:

a. An activity constituting a federal crime or a threat to national security has or may have occurred, is or may be occurring, or will or may occur, and the investigation may obtain information relating to the activity or the involvement or role of an individual, group, or organization in such activity.

b. An individual, group, organization, entity, information, property, or activity is or may be a target of attack, victimization, acquisition, infiltration, or recruitment in connection with criminal activity in violation of federal law or a threat to national security, and the investigation may obtain information that would help to protect against such activity or threat.

c. The investigation may obtain foreign intelligence that is responsive to a foreign intelligence requirement.

d. Preliminary and Full Investigations

A predicted investigation relating to a federal crime or threat to national security may be conducted as a preliminary investigation or a full investigation. A predicted investigation that is based solely on the authority to collect foreign intelligence may be conducted only as a full investigation.

a. Preliminary investigations

i. Predication Required for Preliminary Investigations

A preliminary investigation may be initiated on the basis of information or an allegation indicating the existence of a circumstance described in paragraph 3.a.-.b.

ii. Duration of Preliminary Investigations

PREDICATED INVESTIGATIONS

1. Purposes

Predicated investigations may be carried out to detect, obtain information about, prevent or protect against federal crimes or threats to national security or to collect foreign intelligence.

2. Approval

The initiation of a predicated investigation requires supervisory approval at a level or levels specified by FBI policy. A predicated investigation based on paragraph

3.c. (relating to foreign intelligence) must be approved by a Special Agent in Charge or by an FBI Headquarters official as provided in such p.

Circumstances Warranting Investigation

A predicated investigation may be initiated on the basis of any of the following circumstances:

a. An activity constituting a federal crime or a threat to national security has or may have occurred, is or may be occurring, or will or may occur, and the investigation may obtain information relating to the activity or the involvement or role of an individual, group, or organization in such activity.

b. An individual, group, organization, entity, information, property, or activity is or may be a target of attack, victimization, acquisition, infiltration, or recruitment in connection with criminal activity in violation of federal law or a threat to national security, and the investigation may obtain information that would help to protect against such activity or threat.

c. The investigation may obtain foreign intelligence that is responsive to a foreign intelligence requirement.

d. Preliminary and Full Investigations

A predicated investigation relating to a federal crime or threat to national security may be conducted as a preliminary investigation or a full investigation. A predicated investigation that is based solely on the authority to collect foreign intelligence may be conducted only as a full investigation.

a. Preliminary investigations

i. Predication Required for Preliminary Investigations

A preliminary investigation may be initiated on the basis of the following:

RETENTION OF INFORMATION

1. The FBI shall retain records relating to activities under these Guidelines in accordance with a records retention plan approved by the National Archives and Records Administration.

2. The FBI shall maintain a database or records system that permits, with respect to each predicated investigation, the prompt retrieval of the status of the investigation (open or closed), the dates of opening and closing, and the basis for the investigation

INFORMATION RELATING TO CRIMINAL MATTERS

1. Coordination with Prosecutors

In an investigation relating to possible criminal activity in violation of federal law, the agent conducting the investigation shall maintain periodic written or oral contact with the appropriate federal prosecutor as circumstances warrant and as requested by the prosecutor. When, during such an investigation, a matter appears arguably to warrant prosecution, the agent shall present the relevant facts to the appropriate federal prosecutor. Information on investigations that have been closed shall be available on request to a United States Attorney or his or her designee or an appropriate Department of Justice official.

INFORMATION RELATING TO CRIMINAL MATTERS

Special Statutory Requirements

a. Dissemination of information acquired under the Foreign Intelligence Surveillance Act is, to the extent provided in that Act, subject to minimization procedures and other requirements.

In plain English, the FBI cannot open a case or close a case without approval from the DOJ. An FBI Agent cannot open or close a case without approval from an FBI supervisor.

Part Two

FBI activity after receiving Collusion information from CIA Director

John Brennan

FBI AGENT ROTH

The FBI should have interviewed Hillary as soon she stated to the public that she was convinced there was collusion with the Russians and the Trump campaign and as soon as the FBI received the collusion information from Director Brennan. Who was the source, and what was the basis of her allegations? Either way, Hillary would have been boxed in. If she chose to try and fool the FBI with false information, she would have been open to making a false statement to an FBI agent charge. If she had declined to speak to the FBI, she could not have continued to peddle this false information to the American public and the Fake Media.

What did the FBI do?

NOTHING. NO INTERVIEW OF CLINTON (Just like JFK case.)

HILLARY'S ALLEGATIONS WERE SERIOUS NATIONAL SECURITY ALLEGATIONS. HOW COULD THE FBI IGNORE THEM? AFTER WORKING FOR THE FBI AS SPECIAL AGENTS, SHELTON AND ROTH OPINE THAT THIS CASE WOULD HAVE GONE UP THE FBI CHAIN OF COMMAND LIKE A ROCKET. THIS BEGAN THE INEPT OR, WORSE YET, DELIBERATE APPROACH BY THE FBI OF FAILING TO FOLLOW UP ON OBVIOUS LEADS.

Steele Dossier

Published December 18, 2018, 2:25am EST

The reporter who broke the news of the Steele dossier used to surveil ex-Trump aides calls its claims largely 'false.'

By Gregg Re | Fox News

Why was the dossier not verified before the FISA warrant?

Sen. Lindsey Graham weighs in on FISA abuses, Mueller filings on 'Hannity.'

The salacious and unverified opposition research dossier cited by the FBI as its main justification to surveil a top Trump aide contains several claims that are "likely false," according to the Yahoo News reporter who was among the first to break the news of the dossier's existence.

Michael Isikoff's statements on John Ziegler's Free Speech Broadcasting podcast came a day before Michael Cohen's adviser Lanny Davis reiterated that Cohen had never been to Prague -- where, according to the dossier, he traveled to arrange a payment to Russian hackers during the 2016 presidential campaign.

The dossier was created by British ex-spy Christopher Steele and funded by the firm Fusion GPS -- which was retained by the Democratic National Committee (DNC) and the Hillary Clinton presidential campaign.

"In broad strokes, Christopher Steele was clearly onto something, that there was a major Kremlin effort to interfere in our elections, that they were trying to help Trump's campaign, and that there were multiple contacts between various Russian figures close to the government and various people in Trump's campaign," Isikoff said.

But he added: "When you actually get into the details of the Steele dossier, the specific allegations, we have not seen the evidence to support them, and, in fact, there are good grounds to think that some of the more sensational allegations will never be proven and are likely false."

On four occasions, the FBI told the Foreign Intelligence Surveillance (FISA) court that it "did not believe" Steele was the direct source for Isikoff's September 23, 2016, Yahoo News article implicating former Trump aide Carter Page in Russian collusion.

DEFIANT FIRED FBI DIRECTOR COMEY LASHES OUT AT GOP AFTER 'FRUSTRATING' HEARING

Carter Page on why he is suing the DNC

Key players in the Russia investigation are being sued for defamation by Page; former Trump campaign aide speaks out on 'Hannity.'

Instead, the FBI suggested to the court that the article by Michael Isikoff was independent corroboration of the salacious, unverified allegations against Trump in the infamous Steele dossier. Federal authorities used both the Steele dossier and the Yahoo News article to convince the FISA court to authorize a surveillance warrant for Page.

But London court records show that contrary to the FBI's assessments, Steele briefed Yahoo News and other reporters in the fall of 2016 at the direction of Fusion GPS -- the opposition research firm behind the dossier. The revelations contained heavily redacted documents released earlier this year after a Freedom of Information Act lawsuit by the organization Judicial Watch.

"The FBI does not believe that Source #1 [Steele] directly provided this information to the identified news organization that published the September 23 News Article," the FBI stated in one of the released FISA documents. "Source #1 told the FBI that he/she only provided this information to the business associate and the FBI."

The documents describe Source #1 as someone "hired by a business associate to conduct research" into Trump's Russia ties -- but do not mention that Fusion GPS was funded by the DNC and Clinton campaign.

Instead, the documents say only: "The FBI speculates that the identified U.S. person was likely looking for information that could be used to discredit [Trump's] campaign." Fox News believes that the U.S. person is Glenn Simpson, co-founder of Fusion GPS.

SPECIAL AGENTS ROTH- What the hell is a news reporter's article doing in a FISA warrant?

Senior Justice Department official Bruce Ohr continued to communicate with former British spy Christopher Steele, even after the FBI cut ties with him. (AP)

Page announced in October he is filing a defamation lawsuit against the DNC over the dossier's claims. He is also suing Perkins Coie and its partners, the law firm that represented Clinton's campaign and hired Fusion GPS.

Page told Fox News' "Hannity" at the time that his lawsuit goes "beyond any damages or any financial aspects."

"There have been so many lies as you're alluding to, and you look at the damage it did to our Democratic systems and our institutions of government back in 2016. And I'm just trying to get some justice," he said.

Meanwhile, ex-Cohen attorney Lanny Davis laughed off a suggestion during an MSNBC interview on Sunday that his former client had ever made a trip to Prague to pay Russian hackers.

"No, no Prague, ever, never," Davis said.

While Cohen's team has long denied he made the trip, the latest denial comes after Cohen pleaded guilty in two separate prosecutions linked to his work for President Trump. Cohen has pledged to cooperate with federal authorities, and Special Counsel, Robert Mueller's team, has said he has largely done so.

ANTI-TRUMP EX-FBI AGENT STRZOK'S PHONE WAS WIPED AFTER HE WAS FIRED FROM MUELLER'S TEAM

Fox News reported in August that embattled Justice Department official Bruce Ohr had contact in 2016 with then-colleague Andrew Weissmann, who is now a top Mueller deputy, as well as other senior FBI officials about the controversial anti-Trump dossier and the individuals behind it.

The sources said Ohr's outreach about the dossier – as well as Steele, the opposition research firm behind it, Glenn Simpson's Fusion GPS, and his wife Nellie Ohr's work for Fusion – occurred before and after the FBI fired Steele as a source over his media contacts. Ohr's network of contacts on the dossier included: anti-Trump former FBI agent Peter Strzok; former FBI lawyer Lisa Page; former deputy director Andrew McCabe; Weissmann and at least one other DOJ official; and a current FBI agent who worked with Strzok on the Russia case.

Weissmann was kept "in the loop" on the dossier, a source said, while he was chief of the criminal fraud division. He is now assigned to Mueller's team.

SPECIAL AGENT ROTH- What did Weismann do with this information?

Did he brief anybody? Did he direct the FBI to do anything with the information?

Since Weismann already knew some information about the case, should he have recused himself?

Ohr's broad circle of contacts indicates members of FBI leadership knew about his backchannel activities regarding the dossier and Steele.

Congressional Republicans are still trying to get to the bottom of Ohr's role in circulating the unverified dossier, which became a critical piece of evidence in obtaining a surveillance warrant for Page in October 2016.

Is Gregg Re a producer of "Tucker Carlson Tonight" on the Fox News Channel?

After the Steele dossier was discredited, Democrats changed their story and

Said it was the Papadopoulos meeting that was the predicate.

How the Russia Inquiry Began: A Campaign Aide, Drinks, and Talk of Political DirtTop of Form

By Sharon LaFraniere, Mark Mazzetti and Matt Apuzzo

Dec. 30, 2017

WASHINGTON — during a night of heavy drinking at an upscale London bar in May 2016, George Papadopoulos, a young foreign policy adviser to the Trump campaign, made a startling revelation to Australia's top diplomat in Britain: Russia had political dirt on Hillary Clinton.

About three weeks earlier, Mr. Papadopoulos had been told that Moscow had thousands of emails that would embarrass Mrs. Clinton, apparently stolen in an effort to try to damage her campaign.

Exactly how much Mr. Papadopoulos said that night at the Kensington Wine Rooms with the Australian, Alexander Downer, is unclear. But two months later, when leaked Democratic emails began appearing online, Australian officials passed the information about Mr. Papadopoulos to their American counterparts, according to four current and former American and foreign officials with direct knowledge of the Australians' role.

The hacking and the revelation that a member of the Trump campaign may have had inside information about it were driving factors that led the F.B.I. to open an investigation in July 2016 into Russia's attempts to disrupt the election and whether any of President Trump's associates conspired.

If Mr. Papadopoulos, who pleaded guilty to lying to the F.B.I. and is now a cooperating witness, was the improbable match that set off a blaze that has consumed the first year of the Trump administration, his saga is also a tale of the Trump campaign in miniature. He was brash, boastful, and underqualified, yet he exceeded expectations. And, like the campaign itself, he proved to be a tantalizing target for a Russian influence operation.

While some of Mr. Trump's advisers have derided him as an insignificant campaign volunteer or a "coffee boy," interviews and new documents show that he stayed influential throughout the campaign. Two months before the election, for instance, he helped arrange a New York meeting between Mr. Trump and President Abdel Fattah el-Sisi of Egypt.

The information that Mr. Papadopoulos gave to the Australians answers one of the lingering mysteries of the past year: What so alarmed American officials to provoke the F.B.I. to open a counterintelligence investigation into the Trump campaign months before the presidential election?

It was not, as Mr. Trump and other politicians have alleged, a dossier compiled by a former British spy hired by a rival campaign. Instead, it was firsthand information from one of America's closest intelligence allies.

Interviews and previously undisclosed documents show that Mr. Papadopoulos played a critical role in this drama and revealed a Russian operation that was more aggressive and widespread than previously known. They add to an emerging portrait, gradually filled in over the past year in revelations by federal investigators, journalists, and lawmakers, of Russians with government contacts trying to establish secret channels at various levels of the Trump campaign.

15

The F.B.I. investigation, which was taken over seven months ago by the special counsel, Robert S. Mueller III, has cast a shadow over Mr. Trump's first year in office — even as he and his aides repeatedly played down the Russian efforts and falsely denied campaign contacts with Russians.

They have also insisted that Mr. Papadopoulos was a low-level figure. But spies frequently target peripheral players as a way to gain insight and leverage.

F.B.I. officials disagreed in 2016 about how aggressively and publicly to pursue the Russia inquiry before the election. But there was little debate about what seemed to be afoot. John O. Brennan, who retired this year after four years as C.I.A. director, told Congress in May that he had been concerned about multiple contacts between Russian officials and Trump advisers.

Russia, he said, had tried to "suborn" members of the Trump campaign.

Mr. Papadopoulos, then an ambitious 28-year-old from Chicago, was working as an energy consultant in London when the Trump campaign, desperate to create a foreign policy team, named him as an adviser in early March 2016. His political experience was limited to two months on Ben Carson's presidential campaign before it collapsed.

Mr. Papadopoulos had no experience with Russia issues. But during his job interview with Sam Clovis, a top early campaign aide, he saw an opening. He was told that improving relations with Russia was one of Mr. Trump's top foreign policy goals, according to court papers, an account Mr. Clovis has denied.

Traveling in Italy that March, Mr. Papadopoulos met Joseph Mifsud, a Maltese professor at a now-defunct London academy who had valuable contacts with the Russian Ministry of Foreign Affairs. Mr. Mifsud showed little interest in Mr. Papadopoulos at first.

Sam Clovis, a former co-chairman of Mr. Trump's presidential campaign, denies that he told Mr. Papadopoulos that improving relations with Russia was one of Mr. Trump's top foreign policy goals during Mr. Papadopoulos's interview for a job with the campaign.

But when he found out he was a Trump campaign adviser, he latched onto him, according to court records and emails obtained by The New York Times. Their joint goal was to arrange a meeting between Mr. Trump and President Vladimir V. Putin of Russia in Moscow or between their respective aides.

In response to questions, Mr. Papadopoulos's lawyers declined to provide a statement.

Before the end of the month, Mr. Mifsud had arranged a meeting at a London cafe between Mr. Papadopoulos and Olga Polonskaya, a young woman from St. Petersburg whom he falsely described as Mr. Putin's niece. Although Ms. Polonskaya told The Times in a text message that her English skills are poor, her emails to Mr. Papadopoulos were largely fluent. "We are all very excited by the possibility of a good relationship with Mr. Trump," Ms. Polonskaya wrote in one message.

More important, Mr. Mifsud connected Mr. Papadopoulos to Ivan Timofeev, a program director for the prestigious Valdai Discussion Club, a gathering of academics that meets annually with Mr. Putin. The two men corresponded for months about how to connect the Russian government and the campaign. Records suggest that Mr. Timofeev, who has been described by Mr. Mueller's team as an intermediary for the Russian Foreign Ministry, discussed the matter with the ministry's former leader, Igor S. Ivanov, who is widely viewed in the United States as one of Russia's elder statesmen.

When Mr. Trump's foreign policy team gathered for the first time at the end of March in Washington, Mr. Papadopoulos said he had the contacts to set up a meeting between Mr. Trump and Mr. Putin. Mr. Trump listened intently but apparently deferred to Jeff Sessions, then a senator from Alabama and head of the campaign's foreign policy team, according to participants in the meeting.

Mr. Sessions, now the attorney general, initially did not reveal that discussion to Congress because he has said he did not recall it. More recently, he said he pushed back against Mr. Papadopoulos's proposal, at least partly because he did not want someone so unqualified to represent the campaign on such a sensitive matter.

If the campaign wanted Mr. Papadopoulos to stand down, previously undisclosed emails obtained by The Times show that he either did not get the message or failed to heed it. He continued for months to try to arrange some kind of meeting with Russian representatives, keeping senior campaign advisers abreast of his efforts. Mr. Clovis ultimately encouraged him and another foreign policy adviser to travel to Moscow, but neither went because the campaign would not cover the cost.

Mr. Papadopoulos was trusted enough to edit the outline of Mr. Trump's first major foreign policy speech on April 27, an address in which the candidate said it was possible to improve relations with Russia. Mr. Papadopoulos flagged the speech to his newfound Russia contacts, telling Mr. Timofeev that it should be taken as "the signal to meet."

"That is a statesman speech," Mr. Mifsud agreed. Ms. Polonskaya wrote that she was pleased that Mr. Trump's "position toward Russia is much softer" than that of other candidates.

Stephen Miller, then a senior policy adviser to the campaign and now a top White House aide, was eager for Mr. Papadopoulos to serve as a surrogate, someone who could publicize Mr. Trump's foreign policy views without officially speaking for the campaign. But Mr. Papadopoulos's first public attempt to do so was a disaster.

In a May 4, 2016, interview with The Times of London, Mr. Papadopoulos called on Prime Minister David Cameron to apologize to Mr. Trump for criticizing his remarks on Muslims as "stupid" and divisive. "Say sorry to Trump or risk special relationship, Cameron said," the headline read. Mr. Clovis, the national campaign co-chairman, severely reprimanded Mr. Papadopoulos for failing to clear his explosive comments with the campaign in advance.

From then on, Mr. Papadopoulos was more careful with the press — though he never regained the full trust of Mr. Clovis or several other campaign officials.

Mr. Mifsud proposed to Mr. Papadopoulos that he, too, serve as a campaign surrogate. He could write op-eds under the guise of a "neutral" observer, he wrote in a previously undisclosed email, and follow Mr. Trump to his rallies as an accredited journalist while receiving briefings from inside the campaign.

In late April, at a London hotel, Mr. Mifsud told Mr. Papadopoulos that he had just learned from high-level Russian officials in Moscow that the Russians had "dirt" on Mrs. Clinton in the form of "thousands of emails," according to court documents. Although Russian hackers had been mining data from the Democratic National Committee's computers for months, that information was not yet public. Even the committee itself did not know.

Whether Mr. Papadopoulos shared that information with anyone else in the campaign is one of many unanswered questions. He was mostly in contact with the campaign over emails. The day after Mr. Mifsud's revelation about the hacked emails, he told Mr. Miller in an email only that he had "interesting messages coming in from Moscow" about a possible trip. The emails obtained by The Times show no evidence that Mr. Papadopoulos discussed the stolen messages with the campaign.

Not long after, however, he opened up to Mr. Downer, the Australian diplomat, about his contacts with the Russians. It is unclear whether Mr. Downer was fishing for that information that night in May 2016. The meeting at the bar came about because of a series of connections, beginning with an Israeli Embassy official who introduced Mr. Papadopoulos to another Australian diplomat in London.

It is also not clear why, after getting the information in May, the Australian government waited two months to pass it to the F.B.I. In a statement, the Australian Embassy in Washington declined to provide details about the meeting or confirm that it occurred.

"As a matter of principle and practice, the Australian government does not comment on matters relevant to active investigations," the statement said. The F.B.I. declined to comment.

A House Judiciary Committee session last month at which Attorney General Jeff Sessions testified. Mr. Sessions was head of the Trump campaign's foreign policy team.

Credit...Al Drago for the New York Times

Once the information Mr. Papadopoulos had disclosed to the Australian diplomat reached the F.B.I., the bureau opened an investigation that became one of its most closely guarded secrets. Senior agents did not discuss it at the daily morning briefing, a classified setting where officials normally speak freely about highly sensitive operations.

Besides the information from the Australians, the investigation was also propelled by intelligence from other friendly governments, including the British and Dutch. A trip to Moscow by another adviser, Carter Page, also raised concerns at the F.B.I.

With so many strands coming in — about Mr. Papadopoulos, Mr. Page, the hackers, and more — F.B.I. agents debated how aggressively to investigate the campaign's Russia ties, according to current and former officials familiar with the debate. Issuing subpoenas or questioning people, for example, could cause the investigation to burst into public view in the final months of a presidential campaign.

It could also tip off the Russian government, which might try to cover its tracks. Some officials argued against taking such disruptive steps, especially since the F.B.I. would not be able to unravel the case before the election.

Others believed that the possibility of a compromised presidential campaign was so serious that it warranted the most thorough, aggressive tactics. Even if the odds against a Trump presidency were long, these agents argued, it was prudent to take every precaution.

That included questioning Christopher Steele, the former British spy who was compiling the dossier alleging a far-ranging Russian conspiracy to elect Mr. Trump. A team of F.B.I. agents traveled to Europe to interview Mr. Steele in early October 2016. Mr. Steele had shown some of his findings to an F.B.I. agent in Rome three months earlier, but that information was not part of the justification to start a counterintelligence inquiry, American officials said.

Ultimately, the F.B.I. and Justice Department decided to keep the investigation quiet, a decision that Democrats, in particular, have criticized. And agents did not interview Mr. Papadopoulos until late January.

Opening Doors to the Top

He was hardly central to the daily running of the Trump campaign, yet Mr. Papadopoulos continuously found ways to make himself useful to senior Trump advisers. In September 2016, with the United Nations General Assembly approaching and stories circulating that Mrs. Clinton was going to meet with Mr. Sisi, the Egyptian president, Mr. Papadopoulos sent a message to Stephen K. Bannon, the campaign's chief executive, offering to broker a similar meeting for Mr. Trump.

After days of scheduling discussions, the meeting was set, and Mr. Papadopoulos sent a list of talking points to Mr. Bannon, according to people familiar with those interactions. Asked about his contacts with Mr. Papadopoulos, Mr. Bannon declined to comment.

Mr. Trump's improbable victory raised Mr. Papadopoulos's hopes that he might ascend to a top White House job. The election win also prompted a business proposal from Sergei Millian, a naturalized American citizen born in Belarus. After he had contacted Mr. Papadopoulos out of the blue over LinkedIn during the summer of 2016, the two repeatedly met in Manhattan.

Mr. Millian has bragged of his ties to Mr. Trump — boasts that the president's advisers have said are overstated. He headed an obscure organization called the Russian-American Chamber of Commerce, some of whose board members and clients are difficult to confirm. Congress is investigating where he fits into the swirl of contacts with the Trump campaign, although he has said he is unfairly being scrutinized only because of his support for Mr. Trump.

Mr. Millian proposed that he and Mr. Papadopoulos form an energy-related business that would be financed by Russian billionaires "who are not under sanctions" and would "open all doors for us" at "any level all the way. To the top."

One billionaire, he said, wanted to explore the idea of opening a Trump-branded hotel in Moscow. "I know the president will distance himself from business, but his children might be interested," he wrote.

Nothing came of his proposals, partly because Mr. Papadopoulos was hoping that Michael T. Flynn, then Mr. Trump's pick to be national security adviser, might give him the energy portfolio at the National Security Council.

The pair exchanged New Year's greetings in the final hours of 2016. "Happy New Year, sir," Mr. Papadopoulos wrote.

"Thank you, and same to you, George. Happy New Year!" Mr. Flynn responded ahead of a year that seemed to hold great promise.

But 2017 did not unfold that way. Within months, Mr. Flynn was fired, and both men were charged with lying to the F.B.I. And both became important witnesses in the investigation Mr. Papadopoulos had played a critical role in starting.

Adam Goldman, Eileen Sullivan, and Matthew Rosenberg contributed reporting.

A version of this article appears in print on December 31, 2017, in Section A, Page 1 of the New York edition with the headline: Unlikely Source Propelled Russian Meddling Inquiry. Order Reprints | Today's Paper | Subscribe

The Australian diplomat whose tip prompted the FBI's Russia probe has a tie to the Clintons

By John Solomon and Alison Spann - *03/05/18 7:13* pm ET HILL

The Australian diplomat whose tip in 2016 prompted the Russia-Trump investigation previously arranged one of the largest foreign donations to Bill and Hillary Clinton's charitable efforts, documents show.

Former Australian Foreign Minister Alexander Downer's role in securing $25 million in aid from his country to help the Clinton Foundation fight AIDS is chronicled in decade-old government memos archived on the Australian foreign ministry's website.

Downer and former President Clinton jointly signed a Memorandum of Understanding in February 2006 that spread out the grant money over four years for a project to provide screening and drug treatment to AIDS patients in Asia.

The money was initially allocated to the Clinton Foundation but later was routed through an affiliate of the charity known as the Clinton Health Access Initiative (CHAI), officials said. Australia was one of four foreign governments to donate more than $25 million to CHAI, records show.

In the years that followed, the project won praise for helping thousands of HIV-infected patients in Papua New Guinea, Vietnam, China, and Indonesia but also garnered criticism from auditors about "management weaknesses" and inadequate budget oversight, and memos show.

Downer, now Australia's ambassador to London, provided the account of a conversation with Trump campaign adviser George Papadopoulos at a London bar in 2016 that became the official reason the FBI opened the Russia counterintelligence probe.

But lawmakers say the FBI didn't tell Congress about Downer's prior connection to the Clinton Foundation. Republicans say they are concerned the new information means nearly all of the early evidence the FBI used to justify its election-year probe of Trump came from sources supportive of the Clintons, including the controversial Steele dossier.

"The Clintons' tentacles go everywhere. So, that's why it's important," said Rep. Jim Jordan (R-Ohio), chairman of a House Oversight and Government Reform subcommittee that has been taking an increasingly visible role in defending the Trump administration in the Russia probe. "We continue to get new information every week. It seems that sort of underscores the fact that the FBI hasn't been square with us."

A spokesman for the FBI and Russia special counsel Robert Mueller declined to comment.

The Australian Foreign Ministry says the Clinton grant was handled like all its other $2 billion annual foreign aid awards, and it ultimately helped thousands in Asia gain access to antiretroviral AIDS medications.

Democrats accuse the GOP of overreaching, saying Downer's role in trying to help the Clinton Foundation fight AIDS shouldn't be used to question his assistance to the FBI.

"The effort to attack the FBI and DOJ as a way of defending the President continues," said Rep. Adam Schiff (D-Calif.), the top Democrat on the House Intelligence panel. "Not content to disparage our British allies and one of their former intelligence officers, the majority now seeks to defame our Australian partners as a way of undermining the Russia probe. It will not succeed but may do lasting damage to our institutions and allies in the process."

Nick Merrill, Hillary Clinton's spokesman, said any effort to connect the 2006 grant with the current Russia investigation was "laughable."

Craig Minassian, a spokesman for the Bill, Hillary, and Chelsea Clinton Foundation, said the focus should be on the foundation's success in helping tens of thousands of AIDS patients.

EARLY INFORMATION WHICH DEBUNKED TRUMP-RUSSIA COLLUSION

Dossier Not What 'Started All of This'

By Lori Robertson

Posted on March 27, 2019

In an interview about the special counsel's report, Rep. John Ratcliffe said that what "started all of this" was "a fake, phony dossier." But a House Republican intelligence committee memo said it was information about a Trump campaign foreign policy adviser that sparked the FBI's counterintelligence investigation into Russian interference in the election.

Ratcliffe, a Texas Republican who is a member of the House intelligence committee, said in the interview on Fox Business Network that "I had seen every classified document that any member of Congress was allowed to see. So, I wasn't surprised at all at the findings" of the special counsel investigation, as revealed in a four-page memo on March 24 by Attorney General William P. Barr. He then turned to the dossier.

Ratcliffe, March 25: *That this was a fake, phony dossier that started all of this, funded by the Democrats. ... It wasn't real, and now Bob Mueller says it wasn't real.*

The "dossier" is a series of memos compiled by former British intelligence officer Christopher Steele on supposed contacts between Russian officials and members of the Trump campaign. It alleged the Russian government had compromising information on then-Republican presidential candidate Donald Trump. Steele was hired by the research firm Fusion GPS, which had been hired by a law firm representing Hillary Clinton's presidential campaign and the Democratic National Committee. (See "Q&A on the Nunes Memo" for more information.)

We don't know what special counsel Robert S. Mueller III said or didn't say about the dossier in his report to Barr. For now, Mueller's report remains confidential. But we do know, according to Barr's summary of it, that Mueller's report said:" [T]he investigation did not establish that members of the Trump Campaign conspired or coordinated with the Russian government in its election interference activities."

Barr wrote in his memo that "the Special Counsel did not find that the Trump campaign, or anyone associated with it, conspired or coordinated with the Russian government in these efforts, despite multiple offers from Russian-affiliated individuals to assist the Trump campaign."

But Ratcliffe is wrong to say the dossier "started all of this." Competing memos from the Republicans and the Democrats on the House intelligence committee both say that information about George Papadopoulos, a Trump campaign foreign policy adviser, had prompted the FBI investigation in July 2016.

Papadopoulos had contacts with Russian intermediaries during the campaign, according to the Justice Department, and later pleaded guilty to lying to the FBI about those contacts. While he was a Trump campaign adviser, Papadopoulos met with a professor with connections to Russian government officials who told him "about the Russians possessing 'dirt' on then-candidate Hillary

Clinton in the form of 'thousands of emails,'" and he tried to arrange a meeting between the Russian government and the campaign, the DOJ's statement of the offense said.

A memo released on February 2, 2018, by the Republicans on the House intelligence committee raised concerns about the use of the dossier in an application from the DOJ and FBI under the Foreign Intelligence Surveillance Act to conduct electronic surveillance on Carter Page, another Trump campaign foreign policy adviser. But it said the "Papadopoulos information triggered the opening of an FBI counterintelligence investigation in late July 2016."

The Democrats on the House intelligence committee agreed with that, saying in a memo released on February 24, 2018, that the FBI investigation started "more than seven weeks" before the FBI received Steele's intelligence reporting in mid-September of that year.

The two sides disagree about how essential the dossier was to the FISA court application to monitor Page. But one of the few points of agreement is that the FBI investigation began with information on Papadopoulos.

After the GOP memo was released, Republican Rep. Trey Gowdy, also a member of the intelligence committee, said the dossier didn't have any effect on the Russia investigation. "I actually don't think it has any impact on the Russia probe," Gowdy said on February 4, 2018, on CBS' "Face the Nation."

Gowdy mentioned other incidents that had nothing to do with the dossier, including Papadopoulos' contacts with the professor and June 9, 2016, Trump Tower meeting Donald Trump Jr. arranged with what he was told was a "Russian government attorney" offering incriminating information on Hillary Clinton. "So there's going to be a Russia probe, even without a dossier."

We asked Ratcliffe's office how he could claim that "a fake, phony dossier … started all of this." His office responded: "Very easily. Both statements are true. The Papadopoulos information is the stated basis for FBI Agent Peter Strzok's opening of the FBI's Crossfire Hurricane counterintelligence investigation on Sunday, July 31, 2016. The Steele dossier, funded By the Democrats, started many months before that date. Further to that point, the sworn testimony of then DOJ ADAG Bruce Ohr is that he met directly with and was personally briefed on the dossier Christopher Steele at the Mayflower Hotel on Saturday, July 30, 2016, the day before the FBI officially opened its investigation."

Ratcliffe's office added: "The 'Trump-Russia collusion' narrative (which Mueller's findings conclude is false) was started by and through the Steele dossier months and months before the FBI investigation was opened." But that's not correct.

The Steele dossier didn't start "many months" before the FBI launched its counterintelligence investigation. Glenn R. Simpson of Fusion GPS testified to Congress that he hired Steele in May or June 2016, asking Steele to "find out about Donald Trump's business activities in Russia." The first of a series of memos from Steele was dated June 20, 2016, and Simpson said he would have received it "within a couple of days" of that date. That was one month before the FBI counterintelligence investigation began.

There's also no evidence that Ohr's late July 2016 meeting with Steele precipitated the FBI investigation. Ohr, a former associate deputy attorney general with the Department of

Justice, testified to Congress that he didn't know about the FBI investigation at the time. Ohr said he reached out to then-FBI Deputy Director Andrew McCabe and met with McCabe in August 2016 to provide the information Steele had given him. "I don't recall the exact date. I'm guessing it would have been in August since I met with Chris Steele at the end of July, and I'm pretty sure I would have reached out to Andrew McCabe soon afterward," Ohr said in his August 2018 testimony.

SPECIAL AGENT ROTH-Where is the opening serial to the Trump Investigation? The serial would clear up the question as to what information was the basis for opening the case.

Other Republicans Point to the Dossier

Ratcliffe wasn't the only Republican to bring up the dossier after Barr released his memo summarizing the special counsel's report.

Jay Sekulow, an attorney for the president, said in a March 25 interview on Fox News: "The whole impetus upon which this inquiry engaged, where it came out of, was this dossier, this counterintelligence investigation regarding collusion." And Ronna McDaniel, chair of the Republican National Committee, said the same day on the cable network: "And it's really shameful that for two years this cloud has been upon his presidency, and it was precipitated by this fake dossier paid for by the Hillary Clinton and the DNC that the Justice Department ran with, that Democrats for two years have accused our president of being an agent for a foreign country."

As we explained, dueling House intelligence committee memos agree it was the Papadopoulos information that triggered the FBI investigation.

Also, on Fox News, Rep. Matt Gaetz claimed that "even [former FBI Deputy Director] Andrew McCabe indicated that in the absence of the dossier, the Papadopoulos meeting would not have been enough to continue the investigation."

Gaetz is referring to the February 2018 Republican memo, which claimed that McCabe had testified in December "that no surveillance warrant would have been sought from the FISC without the Steele dossier information." But that has been disputed, including By McCabe.

Democrats said at the time that the memo's description of McCabe's closed-door testimony was incorrect. In an interview with CNN, McCabe said his testimony had been "selectively quoted" and "mischaracterized" in the GOP memo.

"We started the investigations without the dossier. We were proceeding with the investigations before we ever received that information," McCabe told CNN. "Was the dossier material important to the [FISA] package? Of course, it was. As was every fact included in that package. Was it the majority of what was in the package? Absolutely not."

As for the special counsel's investigation, Mueller was appointed by Rod Rosenstein, in his capacity as acting attorney general, on May 17, 2017, eight days after President Donald Trump had fired then-FBI Director James Comey. Rosenstein said in a statement that "the public interest requires me to place this investigation under the authority of a person who exercises a degree of independence from the normal chain of command."

"I determined that a Special Counsel is necessary in order for the American people to have full confidence in the outcome" of the Russia investigation, he said. "Our nation is grounded on the rule of law, and the public must be assured that government officials administer the law fairly."

Special Agent Roth- The next article By former AUSA Andy McCarthy is the basis for most of the criticism cited By the author. The FBI had multiple occasions to bring this investigation to a logical conclusion but simply failed to do so.

FBI knew 'collusion' was a nothing-burger but kept fake scandal alive anyway

By Andrew C. McCarthy

July 20, 2020, 7:48 pm

"We have not seen evidence of any individuals affiliated with the Trump team in contact with [Russian intelligence officers]."

How much wasted time on pointless investigations could have been prevented had Peter Strzok, then one of the FBI's top counterintelligence officials who was spearheading the bureau's Trump-Russia investigation, said this publicly one month into President Trump's term?

But no, it was a private note By Strzok for consumption within the FBI to debunk a February 14, 2017, New York Times article. The news story, a compilation By five of the Times' top reporters, working with four unnamed sources (the usual "current and former American officials"), claimed that members of the Trump campaign had "repeated contacts with senior Russian intelligence officials" before the 2016 election.

This was false. Just as important, the FBI knew it was false.

But we, the American people, only know that now, in 2020, because Strzok's notes were finally made public on Friday.

The Times article centrally identified former Trump campaign chairman Paul Manafort as a key adviser in communication with Kremlin spies. Strzok, however, countered that the bureau was "unaware of any calls with any Russian government official in which Manafort was a party."

Significantly, the Times report was part of a tireless campaign of government leaks, mostly from current and former intelligence operatives (undoubtedly from officials who either worked in agencies still teeming with Obama holdovers or left government after serving the Obama administration).

The story was published just after the firing of Michael Flynn, Trump's first national security adviser. As part of the Trump transition, Flynn had engaged in perfectly appropriate contacts with Russia's ambassador to the United States but had been publicly portrayed as if he were a clandestine agent working for Moscow against the country he'd bled for as a decorated US Army commander.

The narrative of "Trump collusion with Russia" was pure fiction. The public officials who peddled it to a voracious anti-Trump press had to know it was bunk. Yet they fed the beast anyway, regardless of the cloud this created, regardless of how much it harmed the administration's capacity to govern.

Worse: This was not merely a media scam. The FBI and the Obama Justice Department made similar representations, under oath, to the federal court that oversees secret government surveillance programs.

By the time of the Times report, the bureau and Obama DOJ had obtained warrants to monitor former Trump campaign adviser Cater Page in October 2016 and January 2017.

In each warrant, the court was told: "The FBI believes that the Russian Government's efforts to influence the 2016 presidential campaign were being coordinated with Page and perhaps other individuals associated with [Trump's] campaign." Moreover, the warrant applications painted a picture of a "conspiracy of cooperation" between Donald Trump and the Putin regime, with Manafort at the hub, using such underlings as Page and Trump's former lawyer, Michael Cohen, as intermediaries.

The media told America FBI had proof of collusion as the bureau realized it had nothing

It was complete nonsense, largely based on the so-called dossier compiled By former British spy Christopher Steele, working on behalf of the Hillary Clinton campaign. Strzok's notes attest that the FBI knew Steele's reporting was highly suspect.

And that's not half of it. The Senate Judiciary Committee, at the same time it disclosed Strzok's notes, also released a lengthy internal FBI memorandum detailing that Steele had immense credibility problems. In particular, his reporting was based on third-hand (or even less reliable) hearsay and innuendo. It was funneled to him through a sub-source who told the FBI, in a lengthy February 2017 interview, that the dossier claims were exaggerations and innuendo gussied up to seem like real intelligence.

Special Agents Shelton and Roth- Yet, despite knowing that, far from dropping its bogus investigation, the FBI doubled down, seeking new warrants in April and June, failing to correct its misrepresentations.

It is a shocking black eye for American law enforcement and intelligence agencies. The Justice Department's criminal investigation is said to be reaching its conclusion. Americans need answers.

Andrew C. McCarthy is a former federal prosecutor, National Review contributing editor, and author of "Ball of Collusion: The Plot to Rig an Election and Destroy a Presidency."

FBI Chief Comey Misled Congress's 'Gang of 8' Over Russiagate, Lisa Page Memo Reveals

Paul Sperry | RealClearWire

June 13, 2022, Updated 1 hr ago

Above, Lisa Page, as an FBI lawyer in 2017, wrote "talking points" for Director James Comey ahead of a briefing to Congress -- a memo now exposed for its deceptions. Her lawyer at right, Amy Jeffress, is the wife of the judge for the trial of recently acquitted ex-Clinton lawyer Michael Sussmann.

By Paul Sperry, RealClearInvestigations
June 9, 2022

The FBI deceived the House, Senate, and the Justice Department about the substance and strength of evidence undergirding its counterintelligence investigation of President Trump, according to a recently declassified document and other material.

A seven-page internal FBI memo dated March 8, 2017, shows that "talking points" prepared for then-FBI Director James Comey for his meeting the next day with the congressional leadership were riddled with half-truths, outright falsehoods, and critical omissions. Both the Senate and the House opened investigations and held hearings based in part on the misrepresentations made in those FBI briefings, one of which was held in the Senate that morning and the other in the House later that afternoon. RealClearInvestigations reached out to every member of the leadership, sometimes known as the "Gang of Eight." Some declined to comment, while others did not respond to queries.

The talking points were prepared by Lisa Page, a senior FBI lawyer who later resigned from the bureau amid accusations of anti-Trump bias, and were used by Comey in his meeting with Hill leaders. They described reports the FBI received in 2016 from "a former FBI CHS," or confidential human source, about former Trump campaign officials Paul Manafort and Carter Page (no relation to Lisa Page) allegedly conspiring with the Kremlin to hack the election.

Quoting from the reports, Comey told congressional leaders that the unidentified informant told the FBI that Manafort "initially 'managed' the relationship between Russian government officials and the Trump campaign, using Carter Page as an intermediary." He also told them that "Page was reported to have had 'secret meetings' in early July 2016 with a named individual in Russia's presidential administration during which they discussed Russia's release of damaging information on Hillary Clinton in exchange for alterations to the GOP platform regarding U.S. policy towards Ukraine."

But previous FBI interviews with Carter Page and other key sources indicated that none of that was true – and the FBI knew it at the time of the congressional briefings.

The Lisa Page memo anticipated concerns about the quality of information Comey was relaying to Congress and suggested he preempt any concerns with another untruth. The memo advised Comey to tell lawmakers that "some" of the reporting "has been corroborated" and to point out that the informant's "reporting in this matter is derived primarily from a Russian-based source," which made it sound more credible.

By this point, however, the FBI knew that the main source feeding unsubstantiated rumors to the informant, Christopher Steele, a former British intelligence agent paid By Hillary Clinton's campaign to dig up dirt on Trump, was American-based.

The FBI first interviewed that source – a Russian national named Igor Danchenko, who was living in the U.S. and had worked at the Brookings Institution – in January 2017. Danchenko had told them that the anti-Trump dirt he funneled to Steele was dubious hearsay passed along over drinks with his high school buddies and an old girlfriend named Olga Galkina, who had made up the accusations about Carter Page and Manafort that the FBI relayed to Congress.

Danchenko is now under criminal indictment in Special Counsel John Durham's ongoing investigation for lying about the sourcing for his information. The source to whom he attributed spurious charges against Trump – including his being compromised by a sex tape held by the Kremlin – was a fabrication, according to the indictment. He never spoke with the person, as he claimed. Another source turned out to be a longtime Hillary Clinton campaign adviser.

The FBI did not tell the Gang of Eight that Danchenko was working for Steele and did not really have any sources inside the Kremlin, according to the script prepared for Comey, which was recently declassified as part of pre-trial discovery in Special Counsel John Durham's probe. The FBI also concealed Steele's identity and the fact he was working for the Clinton campaign.

'Crowning' Deception

Adding to the deception, Comey referred to the unnamed informant by the codename "CROWN," making it appear as if Steele's dossier was a product of British intelligence, although Steele had not worked for the British government for several years and was reporting entirely in a private capacity. **According to the talking points memo, Comey also withheld from Congress the fact that Steele had been fired By the FBI for leaking information to the media. Instead of sharing that critical information about his reliability and credibility – to say nothing of his political and financial motivations – Comey hid the truth about his star informant from the nation's top lawmakers.**

"If asked about CROWN/Steele" during the briefing, the memo anticipated, Comey was to tell lawmakers only that "CROWN, a former FBI CHS, is a former friendly foreign intelligence service employee who reported for about three years, and some of whose reporting has been corroborated."

Meanwhile, FBI headquarters officials were duping the Foreign Intelligence Surveillance Act (FISA) court in a similar fashion in order to continue to obtain warrants to spy on Carter Page. They led judges on the secret surveillance court to believe Danchenko was "Russian-based" – and, therefore, presumably more credible.

The official in charge of vetting the Steele dossier at the time – and interviewing him and his primary source, Danchenko, to corroborate their allegations – was FBI Supervisory Intelligence Analyst Brian Auten. By March 2017, Auten knew the "Russian-based" claim was untrue, and yet he let case agents slip it into two FISA renewal requests targeting Page.

Auten seemed to become concerned about the falsehood only when the Senate Judiciary Committee asked to see the Page spy warrants. He then reviewed the FISA applications in advance of Comey briefing the panel on March 15 and raised concerns with then-FBI attorney Kevin Clinesmith, who was assisting with redactions to the documents before

sharing them with Congress. Auten wondered in text messages whether a correction should be reported to the court. But no amendment was ever made.

Years later, in a closed-door 2020 hearing, Senate Judiciary Committee investigators finally caught up with Auten and asked him about it.

"The FISA applications all say that he's Russian-based," then-chief Senate Judiciary Committee investigative counsel Zach Somers pressed Auten. "Do you think that should have been corrected with the Foreign Intelligence Surveillance Court?"

Auten said he raised the issue with Clinesmith, who was convicted last year By Durham on charges related to falsifying evidence in the FISA application process. "And what response did you get back?" Somers asked. "I did not get a response back," Auten replied.

Fraud and More Fraud

And so, the "Russian-based" fraud lived on through the FISA renewals, which also swore to the court that Danchenko was "truthful and cooperative." (Attempts to reach Auten for comment were unsuccessful. The FBI declined to comment.)

The five-year statute of limitations for criminal liability related to invalid FISA applications expires at the end of this month. It has already expired regarding false statement offenses that may have been committed during the March 2017 Gang of Eight briefings.

However, legal experts say Durham could bypass the statute by filing conspiracy charges. Some former FBI attorneys and prosecutors believe the special counsel is building a "conspiracy to defraud the government" case against former FBI officials and others.

Around the same time, the FBI similarly misled high-ranking officials at the Justice Department.

In a March 6, 2017 briefing on the Russiagate probe to acting Attorney General Dana Boente, Comey's deputy Andrew McCabe and counterintelligence official Peter Strzok suggested that Steele's material came from the British government rather than the Clinton campaign by referring to it as "CROWN source reporting," according to handwritten notes taken during the meeting.

Strzok falsely suggested to Boente that the probable cause for his opening the Russiagate investigation, codenamed Crossfire Hurricane, included Trump asking Russia during a July 2016 public campaign appearance to find Clinton's 30,000 missing State Department emails she had deleted from a private server. The electronic communication Strzok personally wrote to officially open the investigation made no mention of this incident. What's more, Trump made the sarcastic remark *after* the date when Strzok stated the FBI determined probable cause.

Strzok, who did not respond to requests for comment, spread the same false claim in his book. He recently admitted in a Georgetown University forum he got that detail wrong while blaming a faulty memory. Strzok was fired by Special Counsel Robert Mueller after the Justice inspector general alerted Mueller to virulently anti-Trump texts he had exchanged with Lisa Page, with whom he was having an illicit affair.

During the high-level briefing, Strzok and McCabe shaded other facts to make it seem as if the case against Trump and his advisers were stronger than it was in order to convince the attorney general they had justifiable cause to continue their "sensitive" political investigations. For instance, they told Boente that the secret FISA monitoring of Page's phone and emails was "fruitful" when in fact, collections failed to corroborate the dossier allegations against Page.

The next month, Boente approved and signed the third application to surveil the Trump adviser. Carter Page was never charged with a crime. But the year-long surveillance, which didn't end until Sept. 22, 2017, allowed FBI headquarters to potentially monitor the Trump presidency through what is known as "incidental collections" of emails, texts, and phone and Skype conversations.

On March 20, 2017, Comey went to Capitol Hill and publicly announced for the first time the existence of the FBI's Crossfire Hurricane investigation into Trump and his campaign.

"The FBI, as part of our counter-intelligence mission, is investigating the Russian government's efforts to interfere in the 2016 presidential election, and that includes investigating the nature of any links between individuals associated with the Trump campaign and the Russian government and whether there was any coordination between the campaign and Russia's efforts," Comey testified.

The unusual public disclosure of an active investigation opened the floodgates to media hysteria about possible Trump's "collusion" with Russia and triggered years of congressional hearings and investigations that dragged Trump figures into countless hours of depositions under subpoena.

Two months later, Mueller took over where fired Comey left off and breathed new life into the counterintelligence and criminal investigations. **In the end, Mueller found no evidence Trump or any Trump official or associate conspired with any Russians to interfere in the election or conduct other espionage. The case, like the Clinton campaign-funded dossier that inspired it, was a bust.**

Tellingly, Lisa Page also personally briefed Mueller about the FBI's investigation when the special counsel took over the case in May 2017. She boasted that Mueller was so impressed with her "overview" that he hired her on the spot. "I want her on my team," she said Mueller told her immediate boss McCabe.

Page did not return requests for comment through her Washington attorney.

Special agent D. Roth- again, the FBI knew that there was no collusion between Trump and Russians

DNI declassifies Brennan notes, CIA memo on Hillary Clinton 'stirring up' scandal between Trump, Russia

A source said Brennan's handwritten notes were taken after briefing Obama on the matter

By **Brooke Singman | Fox News**

EXCLUSIVE: Director of National Intelligence John Ratcliffe on Tuesday declassified documents that revealed former CIA Director John Brennan briefed former President Obama on Hillary Clinton's purported "plan" to tie then-candidate, Donald Trump, to Russia as "a means of distracting the public from her use of a private email server" ahead of the 2016 presidential election, Fox News has learned.

Ratcliffe declassified Brennan's handwritten notes – which were taken after he briefed Obama on the intelligence the CIA received – and a CIA memo, which revealed that officials referred the matter to the FBI for potential investigative action.

The Office of the Director of National Intelligence transmitted the declassified documents to the House and Senate Intelligence Committees on Tuesday afternoon.

"Today, at the direction of President Trump, I declassified additional documents relevant to ongoing Congressional oversight and investigative activities," Ratcliffe said in a statement to Fox News Tuesday.

A source familiar with the documents explained that Brennan's handwritten notes were taken after briefing Obama on the matter.

"We're getting additional insight into Russian activities from [REDACTED]," Brennan notes read. "CITE [summarizing] alleged approved by Hillary Clinton a proposal from one of her foreign policy advisers to vilify Donald Trump by stirring up a scandal claiming interference by the Russian security service," Brennan's notes read.

The notes state, "on 28 of July." In the margin, Brennan writes "POTUS," but that section of the notes is redacted.

"Any evidence of collaboration between Trump campaign + Russia," the notes read.

The remainder of the notes is redacted, except in the margins, which read: "JC," "Denis," and "Susan." "

The notes don't spell out the full names, but "JC" could be referring to then-FBI Director James Comey, "Susan" could refer to National Security Adviser Susan Rice, and "Denis" could refer to Obama chief of staff Denis McDonough.

The declassification comes after Ratcliffe, last week, shared newly-declassified information with the Senate Judiciary Committee, which revealed that in September 2016, U.S. intelligence officials forwarded an investigative referral on Hillary Clinton purportedly approving "a plan concerning U.S. presidential candidate Donald Trump and Russian hackers hampering U.S. elections" in order to distract the public from her email scandal.

31

That referral was sent to Comey and then-Deputy Assistant Director of Counterintelligence Peter Strzok.

"The following information is provided for the exclusive use of your bureau for background investigative action or lead purposes as appropriate," the CIA memo to Comey and Strzok stated.

SPECIAL AGENTS ROTH- Again, Comey is on notice that Hillary Clinton is behind the fake Russian-Trump collusion story.

"This memorandum contains sensitive information that could be source-revealing. It should be handled with particular attention to compartmentation and need-to-know. To avoid the possible compromise of the source, any investigative action taken in response to the information below should be coordinated in advance with Chief Counterintelligence Mission Center, Legal," the memo, which was sent to Comey and Strzok, read. "It may not be used in any legal proceeding— including FISA applications—without prior approval..."

"Per FBI verbal request, CIA provides the below examples of information the CROSSFIRE HURRICANE fusion cell has gleaned to date," the memo continued. "An exchange [REDACTED] discussing US presidential candidate Hillary Clinton's approval of a plan concerning US presidential candidate Donald Trump and Russian hackers hampering US elections as a means of distracting the public from her use of a private email server."

The memo is heavily redacted.

COMEY SAYS NEW INFORMATION THAT HILLARY CLINTON DRUMMED UP RUSSIA CONTROVERSY TO VILIFY TRUMP 'DOESN'T RING A BELL'

Ratcliffe informed the committee last week that the Obama administration obtained Russian intelligence in July 2016 with allegations against Clinton but cautioned that the intelligence community "does not know the accuracy of this allegation or the text to which the Russian intelligence analysis may reflect exaggeration or fabrication."

According to Ratcliffe's letter, the intelligence included the "alleged approval by Hillary Clinton on July 26, 2016, of a proposal from one of her foreign policy advisers to vilify Donald Trump by stirring up a scandal claiming interference by Russian security services."

Nick Merrill, Clinton's spokesperson, called the allegations "baseless b———t."

But Ratcliffe, in a statement released after the information was made public, pushed back on the idea he was advancing "Russian disinformation."

"To be clear, this is not Russian disinformation and has not been assessed as such by the Intelligence Community," Ratcliffe said in a statement to Fox News. "I'll be briefing Congress on the sensitive sources and methods by which it was obtained in the coming days."

A source familiar with the documents told Fox News on Tuesday that the allegation was "not disinformation."

"This is not Russian disinformation. Even Brennan knew, or he wouldn't be briefing the president of the United States on it," the source said. "There is a high threshold to orally brief the president of the United States, and he clearly felt this met that threshold."

Another source familiar with the documents told Fox News that "this information has been sought by hundreds of congressional requests for legitimate oversight purposes and was withheld for political spite—and the belief that they'd never get caught."

The source added that the Brennan notes are significant because it is "their own words, written and memorialized in real-time."

Meanwhile, last week, during a hearing before the Senate Judiciary Committee, Comey was asked whether he received an investigative referral on Clinton from 2016, but he said it didn't "ring any bells."

"You don't remember getting an investigatory lead from the intelligence community? On Sept. 7, 2016, U.S. intelligence officials forwarded an investigative referral to James Comey and Strzok regarding Clinton's approval of a plan [about] Trump…as a means of distraction?" Graham asked Comey.

"That doesn't ring any bells with me," Comey said.

"That's a pretty stunning thing that it doesn't ring a bell," Graham fired back. "You get this inquiry from the intelligence community to look at the Clinton campaign trying to create a distraction, accusing Trump of being a Russian agent or a Russian stooge."

Graham questioned, "how far-fetched is that," citing the fact that the Clinton campaign and the Democratic National Committee, through law firm Perkins Coie, hired Fusion GPS and ex-British intelligence officer Christopher Steele to the author and compiled information for the controversial and unverified anti-Trump dossier.

The Clinton campaign and the Democratic National Committee, through law firm Perkins Coie, hired Fusion GPS and ex-British intelligence officer Christopher Steele to author and compile information for the controversial and unverified anti-Trump dossier.

The dossier contains claims about alleged ties between Donald Trump and Russia that served as the basis for Foreign Intelligence Surveillance Act (FISA) warrants obtained against former Trump campaign aide Carter Page.

OBAMA ADMINISTRATION BRIEFED ON CLAIMS HILLARY CLINTON DRUMMED UP RUSSIA CONTROVERSY TO VILIFY TRUMP, DISTRACT FROM EMAILS

Comey maintained that the referral did not "sound familiar."

Meanwhile, House Intelligence Committee Ranking Member Devin Nunes, R-Calif., called the information and potentially forthcoming documents "smoking guns."

"The documents that are underlying that we now have seen, I have only seen a few of those – they're smoking guns," Nunes said on "Sunday Morning Futures" this week. "That information definitely needs to be made available to the American public."

Nunes added that there is "even more underlying evidence that backs up" the information Ratcliffe released and called the amount of time it took for allies of the president to get the information declassified and made public "mind-boggling."

"This has been a very difficult task for us to get to the bottom of because you have corrupt officials," Nunes said.

Attorney General Bill Barr last year appointed U.S. Attorney of Connecticut John Durham to investigate the origins of the FBI's Russia probe shortly after special counsel Robert Mueller completed his years-long investigation into whether the campaign colluded with the Russians to influence the 2016 presidential election.

It is unclear whether this information will be considered part of Durham's investigation.

Brooke Singman is a Fox News Digital politics reporter. You can reach her at Brooke.Singman@Fox.com or @BrookeSingman on Twitter.

Special Agent Roth- again, the FBI knew that there was no collusion.

Again, the FBI ignored this information. Again, the case could have been closed after a few interviews.

EARLY INFORMATION WHICH DEBUNKED TRUMP-RUSSIA COLLUSION

Steele dossier is debunked

George Papadopoulos Australian diplomat $10 million contribution to Clinton Foundation

Dossier Not What 'Started All of This'

FBI knew 'collusion' was a nothing-burger but kept fake scandal alive anyway

DNI declassifies Brennan notes, CIA memo

CIA has known Trump-Russia collusion data not 'technically plausible.'

DOJ FBI RESPONSE

SPECIAL AGENT ROTH

Did the FBI interview Mrs. Clinton or any of her campaign staff regarding **The Steele Dossier?**

Again, No.

Part Three

Clinton Campaign Officials Spread Her False Allegations

To mine the data, the Clinton campaign enlisted a team of Beltway computer contractors as well as university researchers with security clearance who often collaborate with the FBI and the intelligence community. They worked from a five-page campaign document called the "Trump Associates List."

The tech group also pulled logs purportedly from servers for a Russian bank and Trump Tower, and the campaign provided the data to the FBI on two thumb drives, along with three "white papers" that claimed the data indicated the Trump campaign was secretly communicating with Moscow through a server in Trump Tower and the Alfa Bank in Russia. Based on the material, the FBI opened at least one investigation, adding to several others it had already initiated targeting the Trump campaign in the summer of 2016.

Michael Sussmann: Indicted former Clinton campaign lawyer allegedly coordinated with Jake Sullivan on dubious materials provided to the FBI and media.

Perkinscoie.com

The indictment states that Sussmann, as well as the cyber experts recruited for the operation, "coordinated with representatives and agents of the Clinton campaign with regard to the data and written materials that Sussmann gave to the FBI and the media."

One of those campaign agents was Sullivan, according to emails Durham obtained. On Sept. 15, 2016 – just four days before Sussmann handed off the materials to the FBI – Marc Elias, his law partner and fellow Democratic Party operative, "exchanged emails with the Clinton campaign's foreign policy adviser concerning the Russian bank allegations," as well as with other top campaign officials, the indictment states.

The sources close to the case confirmed the "foreign policy adviser" referenced by the title is Sullivan.

They say he was briefed on the development of the opposition-research materials tying Trump to Alfa Bank and was aware of the participants in the project. These included the Washington opposition-research group Fusion GPS, which worked for the Clinton campaign as a paid agent and helped gather dirt on Alfa Bank and draft the materials Elias discussed with Sullivan, the materials Sussmann would later submit to the FBI. Fusion researchers were in regular contact with both Sussmann and Elias about the project in the summer and fall of 2016. Sullivan also personally met with Elias, who briefed him on Fusion's opposition research, according to the sources.

Sullivan maintained in congressional testimony in December 2017 that he didn't know of Fusion's involvement in the Alfa Bank opposition research. In the same closed-door testimony before the House Intelligence Committee, he also denied knowing anything about Fusion in 2016 or who was conducting the opposition research for the campaign.

"Marc [Elias] ... would occasionally give us updates on the opposition research they were conducting, but I didn't know what the nature of that effort was – inside effort, outside effort, who was funding it, who was doing it, anything like that," Sullivan stated under oath.

MS. SPEIER: And so, during the campaign, outside of reporters calling and asking questions, you never actually saw the dossier?

MR. SULLIVAN: I never saw the dossier. As I was telling counsel in response to his questions, Mark, and without going into privilege, would occasionally give us updates on the opposition research they were conducting. But I didn't know what the nature of that effort was, inside effort, outside effort, who was funding it, who was doing it, anything like that, nor was I sort of centrally responsible for figuring out how to deal with or use opposition research. My job was to put everything in a policy context. So that's where my focus was. So Christopher Steele, Orbis, all of that, those were things that I came to learn about and know about their role after the campaign ended.

Jake Sullivan's December 2017 House testimony may put him in perjury jeopardy.

House Permanent Select Committee on Intelligence

Sullivan also testified he didn't know that Perkins Coie, the law firm where Elias and Sussmann were partners, was working for the Clinton campaign until October 2017, when it was reported in the media as part of stories revealing the campaign's contract with Fusion, which also produced the so-called Steele dossier. Sullivan maintained he didn't even know that the politically prominent Elias worked for Perkins Coie, a well-known Democratic law firm. Major media stories from 2016 routinely identified Elias as "general counsel for the Clinton campaign" and a "partner at Perkins Coie."

"To be honest with you, Marc wears a tremendous number of hats, so I wasn't sure who he was representing," Sullivan testified. "I sort of thought he was, you know, just talking to us as, you know, a fellow traveler in this — in this campaign effort."

Marc Elias: Prominent Democrat lawyer allegedly also coordinated with Sullivan. Sullivan would later plead ignorance under oath about Elias's role.

Perkins Coie

Although he acknowledged knowing Elias and his partner were marshaling opposition researchers for a campaign project targeting Trump, Sullivan insisted, "They didn't do something with it." In truth, they used the research to instigate a full-blown investigation at the FBI and seed a number of stories in the Washington media, which Elias discussed in emails.

Lying to Congress is a felony. Though the offense is rarely prosecuted, former Special Counsel Robert Mueller won convictions of two of Trump's associates on charges of that very offense.

An attorney for Sullivan did not respond to questions, while a spokeswoman for the National Security Council declined to comment. **After the 2016 election, Sullivan continued to participate in the anti-Trump effort, which enlisted no fewer than three Internet companies and two university computer researchers, who persisted in exploiting nonpublic Internet data to conjure up "derogatory information on Trump" and his associates, according to the indictment.**

Prosecutors say the operation ran through at least February 2017, when Sullivan met with another central figure in the plot to plant the anti-Trump smear at the FBI. But now, the goal was to compel agents to continue investigating the false rumors in the wake of the election, thereBy keeping Trump's presidency under an ethical cloud.

Daniel Jones: One of the lead figures in helping resurrect the Trump-Russia collusion narrative after Trump's election, Jones coordinated with Sullivan in hatching the effort.

McCain Institute/YouTube

On Feb. 10, 2017, Sullivan huddled with two Fusion operatives and their partner Daniel Jones, a former FBI analyst and Democratic staffer on the Hill, to hatch the post-election plan to resurrect rumors Trump was a tool of the Kremlin. As RealClearInvestigations first reported, the meeting, which lasted about an hour and took place in a Washington office building, also included former Clinton campaign chairman John Podesta. The group discussed raising money to finance a multimillion-dollar opposition research project headed By Jones to target the new president. In effect, Jones' operation would replace the Clinton campaign's operation, continuing the effort to undermine Trump.

It's not clear if Sussmann attended the Feb. 10 meeting, but he was apparently still involved in the operation, along with his crew of data miners. The day before the meeting attended by Sullivan, Sussmann paid a visit to the CIA's Langley headquarters to peddle the disinformation about the secret server – this time to top officials there, according to the sources familiar with Durham's investigation. During a roughly 90-minute meeting, Sussmann provided two officials at the intelligence headquarters "updated" documents and data he'd provided the FBI before the election, RealClearInvestigations has learned exclusively.

Then, on March 28, 2017, Jones met with the FBI to pass on supposedly fresh leads he and the cyber researchers had learned about the Alfa Bank server and Trump, and the FBI looked into the new leads after having closed its investigation a month earlier. That same month, FBI Director James Comey publicly announced the bureau was investigating possible "coordination" between Moscow and the newly sworn-in president's campaign.

Despite the renewed push By Jones, the FBI debunked the tip of a nefarious Russian back channel. Agents learned the email server in question wasn't even controlled By the Trump Organization. "It wasn't true," Mueller confirmed in their 2019 testimony.

It turns out that the supposed "secret server" was housed in the small Pennsylvania town of Lititz and not in Trump Tower in New York City, and it was operated by a marketing firm based in Florida called Cendyn that routinely blasts out emails promoting multiple hotel chains. Simply put, the third-party server sent spam to Alfa Bank employees who used Trump hotels. The bank had maintained a New York office since 2001.

"The FBI's investigation revealed that the email server at issue was not owned or operated By the Trump Organization but, rather, had been administrated By a mass-marketing email company that sent advertisements for Trump hotels and hundreds of other clients," Durham wrote in his indictment.

Nonetheless, Jones and Sullivan kept promoting the canard as true.

With help from Sullivan and Podesta in 2017, Jones launched a nonprofit group called The Democracy Integrity Project, which raised some $7 million, mainly from Silicon Valley tech executives. TDIP hired computer researchers, as well as Fusion opposition researchers and Christopher Steele, the British author of the now-discredited Steele dossier, to "prove" the rumors in the dossier. As they sought new dirt on Trump, they fed their information to media outlets, leading Democrats on the Senate Intelligence Committee (namely Sens. Mark Warner and Ron Wyden), and the FBI. Jones previously worked on the Senate intelligence panel, which had launched a major investigation of Trump and Russia, and he provided a pipeline of information for the committee, according to the sources.

As RCI first reported, Jones, emailed a daily news bulletin known as "TDIP Research" to prominent Beltway journalists to keep the Trump-Russia "collusion" rumor mill going, including the debunked rumor about the "secret server." Durham has subpoenaed Jones to testify before his grand jury hearing the case, along with computer experts and researchers recruited by Sussmann for the Clinton campaign project, persons close to the investigation said. Attempts to reach Jones for comment were unsuccessful.

In a statement, Durham said his investigation "is ongoing."

Special Counsel John Durham: Lengthy single count "speaking" indictment of Sussmann suggests a broader conspiracy case in the works.

AP

Indictments for a single-count process crime, such as making a false statement, normally run a page or two. But Durham's filing charging Sussmann spans 27 pages and is packed with detail. FBI veterans say the 40-year prosecutor used the indictment to outline a broader conspiracy case he's building that invokes several other federal statutes.

"That is what we call a 'speaking indictment,' meaning it is far more detailed than is required for a simple indictment under [federal statute] 1001," which outlaws are making false statements and representations to federal investigators, former assistant FBI Director Chris Swecker said in an interview with RealClearInvestigations.

"It is damning," he added. "And I see it as a placeholder for additional indictments, such as government grant and contract fraud, computer intrusion, the Privacy Act and other laws against dissemination of personally identifiable information, and mail fraud and wire fraud – not to mention conspiracy to commit those offenses."

40

Chris Swecker: The Sussmann indictment "is damning," and "I definitely see more to come," says the ex-top FBI investigator.

Miller & Martin

"I definitely see more [indictments] to come," emphasized Swecker, who knows Durham personally and worked with him on prior investigations. The sources close to the case said former FBI general counsel James Baker, who accepted the sketchy materials from Sussmann and passed them on to agents for investigation, is cooperating with Durham's investigation, along with former FBI counterintelligence chief Bill Priestap, who has provided prosecutors contemporaneous notes about what led the bureau to open an investigation into the allegations Trump used Alfa Bank as a conduit between his campaign and Russian President Vladimir Putin to steal the election.

According to the sources, Durham also has found evidence that Sussmann misled the CIA, another front in the scandal being reported here for the first time. In December 2016, the sources said Sussmann phoned the general counsel at the agency and told her the same story about the supposed secret server – at the same time, the CIA was compiling a national intelligence report that accused Putin of meddling in the election to help Trump win.

Sussmann told Caroline Krass, then the agency's top attorney, that he had information that may help her with a review President Obama had ordered of all intelligence related to the election and Russia, known as the Intelligence Community Assessment. The review ended up including an annex with several unfounded and since-debunked allegations against Trump developed by the Clinton campaign.

It's not clear if the two-page annex, which claimed the allegations were "consistent with the judgments in this assessment," including the Alfa Bank canard. Before it was made public, several sections had been redacted. But after Sussmann conveyed the information to Krass, an Obama appointee, she told him she would consider it for the intelligence review of Russian interference, which tracks with Sussmann's 2017 closed-door testimony before the House Intelligence Committee. (Krass' name is blacked out in the declassified transcript, but sources familiar with Sussmann's testimony confirmed that he identified her as his CIA contact.)

Caroline Krass: Michael Sussmann also gave Trump-Russia material to this CIA lawyer.

CIA/Wikipedia

"We're interested," said Krass, who left the agency several months later. "We're doing this review, and I'll speak to someone here."

It's not known if Sussmann failed to inform the top CIA lawyer that he was working on behalf of the Clinton campaign, as he's alleged to have done at the FBI. Attempts to reach Krass, who now serves as Biden's top lawyer at the Pentagon, were unsuccessful.

But in his return trip to the CIA after the election, Sussmann "stated falsely – as he previously had stated to the FBI general counsel – that he was 'not representing a particular client,' " according to the Durham indictment, which cites a contemporaneous memo drafted by two agency officials with whom Sussmann met that memorialize their meeting. (The document refers to the CIA by the pseudonym "Agency-2." Sources confirm Agency-2 is the CIA.)

Remarkably, the CIA did not ask for the source of Sussmann's walk-in tip, including where he got several data files he gave the agency. The FBI exhibited a similar lack of curiosity when Sussmann told it about the false Trump/Alfa Bank connection.

SPECIAL AGENT ROTH- Again, the FBI never asked Sussman where he obtained the information. A truthful answer by the FBI could have ended this Russian-Trump collusion scheme.

Attempts to reach Sussmann to get his side of the additional CIA allegations leveled by Durham were unsuccessful. The 57-year-old attorney pleaded not guilty to a single felony count and was released on a $100,000 bond Friday. If convicted, he faces up to five years in prison.

The prominent Washington lawyer quietly resigned from Perkins Coie, which has scrubbed all references to him from its website. And late last month, as rumors of the indictment swirled, the powerhouse law firm divested its entire Political Law Group, formerly headed by Marc Elias – who commissioned the Steele dossier. Elias, who worked closely with Sussmann on the Trump-Alfa Bank project, also is no longer employed by the firm.

In late July 2016, during the Democratic National Convention in Philadelphia, the CIA picked up Russian chatter about a Clinton foreign policy adviser who was trying to develop allegations to "vilify" Trump. The intercepts said Clinton herself had approved a "plan" to "stir up a scandal" against Trump by tying him to Putin. According to hand-written notes, then-CIA chief John Brennan warned President Obama that Moscow had intercepted information about the "alleged approval by Hillary Clinton on July 26, 2016, of a proposal from one of her foreign policy advisers to vilify Donald Trump." That summer, Brennan had personally briefed Democrats, including then-Senate Majority Leader Harry Reid, on the Alfa Bank-Trump server rumors, according to congressional reports. Reid fired off a letter to Comey demanding that the FBI do more to investigate Trump's ties to Russia.

During that convention, Sullivan drove a golf cart from one TV-network news tent in the parking lot to another, pitching producers and anchors a story that Trump was conspiring with Putin to steal the election. CNN, ABC News, CBS News, and NBC News, as well as Chris

Wallace of Fox News gave him airtime to spin the Clinton campaign's unfounded theories. Sullivan also gave off-camera background briefings to reporters.

"We were on a mission," Clinton campaign spokeswoman Jennifer Palmieri later admitted in a Washington Post column. "We wanted to raise the alarm."

Then, on the eve of the election, Sullivan claimed in a written campaign statement that Trump and the Russians had set up a "secret hotline" through Alfa Bank, and he suggested "federal authorities" were investigating "this direct connection between Trump and Russia." He portrayed the shocking discovery as the work of independent experts — "computer scientists" — without disclosing their attachment to the campaign.

"This could be the most direct link yet between Donald Trump and Moscow," Sullivan claimed.

Clinton teed up his statement on Oct. 31, 2016, tweet, which quickly went viral. Also, that day, Clinton tweeted, "It's time for Trump to answer serious questions about his ties to Russia," while attaching a meme that read: "Donald Trump has a secret server. It was set up to communicate privately with a Putin-tied Russian bank called Alfa Bank."

Hillary Clinton ✓
@HillaryClinton

···

Computer scientists have apparently uncovered a covert server linking the Trump Organization to a Russian-based bank.

Statement from Jake Sullivan on New Report Exposing Trump's Secret Line of Communication to Russia

In response to a new report from Slate showing that the Trump Organization has a secret server registered to Trump Tower that has been covertly communicating with Russia, Hillary for America Senior Policy Adviser Jake Sullivan released the following statement Monday:

"This could be the most direct link yet between Donald Trump and Moscow. Computer scientists have apparently uncovered a covert server linking the Trump Organization to a Russian-based bank.

"This secret hotline may be the key to unlocking the mystery of Trump's ties to Russia. It certainly seems the Trump Organization felt it had something to hide, given that it apparently took steps to conceal the link when it was discovered by journalists.

"This line of communication may help explain Trump's bizarre adoration of Vladimir Putin and endorsement of so many pro-Kremlin positions throughout this campaign. It raises even more troubling questions in light of Russia's masterminding of hacking efforts that are clearly intended to hurt Hillary Clinton's campaign. We can only assume that federal authorities will now explore this direct connection between Trump and Russia as part of their existing probe into Russia's meddling in our elections."

8:36 PM · Oct 31, 2016 · TweetDeck

11.8K Retweets **4,183** Quote Tweets **15.5K** Likes

The Clinton campaign played up the bogus Trump-Alfa Bank story on the eve of the 2016 election.

Twitter/@HillaryClinton

It's not immediately apparent if then-Vice President Joe Biden was briefed about the Alfa Bank tale or other Trump-Russia rumors and investigations.

Biden has never been questioned about his own role in the investigation of Trump. However, it was the former vice president who introduced the idea of prosecuting Trump's national security adviser appointee, Gen. Flynn, under the Logan Act of 1799, a dead-letter statute that prohibits private citizens from interfering in U.S. foreign policy and which hasn't been used to prosecute anyone in modern times. According to notes taken by then-FBI counterintelligence official Peter Strzok, who attended a Jan. 5, 2017, Oval Office meeting with Obama and Biden, in which Trump, Flynn, and Russia were discussed, Biden raised the idea: "VP: Logan Act," the notes read.

Sullivan has argued in congressional testimony and elsewhere that Flynn violated the Logan Act, raising suspicions he may have put the idea in Biden's head. Sullivan had advised the vice president before joining the Clinton campaign.

This and all other original articles created by RealClearInvestigations may be republished for free with attribution. (These terms do not apply to outside articles linked on the site.)

Biden Security Adviser Jake Sullivan Tied to Alleged 2016 Clinton Scheme to Co-Opt the CIA and FBI to Tar Trump

By Paul Sperry, RealClearInvestigations

September 23, 2021

ALFA BANK RUSSIA/JAKE SULLIVAN

Jake Sullivan repeatedly promoted the Alfa Bank story at the center of the Durham indictment

The other two who appeared at the meeting were Fusion co-founder Peter Fritsch and Democratic Sen. Dianne Feinstein's former aide, Dan Jones.

Sullivan admitted he was in meetings where Elias briefed the campaign on opposition research, saying some of it was related to the Steele allegations.

Baker briefed Comey, McCabe

FBI concerns about media

FBI finds no 'surreptitious communications channel' after weeks of investigation

'Frustrated' Clinton lawyer shopped phony Trump-Russia data to CIA in '17: witnesses

By Ben Feuerherd and Bruce Golding

May 20, 2022 9:15pm

WASHINGTON, DC — Former Hillary Clinton campaign lawyer Michael Sussmann denied he was "representing a client" when he gave the CIA faulty data linking Donald Trump to Russia — and appeared "frustrated" that officials weren't taking the information seriously, two former agency employees testified Friday.

One ex-spy — identified in court only as "Kevin P." — recalled that he and a colleague met with Sussmann at CIA headquarters in Langley, Va., in February 2017, shortly after Trump took office.

Sussmann gave the men two thumb drives that he said came from unidentified "contacts" and showed a secret cyber back channel between a Trump Organization server and Russia's Alfa Bank; Kevin P. said, "He said he was not representing a client," the witness testified, adding that Sussmann also said he'd previously given "similar but unrelated" information to the FBI.

Sussmann, 57, is on trial in Washington, DC, the federal court for allegedly denying that he was acting on behalf of a client when he gave two thumb drives and three "white papers" on the purported Trump-Russia ties to then-FBI general counsel James Baker on Sept. 19, 2016.

Sussmann is charged with a single count of lying to the government, with special counsel John Durham alleging that he was actually working for the Clinton campaign and another client, tech executive Rodney Joffe, who told Sussmann about the data.

Sussman worked as Hillary Clinton's campaign lawyer. Andrew Schwartz / SplashNews.com

Following the meeting at CIA headquarters, Kevin P.'s colleague — identified as "Steve M." — drafted a memo summarizing what took place and noting that Sussmann had been there on behalf of a client, according to evidence shown to jurors.

But Kevin P. edited the memo to take out the word "client" and replaced it with "contacts," another exhibit showed.

Sussmann's meeting in Langley appeared to be the result of an earlier sit-down with retired CIA official Mark Chadason, former station chief in both Europe and North Africa, who testified that he met with a Sussmann at a hotel in northern Virginia on Jan. 31, 2017, at the request of a mutual friend.

Sussman gave the CIA faulty data linking the Trump Organization and Russia's Alfa Bank in 2017.

Sussmann told Chadason that he wanted to give the CIA information about a national security issue and had previously reached out to the agency's general counsel in an attempt to do so, Chadason said.

Sussmann said he got the information from a Republican client but added that he wasn't "sure if he would reveal himself to the CIA," the former spook said.

Sussmann also said he planned to go to the New York Times if the CIA didn't pursue the matter, Chadason recalled.

Under cross-examination, Chadason said he didn't view Sussmann's remark as a threat but an act of desperation.

Part Four

Attempts By Democrats to Remove Trump

IMPEACHMENTS OF TRUMP

Inauguration Day in January 2017.

The campaign to impeach President Trump has begun.

Anti-Trump protesters chant during the swearing-in ceremony

Protesters broke out in chants against President Trump during his swearing-in ceremony at the U.S. Capitol. (Claritza Jimenez/the Washington Post)

By Matea Gold

Enterprise/investigations editor

Jan. 20, 2017, at 12:19 p.m. EST

The effort to impeach President Donald John Trump is already underway.

At the moment the new commander-in-chief was sworn in, a campaign to build public support for his impeachment went live at ImpeachDonaldTrumpNow.org, spearheaded by two liberal advocacy groups aiming to lay the groundwork for his eventual ejection from the White House.

The organizers behind the campaign, Free Speech for People and RootsAction, are hinging their case on Trump's insistence on maintaining ownership of his luxury hotel and golf course business while in office. Ethics experts have warned that his financial holdings could potentially lead to constitutional violations and undermine public faith in his decision-making.

Their effort is early, strategists admit. But they insist it is not premature — even if it triggers an angry backlash from those who will argue that they are not giving the new president a chance.

"If we were to wait for all the ill effects that could come from this, too much damage to our democracy would occur," said Ron Fein, legal director at Free Speech for People. "It will undermine faith in basic institutions. If nothing else, it's important for Americans to trust that the president is doing what he thinks is the right thing … not that it would help jump-start a stalled casino project in another country."

Michael Moore: 'Donald Trump will not last these four years'

Documentary filmmaker Michael Moore spoke at a protest at McPherson Square in Washington, D.C., following President Trump's inauguration. (The Washington Post)

The impeachment drive comes as Democrats and liberal activists are mounting broad opposition to stymie Trump's agenda. Among the groups organizing challenges to the Trump administration is the American Civil Liberties Union, which plans to wield public-records requests and lawsuits as part of an aggressive action plan aimed at protecting immigrants and pushing for government transparency, among other issues.

"We think that President Trump will be in violation of the Constitution and federal statutes on day one, and we plan a vigorous offense to ensure the worst of the constitutional violations do not occur," said Anthony D. Romero, the ACLU's executive director

.

"We may have a new president, but we have the same old system of checks and balances," he added.

Strategists behind the campaign for impeachment said they are confident that other groups will soon join their cause. They argue that Trump will immediately be in violation of the U.S. Constitution's Foreign Emoluments Clause, which prohibits a president from accepting a gift or benefit from a foreign leader or government.

Fein cited several examples, including rent paid by the Industrial & Commercial Bank of China for its space in Trump Tower in New York and potential ongoing spending by foreign diplomats at the Trump International Hotel in Washington and other Trump properties. In addition, he said, royalties collected by the Trump organization from the president's business partner in the Philippines, who was recently named a special envoy to the United States, could violate the clause.

Trump's Washington hotel is the hub of inaugural action — and potential conflicts

Trump said this month that he would donate "profits" from foreign business clients to the U.S. Treasury. However, neither Trump nor representatives of the Trump Organization have provided details on how such payments would be tracked, collected, and disbursed.

The foreign emoluments clause has never been tested in the courts, and some scholars argue that violating it would not qualify as "treason, bribery or other high crimes and misdemeanors," the grounds for impeachment of a federal official.

But Fein noted that former Virginia governor Edmund Jennings Randolph, a delegate to the Constitutional Convention and later the first U.S. attorney general, argued during Virginia's debate over ratifying the constitution that a president who was found to have taken a foreign emolument "may be impeached."

His group has mapped out a long-shot political strategy to build support for a vote in the House on articles of impeachment.

The first step is fairly simple: getting a resolution introduced that calls for the House Judiciary Committee to investigate whether there are grounds to impeach Trump — a move that Fein said a number of members of Congress are interested in taking.

"Getting it introduced is not going to be a problem," he said.

Still, the idea that a majority of the GOP-controlled House members would ultimately vote to launch an investigation of the new president seems highly improbable. Fein said he is confident the political climate will change and lawmakers will eventually support the effort.

"I think that at a certain point, the combination of new revelations coming out and, importantly, calls and pressure from constituents in their own districts will be a deciding factor," he said. "And, at some point, they will decide it is in their own interests to support this."

While half a dozen federal judges in American history have been impeached by the House and successfully convicted in the Senate, no U.S. president has ever been removed from office through such a process. The closest was Andrew Johnson, who narrowly avoided conviction in the Senate in 1868 after the House charged him with removing the secretary of war in violation of the Tenure of Office Act.

In 1974, the House Judiciary Committee approved articles of impeachment against then-President Richard Nixon, but he resigned before they could be voted on by the full House. President Bill Clinton was impeached by the House on charges of perjury and obstruction of justice, but the articles of impeachment were defeated in the Senate in 1999.

Matea Gold is the national political enterprise and investigations editor for The Washington Post. She previously covered money and influence as a national political reporter.

Special Agent Roth-Trump met with President Obama in the White House on the day of the Inauguration. The meeting usually lasts for 40 minutes, but this meeting lasted 1.5 hours.

Trump said "President Obama" is a nice man. President Obama gave Trump a letter that was found in Trump's Mara-La-Go house.

Michael Moore, is this the way to start a change of government?

Impeachment Ukraine

The Trump–Ukraine scandal revolves around efforts by U.S. President Donald Trump to coerce Ukraine and other foreign countries into providing damaging narratives about 2020 Democratic Party presidential primary candidate Joe Biden, as well as information relating to the origins of previous political attacks against him, such as the claims investigated by Robert Mueller. Trump allegedly enlisted surrogates within and outside his official administration, including his personal lawyer, Rudy Giuliani , and Attorney General William Barr, to pressure Ukraine and other foreign governments to cooperate in investigating conspiracy theories concerning American politics. Trump blocked but later released payment of a congressionally mandated $400 million military aid package to allegedly obtain *quid pro quo* cooperation from Volodymyr Zelenskyy, the president of Ukraine. A number of contacts were established between the White House and the government of Ukraine, culminating in a phone call between Trump and Zelenskyy on July 25, 2019. Less than two hours later, on behalf of the president, senior executive budget official Michael Duffey discreetly instructed the Pentagon to continue withholding military aid to Ukraine.

The scandal reached public attention in mid-September 2019 after a whistleblower complaint was made in August 2019. The complaint raised concerns about Trump using presidential powers to solicit foreign electoral intervention in the 2020 U.S. presidential election. The Trump White House has corroborated several allegations raised by the whistleblower. A non-verbatim transcript of the Trump–Zelenskyy call confirmed that Trump requested investigations into Joe Biden and his son Hunter, as well as a discredited conspiracy theory involving a Democratic National Committee server, while repeatedly urging Zelenskyy to work with Giuliani and Barr on these matters. The White House also confirmed that the record of the call had been transferred to a highly classified system.

White House acting chief of staff Mick Mulvaney said one reason why Trump withheld military aid to Ukraine was Ukrainian "corruption related to the DNC server," referring to a debunked theory that Ukrainians framed Russia for hacking into the DNC computer system. After the impeachment inquiry began, Trump publicly urged Ukraine and China to investigate the Bidens. Bill Taylor, the Trump administration's top diplomat to Ukraine, testified that he was told that U.S. military aid to Ukraine and a Trump–Zelenskyy White House meeting was conditioned on Zelenskyy publicly announcing investigations into the Bidens and alleged Ukrainian interference in the 2016 U.S. elections.[37] United States Ambassador to the European Union Gordon Sondland testified that he worked with Giuliani at Trump's "express direction" to arrange a *quid pro quo* with the Ukraine government.

Acquittal

Under the U.S. Constitution, a two-thirds majority of the Senate is required to convict the president. The possible penalties are the removal from office and disqualification from holding office in the future. On February 5, 2020, the Senate acquitted Trump on both counts. The votes were 52–48 to acquit on the first count and 53–47 to acquit on the second count. The votes were sharply divided along party lines. [195] Mitt Romney became the first senator in history from an impeached president's party to vote to convict, voting "guilty" on the first count.

Public opinion

Before the trial, in mid-January 2020, Americans were sharply divided on whether Trump should be removed from office, with Democrats largely supporting removal, Republicans largely opposing, and independents divided. A *USA Today*/Suffolk University poll conducted between December 10 and 14, 2019, found that 45% of respondents supported the impeachment and removal of Trump from office, while 51% opposed it. A CNN poll conducted from December 12 to 15 also found that 45% supported impeachment and removal, compared to 47% who opposed the idea. A Gallup poll released on the day of Trump's impeachment found that the president's approval rating increased by six points during the impeachment process while support for the impeachment fell. Another CNN poll conducted between January 16 and 19, 2020, found that 51% supported Trump's removal from office, compared to 45% who opposed it. An NBC/*Wall Street Journal* poll released on January 2, 2020, showed 46% favored removal from office and 49% opposed, with the in favor/opposed being almost exclusively along party lines.[203]

Impeachment January 6

Donald Trump, the 45th president of the United States, was impeached for the second time on January 13, 2021, one week before his term expired. It was the fourth impeachment of a U.S. president and the second for Trump after his first impeachment in December 2019. Ten Republican representatives voted for the second impeachment, the most pro-impeachment votes ever from a president's party. This was also the first presidential impeachment in which all majority caucus members voted unanimously for impeachment.

The House of Representatives of the 117th U.S. Congress adopted one article of impeachment against Trump for "incitement of insurrection," alleging that he had incited the January 6 attack on the U.S. Capitol. These events were preceded by numerous unsuccessful attempts by Trump to overturn the 2020 presidential election, as well as his pushing of voter fraud conspiracy theories on his social media channels before, during, and after the election A single article of impeachment charging Trump with "incitement of insurrection" against the U.S. government and "lawless action at the Capitol" was introduced to the House of Representatives on January 11, 2021 The article was introduced with more than 200 co-sponsors.The same day, House Speaker Nancy Pelosi gave Vice President Mike Pence an ultimatum to invoke Section 4 of the 25th Amendment to assume the role of acting president within 24 hours, or the House would proceed with impeachment proceedings. Pence stated that he would not do so in a letter to Pelosi the following day, arguing that to do so would not "be in the best interest of our Nation or consistent with our Constitution." Nevertheless, a House majority, including Republican Adam Kinzinger, passed a resolution urging Pence to invoke the 25th Amendment.

The House impeachment managers formally triggered the start of the impeachment trial on January 25 by delivering to the Senate the charge against Trump. The nine managers walked into the Senate chamber led by the lead impeachment manager, Representative Jamie Raskin, who read the article of impeachment. The trial in the Senate was scheduled to start on February 9. The trial was the first of its kind for a departed U.S. president, with Andrew Johnson, Bill Clinton, and Trump having each been the incumbent in prior impeachment trials; as a result, Chief Justice John Roberts chose not to preside as he had done for Trump's first impeachment trial (the president pro tempore of the Senate, Vermont senator Patrick Leahy, presided instead, and arguments favoring the conviction of Trump cited the Senate's 1876 conviction of Ulysses S. Grant's Secretary of War William W. Belknap, who was impeached, but was not convicted, after leaving office. At the trial, 57 senators voted "guilty," which was less than the two-thirds majority needed (67) to convict Trump, and 43 senators voted "not guilty," resulting in Trump being acquitted of the charges on February 13, 2021.

At the conclusion of the trial, the Senate voted 57–43 to convict Trump of inciting insurrection, falling 10 votes short of the two-thirds majority required by the Constitution, and Trump was therefore acquitted. Seven Republican senators joined all Democratic and independent senators in voting to convict Trump, the largest bipartisan vote for an impeachment conviction of a U.S. president or former U.S. president. After the vote on the acquittal, Mitch McConnell said it is no doubt that Trump was practically and morally responsible for inciting the events at the Capitol, but he voted against conviction due to his interpretation of the United States Constitution.

SPECIAL AGENT ROTH- Acknowledge that the Impeachment of a President is a political exercise.

Add Jan. 6 hearing

Robert Mueller, Special Council

Mueller finds no proof of Trump collusion with Russia; AG Barr says evidence 'not sufficient' to prosecute

"(W)hile this report does not conclude that the President committed a crime, it also does not exonerate him," the special counsel said in his report.

March 24, 2019, 3:09 PM EDT / Updated March 24, 2019, 6:14 PM EDT

By Pete Williams, Julia Ainsley and Gregg Birnbaum

Special counsel Robert Mueller found no proof that President Donald Trump criminally colluded with Russia and reached no conclusion about whether Trump obstructed justice, Attorney General William Barr told Congress on Sunday while also announcing that he found insufficient evidence to pursue the matter further.

The bombshell findings were contained in a letter that Barr sent to lawmakers summarizing Mueller's report, and that was made public.

Barr quoted Mueller's report, which he said stated: "(T)he investigation did not establish that members of the Trump campaign conspired or coordinated with the Russian government in its election interference activities."

The report makes it clear that Trump was not exonerated in his behavior but simply found insufficient criminal evidence to prosecute.

On obstruction of justice, Barr wrote that the special counsel declined "to make a traditional prosecutorial judgment," leaving it up to the attorney general to choose whether to bring obstruction charges against the president. Barr declined to do so, he said in the letter to Congress, based on the evidence presented and Department of Justice guidelines around prosecuting a sitting president.

Mueller report: 'Evidence...not sufficient' that Trump obstructed justice

MARCH 24, 201901:20

Mueller did not, Barr said, "draw a conclusion — one way or the other — as to whether the examined conduct constituted obstruction."

"Instead, for each of the relevant actions investigated, the (Mueller) report sets out the evidence on both sides of the question and leaves unresolved what the Special Counsel views as 'difficult issues' of law and fact concerning whether the President's actions and intent could be viewed as obstruction," Barr wrote. "The Special Counsel states that 'while this report does not conclude that the President committed a crime, it also does not exonerate him.'"

Trump tweeted a short time later, "Complete and Total EXONERATION."

No Collusion, No Obstruction, Complete and Total EXONERATION. KEEP
AMERICA GREAT!

— Donald J. Trump (@realDonaldTrump) March 24, 2019

Providing Mueller's "principal conclusions," as Barr has referred to them, to lawmakers came after the transmission of the special counsel's report to Barr on Friday that concluded an investigation that has resulted in the indictments of 34 people infuriated the president and threw the administration into turmoil.

It remains unclear whether Mueller's full report will ever be made public.

The long-awaited end of the probe came almost two years after Mueller was appointed by Deputy Attorney General Rod Rosenstein to investigate "any links and/or coordination between the

Russian government and individuals associated with the campaign of President Donald Trump" and "any matters that arose or may arise directly from the investigation."

Among those who have been criminally charged are Trump's former national security adviser Michael Flynn; former campaign chairman Paul Manafort; longtime ex-political adviser Roger Stone; former personal lawyer Michael Cohen; and numerous Russian nationals. There have been a number of guilty pleas and convictions — but none of the charges have directly accused Trump or anyone in his orbit of conspiring with Russians to help Trump get elected in 2016.

There will be no more indictments now that the probe is over, NBC News has learned.

Emily Compagno blasts Robert Mueller following Clinton bombshell: His team should be 'extremely embarrassed.'

Former Clinton campaign manager RobBy Mook testified Friday that Hillary Clinton approved of leaking Trump-Russia allegations to the media.

Emily Compagno: Robert Mueller should be embarrassed

'Outnumbered' co-host Emily Compagno argues it is 'absolutely unacceptable' that Robert Mueller's report didn't include that Hillary Clinton approved the leak of Trump-Russia allegations to the media.

Emily Compagno sounded off on special counsel Robert Mueller following the bombshell testimony from former Clinton campaign manager RobBy Mook. The "Outnumbered" co-host said Monday it is "absolutely unacceptable" that Mueller's report didn't mention Hillary Clinton approved of leaking the Trump-Russia allegations to the media, given the extensive resources for Mueller's investigation.

TRUMP REACTS TO TESTIMONY THAT CLINTON SPREAD RUSSIA ALLEGATIONS: 'WHERE DO I GET MY REPUTATION BACK?'

EMILY COMPAGNO: *They used 19 special prosecutors and more than 40 FBI agents. We footed that entire bill. They produced three separate reports that basically said, 'well, we can't prove a connection between Trump and Russia, but we can't disprove it.' All it would have taken is five minutes spent in a room with this guy who could have said, 'yes, actually, it was greenlit By Hillary Clinton. Actually, yes. There was not one modicum of truth to this.'*

And instead, this really important person is the one who approved of and spearheaded it being leaked to the media. And listen, if I was one of the attorneys on Mueller's team, I would not only be extremely embarrassed right now, but I would have a lot of questions. Because either they did know, and it didn't make it into the report, or they didn't know. And either of those answers is absolutely unacceptable.

SPECIAL AGENT ROTH AND EMILY COMPAGNO FOX NEWS - Great minds think alike.

The entire theme of this book is how easily and quickly the Clinton Collusion scam could have been stopped. All it took was one interview.

RUSSIA GATE PROBE

By Post-Editorial Board

August 26, 2022, 7:03 pm

Contrary to Special Counsel Robert Mueller's remarks, a memo from the DOJ's Office of Legal Counsel said there was not enough evidence to support an obstruction of justice charge against President Donald Trump. EPA

In a final blow to the credibility of RussiaGate special counsel Robert Mueller, a newly released 2019 memo shows he was blowing smoke in pretending that, even though the whole Russia-collusion case was utterly baseless, then-President Donald Trump *could* still be prosecuted for obstruction of justice over how he dealt with the investigation.

Naturally, the media have greeted the memo from the Justice Department's Office of Legal Counsel with dead silence.

The DOJ found no evidence of collusion between Trump and Russia.

Dems' war on ex-President Donald Trump is without precedent

When Mueller finally testified publicly about his findings, he turned out to be sadly diminished from his salad days, enormously challenged in even explaining the work he'd supposedly supervised for nearly two years. It was evident he'd simply served as a figurehead for the partisan Democrats who actually did the investigation — which, he admitted, found zero serious evidence of Trump-Russia collusion.

But he still hedged, saying that if his office "had confidence that the president clearly did not commit a crime, we would have said that."

In other words, they couldn't prove a negative (not that they *wanted* to). And that's basically what the 2019 memo said: Mueller's minions not only didn't have evidence to support obstruction charges but "certain of the conduct examined by the Special Counsel could not, as a matter of law, support an obstruction charge" — meaning they were trying to treat completely *legal* Trump actions as obstruction.

Then-Attorney General Bill Barr duly announced as much and was pilloried by the Trump-hating press as covering for Orange Man.

Mueller's staff delivered their report to Barr (contrary to his request) in such a way that he couldn't immediately release it to the public; he had to have *his* staff take days to redact various confidential information. And that delay, too, fed the "Barr coverup" hysteria.

The newly released memo reveals that the whole investigation was utterly weaponized against Trump: Mueller's minions came up empty-handed yet still tried to paint him as a crook.

All part and parcel of the overall RussiaGate insanity, where democracy, we were told, was at stake. Out the door went the normal rules of journalism *and* justice, as insiders leaked "scoop" after empty scoop to eagerly gullible "news" outlets — only for all of it to evaporate on contact with reality.

Recent months have brought an avalanche of revelations wrecking every major prop of the Russia Gate claims. The Steele Dossier was bunk based on nothing but speculative gossip among a "researcher" and his pals.

And the FBI and Justice Department *knew* it but acted on the bogus information anyway — moved in part by the hysteria the media were creating on the basis of deceitful leaks from Democratic government insiders.

Democracy *was* at stake, but the press and relevant parts of Justice were on the wrong side. No wonder no one (except the willfully deceived) trusts them anymore.

DEMOCRATS CALL TRUMP A RACIST

Charles Payne Fox News FINANCIAL

Special Agent Roth- I respect Charles' integrity so much that if he told me to throw all my money off the Empire State Building, I would do it without hesitation.

My next guest says creating the Juneteenth holiday will unite Americans. Alveda King is the niece of Martin Luther King Jr., and she joins me now.

Alveda, it is always a pleasure to have you on.

Just share your thoughts. I mean, I can imagine a number of things running through your mind watching this event.

DR. ALVEDA KING, FOX NEWS CONTRIBUTOR: Absolutely, Charles.

I was a state legislator when the Martin Luther King bill became a holiday, and I was very instrumental in Georgia as a state legislator in helping to get that passed. So, I feel just as excited today as I did then. However, I remember being at the White House in 2020 with President Trump and some black leaders. And he supported us fully in having Juneteenth to be a holiday. I have been working at Priests for Life as a pastoral associate for many, many years.

NEWSWEEK

Alveda King

President Donald Trump responds to Dr. Alveda King, niece of Dr. Martin Luther King Jr., during a meeting with inner city pastors at the White House in Washington, D.C., on August 1, 2018

JIM WATSON/AFP

"You know, we all believe the same. That's something the president has said, one race, one human race," King said. "So, he's not a racist, absolutely is not," she continued, "and the programs that he has moved forward, the higher job market is helping African Americans. The criminal justice reform **MLK's Niece Defends**

Donald Trump against Racism Accusations: 'All That News Is Absolutely Fake'

BY JASON LEMON ON *7/30/19 AT 10:20 AM EDT*

Alveda King, the niece of iconic Civil Rights activist Dr. Martin Luther King Jr., told Fox News on Tuesday that claims by Democrats, pundits, and activists that President Donald Trump is a racist are inaccurate.

During a Tuesday morning segment of Fox & Friends, King appeared for an interview with the morning show's co-host Steve Doocy to discuss a meeting she and other African American pastors had with Trump at the White House and to comment on the president's recent attacks on Democratic Representative Elijah Cummings and his city, Baltimore. After Doocy played a clip of politicians and analysts criticizing the president and arguing that he is racist, King disagreed strongly.

"All of that news is absolutely fake," King, who formerly served as a representative in Georgia's State House, insisted. She told Doocy that the president told her and the others in their meeting this week that "he cares about all Americans." helping African Americans."

Trump on Saturday lashed out at Cummings, who represents Maryland's 7th District which includes more than half of Baltimore, arguing that the representative's city is a place where "No human being would want to live."

"Cumming [sic] District is a disgusting, rat and rodent-infested mess. If he spent more time in Baltimore, maybe he could help clean up this very dangerous & filthy place," the president wrote.

That was my first initiative when I joined Priests for Life. Let's get Juneteenth for not only African-Americans but for babies. And so that has been an initiative. I'm very happy that it has been signed; been working on it for a very, very long time.

I see that President Biden did sign it. And I'm glad he signed it. We have been working on it for a long time, even with President Trump. And I'm just so very happy to see it passed.

You know, what happens, a new president comes in, and they get to take credit, not only for what they're doing but the good things that the president before them did, like the vaccines, for instance, with President Trump.

PAYNE: Sure. Right.

WALL STREET JOURNAL

The Trump Boom Lifted Black Americans

Before the pandemic, the economy grew in ways that mostly benefited low-income and middle-class households.

WSJ Opinion: Identity Politics at the Supreme Court

Joe Biden began his presidency with a promise to advance equity, which means favoring some races and ethnicities over others to shrink outcome disparities. Like many of his fellow liberal Democrats, Mr. Biden is tethered to the belief that black upward mobility won't happen without coddling and special treatment from the government. Donald Trump's record complicates such claims.

One of the most underreported stories of the Trump presidency is the extent to which black economic fortunes improved. The mainstream media presented Mr. Trump daily as a bigot whose policies would harm the interests of racial and ethnic minorities. Meantime, black economic advancement occurred to an extent unseen not only under Barack Obama but going back several generations—until the pandemic shutdowns brought progress to a halt.

Part Five

Fake Media

CNN's Brian Stelter flip-flops on the Hunter Biden scandal By saying it's 'not just a right-wing media story.'

Joseph Wulfsohn, Brian Flood - 2h ago

CNN's media correspondent Brian Stelter had an apparent epiphany about the severity of the Hunter Biden scandal, which turned out not to be a dismissable "right-wing media story" like the liberal pundit insisted in 2020.

On Sunday's installment of "Reliable Sources," Stelter suggested President Biden's 2024 ambitions could be derailed by the ongoing federal investigations into his son during an interview with Michael LaRosa, the former press secretary for First Lady Jill Biden.

"What about his son? What about Hunter?" Stelter asked. "Hunter is under federal investigation; charges can be coming at any time; this is not just a right-wing media story. This is a real problem for the Bidens."

"Could he decide not to run for re-election given his son?" Stelter followed, marking a dramatic tonal shift from what he expressed in 2020 under different CNN ownership.

FORMER FBI SPECIAL AGENT ROTH – This is evidence of Biden rigging 2020

Election.

TRUMP SAYS CNN HAS 'GOTTEN WORSE' UNDER NEW OWNERSHIP: 'THEY LOST TREMENDOUS CREDIBILITY'

© Provided by FOX News Brian Stelter has changed his stance on Hunter Biden's laptop as CNN's new management wants to focus on "news." Matt Winkelmeyer/Getty Images for Vanity Fair

In October 2020, just days after the New York Post published its reporting on the contents of Hunter Biden's laptop, which included emails shedding light on his questionable business dealings overseas, Stelter accused conservatives of "whataboutism," even peddling the unsubstantiated claims that the laptop's contents were "tied to a Russian disinformation effort" attacking his father.

He then attempted to cast doubt on the Post's reporting by stressing the involvement of Steve Bannon and Rudy Giuliani as well as questioning the legitimacy of John Paul Mac Isaac, the Delaware computer repair store owner who first obtained Hunter Biden's laptop.

CNN WILL 'REIMAGINE' LONG-STRUGGLING MORNING SHOW 'NEW DAY,' CEO SAYS

"There's a lot about this story that does not add up," Stelter told his viewers at the time. "And, I mean, for all we know, these emails were made up, or maybe some are real, and some are fakes, we don't know. But we do know that this is a classic example of the right-wing media machine."

After complaining about the coverage of the emerging scandal that was virtually ignored by the liberal media, Stelter went on to call the Post's reporting of Hunter Biden's laptop a "manufactured scandal," a "so-called scandal" and suggested the newspaper is not a "fully reliable source."

Stelter pushed out a CNN story that echoed the common media narrative at the time: the story was a possible Russian disinformation effort.

"That might be because the details of the story have been denied by a credible former Joe Biden staffer and the Biden campaign, and US authorities are investigating whether the emails are part of an ongoing Russian disinformation effort," CNN's Alexis Benveniste wrote at the time.

In April, Stelter defended the media's collective decision not to cover the Hunter Biden scandal when it first emerged in the final weeks of the 2020 presidential election.

"I think there's a tension between big American newsrooms that want to check something out themselves, that don't want to rely on other outlets, that don't want to just repeat and regurgitate, but then there's an audience expectation of being able to instantly cover every story and have every answer," Stelter said during a panel discussion at the "Disinformation and the Erosion of Democracy" conference in Chicago. "And so in September or October of 2020, when the New York Post has something, other outlets can't match it, there's this pressure – 'Why aren't you confirming this? Why aren't you focusing on this? Why aren't you leading on this?' Because we haven't matched it, we haven't confirmed it."

CNN'S BRIAN STELTER AND JIM ACOSTA SINGLED OUT AS LIBERAL HOSTS WHO COULD BE 'OUSTED' BY THE NEW REGIME

"Now lately, the [New York] Times and the [Washington] Post have, and that's notable, and CNN had a story last week about the federal investigation into Hunter, but I think there's this tension between fast and slow journalism, perhaps, between people who know how newsrooms work and the vast majority of those who don't."

What's also "notable" is that Stelter has yet to acknowledge how Politico, The New York Times, The Washington Post, and NBC News have verified the authenticity of Hunter Biden's laptop on "Reliable Sources," according to Grabien transcripts.

However, Stelter suddenly feels the scandal is legitimate.

"He's pretending like he's actually never said these things and thinks that it could be a big problem for the president in 2024. Yeah, welcome to the party, pal. We've been talking about this for some time, and don't pretend like you tried to dismiss this story as a manufactured scandal, and now, because you have a new boss, I guess he's trying to keep his job by actually doing his job by talking about this story the way it should be talked about," Fox News contributor Joe Concha said Monday on "FOX & Friends First."

Stelter didn't respond to a request for comment.

Stelter's about-face comes as recently appointed CNN CEO Chris Licht is evaluating all CNN talent and executives to determine who should stick around as he attempts to focus on "news," as opposed to the liberal opinion programming that the network became known for under previous management.

CNN BOSS CHRIS LICHT 'HAS A BIG CHORE' FIXING STRUGGLING PRIMETIME LINEUP: 'END THE BUFFOONERY'

Jeff Zucker, who was largely responsible for the network's shift from a just-the-facts news operation to liberal opinion programming, was forced to step down earlier in 2022 ahead of the long-planned merger that put CNN under the control of Warner Bros. Discovery.

Zucker and Stelter were known to be close, and the network even enlisted its in-house media pundit to deliver the news that his former boss was stepping down to viewers. Earlier this year, Axios named Stelter, along with Jim Acosta, as CNN hosts seen as the "face of the network's liberal shift" in the eyes of conservatives.

Licht, who took over the network last spring, hasn't made significant changes to the network's programming aside from toning down the network's use of the "Breaking News" on-screen graphic.

Former President Trump told Fox News Digital over the weekend at CPAC Texas that CNN has actually "gotten worse" since Warner Bros. Discovery took control.

CIA OPINION OF THE MEDIA

Operation Mockingbird

- On the one hand, the print media's heavy bias toward the lone–gunman account,

- and, on the other hand, the strong rejection of that account by the general population and, perhaps even more so, by knowledgeable writers. The CIA document claimed in 1967 that "46% of the American public did not think that Oswald acted alone." In 1976, the figure was 81%.

Much of the media's behavior can be explained by simple institutional analysis without needing to invoke corruption or conspiracy. The media's coverage of political events is necessarily influenced by its identification with established political institutions and, in some cases, by its owners' membership in such institutions. Nevertheless, the CIA's widespread use of full–time and freelance employees within the media, sometimes known as Operation Mockingbird, surely influences any story in which the CIA's reputation might be directly affected.

The extent of the CIA's influence over the media became clear with the publication of the Church Committee's findings in 1976:

Special Agent Roth-Does this sound familiar?

CIA had the media "figured out" in the 1960s and the 1970s

22 November 1963

The Role of the Media

Documents made public many years later reveal the extent to which senior figures in the print and broadcast media were involved in shaping the official response to the assassination. One such figure was the syndicated newspaper columnist Joe Alsop. A telephone conversation between Alsop and Johnson is reproduced in Section 2, JFK Assassination.

The conversation gives an insight into Johnson's juggling of the various investigatory options: the Texas court of inquiry, the FBI report, and Katzenbach's proposed presidential commission. It also gives an insight into the relationship between the media and the government:

- The importance of the media to the presidency was such that a president would take a phone call from a member of the public on the morning of his predecessor's funeral.

- Also uses what appears to be outrageous flattery, but which may simply reflect his identification with the needs of governmental institutions: "you're going to make a marvelous … well, you've already made a marvelous start … you haven't put a damned foot one–a quarter of an inch wrong … and I've never seen anything like it, you've been simply marvelous." Similar remarks found their way into newspaper editorials and were later applied to the Warren Report.

- The media were centrally involved in creating policy. Alsop tries to persuade Johnson of the need for the results of the criminal investigation to be sanctified by a number of august figures. He mentions that he has recently spoken on this subject to several influential people, including Nicholas Katzenbach, Dean Acheson, the former Secretary of State, Fred Friendly, the president of CBS, and Bill Moyers, an assistant to Johnson.

- Both Johnson and Alsop assume that the role of the media is to persuade the general public of the government's point of view. In Alsop's words, "what I'm really honestly giving you is public relation[s] advice."

Phone Call Transcript[1]

Monday 25 November, 1963, 10:40am

22 November

The Washington Post was accused of bias on Monday after publishing a piece that claimed there is "no evidence" Hillary Clinton triggered the Russian probe despite her former campaign manager testifying that she approved distributing materials alleging a secret communications channel between the Trump Organization and Russia's Alfa Bank to the media. (Mike Smith/NBC/NBCU Photo Bank via Getty Images)

Bump attempted to make the case that things including WikiLeaks publishing Democratic National Committee emails, George Will pondering why Trump wouldn't release his taxes, and ex-

---

[1] http://www.maryferrell.org/mffweb/archive/viewer/showDoc.do?docId=838

campaign manager Paul Manafort all helped the public believe there could have been more to the Trump-Russia story.

FALSE INFORMATION ABOUT TRUMP

Michael Sussmann trial: ABC, NBC, CBS, MSNBC ignore case at the center of Trump-Russia probe

Brian Flood - Friday

Some of the mainstream media organizations that were obsessed with the Russia gate scandal have suddenly decided a trial at the center of the investigation's origins isn't worth covering. Special counsel's team accuses him of Mr. Sussman of manipulating the Lno idea.

Since May 15, the eve of the trial, ABC News, NBC News, CBS News, and MSNBC all ignored the trial on air through Thursday evening, according to a search of transcripts.

CNN spent less than 10 minutes covering the trial from May 15 through Thursday and didn't mention it on air at all on Wednesday or Thursday as testimony intensified. None of CNN's coverage has come during primetime.

Sussmann has been charged with making a false statement to the FBI when he told former FBI General Counsel James Baker in September 2016, less than two months before the presidential election, that he was not doing work "for any client" when he requested and attended a meeting where he presented "purported data and 'white papers' that allegedly demonstrated a covert communicates channel" between the Trump Organization and Alfa Bank, which has ties to the Kremlin.

The media told America that the FBI had proof of collusion as the bureau realized it had nothing. The FBI did nothing to stop the media. And actually encouraged it.

SPECIAL AGENT ROTH- New York Times and Washington Post got away with false information during the JFK Assassination. They simply thought that they could get away with it again. Fortunately, the New York Post and Fox News were here this time.

Justice Dept. Strongly Discouraged Comey on Move in Clinton Email Case New York Times

"Director Comey's letter refers to emails that have come to light in an unrelated case, but we have no idea what those emails are, and the Director himself notes they may not even be significant," he said.

It is extraordinary that we would see something like this just 11 days out from a presidential election."

Mrs. Clinton's running mate, Sen. Tim Kaine of Virginia, said Mr. Comey owes the campaign and the public a "clearer accounting" of the new information.

"When you do this 11 days before a presidential election, and you don't provide many details — but details apparently are being given by the FBI to the press — this is very, very troubling," Mr. Kaine told VICE News. "We hope that the director, and we really think that he should, give a clearer accounting of exactly what's going on right now."

Mr. Podesta predicted the FBI would come to the same conclusion this time as it did in July, and he pointedly noted that the letter was sent to eight Republican committee chairmen in Congress. But it was also carbon-copied to the ranking Democrats.

Mr. Comey did not explain in his letter what information the new emails contain, how long it will take to evaluate them, nor how they were obtained.

The New York Times reported Friday that the emails were snagged as part of an investigation into former Rep. Anthony Weiner and allegations he sent illicit messages through text and social media applications to a 15-year-old North Carolina girl. The paper reported that law enforcement officials seized at least one device shared by Mr. Weiner and his now estranged wife, Huma Abedin — a top personal aide to Mrs. Clinton. The couple announced they were separating in August amid Mr. Weiner's involvement in another sexting scandal, but before the 15-year-old girl's allegations surfaced.

As Mrs. Clinton's top personal aide, Ms. Abedin also had an account on the secret Clinton email server and exchanged classified information with her boss.

Mr. Comey said he was briefed on the new emails on Thursday and felt it was important to promptly alert Congress of investigators' latest efforts.

Republican leaders who were among the eight recipients of the letter called for further disclosures by the FBI director, with Sen. Richard C. Shelby urging him to provide additional information before voters go to the polls on Nov. 8.

"While I am pleased that the FBI is re-opening this case in light of new information, it is imperative that the Bureau immediately evaluate the material to complete this investigation," said Mr. Shelby, chairman of the Appropriations Subcommittee on Commerce, Justice, Science, and Related Agencies. "The American people are electing their next Commander-in-Chief only days from now, and they deserve to know the conclusion of your review prior to Election Day."

Sen. Charles E. Grassley, who, as chairman of the Senate Judiciary Committee, was one of the letter's recipients, said Mr. Comey owes the country more of an explanation about what he's found.

"The letter from Director Comey was unsolicited and, quite honestly, surprising. But it's left a lot more questions than answers for both the FBI and Secretary Clinton," the Iowa Republican said.

GOP presidential nominee Donald Trump, campaigning in Manchester, New Hampshire, said he respected the FBI for reversing itself.

"Perhaps, finally, justice will be done," he said.

For her part Mrs. Clinton, campaigning in Cedar Rapids, Iowa, did not address the issue, instead sticking doggedly to her stump speech of attacks on Mr. Trump mixed with a plea to voters to focus on issues.

President Obama, who has been saddled by association with Mrs. Clinton, who was serving him during the time she maintained her secret email server, did not respond to questions shouted by reporters Friday afternoon as he left the White House on a campaign trip to Florida to stump for Mrs. Clinton and Democratic Senate candidate Patrick Murphy.

Briefing reporters on Air Force One, deputy press secretary Eric Schultz said Mr. Obama President Obama expects the FBI to "follow the facts wherever they lead" and to act "irrespective of politics."

Mr. Schultz said the new email development does not affect Mr. Obama's support of Mrs. Clinton.

Libertarian candidate Gary Johnson said on CNN, "Obviously, the FBI didn't do this lightly. There has to be something there."

He lamented the prospect of "a president-elect under criminal investigation."

"That's what's going to now be the case if she is elected," he said. "She will control those jobs [in the Justice Department] that control how this issue moves forward, which points to a special prosecutor. This is a mess. It's a mess. I think Trump is toast, so is Hillary moving forward as president-elect? Four years of this? Ugh."

Congressional Republicans, who have been at odds with Mr. Trump on many issues, found common ground with their nominee in attacking Mrs. Clinton.

"This decision, long overdue, is the result of her reckless use of a private email server and her refusal to be forthcoming with federal investigators," said House Speaker Paul D. Ryan.

He again called for the Obama administration to suspend the classified intelligence briefings Mrs. Clinton is getting as the Democratic nominee.

And Sen. John Cornyn, Texas Republican, wondered whether the Justice Department would now convene a grand jury to pursue the case.

He said the FBI had already cleared Mrs. Clinton of mishandling classified information, so to reopen the case suggests either potential new evidence of intent to mishandle secrets or other potential criminal questions.

"Originally, the FBI focused on 'classification rules' and not broader issues related to government records/obstruction of justice. Will they now?" Mr. Cornyn tweeted.

An FBI spokesman declined Friday to comment on the reopening of the investigation.

The revelation that the investigation is continuing comes too late to affect the 16 million voters who have already cast ballots in absentee or in-person voting.

Republicans have said Mrs. Clinton appeared to mislead Congress in her sworn testimony to the Benghazi probe in 2015.

The staggering reversal by Mr. Comey comes as Mrs. Clinton is reeling from another electronic scandal — the revelations from emails obtained and posted by WikiLeaks from Mr. Podesta's personal email address.

Mrs. Clinton refused to use an official state.gov email account during her four years as secretary, instead setting up an account on a server she kept at her home in New York. That arrangement shielded her emails from public disclosure for six years, thwarting open-records laws.

She belatedly turned over some 30,000 messages she deemed government-related, but the FBI recovered thousands of others she didn't — including some that contained classified information.

Director Comey announced at a press conference on July 5, 2016, that there was not enough evidence to charge Hillary regarding the e-mail scandal.

Special Agent Roth- After Comey's press conference,

some former FBI agents began saying that if an agent couldn't figure out

what Comey and Clinton were doing, he or she should not have been an FBI Agent?

ADAM SCHIFF, Representative California

WSJ Editorial Board: All the Adam Schiff transcripts – Chair knew there was no proof of Russia-Trump collusion

Over the past several years, CNN, MSNBC & the networks just could not get enough of Adam Schiff, who repeatedly pushed the claim about Trump-Russia collusion.

House intelligence committee Chairman Adam Schiff (D-Calif.) insisted Sunday there is no question that evidence points to President Donald Trump's 2016 campaign colluding with Russia, despite what his Republican counterparts in the Senate say.

"You can see evidence in plain sight on the issue of collusion, pretty compelling evidence," the congressman said on CNN's "State of the Union." However, he noted, "there's a difference between seeing evidence of collusion and being able to prove a criminal conspiracy beyond a reasonable doubt."

FBI Special Agent Roth. What sense does Mr. Schiff's statement make?

The only interpretation that we can see is that he cannot prove a criminal conspiracy beyond a reasonable doubt.

Earlier this month, Senate intelligence committee Chairman Richard Burr (R-N.C.) told CBS News his panel had discovered nothing to indicate collusion had occurred, though Schiff has stood firmly against that conclusion.

Schiff cited the 2016 Trump Tower meeting in which Donald Trump Jr. was promised dirt from Russians on then-presidential candidate Hillary Clinton, as well as Trump's soon-to-be national security adviser Michael Flynn discussing sanctions with Russian ambassador Sergey Kislyak during the presidential transition.

"All of this is evidence of collusion, and you either have to look the other way to say it isn't, or you have to have a different word for it because it is a corrupt dealing with a foreign adversary during a campaign," Schiff added. "But again, it will be up to [special counsel Robert] Mueller to determine whether that amounts to criminal conspiracy."

Special Agent Roth. Special Counsel Robert Mueller found no collusion between Trump and Russia. Counsel Mueller and his staff spent a significant amount of time on the 2016 Trump Tower meeting, which Donald Trump Jr. attended.

WSJ Editorial Board: All the Adam Schiff transcripts – Chair knew there was no proof of Russia-Trump collusion

By Wall Street Journal Editorial Board | The Wall Street Journal

Lee Smith: 'Adam Schiff lied, and the media let him.'

Americans expect that politicians will lie, but sometimes the examples are so brazen that they deserve special notice. Newly released Congressional testimony shows that Adam Schiff spread falsehoods shamelessly about Russia and Donald Trump for three years even as his own committee gathered contrary evidence.

The House Intelligence Committee last week released 57 transcripts of interviews it conducted in its investigation into Russia's meddling in the 2016 election. The committee probe started in January 2017 under then-Chair Devin Nunes and concluded in March 2018 with a report finding no evidence that the Trump campaign conspired with the Kremlin. Most of the transcripts were ready for release long ago, but Mr. Schiff oddly refused to release them after he became chairman in 2019. He only released them last week when the White House threatened to do it first.

Now we know why. From the earliest days of the collusion narrative, Mr. Schiff insisted that he had evidence proving the plot. In March 2017 on MSNBC, Mr. Schiff teased that he couldn't "go into particulars, but there is more than circumstantial evidence now."

In December 2017, he told CNN that collusion was a fact: "The Russians offered help, the campaign accepted help. The Russians gave help, and the President made full use of that help." In April 2018, Mr. Schiff released his response to Mr. Nunes's report, stating that it's finding of no collusion "was unsupported by the facts and the investigative record."

Michael Berry

New Documents Prove Adam Schiff Lied About Trump-Russia Collusion

May 13, 2020

Over the past several years, CNN, MSNBC & the networks just could not get enough of Adam Schiff, who repeatedly pushed the claim about Trump-Russia collusion.

However, newly released Congressional testimony shows that Adam Schiff flat-out lied about Russia and Donald Trump for three years.

Last week, the House Intelligence Committee last week released 57 transcripts of interviews it conducted in its investigation into Russia's meddling in the 2020 election

"...from the earliest days of the collusion narrative, Mr. Schiff insisted that he had evidence proving the plot. In March 2017 on MSNBC, Mr. Schiff teased that he couldn't "go into particulars, but there is more than circumstantial evidence now."

In December 2017, he told CNN that collusion was a fact: "The Russians offered help, the campaign accepted help. The Russians gave help, and the President made full use of that help." In April 2018, Mr. Schiff released his response to Mr. Nunes's report, stating that its finding of no collusion "was unsupported by the facts and the investigative record."

None of this was true, and Mr. Schiff knew it. In July 2017, here's what former Director of National Intelligence James Clapper told Mr. Schiff and his colleagues: "I never saw any direct empirical evidence that the Trump campaign or someone in it was plotting/conspiring with the Russians to meddle with the election." Three months later, former Obama Attorney General Loretta Lynch agreed that while she'd seen "concerning" information, "I don't recall anything being briefed up to me." Former Deputy AG Sally Yates concurred several weeks later: "We were at the fact-gathering stage here, not the conclusion stage."

And it wasn't just Schiff who lied and pushed the false collusion narrative. Members of the deep state knew there was no collusion.

The WSJ editorial adds:

"Most remarkable, former FBI Deputy Director Andrew McCabe admitted the bureau's reason for opening the case was nonsense. Asked in December 2017 why the FBI obtained a secret surveillance warrant on former Trump aide Carter Page rather than on George Papadopoulos (whose casual conversation with a foreign diplomat was the catalyst for the probe), Mr. McCabe responded: "Papadopoulos' comment didn't particularly indicate that he was the person that had had—that was interacting with the Russians." No one else was either.

On it went, a parade of former Obama officials who declared under oath they'd seen no evidence of collusion or conspiracy—Susan Rice, Ben Rhodes, Samantha Power. Interviews with the Trump campaign or Administration officials also yielded no collusion evidence. Mr. Schiff had access to these transcripts even as he claimed he had "ample" proof of collusion and wrote his false report."

So what price will Schiff pay for the lies he told repeated over the past three years? Nothing. He'll still be invited back on CNN and MSNBC, along with the networks, and the journalist will complain about why Trump attacks them and why the general public not only doesn't trust them but bitterly despises them.

"He's way up there in direct line to the president. The director of the CIA wouldn't even give us a phone call. So that is in contempt of Congress. So that is now in contempt of the American people because we represent the American people's elected representatives.

"We have oversight responsibilities, and Haspel completely ignored us. That is beyond contempt. And that really tells you all you need to know in terms of her potential complicity in this. Because if she wasn't complicit, she would have honored these requests. Or she would have at least picked up the phone and said, 'Senators, this is why I can't comply with your legitimate oversight requests,' but she didn't do that."

He said: **"That was repeated By (FBI Director) Christopher Wray, who I subpoenaed. And he slow-walked it. We got a tiny fraction of what we requested from him, and I'm sure we didn't get the good stuff. With Haspel at the CIA, we didn't even get the courtesy of blowing us off with a lame excuse. She wouldn't even call us."**

SPECIAL AGENTS ROTH- CONGRESSMAN SCHIFF. CAN YOU SEE THIS EVIDENCE?

Trump and the Russians

The Times Just Won 3 Pulitzers. Read the Winning Work.

Washington Post panned for massive correction to Trump-Georgia election story: 'So, they made up quotes.'

MSNBC, ABC, NBC, and CBS are among the mainstream news outlets that have completely ignored the bombshell testimony, but Washington Post nation correspondent Phillip Bump took a different strategy and provided cover for Clinton.

The Post's piece headlined, "Again: there's no evidence Hillary Clinton triggered the Russian probe," began by criticizing a Wall Street Journal editorial board column that condemned the 2016 Democratic nominee for harming the country by pushing the narrative that Trump's campaign colluded with Russia.

Part Six

Big Tech Censorship of Trump

Published August 25, 2022, 4:57pm EDT

Mark Zuckerberg tells Joe Rogan FBI warned Facebook of 'Russian propaganda' before Hunter Biden laptop story

Mark Zuckerberg defended Facebook's actions in limiting the reach of the Hunter Biden laptop story

By **Joseph A. Wulfsohn | Fox News**

Appearing on Thursday's installment of "The Joe Rogan Experience," Zuckerberg was asked about Facebook's suppression of the New York Post's reporting that shed light on the shady foreign business dealings of the son of then-candidate Joe Biden.

Zuckerberg began by stressing how Facebook took a "different path" than Twitter, which completely censored the Post's reporting while Facebook limited its reach on the platform.

"Basically, the background here is the FBI, I think, basically came to us- some folks on our team and was like, 'Hey, just so you know, like, you should be on high alert… We thought that there was a lot of Russian propaganda in the 2016 election. We have it on notice that, basically, there's about to be some kind of dump of that's similar to that. So just be vigilant,'" Zuckerberg told host Joe Rogan.

FBI OFFICIALS SLOW-WALKED HUNTER BIDEN LAPTOP INVESTIGATION UNTIL AFTER 2020 ELECTION: WHISTLEBLOWERS

Zuckerberg insisted that Facebook users were "still allowed to share" the Post's reporting on the Hunter Biden laptop even as their "third-party fact-checking program" was looking into whether it was misinformation but acknowledged that the "ranking in [the] news feed was a little bit less" and that "fewer people saw it than would've otherwise."

"By what percentage?" Rogan asked.

"I don't know off the top of my head, but it's- it's meaningful," Zuckerberg responded. "But we weren't sort of as black and white about it as Twitter. We just kind of thought they look, if the FBI, which I still view is a legitimate institution in this country, it's a very professional law enforcement- they come to us and tell us that we need to be on guard about something then I want to take that seriously."

MSNBC BURIES NBC NEWS REPORT ON HUNTER BIDEN LAPTOP, OFFERS LESS THAN 4 MINUTES OF COVERAGE

"Did they specifically say you need to be on guard about that story?" Rogan followed.

"No, I don't remember if it was that specifically, but it basically fit the pattern," Zuckerberg said.

When asked if there was any "regret" about suppressing a story that turned out be factual, Zuckerberg replied, "Yeah, yeah. I mean, it sucks."

However, he went on to defend Facebook's practices, telling Rogan its process was "pretty reasonable" since his platform still allowed the New York Post articles to be distributed rather than the complete blackout that Twitter enforced.

BRIAN STELTER DEFENDS MEDIA NOT COVERING HUNTER BIDEN IN 2020, SAYS CRITICS DON'T KNOW 'HOW NEWSROOMS WORK'

Rogan appeared sympathetic to Zuckerberg's predicament, especially regarding the FBI's warning of Russian propaganda.

"It's probably also the case of armchair quarterbacking, right? Or at least Monday morning quarterbacking… because in the moment, you had reason to believe based on the FBI talking to you that it wasn't real and that there was going to be some propaganda. So what do you do?" Rogan said. "And then, if you just let it get out there and what if it changes the election and it turns out to be bulls---, that's a real problem. And I would imagine that those kinds of decisions are the most difficult."

Meta, Facebook's parent company, issued a statement saying "None of this is new. Mark testified before the Senate nearly two years ago that in the lead up to the 2020 election, the FBI warned about the threat of foreign hack and leak operations… We took that seriously, and as Mark said when he testified, we didn't block the New York Post story, we temporarily reduced its distribution to give fact-checking partners time to review it."

In the final weeks of the 2020 presidential election, both Big Tech and the liberal media suppressed the bombshell revelations that emerged from Hunter Biden's laptop.

Both Zuckerberg and then-Twitter CEO Jack Dorsey expressed regret for their actions limiting the distribution of the New York Post's reporting and several news organizations including The New York Times, The Washington Post, NBC News and Politico have since verified the authenticity of the laptop.

Sen. Ron Johnson, R-Wisc., revealed this week in a letter to Department of Justice Inspector General Michael Horowitz that whistleblowers allege FBI officials told agents not to investigate Hunter Biden's laptop for months over concerns it would impact the 2020 election.

According to Johnson, "individuals with knowledge" of the Hunter Biden case told his office that the investigation was intentionally slowed on orders from "local FBI leadership."

Senate Judiciary ranking member Chuck Grassley, R-Iowa said other whistleblower allegations reveal a "deeply rooted political infection" within the FBI.

Fox News' Timothy H.J. Nerozzi contributed to this report.

Joseph A. Wulfsohn is a media reporter for Fox News Digital. Story tips can be sent to joseph.wulfsohn@fox.com and on Twitter: @JosephWulfsohn.

House Oversight ranking member says it's 'unacceptable' for Treasury Department to deny his request for Hunter Biden financial records

Evan Perez – *September 5, 9:28 AM*

The top Republican on the House Oversight Committee criticized the Treasury Department on Saturday for declining his request to provide banking Suspicious Activity Reports on Hunter Biden and others, according to a press statement.

Kentucky Rep. James Comer accused the department of trying to "run cover for the Biden family and possibly hide information about whether Joe Biden benefited financially from his family's business transactions."

Comer's interest in the financial records, shared by several other Republican members of Congress, signals an area of investigative focus for the GOP if the party gains control of the House in the midterm elections.

Jonathan Davidson, the assistant secretary of legislative affairs at the Treasury Department, said in a letter to Comer dated Friday that the department "deeply respects the critical oversight role of Congress and remains committed to responding to appropriate requests from committees of jurisdiction."

Since Republicans are currently in the minority and do not control the agenda of the congressional committees, Comer's request as the ranking member means the department is not obligated to fulfill the request.

Comer called Treasury's response "unacceptable" in the news release.

"We need more information about these transactions and if Joe Biden has benefited financially from his family's dealings with foreign adversaries. It is a matter of national security to know if President Biden is compromised. The American people deserve answers, and Republicans will use the power of the gavel next Congress to get them," he said.

Published August 25, 2022, 11:16 am EDT

FBI officials slow-walked Hunter Biden laptop investigation until after 2020 election: whistleblowers

FBI officials, concerned about influencing the 2020 election, told employees, 'You will not look at that Hunter Biden laptop,' according to whistleblowers

By **Timothy H.J. Nerozzi | Fox News**

FBI officials told agents not to investigate Hunter Biden's so-called "laptop from hell" for months due to concerns about influencing the 2020 presidential election; whistleblowers told Sen. Ron Johnson, R-Wis.

According to Johnson, "individuals with knowledge" of the Hunter Biden case told his office that the investigation was intentionally slowed on orders from "local FBI leadership."

"While I understand your hesitation to investigate a matter that may be related to an ongoing investigation, it is clear to me based on numerous credible whistleblower disclosures that the FBI cannot be trusted with the handling of Hunter Biden's laptop," Johnson claimed in a letter to Department of Justice Inspector General Michael Horowitz.

According to the whistleblowers, FBI officials told employees, "You will not look at that Hunter Biden laptop."

"These new allegations provide even more evidence of FBI corruption and renew calls for you to take immediate steps to investigate the FBI's actions regarding the laptop," Johnson added.

Johnson is not the only lawmaker alleging evidence of recent malpractice from the FBI.

GRASSLEY SAYS NEW WHISTLEBLOWER INFO REVEALS 'DEEPLY ROOTED POLITICAL INFECTION' WITHIN THE FBI

Read the letter from Sen. Johnson:

Senate Judiciary ranking member Chuck Grassley said other whistleblower allegations reveal a "deeply rooted political infection" within the FBI.

In an Aug. 17 letter to FBI Director Christopher Wray, the Iowa Republican demanded an accounting for alleged political bias influencing high-level investigations, particularly out of the FBI's Washington, D.C., office.

An investigation into Hunter Biden's tax affairs, which began in 2018, has reached a "critical stage," a source told Fox News Digital last month. (BACKGRID USA)

Officials are looking into whether to charge Hunter Biden with various tax violations and possible foreign lobBy ing violations. (BACKGRID USA)

"Starting on May 31, 2022, I've written three letters to you regarding political bias that has infected the FBI's Washington Field Office," Grassley, R-Iowa, writes. "Two of those letters provided specific and credible allegations based on numerous whistleblowers that have approached my office with information that one can only conclude is indicative of a deeply rooted political infection that has spread to investigative activity into former President Trump and Hunter Biden."

Hunter Biden was spotted Monday for the first time after the Biden family's big vacation — the first son was seen stopping with his family for ice cream in Los Angeles.

The Biden vacation came the same week Fox News Digital reported that Hunter Biden and his longtime business partner Eric Schwerin were actively working behind the scenes in 2016 to solicit donations for a top former Biden adviser's congressional campaign while also working on Chinese business deals with the adviser's business partner.

In addition, an investigation into Hunter's tax affairs, which began in 2018, has reached a "critical stage," a source told Fox News Digital last month. Officials are looking into whether to charge the first son with various tax violations and possible foreign lobbying violations.

Timothy Nerozzi is a writer for Fox News Digital. You can follow him on Twitter @timothynerozzi and can email him at timothy.nerozzi@fox.com

Big Tech Censorship: The Conservative Purge

Posted on January 12, 2021, by seabreezeeditor

By Max Roemer

Jack Dorsey of Twitter and Mark Zuckerberg of Facebook have told Americans that they can no longer hear from their President. Both Twitter and Facebook have banned President Trump indefinitely. This reporter alone has lost over 5,000 conservative Twitter followers within 48 hours following the conservative purge and gross violation of our First Amendment rights. I have never railed about election fraud or incited violence, yet I was punished for my Right-leaning viewpoints.

The First Amendment states, "Congress shall make no law respecting an establishment of religion or prohibiting the free exercise thereof; or abridging the freedom of speech, or of the press, or the right of the people peaceably to assemble, and to petition the Government for a redress of grievances." It is self-evident that Big Tech has no regard whatsoever for your First Amendment rights. It is being said that these are private companies and that they can do as they please. They are also protected under Section 230 of the Communications Decency Act. A law that Trump tried to do away with as its unlimited powers for Big Tech companies needs revision so that their users are protected.

Millions of conservatives have deleted their accounts and have left Twitter and Facebook since the indefinite suspensions of President Trump. Twitter's stock is down over 12% at the time of this printing. Most have migrated to Parler, known for its promises of free speech, and Big Tech has responded by removing Parler from the Google Play store, claiming an "ongoing and urgent public safety threat," and the Apple App store claiming Parler is not doing enough to squash, "threats of violence and illegal activity." Amazon hosts Parler web services and has removed Parler from the internet on midnight Sunday night. Leaving Parler effectively completely unavailable and unusable.

We get it: The Left feels empowered. They have elected a Democrat president who will enjoy for at least two years a Democrat majority in the House and Senate. At the same time, President Trump will soon leave office a defeated man, subject to endless recriminations by Democrats and non-stop condemnation from the liberal media. Trump is threatened with impeachment once again by House Speaker Nancy Pelosi, D-Calif., whose appetite for partisan nastiness appears insatiable.

Big Tech is empowered, too, having played an important role in the election of Joe Biden. The social media giants lean left politically; their campaign donations to Biden and suppression of negative articles about him and his son Hunter Biden were all in service to electing their favored candidate.

Republicans must find a way to bring Twitter, Facebook, and other social media giants to heel. Given the relentless and increasingly dishonest bias of the liberal media, the availability of social media platforms is one of the few avenues left to push back against the Left's indoctrination of the nation.

Permanent suspension of @realDonaldTrump

By Twitter

Friday, 8 January 2021

After a close review of recent Tweets from the @realDonaldTrump account and the context around them — specifically, how they are being received and interpreted on and off Twitter — we have permanently suspended the account due to the risk of further incitement of violence.

In the context of horrific events this week, we made it clear on Wednesday that additional violations of the Twitter Rules would potentially result in this very course of action. Our public interest framework exists to enable the public to hear from elected officials and world leaders directly. It is built on the principle that the people have a right to hold power to account in the open.

However, we made it clear going back years that these accounts are not above our rules entirely and cannot use Twitter to incite violence, among other things. We will continue to be transparent about our policies and their enforcement.

Below is a comprehensive analysis of our policy enforcement approach in this case.

Overview

On January 8, 2021, President Donald J. Trump Tweeted:

"The 75,000,000 great American Patriots who voted for me, AMERICA FIRST, and MAKE AMERICA GREAT AGAIN, will have a GIANT VOICE long into the future. They will not be disrespected or treated unfairly in any way, shape, or form!!!"

Shortly thereafter, the President Tweeted:

"To all of those who have asked, I will not be going to the Inauguration on January 20th."

Due to the ongoing tensions in the United States, and an uptick in the global conversation in regards to the people who violently stormed the Capitol on January 6, 2021, these two Tweets must be read in the context of broader events in the country and the ways in which the President's statements can be mobilized by different audiences, including to incite violence, as well as in the context of the pattern of behavior from this account in recent weeks. After assessing the language in these Tweets against our Glorification of Violence policy, we have determined that these Tweets are in violation of the Glorification of Violence Policy, and the user @realDonaldTrump should be immediately and permanently suspended from the service.

Assessment

We assessed the two Tweets referenced above under our Glorification of Violence policy, which aims to prevent the glorification of violence that could inspire others to replicate violent acts and determined that they were highly likely to encourage and inspire people to replicate the criminal acts that took place at the U.S. Capitol on January 6, 2021.

This determination is based on a number of factors, including:

President Trump's statement that he will not be attending the Inauguration is being received by a number of his supporters as further confirmation that the election was not legitimate and is seen as him disavowing his previous claim made via two Tweets (1, 2) by his Deputy Chief of Staff, Dan Scavino, that there would be an "orderly transition" on January 20th.

The second Tweet may also serve as an encouragement to those potentially considering violent acts that the Inauguration would be a "safe" target, as he will not be attending.

The use of the words "American Patriots" to describe some of his supporters are also being interpreted as support for those committing violent acts at the US Capitol.

The mention that his supporters had a "GIANT VOICE long into the future" and that "They will not be disrespected or treated unfairly in any way, shape or form!!!" is being interpreted as further indication that President Trump does not plan to facilitate an "orderly transition" and instead that he plans to continue to support, empower, and shield those who believe he won the election.

Plans for future armed protests have already begun proliferating on and off Twitter, including a proposed secondary attack on the US Capitol and state capitol buildings on January 17, 2021.

As such, our determination is that the two Tweets above are likely to inspire others to replicate the violent acts that took place on January 6, 2021, and that there are multiple indicators that they are being received and understood as an encouragement to do so.

Twitter Inc.

Facebook and Twitter Limit Sharing 'New York Post Story About Joe Biden

October 14, 20206:49 PM ET

SHANNON BOND

Updated at 9:14 p.m. ET

Facebook and Twitter took action on Wednesday to limit the distribution of *New York Post* reporting with unconfirmed claims about Democratic presidential nominee Joe Biden, leading President Trump's campaign and allies to charge the companies with censorship.

Both social media companies said the moves were aimed at slowing the spread of potentially false information. But they gave few details about how they reached their decisions, sparking criticism about the lack of clarity and consistency with which they apply their rules.

'Russia Doesn't Have to Make Fake News': Biggest Election Threat Is Closer To Home

The *New York Post* published a series of stories on Wednesday citing emails, purportedly sent by Biden's son Hunter, which the news outlet says it got from Trump's private attorney, Rudy Giuliani, and former Trump adviser Steve Bannon.

Facebook was limiting distribution of the *Post*'s main story while its outside fact-checkers reviewed the claims, spokesman Andy Stone said. That means the platform's algorithms won't place posts linking to the story as highly in people's news feeds, reducing the number of users who see it. However, the story has still been liked, shared, or commented on almost 600,000 times on Facebook, according to data from Crowd Tangle, a research tool owned by the social network.

Stone said Facebook sometimes takes this step if it sees "signals" that something gaining traction is false to give fact-checkers time to evaluate the story before it spreads widely. He did not give more detail on what signals Facebook uses or how often it takes this approach.

Twitter went further. It is blocking users from posting pictures of the emails or links to two of the *New York Post*'s stories referring to them, spokesman Trenton Kennedy said, citing its rules against sharing "content obtained through hacking that contains private information."

Users who try to share the links on Twitter are shown a notice saying, "We can't complete this request because this link has been identified by Twitter or our partners as being potentially harmful."

If a user clicks on links already posted on Twitter, the user is taken to a warning screen saying, "this link may be unsafe," which they have to click past to read the story. Twitter also required the *New York Post* to delete its tweet about the story.

Twitter said it decided to block the links because it couldn't be sure about the origins of the emails. It said its policy "prohibits the use of our service to distribute content obtained without authorization" and that it doesn't want to encourage hacking by allowing people to share "possibly illegally obtained materials."

But the company declined to comment on how it had reached that decision or what evidence it had weighed about the emails in the *Post*'s stories.

The company later gave an additional explanation for why it was blocking the stories.

Its safety team said in a tweet that the images of emails in the articles "include personal and private information — like email addresses and phone numbers — which violate our rules" against unauthorized sharing of such details.

CEO Jack Dorsey acknowledged that the company's communication about why it was blocking the articles "was not great." He tweeted that it was "unacceptable" to prevent people from sharing "with zero context as to why we're blocking."

Asked for comment about the social networks' actions, *New York Post* spokeswoman Iva Benson referred NPR to an article by the paper's editorial board.

"Our story explains where the info came from, and a Senate committee now confirms it also received the files from the same source," the editorial said. "Yet Facebook and Twitter are deliberately trying to keep its users from reading and deciding for themselves what it means."

Twitter and Facebook have been acting more aggressively in recent weeks to curb the spread of false claims and manipulation related to the election as part of efforts to avoid a repeat of 2016 when Russian-linked actors used social media to target American voters.

Facebook has been warning about the possibility of "hack and leak" operations, where stolen documents or other sensitive materials are strategically leaked — as happened in 2016 with hacked emails from the Democratic National Committee and Hillary Clinton's campaign.

But the companies' moves on Wednesday drew criticism from some experts, who said Facebook and Twitter needed to explain more clearly their policies and how often they apply them.

"This story is a microcosm of something that I think we can expect to happen a lot over the next few weeks and, I think, demonstrates why platforms having clear policies that they are prepared to stick to is really important," said Evelyn Douek, a Harvard Law School lecturer who studies the regulation of online speech.

"It's really unclear if they have stepped in exceptionally in this case and, if they have, why they've done so," she said. "That inevitably leads to exactly the kind of outcry that we've seen, which is that they're doing it for political reasons and because they're biased."

Republicans seized on the episode as proof of their long-running assertions that social networks censor conservative voices. There is no statistical evidence to support those claims.

Jack Dorsey says blocking Post's Hunter Biden story was 'total mistake' — but won't say who made it

By Noah Manskar

March 25, 2021 4:04pm

Twitter doesn't have a "censoring department" that blocked The Post from tweeting last fall, CEO Jack Dorsey said Thursday — but he wouldn't reveal who was responsible for the blunder.

At a congressional hearing on misinformation and social media, Dorsey said Twitter made a "total mistake" By barring users from sharing The Post's bombshell October report about Hunter Biden's emails.

Twitter also locked The Post out of its account for more than two weeks over baseless charges that the exposé used hacked information — a decision Dorsey chalked up to a "process error."

"It was literally just a process error. This was not against them in any particular way," Dorsey told the House Energy and Commerce Committee.

"If we remove a violation, we require people to correct it," he added. "We changed that based on their wanting to delete that tweet, which I completely agree with. I see it. But it is something we learn."

But Dorsey dodged a question from Rep. Steve Scalise about who decided to freeze the 200-year-old newspaper's account.

Twitter demanded The Post delete six tweets that linked to stories based on files from the abandoned laptop of President Biden's son. Twitter backed down after the paper refused to remove the posts — a development The Post celebrated on its Oct. 31 front page with the headline "FREE BIRD!"

"Their entire account to be blocked for two weeks by mistake seems like a really big mistake," Scalise, a Louisiana Republican, told Dorsey. "Was anyone held accountable in your censoring department for that mistake?"

"Well, we don't have a censoring department," the bearded and newly bald-headed tech exec replied.

When Scalise interjected to ask who made the decision "to block their account for two weeks," Dorsey claimed, "We didn't block their account for two weeks."

"We required them to delete the tweet, and then they could tweet it again," he said. "They didn't take that action, so we corrected it for them."

Scalise compared Twitter's response to The Post's stories with a Jan. 9 Washington Post article that claimed then-President Donald Trump urged Georgia's lead elections investigator to "find the fraud" in the state's presidential vote and that she'd be a "national hero" if she did.

The paper issued a lengthy correction to the story this month, revealing that Trump never used those words, though he did say the office would find "dishonesty" and that she had "the most important job in the country right now."

"There are tweets today … that still mischaracterize it even in a way where the Washington Post admitted it's wrong, yet those mischaracterizations can still be retweeted," Scalise told Dorsey. "Will you address that and start taking those down to reflect what even the Washington Post themselves has admitted is false information?"

Dorsey would not answer either way affirmatively: "Our misleading information policies are focused on manipulated media, public health, and civic integrity," he said. "That's it."

Part Seven

Additional Cases Regarding Hillary Clinton

Clinton Foundation

JUDGE ORDERS IRS RE CLINTON FOUNDATION opening and closing serials Field Offices on case ordered to stop any further investigation.

FBI launches new Clinton Foundation investigation

BY JOHN SOLOMON - *01/04/18 8:35 PM ET*

The Justice Department has launched a new inquiry into whether the Clinton Foundation engaged in any pay-to-play politics or other illegal activities while Hillary Clinton served as secretary of State, law enforcement officials and a witness tells The Hill.

FBI agents from Little Rock, Ark., where the foundation was started, have taken the lead in the investigation and have interviewed at least one witness in the last month, and law enforcement officials said additional activities are expected in the coming weeks.

The officials, who spoke only on condition of anonymity, said the probe is examining whether the Clintons promised or performed any policy favors in return for largesse to their charitable efforts or whether donors made commitments of donations in hopes of securing government outcomes.

The probe may also examine whether any tax-exempt assets were converted for personal or political use and whether the foundation complied with applicable tax laws, the officials said.

One witness recently interviewed by the FBI described the session to The Hill as "extremely professional and unquestionably thorough" and focused on questions about whether donors to Clinton's charitable efforts received any favorable treatment from the Obama administration on a policy decision previously highlighted in media reports.

The witness discussed his interview solely on the grounds of anonymity. He said the agents were from Little Rock, and their questions focused on government decisions and discussions of donations to Clinton entities during the time Hillary Clinton led President Obama's State Department.

The FBI office in Little Rock referred a reporter Thursday to Washington headquarters, where officials declined any official comment.

Clinton's chief spokesman, Nick Merrill, on Friday morning excoriated the FBI for re-opening the case, calling the probe "disgraceful" and suggesting it was nothing more than a political distraction from President Trump's Russia controversies.

"Let's call this what it is: a sham," Merrill said. "This is a philanthropy that does life-changing work, which Republicans have tried to turn into a political football. It began with a now long-debunked project spearheaded by Steve Bannon during the presidential campaign. It continues with Jeff Sessions doing Trump's bidding by heeding his calls to meddle with a department that is supposed to function independently."

Foundation spokesman Craig Minassian took a more muted response, saying the new probe wouldn't distract the charity from its daily work.

"Time after time, the Clinton Foundation has been subjected to politically motivated allegations, and time after time, these allegations have been proven false. None of this has made us waver in our mission to help people," Minassian said. "The Clinton Foundation has demonstrably improved the lives of millions of people across America and around the world while earning top ratings from charity watchdog groups in the process."

The Wall Street Journal reported late last year that several FBI field offices, including the one in Little Rock, had been collecting information on the Clinton Foundation for more than a year. The report also said there had been pushback to the FBI from the Justice Department.

A renewed law enforcement focus follows a promise to Congress late last year from top Trump Justice Department officials that law enforcement would revisit some of the investigations and legal issues closed during the Obama years that conservatives felt were given short shrift. It also follows months of relentless criticism on Twitter from President Trump, who has repeatedly questioned why no criminal charges were ever filed against the "crooked" Clintons and their fundraising machine.

For years, news media, from The New York Times to The Daily Caller, have reported countless stories on donations to the Clinton Foundation or speech fees that closely fell around the time of favorable decisions by Clinton's State Department. Conservative author Peter Schweizer chronicled the most famous of episodes in his book "Clinton Cash" that gave ammunition to conservatives, including Trump, to beat the drum for a renewed investigation.

Several GOP members of Congress have recently urged Attorney General Jeff Sessions to appoint a special counsel to look at the myriad issues surrounding the Clintons. Justice officials sent a letter to Congress in November suggesting some of those issues were being re-examined, but Sessions later testified the appointment of a special prosecutor required a high legal bar that had not yet been met.

Published May 19, 2022 12:40pm EDT

Second Scandal Hillary Clinton

What Hillary Clinton's email scandal is really about

By Alvin Chang; *@alv9n - alvin@vox.com*

Updated Oct 28, 2016, 1:14pm EDT

The FBI announced Friday it was **renewing its investigation** into Hillary Clinton's use of private email servers after deciding not to press charges in September after their first round of investigation. For months, the "email scandal" has haunted Clinton's campaign, and conservatives have used it to feed into a larger message: that Clinton can't be trusted.

Just look at all the stories Breitbart puts under the" Hillary **Clinton Email Scandal**" tag. It's a mishmash of stories — including ones about her hiding health problems, which have nothing to do with email. All the articles together weave a storyline that seems more egregious than the individual parts that make it up.

But at the core of it, there really are problems. And we should be able to talk about those problems with clarity. **Vox's Jeff Stein created a concise framework** about the scandal, so we made a cartoon that pinpoints the primary issues at play.

First, let's walk through what actually happened

To understand what exactly it was that Clinton did, we need to understand what an email server is. It's the technical underpinning of the controversy.

It's basically like a post office. It's a computer connected to the internet that sorts through letters and delivers them.

And much like a post office, the server has three jobs:

So that means the person in charge of this digital post office — a postmaster, if you will — has an important job. This person has to implement security features to make sure the server can do its job well. This person also has control of the messages coming in and out.

Normally for the secretary of state, this responsibility would've belonged to people in the federal government who have the expertise to maintain email systems.

But when Clinton was offered an email address on State Department servers, her staff refused. Instead, they **used a server in Clinton's home**, maintained part-time by two staffers.

We don't know why Clinton used a private server. **She says** it's because she only wanted to carry one mobile device — and since State Department devices only allowed for State Department email addresses to be added to the phone, she chose to use her personal device and her personal email.

But this is what led to multiple problems — and multiple storylines around those problems.

Problem 1: Clinton made herself vulnerable to hackers

Clinton's private server had **several potential points of vulnerability**, so it was possible for spies to hack into the system — both to view messages or to reroute messages.

There was no evidence that Clinton's server was breached, but hackers are good at covering their tracks, and the **FBI hints that it thinks** a hack was likely.

On her servers, an FBI investigation in July 2016 found **81 email chains** that ranged from confidential to top secret, but intelligence agencies overuse these labels, so it's unclear if revealing these emails would've actually threatened national security.

There was **"gross negligence,"** as the FBI points out.

Eventually, Clinton's staff hired a private company to run their email servers in Secaucus, New Jersey. This was a more secure option but still not ideal. In fact, if we're talking about pure security, it's unclear what the best option would've been.

Even if Clinton used the State Department mail servers, it wouldn't have been foolproof. The State Department has been **accused of having poor institutional security**, which manifested in a **2015 hack of its unclassified email system**.

Problem 2: Clinton may have been trying to skirt transparency laws

Email servers are physical computers — and the person who controls those servers has your data.

When Congress was investigating the terrorist attacks in Benghazi, it asked the State Department for Clinton's emails. But the department **only turned over eight emails**. That's because Clinton's emails were on her own server, not theirs.

That said, Republicans have insisted Clinton did this to avoid having her emails released or subject to the Freedom of Information Act. In other words, the accusation is that she did it so the public couldn't see her communication. This goes to motive, which means it's difficult to prove either way, and anyone who claims otherwise is speculating.

But the idea that she is actively trying to hide her communication feeds into a more absurd accusation that we should dismiss: that Clinton tried to delete emails from her server during the House's Benghazi investigation. Vox's Jeff Stein has a good timeline showing why **this theory makes no sense**.

What has been lumped into this storyline: the idea that Clinton is compromised?

There is another completely separate case that has to do with emails but gets thrown into the "Clinton email scandal" bin as well. The right-wing transparency group Judicial Watch obtained emails between top officials at the State Department and the Clinton Foundation.

Some think it shows that people who donated to the Clinton Foundation received preference from the secretary of state's office. There is no evidence to back this up, and this storyline has nothing to do with her private server. It's another story, like the one about her health, that is woven into the larger narrative that Clinton can't be trusted.

There are two primary problems with Clinton's decision to use a private email server.

The first is cybersecurity. The FBI concluded that Clinton and her staff were not fully aware of the threat they exposed themselves to. It points to a larger problem with government, where public servants outside the intelligence agencies often treat cybersecurity as an afterthought. Last year, Congress did **pass a law** that allows private companies to work with the government to improve cybersecurity, and this year President Barack Obama created a **commission on cyber defense**. But there are still massive **political** and **bureaucratic** problems that the next executive has to deal with.

The second issue is transparency. The Obama administration has been among the **"least transparent"** in recent history, even though Obama promised greater transparency during his 2008 campaign. The administration has kept entire **government programs secret, stonewalled public records requests**, and viciously **gone after those who leak information**.

An Associated Press investigation found that the backlog of public records requests **grew 55 percent** under Obama. So whatever Clinton's motive was for the private server, it brings up concerns about whether the public's right to know will continue to erode under the next administration. And Donald Trump **hasn't exactly been the model** for transparency either, though he has **tried to create the illusion of it**.

Both of these are massive, nuanced issues that raise real questions about how Clinton or Trump would govern. It touches on two increasingly relevant issues about our data — how we should protect it and who should be able to see it. But they've been reframed into this amorphous narrative about trust.

Correction: A previous version of this story said Clinton's server contained 81 emails ranging from "classified to top secret," but it should read "confidential to top secret." There are **three levels of classified information**: confidential, secret, and top secret.

The Washington Times - Friday, October 28, 2016

The FBI has renewed its investigation into Hillary Clinton's secret emails, Director James Comey told Congress in a new letter Friday, heightening the stakes for the Democratic presidential nominee with less than two weeks before Election Day.

Mr. Comey said his agents learned of new emails "pertinent" to their probe while working on an unrelated case. He said his agents need to review those messages to see whether they contain classified information and whether they affect his previous decision.

In July, Mr. Comey announced that while he determined Mrs. Clinton did mishandle classified information, she was too inept to know the risks she was running, so he couldn't prove she did it intentionally — undercutting a criminal case.

TOP STORIES By Stephen Dinan

His new announcement Friday threatened to upend the presidential campaign.

John Podesta, Mrs. Clinton's campaign chairman, demanded Mr. Comey explain what new information he's found and blamed Republicans for "browbeating" the FBI into Friday's decision.

Washington Times

Clinton e-mails Comey

"Director Comey's letter refers to emails that have come to light in an unrelated case, but we have no idea what those emails are, and the Director himself notes they may not even be significant," he said.

"It is extraordinary that we would see something like this just 11 days out from a presidential election."

Mrs. Clinton's running mate, Sen. Tim Kaine of Virginia, said Mr .Comey owes the campaign and the public a "clearer accounting" of the new information.

"When you do this 11 days before a presidential election, and you don't provide many details — but details apparently are being given by the FBI to the press — this is very, very troubling," Mr. Kaine told VICE News. "We hope that the director, and we really think that he should, give a clearer accounting of exactly what's going on right now."

Mr. Podesta predicted the FBI would come to the same conclusion this time as it did in July, and he pointedly noted that the letter was sent to eight Republican committee chairmen in Congress. But it was also carbon-copied to the ranking Democrats.

Mr. Comey did not explain in his letter what information the new emails contain, how long it will take to evaluate them, nor how they were obtained.

The New York Times reported Friday that the emails were snagged as part of an investigation into former Rep. Anthony Weiner and allegations he sent illicit messages through text and social media applications to a 15-year-old North Carolina girl. The paper reported that law enforcement officials seized at least one device shared by Mr. Weiner and his now estranged wife, Huma Abedin — a top personal aide to Mrs. Clinton. The couple announced they were separating in August amid Mr. Weiner's involvement in another sexting scandal, but before the 15-year-old girl's allegations surfaced.

As Mrs. Clinton's top personal aide, Ms. Abedin also had an account on the secret Clinton email server and exchanged classified information with her boss.

Mr. Comey said he was briefed on the new emails on Thursday and felt it was important to promptly alert Congress of investigators' latest efforts.

Republican leaders who were among the eight recipients of the letter called for further disclosures by the FBI director, with Sen. Richard C. Shelby urging him to provide additional information before voters go to the polls on Nov. 8.

"While I am pleased that the FBI is re-opening this case in light of new information, it is imperative that the Bureau immediately evaluate the material to complete this investigation," said Mr. Shelby, chairman of the Appropriations Subcommittee on Commerce, Justice, Science, and Related Agencies. "The American people are electing their next Commander-in-Chief only days from now, and they deserve to know the conclusion of your review prior to Election Day."

Sen. Charles E. Grassley, who as chairman of the Senate Judiciary Committee was one of the letter's recipients, said Mr. Comey owes the country more of an explanation about what he's found.

"The letter from Director Comey was unsolicited and, quite honestly, surprising. But it's left a lot more questions than answers for both the FBI and Secretary Clinton," the Iowa Republican said.

GOP presidential nominee Donald Trump, campaigning in Manchester, New Hampshire, said he respected the FBI for reversing itself.

"Perhaps, finally, justice will be done," he said.

For her part Mrs. Clinton, campaigning in Cedar Rapids, Iowa, did not address the issue, instead sticking doggedly to her stump speech of attacks on Mr. Trump mixed with a plea to voters to focus on issues.

President Obama, who has been saddled by association with Mrs. Clinton, who was serving him during the time she maintained her secret email server, did not respond to questions shouted by reporters Friday afternoon as he left the White House on a campaign trip to Florida to stump for Mrs. Clinton and Democratic Senate candidate Patrick Murphy.

Briefing reporters on Air Force One, deputy press secretary Eric Schultz said Mr. Obama President Obama expects the FBI to "follow the facts wherever they lead" and to act "irrespective of politics."

Mr. Schultz said the new email development does not affect Mr. Obama's support of Mrs. Clinton.

Libertarian candidate Gary Johnson said on CNN, "Obviously, the FBI didn't do this lightly. There has to be something there."

He lamented the prospect of "a president-elect under criminal investigation."

"That's what's going to now be the case if she is elected," he said. "She will control those jobs [in the Justice Department] that control how this issue moves forward, which points to a special prosecutor. This is a mess. It's a mess. I think Trump is toast, so is Hillary moving forward as president-elect? Four years of this? Ugh."

Congressional Republicans, who have been at odds with Mr. Trump on many issues, found common ground with their nominee in attacking Mrs. Clinton.

"This decision, long overdue, is the result of her reckless use of a private email server and her refusal to be forthcoming with federal investigators," said House Speaker Paul D. Ryan.

He again called for the Obama administration to suspend the classified intelligence briefings Mrs. Clinton is getting as the Democratic nominee.

And Sen. John Cornyn, Texas Republican, wondered whether the Justice Department would now convene a grand jury to pursue the case.

He said the FBI had already cleared Mrs. Clinton of mishandling classified information, so to reopen the case suggests either potential new evidence of intent to mishandle secrets or other potential criminal questions.

"Originally, FBI focused on 'classification rules' and not broader issues related to government records/obstruction of justice. Will they now?" Mr. Cornyn tweeted.

An FBI spokesman declined Friday to comment on the reopening of the investigation.

The revelation that the investigation is continuing comes too late to affect the 16 million voters who have already cast ballots in absentee or in-person voting.

Republicans have said Mrs. Clinton appeared to mislead Congress in her sworn testimony to the Benghazi probe in 2015.

The staggering reversal by Mr. Comey comes as Mrs. Clinton is reeling from another electronic scandal — the revelations from emails obtained and posted by WikiLeaks from Mr. Podesta's personal email address.

Mrs. Clinton refused to use an official state.gov email account during her four years as secretary, instead setting up an account on a server she kept at her home in New York. That arrangement shielded her emails from public disclosure for six years, thwarting open-records laws.

She belatedly turned over some 30,000 messages she deemed government-related, but the FBI recovered thousands of others she didn't — including some that contained classified information

His new announcement Friday threatened to upend the presidential campaign.

John Podesta, Mrs. Clinton's campaign chairman, demanded Mr. Comey explain what new information he's found and blamed Republicans for "browbeating" the FBI into Friday's decision.

Justice Dept. Strongly Discouraged Comey on Move in Clinton Email Case New York Times

CLINTON REACTION TO COMEY RE: E-mail shivved me

She writes in her memoir that Comey 'shivved' her by releasing a trove of emails just 11 days before the election.

'My first instinct was that my campaign should hit back hard and explain to the public that Comey had badly overstepped his bounds,' she said.

'My team raised concerns with that kind of confrontational approach. In the end, we decided it would be better to just let it go and try to move on. Looking back, that was a mistake.'

FBI interviews Hillary Clinton over email use as secretary of state

Hillary Clinton has admitted that her private email server was a "mistake," and she "would do it differently" if she could go back.

By Gabriel Debenedetti and Kristen East

07/02/2016 12:36 PM EDT

Updated: 07/02/2016 03:04 PM EDT

Hillary Clinton met with the Federal Bureau of Investigation on Saturday morning for a "voluntary interview" about the investigation into her use of a private email server while serving as secretary of state, her campaign announced.

The interview at FBI headquarters in Washington, which lasted for three and a half hours, according to a campaign aide, is a long-expected development in the months-long email saga that has complicated Clinton's White House bid since before its formal inception. Clinton has steadfastly denied any wrongdoing and pledged to cooperate with the bureau's inquiry, bluntly telling an interviewer in March that an indictment is "not going to happen."

Clinton later Saturday spoke with MSNBC's "Meet the Press" host Chuck Todd about the interview, saying she was "eager to do it" while refusing to speculate on the investigation's timeline or final conclusion.

"Let me just repeat what I have repeated for many months now. I never received nor sent any material that was marked classified, and there is a process for the review of material before it is released to the public, and there were decisions made that material should be classified. I do call that retroactively classifying. So therefore, it would not be publically released. But that doesn't chance [sic] the fact as I've explained many times. ... "I have said that I'm going to continue to put forth my record, what I have stood for, do everything I can to earn the trust of the voters of our country."

The presumptive Democratic nominee also addressed criticism from both parties on her husband, former President Bill Clinton's meeting with attorney general Loretta Lynch at a Phoenix airport, saying "hindsight is 20/20."

The Clinton campaign, in a previous statement, called the meeting with the FBI "voluntary."

An FBI spokeswoman declined to comment on the session.

While her use of a homebrewed email server was not a major issue during Clinton's primary campaign against Vermont Sen. Bernie Sanders -- who effectively took the issue off the table during their first debate -- it has already been a major point of contention with her likely Republican opponent Donald Trump, who refers to her as "Crooked Hillary" and has vowed to put her in jail if he is elected.

The timing of the interview suggests that the Department of Justice's investigation may be nearing its conclusion, just weeks before Clinton formally accepts her party's nomination in Philadelphia later this month. And it comes after a number of her closest confidantes, including top advisers Cheryl Mills and Huma Abedin, have already spoken with the FBI. Bryan Pagliano, a former technology aide to Clinton, also spoke with investigators after striking an immunity deal with federal prosecutors.

In recent months, Mills, Abedin, and Pagliano have also submitted court-ordered depositions about Clinton's email setup. The transcripts of those sessions have been publicly released, showing Pagliano repeatedly invoked his 5th Amendment right against self-incrimination. The conservative group that conducted that questioning as part of a Freedom of Information Act lawsuit, Judicial Watch, has also asked another judge to order Clinton to give a deposition in a separate FOIA lawsuit. No ruling has been made on that request.

The controversy has dogged Clinton repeatedly since the news first broke of her unusual email arrangement in March 2015, and both the candidate and campaign officials have long said they were happy and willing to cooperate with the investigation.

But it has nonetheless long been a drag on Clinton politically, a major cause of her low trustworthiness ratings among voters as Republicans have portrayed her as corrupt. A Quinnipiac University poll published on Wednesday found Trump besting her, 45-37 percent, on the question of who is more honest and trustworthy.

The political furor surrounding the email issue has re-exploded in recent weeks, following the release of a State Department inspector general's report in late May that concluded Clinton had failed to comply with the department's records policies while using her server.

The report noted how some employees who asked questions about the arrangement were told not to question it, and it confirmed that the server was subject to apparent hacking attempts.

"Secretary Clinton should have preserved any federal records she created and received on her personal account by printing and filing those records with the related files in the Office of the Secretary," read that report, which also criticized the agency's record-keeping procedures.

"At a minimum, Secretary Clinton should have surrendered all emails dealing with department business before leaving government service, and because she did not do so, she did not comply with the department's policies that were implemented in accordance with the Federal Records Act."

Clinton has cooperated with the FBI's investigations by turning over more than 30,000 of her emails while deleting around the same number she said were personal in nature. Hundreds of emails turned over during the process were later deemed classified — several dozen of them Secret or Top Secret, the upper tiers of national security classification, and about 2000 designated as Confidential, the lowest level of protection for classified information — in what Clinton has called "an absurdity."

She has said, however, that using a private email server was a "mistake," and she "would do it differently" if she could go back.

"I understand people may have concerns about this. But I hope voters look at the full picture of everything I've done in my career and the full threat posed by a Donald Trump presidency, and if they do, I have faith in the American people that they will make the right choice here," she told CNN's Jake Tapper recently.

The timing of the FBI interview, on the Fourth of July; a weekend when few Americans are likely to be paying much attention is fortunate for Clinton — as is, noted former Obama White House aide David Axelrod, its placement in the lull period between the primaries and the Democratic National Convention.

Timing of FBI interview, between primaries and convention, probably good timing for @HillaryClinton. Best to get it behind her.

— David Axelrod (@davidaxelrod) *July 2, 2016*

Just last week, Clinton's husband, Bill Clinton, came under even more scrutiny from Republicans and Democrats alike for meeting with Lynch aboard a private plane on a Phoenix airport tarmac. The impromptu get-together, which both parties described as a friendly discussion about golf and grandchildren, fueled GOP calls for an independent investigation.

Lynch, a Democratic-appointed by President Barack Obama, acknowledged on Friday that the meeting had "cast a shadow" over the Justice Department's investigation into the candidate's emails, adding that she anticipates accepting whatever conclusion investigators present her.

"The recommendations will be reviewed by career supervisors in the Department of Justice and in the FBI, and by the FBI director," Lynch said at the Aspen Ideas Festival in Colorado. "And then, as is the common process, they present it to me, and I fully expect to accept their recommendations."

The Trump campaign blasted out an email after Lynch's comments with the subject line "FACTS ON CLINTON'S SECRET SERVER." Lynch's unwillingness to formally recuse herself from the FBI investigation, the email said, "raises even more questions about potential political pressure, interference, and bias."

Josh Gerstein contributed.

GOP senators: Comey drafted a statement clearing Clinton before her interview

"Conclusion first, fact-gathering second—that's no way to run an investigation," Sens. Chuck Grassley (right) and Lindsey Graham wrote to FBI Director Christopher Wray. | Brendan Smialowski/AFP/Getty Images

By Josh Gerstein

08/31/2017 03:03 PDT

Updated: 09/01/2017 08:12 AM EDT

Former FBI Director James Comey began drafting a statement rejecting the idea of criminal charges against Democratic presidential candidate Hillary Clinton over her private email account about two months or more before Clinton was interviewed in the FBI probe, according to partial transcripts of interviews released Thursday by two Republican senators.

Senate Judiciary Committee Chairman Chuck Grassley and Sen. Lindsey Graham said they obtained the transcripts from the Office of Special Counsel, a government watchdog agency that launched an investigation into whether Comey's actions violated a federal law against government employees engaging in political activity while on duty.

In a letter sent Wednesday to Comey's successor, FBI Director Christopher Wray, Grassley and Graham said Comey's move to start preparing the statement sometime in April or early May reflected a premature conclusion that Clinton shouldn't be charged.

"Conclusion first, fact-gathering second—that's no way to run an investigation. The FBI should be held to a higher standard than that, especially in a matter of such great public interest and controversy," Grassley and Graham wrote as they demanded all FBI records of the drafts Comey prepared as well as other materials related to the OSC probe.

Grassley and Graham said the OSC—a permanent, independent executive branch agency unrelated to Special Counsel Robert Mueller's Trump-Russia probe—shut down its investigation after Comey was fired in May by President Donald Trump. That's because the key law prohibiting the use of an official position for political purposes, the Hatch Act, is not a criminal statute. As a result, there's no action that can be taken against people who are no longer government employees.

A spokeswoman for the Office of Special Counsel declined to comment on the senators' claims or to discuss the agency's inquiry into Comey's conduct.

An FBI spokeswoman confirmed receipt of the senators' letter and said the agency would provide any response to the lawmakers directly.

On Friday morning, Trump jumped on the disclosure as evidence that the fix was in on the Clinton email probe from the beginning.

"Wow, looks like James Comey exonerated Hillary Clinton long before the investigation was over...and so much more," he tweeted. "A rigged system!"

White House press secretary Sarah Huckabee Sanders said Thursday that if the senators' claims are true, they support Trump's decision to dismiss Comey.

"If it is as accurate as they say it is, that would certainly give cause and reason that Jim Comey was not the right person to lead the FBI," Sanders said before urging reporters to dig into the story.

Congressional Republicans had long suspected that Comey had already decided Clinton

 would not be charged when a team of FBI agents and prosecutors met with her for three-and-a-half hours at FBI headquarters on Saturday, July 2, 2016. Comey's unusual and controversial public statement concluding the investigation came just three days later, on the Tuesday following the Independence Day holiday.

However, the senators say the OSC interviews indicate Comey began drafting the statement at least six weeks earlier, well before FBI agents finished interviewing key witnesses in the investigation, including Clinton lawyers Cheryl Mills and Heather Samuelson, State Department tech aide Bryan Pagliano and State information technology manager John Bentel.

At a House hearing last September, Comey vehemently denied any decision had been made not to charge Clinton before the July 2 interview. He was not asked when he began preparing his public statement.

"If colleagues of ours believe I am lying about when I made this decision, please urge them to contact me privately so we can have a conversation about this," Comey said. "All I can do is tell you again; the decision was made after that because I didn't know what was going to happen in that interview."

The then-FBI chief said it was possible Clinton might lie in the interview, although he also said there was no indication she did.

The GOP senators referred to Comey's statement as "exonerating" Clinton, but it was so critical of her and her aides that it subsequently led Democrats to write to the Office of Special Counsel to seek a probe of whether his comments were intended to damage her prospects in the presidential race.

SPECIAL AGENT ROTH have reviewed the timeline from the date of the Clinton interview on July 2, 2016, to the announcement of James Comey on July 5, 2016. It would be virtually impossible to write the interview form 302 in 4 days, have all FBI Agents who attended the interview read it and initial it, send the 302 to the DOJ for review, and then forward the 302 to Comey to read it and make a momentous decision in 2 and one-half days.

The fix was in.

Part Eight

Family Members Are Targeted

DONALD TRUMP, JR.

Mueller Trump Tower

Mueller declined to charge Donald Trump Jr. for meeting with a Russian lawyer

Once it became clear the meeting between Donald Trump Jr. and a Russian lawyer would become public knowledge, senior aides scrambled to respond.

The Mueller report was released Thursday.NBC News / AP / Getty Images

April 18, 2019, 2:05 PM EDT

By Allan Smith

Donald Trump Jr. and other Trump campaign officials involved in the June 2016 meeting with a Kremlin-linked lawyer were not charged with campaign finance violations in part because it would be difficult to prove the participants knew their conduct was unlawful, special counsel Robert Mueller's redacted report, released Thursday, said.

The meeting, which took place at Trump Tower in New York City on June 9, 2016, was pitched to Trump Jr. as the opportunity for members of Trump's presidential campaign to receive damaging information about Democratic nominee Hillary Clinton from a Russian lawyer Natalia Veselnitskaya.

It is illegal for campaigns to accept help from a foreign government or from foreign nationals.

"On the facts here, the government would unlikely be able to prove beyond a reasonable doubt that the June 9 meeting participants had general knowledge that their conduct was unlawful," the report reads. "The investigation has not developed evidence that the participants in the meeting were familiar with the foreign-contribution ban or the application of federal law to the relevant factual context. The government does not have strong evidence of surreptitious behavior or efforts at concealment at the time of the June 9 meeting."

Rob Goldstone, a British music publicist who helped coordinate the meeting, told Trump Jr. in an email that the "crown prosecutor of Russia" would provide official documents and information that would incriminate Clinton and her connections with Russia as "part of Russia and its government's support for Mr. Trump."

Trump Jr. wrote of the possible dirt, "Seems we have some time, and if it's what you say, I love it especially later in the summer."

Mueller said in his report that investigators did not believe they could prove Trump Jr. acted "willfully" when he possibly violated campaign finance law.

"The Report confirms that the June 9, 2016 meeting was just what Don said it was, and nothing more, and that there was nothing improper about potentially listening to information," Trump Jr.'s attorney, Alan Futerfas, said in a statement Thursday, responding to the release of Mueller's report.

As a source for the Trump campaign, Veselnitskaya proved disappointing, as she did not provide the damaging information about Clinton that was promised.

Mueller also said in his report that his investigation found no "documentary" evidence that then-candidate Trump knew about the meeting in advance.

"According to written answers submitted by President Trump, he has no recollection of learning of the meeting at the time, and the Office found no documentary evidence showing that he was made aware of the meeting — or its Russian connection — before it occurred," Mueller wrote in his report.

That was an outstanding question, given some conflicting statements from those close to the matter. In a 2017 testimony to the Senate Judiciary Committee, Trump Jr. said he could not remember if he had told his father in advance. Last year, Trump's personal attorney, Rudy Giuliani, said he "would be surprised if [Trump] could remember" if he was informed in advance of the meeting.

The president's former longtime attorney Michael Cohen, who is set to start a three-year prison sentence after pleading guilty to a list of federal felonies, including two relating to paying off women who alleged affairs with the president on Trump's behalf, told Congress this year that he remembered Trump Jr. telling his father in advance.

Mueller wrote in his report that although Cohen "believed that Trump Jr. had previously discussed the meeting with his father," the attorney "was not involved in any such conversation."

Trump's misleading statement to the press

According to Mueller's report, Trump was aware of the existence of emails related to the Trump Tower meeting by June 2017.

In July 2017, senior White House aide Hope Hicks informed the president that The New York Times planned to publish a story about the meeting, Mueller wrote, and Trump became involved in the effort to craft a response.

In the days leading up to The Times' story, senior aides sought to fill Trump in on just how damaging the emails between Trump Jr. and Goldstone were and scrambled to coordinate a message.

Hicks warned Trump that the emails were "really bad" and the story surrounding them would be "massive" once it broke, Mueller wrote, but Trump was "insistent that he did not want to talk about it and said he did not want details."

Mueller's report shows he chose not to charge Trump because obstruction was in plain view

Trump at first instructed her to provide no comment, which she thought was "odd because he usually considered not responding to the press to be the ultimate sin," Mueller wrote.

Trump asked Hicks what the meeting had been about, to which Hicks said she was told it was "about Russian adoption."

"Then just say that," Trump responded, according to the report.

According to the report, Trump Jr. wanted the statement to say it was to "primarily" talk about the issue of Russian adoption. In text messages provided to Mueller, Hicks agreed with Trump Jr. But said his father didn't want that word included in the statement because "he was worried it invites questions."

Trump Jr. said that if the caveat was not included, it would appear "as though I'm lying later when they inevitably leak something."

The statement ultimately given to The Times for their story published on July 8, 2017, was the president's version — the one that declared the meeting was about adoption policy.

Trump Jr. had to issue subsequent statements once it became clear the initial response was misleading and eventually disclosed the emails publicly once he became aware The Times was about to publish them in a subsequent story.

But Mueller concluded that because each of these misleading efforts was directed at the press and that there was no evidence Trump sought to withhold information from or mislead Congress or the special counsel, it did not constitute obstruction of justice.

Allan Smith

Allan Smith is a political reporter for NBC News.

Part Nine

2020 Election Fraud

FBI Tipped 2020 Election for Biden

By Larry Bell

Wednesday, 31 August 2022 12:02 PM

According to an August survey of 1,335 adults conducted by the New Jersey-based Techno Metrica Institute of Policy and Politics, a whopping 79 percent believed that Donald Trump would have been reelected for a second term had they known the dirty demons lurking in Hunter Biden's laptop from hell that the FBI and DOJ had been dismissing as "Russian disinformation."

In addition, 47 percent of those polled said that knowing before the election that the laptop contents were real and not "disinformation" would have changed their voting decision —including more than two-thirds (71 percent) of Democrats.

The FBI clearly knew the contents were real. They had been sitting on that knowledge since December 2019 and revealed nothing throughout the election season.

The New York Post broke the story in October 2020 exposing emails on the hard drive of an abandoned Apple computer that Hunter Biden had abandoned at a Wilmington, Delaware, repair shop indicating the Biden family may have participated in illicit business deals in Ukraine, China and other countries.

Immediately after the story broke, more than 50 former U.S. intelligence officials, including CIA Director John Brennan, signed a public letter claiming the material published by the Post from Hunter's hard drive "has all the classic earmarks of a Russian disinformation operation."

Joe Biden cited their letter in the presidential debates to deflect questions, and social media censored the story, denying voters critical information on the eve of the election.

We have since learned that the FBI not only buried the laptop story, the bureau also ran active interference for the Biden administration and Democratic Party in getting it banned on social media.

Facebook CEO Mark Zuckerberg admitted during a media interview on the Joe Rogan podcast that the FBI had approached his staff telling them in advance to expect a big story that the Russians had planted which he now believes was about the laptop.

Zuckerberg told Rogan: "The background here is that the FBI came to us — some folks on our team — and was like 'Hey, just so you know, you should be on high alert. We thought there was a lot of Russian propaganda in the 2016 election, we have it on notice that basically there's about to be some kind of dump that's similar to that'."

Although Zuckerberg said the FBI did not warn Facebook about the Biden story in particular — Facebook thought it "fit that pattern."

This was indeed part of an FBI "pattern."

The FBI was also fully aware that Trump Russia collusion charges cooked up by Hillary Clinton to deflect attention away from her "deleted email problem" presented to their general counsel by her attorney as a "good citizen" were "not technically plausible," but nevertheless allowed him to be continually hounded by these false allegations throughout his presidency.

Then there's the murky matter of the agency's Crossfire Hurricane spying operation entirely premised upon a phony "dirty dossier" report sponsored and funded by the Clinton campaign containing salacious references to an imaginary Trump "pee tape" Russian hotel episode that would make even the fictional prostitutes blush.

That FBI espionage on Trump began before he was elected, and continued with tacit approval by the Obama White House after he was sworn into office.

In their FISA court spying filings, the agency omitted known facts that the dossier information used in 2017 to conduct surveillance on Trump campaign aide Carter Page was bogus. Kevin Clinesmith, a low-level FBI lawyer, copped a guilty plea of altering evidence in exchange for skating on serious federal prison time.

Carter Page wasn't the only Trump associate targeted.

A sting setup admitted by former FBI Director James Comey produced criminal charges that bankrupted Trump's incoming national security director, retired Lt. Gen. Michael Flynn, for making false statements to the FBI involving conversations with Russian Ambassador Sergey Kislyak. The DOJ later filed a motion to dismiss asserting that it no longer believed it could prove beyond a reasonable doubt the statements were untruthful.

In the run-up to the 2016 elections, text messages between a mating pair of nesting high-level FBI lovebirds in the eye of the Crossfire Hurricane storm made it clear they shared no affection for then-candidate Donald Trump whatsoever.

Peter Strzok, who led the investigation, assured Lisa Page, a lead attorney on the matter, that the agency wouldn't allow Trump to win the presidency.

Strzok had referred to Donald Trump in a text as "a f---ing idiot." And when Page worried about Trump winning, Strzok wrote to her, "No, he won't. We'll stop it."

The previously unprecedented recent FBI document raid on former President Trump's private Mar-a-Lago residence over publicly undisclosed investigations has many Americans legitimately terrified about a politicized two-tier justice system run amok.

There was no comparable DOJ or FBI interest in pursuing clear evidence that Hillary Clinton had deleted 33,000 emails — many containing national security-sensitive classified information subpoenaed by Congress following her term as secretary of state — going so far as having some records "wiped with BleachBit," and cellphones destroyed with hammers.

Any thought of the FBI invading the Clintons' Chappaqua home to seize documents would have been unthinkable.

Also recall that former FBI Director Comey not only took his handwritten notes when he was fired by Trump in 2017, but even leaked confidential information to The New York Times without any legal repercussions.

This is the same Comey whose conclusion during a July 2016 press briefing stated: "Although there is evidence of potential violations of the statutes regarding the handling of classified information, our judgment is that no reasonable prosecutor would bring such a case (against Hillary)."

Obama Attorney General Loretta Lynch let Mr. Comey's judgment stand, leaving Hillary free to continue her run for the White House.

Nevertheless, there is ample evidence that those who head the deep state are determined and prepared to do anything in their power to make Donald Trump ineligible for a second term through discovery of any potentially indictable offenses.

Attorney General Merrick Garland, who ordered the Mar-a-Lago raid, will now be compelled to make a convincing case that Trump's transgressions are greater than Clinton's.

Far more than Donald Trump, the American justice system is already on trial.

La Jolla Provocateur Dinesh D'Souza Disputes 2020 Election in New Film

*by **Debbie L. Sklar** | May 7, 2022*

The video platform Rumble announced conservative author and filmmaker Dinesh D'Souza, a La Jolla resident, would release his movie *2000 Mules* on Saturday through the Locals subscription-service.

"The documentary film created by Dinesh D'Souza, exposes widespread, coordinated voter fraud in the 2020 election, sufficient to change the overall outcome," according to the producers.

The film is said to draw on a database of 10 trillion cellphone pings provided by the election integrity group True the Vote. The "mules" are paid professional operatives that D'Souza claims delivered fraudulent and illegal votes to mail drop boxes in the five key states.

Allegations of election fraud have been dismissed by courts across the country, but former President Trump continues to claim that he won reelection. Trump pardoned D'Souza, who was on probation for campaign finance violations, in 2018.

The new film has already been criticized for "flawed analysis" of the cellphone data it cites. But it has also by praised by conservative media.

D'Souza, who has more than 1.5 million followers on Rumble, previously produced several conservative films, including *2016: Obama's America* and *Death of a Nation,* and written multiple books, including *What's So Great About America* and *The End of Racism.*

"Locals allows me to reach a broad audience with this important movie," D'Souza said. "I know that I will be able to say what I believe without worrying about being canceled or censored."

"Supporting creative independence is core to our values. Together with Rumble, we are excited to offer creators a new way to distribute and sell movies directly to their audience" said Assaf Lev, president of Locals.

Why any solution to Ginni Thomas' partisan lobBy ing would be worse than the problem

***Opinion* By Jessica Levinson** - *Yesterday 5:37 AM*

New reports indicate that Ginni Thomas, who's married to Supreme Court Justice Clarence Thomas, was even more involved than we knew in systematic efforts to overturn Joe Biden's 2020 victory over Donald Trump. We knew that she had sent a barrage of texts to Trump's White House chief of staff Mark Meadows in an effort to overturn the 2020 election. We knew she'd reportedly emailed the aide of a prominent conservative in the U.S. House of Representatives and said his group needed to be "out in the streets."

Ginni Thomas was even more involved than we knew in efforts to overturn Joe Biden's 2020 victory.

We knew that she'd reportedly sent emails to John Eastman, one of Trump's attorneys, who provided a roadmap for the fake electors scheme. We knew she'd attended the rally that occurred right before the riot on Jan. 6, 2021. According to past reports, she emailed 29 Republican lawmakers in Arizona urging them to contest Biden's win there. The latest development is that she also contacted Wisconsin lawmakers in an effort to overturn the election.

Even so, we should be careful not to make systemic changes to the Supreme Court because of what Ginni Thomas did while married to Justice Clarence Thomas.

Let's be clear, for the reasons listed above, Justice Clarence Thomas should have recused himself from weighing in on at least some of the litigation related to the 2020 presidential election. His spouse, Ginni Thomas, didn't just vocally support one candidate. She lobbied for people across the country to help to overturn her candidate's loss.

Narrow Wins in These Key States Powered Biden to The Presidency

December 2, 20205:00 AM ET

Benjamin Swasey & Connie Hanzhang Jin

In a contest with historic turnout, President-elect Joe Biden topped President Trump by nearly 7 million votes, and 74 votes in the Electoral College, but his victory really was stitched together with narrow margins in a handful of states.

Trump's legal team has mounted dubious and so-far-unsuccessful efforts to overturn the results in six key states Biden won. All six of those states have now certified their results, providing an opportunity to look back at the final tallies.

The graphic below shows the results in those six swing states, illustrating the especially close margins in Arizona, Georgia and Wisconsin.

POLITICS

President-Elect Joe Biden Hits 80 million Votes In Year of Record Turnout

The tight races in the trio of states had a big electoral impact. As NPR's Domenico Montanaro has put it, "just 44,000 votes in Georgia, Arizona and Wisconsin separated Biden and Trump from a tie in the Electoral College."

Of course, Trump is no stranger to narrow victories. He won the 2016 election thanks to just under 80,000 combined votes in three of those six key states.

Justice Department has issued dozens of subpoenas in the last week related to Trump and the Capitol riot

Ken Dilanian And Michael Kosnar and Zoë Richards and Jonathan Dienst and Marc Caputo

September 12, 2022, 8:25 PM

The Justice Department has issued about 40 subpoenas in the last week related to the actions of former President Donald Trump, his allies and efforts to overturn the 2020 election, according to sources familiar with the matter.

It also seized two telephones, the sources said.

The subpoenas and phone seizures, first reported by The New York Times, are the latest developments in the sprawling investigation into the former president.

The Times, citing people familiar with the investigation, reported that Trump adviser Boris Epshteyn was one of the people whose phone was seized. A source who spoke to Epshteyn confirmed to NBC News that his phone was taken last week.

The House committee investigating the Jan. 6 Capitol riot subpoenaed Epshteyn and three other Trump associates — Rudy Giuliani, Jenna Ellis and Sidney Powell — in January.

Former New York City Police Commissioner Bernard Kerik's lawyer confirmed to NBC News that he received a subpoena last week.

Kerik's attorney, Timothy Parlatore, called it "the widest and most obtuse subpoena I have seen in my years practicing criminal law."

Parlatore said he also represents Trump in the investigation.

The Justice Department declined to comment Monday night.

Separately, the department is engaged in a legal battle with Trump and his counsel over documents retrieved during the FBI's search of the former president's Florida estate on Aug. 8.

Trump lawyers asked a judge Monday to continue blocking the Justice Department from reviewing the documents, some of which bore classification markings.

January 6 hearing: Former Trump-appointed US attorney testifies he found no widespread voter fraud in Georgia

By FOX 5 Atlanta Digital Team

Published June 13, 2022, 6:28 AM

Updated 1:04 PM

Capitol Riot

Liz Cheney Throws a Tantrum After January 6 Panel Chairman Bennie Thompson Rules out Trump Criminal Referral

By Cristina Laila

Published June 13, 2022, at 9:31 pm

Monday marked day two of Liz Cheney's Maoist January 6 show trial.

January 6 panel Chairman Bennie Thompson (D-MS) on Monday evening said the committee will not be making criminal referrals to the Justice Department.

"If the Department of Justice looks at it and assumes that there's something that needs further review. I'm sure they'll do it," Thompson said to reporters.

Then asked again if the January 6 committee would ever make a criminal referral. "No, that's not our job. Our job is to look at the facts and circumstances around January 6, what caused it, and make recommendations after that."

"They're the prosecutors, not the legislative branch," Rep. Zoe Lofgren said to reporters, backing up Bennie Thompson's statement.

BioShield.Com

Liz Cheney threw a tantrum after Rep. Thompson confirmed his committee would never criminally refer President Trump to the Justice Department.

Cheney immediately released a statement contradicting Bennie Thompson.

FBI Finally Proves That Donald Trump Had Nothing to Do with Jan. 6 'Insurrection'

By Admin

Published on August 20, 2021

RTBS Offer

The Federal Bureau of Investigation did not set out to prove Donald Trump had nothing to do with the January 6 events that have been characterized as an "insurrection" and a "coup." But a new exclusive report from Reuters obliterates the essential claims that Donald Trump directed extremists to attack the Capitol building and urged protesters to thwart a peaceful transfer of power.

"The FBI has found scant evidence that the Jan. 6 attack on the U.S. Capitol was the result of an organized plot to overturn the presidential election result, according to four current and former law enforcement officials," Reuters reported.

> *The Nation will indeed remember January 6, 2021—and President Trump's singular responsibility for that tragedy. It is impossible to imagine the events of January 6 occurring without President Trump creating a powder keg, striking a match, and then seeking personal advantage from the ensuing havoc.*

However, President Trump could not have "incited" the Capitol attack that was planned before his speech was given. The New York Times reports that the "first barriers were breached" at 12:53 p.m. at the Northwest side of the Capitol. The NY Times then claims that Trump's "call to action" was at 1:12 p.m. Of course, this is nearly twenty minutes after the purported first "breach" of the barricades. The speech was given a mile and a half away.

Trump's speech was standard political fare, and he even told the audience at his speech to "peacefully and patriotically make their voices heard." He also deliberately said "fight" in the commonplace political context:

> *For years, Democrats have gotten away with election fraud and weak Republicans. And that's what they are. There are so many weak Republicans. And we have great ones. Jim Jordan and some of these guys they're out there fighting. The House guys are fighting. But it's, it's incredible.*

The Commander-in-Chief and head of powerful intelligence and law enforcement agencies did *not* select a motley rabble of disparate extremist elements to carry out a "coup" to disrupt the objections of the Electoral College. The extremists in the Capitol building were not even found to be armed with firearms. This was a ludicrous argument from the very beginning, but that did not stop major news outlets from promoting it.

Reuters itself had put forth the claim that Donald Trump had attempted to 'thwart' a peaceful transfer of power in a tendentious article it published on January 6.

"Trump has sought for weeks to thwart a peaceful transfer of power, aided by groups such as 'Stop the Steal,' which promoted stopthesteal.us the day's protest and peddled false claims about voter fraud on Facebook and other social media," Reuters reported.

"In a statement posted on Twitter by White House spokesman Dan Scavino on Thursday, Trump said there would be an orderly transition of power 'though I totally disagree with the outcome of the election,'" the report continued.

"But Wednesday's events were the culmination of his efforts to thwart a peaceful transfer," Reuters claimed. "About 50 minutes into the speech, some of his supporters, waving Trump flags, began heading toward Capitol Hill, where unprecedented mayhem ensued."

This is a deceptive narrative on many accounts, even setting aside that Democrats for decades had been putting forth arguments that elections were 'stolen or had otherwise contested election results. An article in USA Today is indicative of the kinds of misleading narratives the media spread about January 6 and Donald Trump's purported role in it.

"As the cases against nearly 200 of the Capitol rioters begin to wind through federal court, many of the defendants blame the commander in chief they followed for the violence that left five dead during the insurrection Jan. 6," USA Today earlier reported.

"In court documents, media interviews, and through official attorney statements, staunch supporters of former President Donald Trump who carried out the attempted coup argue they were merely doing what they thought the nation's leader had asked, some citing a cult-like loyalty."

Yet none of the January 6 defendants have been charged with "insurrection." None of them have been charged with "treason" for attempting to overturn an election. In fact, many of those who were charged with even violent crimes are getting plea deals, apparently to prevent the release of exculpatory evidence in discovery, such as nearly 14,000 hours of video footage of the event.

The FBI is coming clean that when it comes to January 6, the agency has found nothing against the 550 defendants to suggest it was an organized "coup" attempt. Nor is there anything to suggest that Donald Trump 'incited' the riot or had 'directed' the extremists.

The lack of evidence, however, did not stop a partisan and deceptive impeachment trial against the former president. It shows that the Democratic Party does not care about dividing the country with its extreme and unfounded claims against its political opponents.

January 6 hearing: Former Trump-appointed US attorney BJay Pak testifies

WASHINGTON, D.C. - The Jan. 6 committee is investigating the U.S. Capitol riot on Jan. 6, 2021, and will hold its second public meeting today. Lawmakers said they would show evidence that former President Donald Trump "engaged in a massive effort to spread false and fraudulent information" about a stolen election despite repeatedly being told by advisers and allies that he had lost.

Former U.S. Attorney for the Northern District of Georgia, BJay Pak, testified during the hearing. Pak said his office investigated a video in which Trump allies claimed a person smuggled fraudulent ballots into State Farm Arena. Pak said his office did not find sufficient evidence of widespread fraud during the 2020 election in Georgia.

Pak was sworn in as a U.S. attorney in the Atlanta-based Northern District of Georgia in October 2017. From January 2011 to January 2017, Pak was a State Representative from the 108th District in the Georgia General Assembly. Pak was a Republican state lawmaker from 2011 to 2017, had previously served as an assistant U.S. attorney from 2002 to 2008, and was working in private practice at the time of his appointment.

Raffensperger and Secretary of State's Office COO Gabriel Sterling are also expected to provide testimony.

The White House said that Pak and five other nominees for U.S. attorney shared "the president's vision for 'Making America Safe Again.'"

The House committee investigating the Capitol riot said Sunday they have uncovered enough evidence for the Justice Department to consider a criminal indictment against former President Donald Trump for seeking to overturn the results of the 2020 election.

The Associated Press contributed to this report.

Bill Donahue, DOJ, Truck Ballots Pennsylvania on Jan. 6 hearing

Jan. 6 hearing: Key takeaways from 2nd day of testimony

CAITLIN DICKSON - Yahoo NEWS

June 13, 2022, 3:05 PM

The Jan. 6 committee investigating the attack on the U.S. Capitol continued its public hearings on Monday morning with testimony that shed new light on how former President Trump deliberately sought to undermine the results of the 2020 election by spreading allegations of widespread voter fraud that he knew were false.

Following opening remarks from the committee chairman, Rep. Bennie Thompson, D-Miss., and vice chair Rep. Liz Cheney, R-Wyo., Rep. Zoe Lofgren, D-Calif., took the lead in questioning witnesses and presenting the committee's examination of "the false narrative that the 2020 election was 'stolen.'"

"Former President Trump's plan to overturn the election relied on a sustained effort to deceive Americans with knowingly false claims of election fraud," Lofgren said. "All elements of the plot relied on convincing his supporters of these false claims."

What were some of the most shocking revelations?

"There was never an indication of interest in what the actual facts were."

In taped depositions given to the select committee, former Trump advisers and administration officials detailed their efforts to substantiate the various voter fraud claims that were promoted by

111

Trump and his allies in the aftermath of the 2020 election and to relay their findings to the former president.

One after another, officials, including former Attorney General William Barr and former acting Deputy Attorney General Richard Donoghue, recalled multiple conversations with Trump in which they explained exactly why specific allegations such as those about suitcases of ballots in Georgia or rigged Dominion voting machines in Michigan weren't true, only for him to move on to the next bogus claim. Barr likened the Justice Department's effort to investigate the "avalanche of fraud allegations" to "playing whack-a-mole" and noted that Trump continued to publicly promote bogus claims even after his attorney general told him they were "bulls***."

"There was never an indication of interest in what the actual facts were," Barr said.

"The 'big lie' was also a big ripoff."

Lofgren argued that Trump deliberately used claims that he knew were false to "raise hundreds of millions of dollars" from his supporters between the election and Jan. 6.

"The 'big lie' was also a big ripoff," Lofgren said, noting that after the election, the Trump campaign flooded supporters' inboxes with emails requesting donations to the "Official Election Defense Fund." However, in a taped deposition shown at Monday's hearing, former Trump campaign staffer Hanna Allred acknowledged that this supposed fund was nothing more than a "marketing tactic."

A "definitely intoxicated" Rudy Giuliani advised Trump to declare victory on election night, according to testimony.

The committee aired clips of videotaped depositions given by a variety of people who were with the former president on election night in 2020, including his former campaign manager, Bill Stepien, and former senior campaign adviser, Jason Miller. They testified about how the former New York City mayor influenced Trump's decision to publicly declare victory on election night before all of the votes had been counted. Stepien had originally been scheduled to testify in person at the hearing, pursuant to a subpoena from the committee, but his appearance was canceled after his wife went into labor early onday morning.

Miller said that Giuliani, who would go on to pursue a variety of unsuccessful legal challenges to the election results, was " definitely intoxicated" during a discussion about what the president should say when he addressed the nation that night. (An attorney for Giuliani has since disputed that he was drunk on election night.)

"There were suggestions by, I believe it was Mayor Giuliani to go and declare victory and say that we won it outright," Miller said, adding, "I think, effectively, Mayor Giuliani was saying, 'We won it. They're stealing it from us. Where did all the votes come from? We need to go say that we won.' And essentially anyone who didn't agree with that position was being weak."

Though Stepien said he thought it was "far too early to be making any calls like that," Giuliani's idea clearly resonated with Trump, who began pushing the narrative that Biden and the Democrats

112

were stealing the election from him when he erroneously declared in the early hours of Nov. 4: "Frankly, we did win this election."

Trump attorney Rudy Giuliani at a news conference in which he discussed legal challenges to vote counting after the 2020 presidential election. (Matt Slocum/AP)

As with last week's inaugural primetime hearing, Monday's hearing featured a mix of live and taped testimony from a wide variety of witnesses.

Those who appeared in person were Chris Stirewalt, a former Fox News political editor who made the controversial decision to accurately call Arizona for Biden on election night in 2020, and conservative election attorney Benjamin Ginsberg, who explained how Trump's legal challenges to the 2020 election results differed from the way such challenges are typically litigated in court; B.J. Pak, the former U.S. attorney for the Northern District of Georgia and former Philadelphia commissioner Al Schmidt, both of whom investigated allegations of voter fraud in their state.

Chris Stirewalt, a former Fox News political editor, is testifying at the House select committee hearing on Monday. (Susan Walsh/AP)

Some of the most compelling testimony, however, came from the taped depositions of those who watched Trump's stolen election narrative take shape in real-time. In addition to Barr, Donoghue, Stepien, and Miller, other notable witnesses who appeared via video Monday include Trump's daughter Ivanka and her husband, Jared Kushner; Trump White House lawyer Eric Herschmann; and Trump campaign lawyer Alex Cannon.

The committee also showed brief clips of depositions given by Rudy Giuliani and lawyer Sidney Powell, who replaced what Stepien referred to as "team normal" after the election, and quickly took the lead in pursuing a series of unsuccessful legal challenges to the election based on far-flung, unsubstantiated allegations of voter fraud.

Asked for his assessment of the more than 60 court cases lodged by Trump's legal team to challenge the 2020 election, Ginsberg told the committee, "The simple fact is that the Trump campaign did not make its case."

In her closing statement, committee Vice Chair Liz Cheney, R-Wyo., said that in the coming days, the panel will present evidence of Trump's "broader planning for Jan. 6," including his plan to try to use the Justice Department to sow doubt about the legitimacy of the election results, and his "detailed planning with John Eastman to pressure the vice president, state legislatures, state officials and others to overturn the election."

The committee's third hearing will take place on Wednesday, June 15th, at 10 a.m. ET.

Jan. 6 committee setting its sights on Pence, Ginni Thomas

Hope Yen

June 19, 2022, 4:29 PM

113

WASHINGTON (AP) — Members of the House committee investigating the Capitol riot said Sunday they may subpoena former Vice President Mike Pence and are waiting to hear from Virginia "Ginni" Thomas, the wife of Supreme Court Justice Clarence Thomas, about her role in the illegal plot to overturn the 2020 election.

Lawmakers indicated they would release more evidence about Donald Trump's alleged effort to defraud supporters by fundraising off false claims of a stolen presidential election. They also pledged to provide pertinent material to the Justice Department by the end of the month for its criminal investigation. The department complained in a letter last week that the committee was complicating its investigation by not sharing transcripts from its 1,000 interviews.

"We're not taking anything off the table in terms of witnesses who have not yet testified," said Rep. Adam Schiff, who described a Pence subpoena as "certainly a possibility."

"We would still, I think, like to have several high-profile people come before our committee," said Schiff, D-Calif.

For example, the committee has been able to document most of Trump's end of his call to Pence on the morning of the insurrection on Jan. 6, 2021, when the then-president made his final plea for Pence to stop the certification of Joe Biden's victory when Pence presided over the Electoral College count in Congress. Members have not yet documented directly what Pence said in response.

The committee chairman, Rep. Bennie Thompson, D-Miss., recently said the committee was still "engaging" with Pence's lawyers while also suggesting it may not be necessary for him to appear because of testimony from many of Pence's closest aides.

Committee members also hope to learn more about Ginni Thomas' own effort to keep Trump in office and the potential conflicts of interest posed on her husband as a result of the Jan. 6 cases that come before the Supreme Court.

Republican state Rep. Rusty Bowers, the Arizona House speaker, is scheduled to testify at the committee's hearing Tuesday, focusing on state officials who were contacted by Trump and the White House as Trump tried to overturn the results. Bowers is likely to be asked about emails he received from Thomas urging him and other state officials to set aside Biden's 2020 win and choose their own set of electors.

"We have questions for her, and we may have questions for him as well," said Rep. Zoe Lofgren, D-Calif.

Thomas has publicly indicated that she "can't wait" to appear before the committee after receiving their request by letter last week.

Along with emailing Arizona officials, Thomas, who attended a rally Trump held just before the Capitol riot, also had written to then-White House chief of staff Mark Meadows in the weeks after the election encouraging him to work to overturn Biden's victory. Emails recently obtained by the committee also show Thomas had email communications with John Eastman, the lawyer who played a key role on behalf of Trump in efforts to pressure Pence to overturn the election.

"I think the committee will be interested, in among other things, whether this was discussed with Justice Thomas, given that he was ruling on cases impacting whether we would get some of this information," Schiff said.

This past January, Thomas was the lone member of the court who supported a bid by Trump to withhold documents from the Jan 6. committee.

Lofgren said the committee would release additional evidence it has gathered on the "big rip-off," in which the committee alleges Trump may have committed fraud by fundraising by making a false claim the election was stolen.

Rep. Adam Kinzinger, R-Ill., said that in the end, the public would have a clear picture of a "failure of the oath" by Trump.

"I think what we're presenting before the American people certainly would rise to a level of criminal involvement by a president," he said.

Kinzinger also said that he and his family had received threats because of his role on the committee. He spoke of his concern that "there's violence in the future. ... And until we get a grip on telling people the truth, we can't expect any differently."

Schiff appeared on CNN's "State of the Union," Lofgren was on CBS' "Face the Nation," and Kinzinger spoke on ABC's "This Week."

Barr Disputes U.S. Attorney's Vote Fraud Claim

By Robert Farley

Posted on July 14, 2021

Former President Donald Trump says a former U.S. attorney in Pennsylvania was forbidden by then-Attorney General Bill Barr to investigate voter fraud in the presidential election. Barr says that's false.

A day after making a claim, Trump released a letter from former U.S. Attorney Bill McSwain — dated June 9 — in which McSwain writes that although he "received various allegations of voter fraud and election irregularities" after the election, he was "given a directive to pass along serious allegations to the State Attorney General for investigation."

On the contrary, Barr notes that he sent a memo on Nov. 9 authorizing U.S. attorneys around the country to "pursue substantial allegations of voting and vote tabulation irregularities."

And a spokesperson for Pennsylvania Attorney General Josh Shapiro says his office never received any referrals from McSwain.

This story is still unfolding, and we'll lay out here what we know and don't know so far about the dispute.

Trump first teased the issue during a rally in Sarasota, Florida, on July 3, saying, "We have a U.S. attorney in Philadelphia that says he wasn't allowed to go and check Philadelphia." Trump promised he'd reveal at his next rally "who didn't allow him."

In a speech at the annual Conservative Political Action Conference in Dallas on July 11, Trump said that person was his former attorney general, Barr.

"But I just a day ago received a statement from the U.S. attorney, highly respected, in Pennsylvania, that Bill Barr would not allow him to investigate voter fraud. Can you believe it?" Trump said. "Now, you have to understand, Philadelphia is the second most corrupt place, so I understand, okay? So, I understand, in the nation. Do you know what first is? Detroit. Detroit was so corrupt. Philadelphia was so corrupt. But the U.S. attorney was not allowed to investigate what … this just came out in a letter. …He was not allowed to do his job. And I saw that. He was all enthused, and then all of a sudden, it was like he was turned off. And so were others."

Trump added, "You'll have to get it [the letter] from him because I want to stay out of it." But the next day, he publicly released the letter, commenting, "U.S. Attorney from the Eastern District of Pennsylvania was precluded from investigating election fraud allegations. Outrageous!"

McSwain, who was appointed U.S. attorney by Trump, wrote to the former president on June 9, seeking his support in the Pennsylvania governor's race. McSwain said via Twitter that he was "pleased that he [Trump] shared my letter."

In the letter, McSwain wrote that Trump was "right to be upset about the way the Democrats ran the 2020 election in Pennsylvania – it was a partisan disgrace." But McSwain, who was the top federal prosecutor in the Philadelphia area until he stepped down in January, claimed his hands were tied.

McSwain, June 9: On Election Day and afterward, our Office received various allegations of voter fraud and election irregularities. As part of my responsibilities as U.S. Attorney, I wanted to be transparent with the public and, of course, fully investigate any allegations. Attorney General Barr, however, instructed me not to make any public statements or put out any press releases regarding possible election irregularities. I was also given a directive to pass along serious allegations to the State Attorney General for investigation – the same State Attorney General who had already declared that you could not win.

I disagreed with that decision, but those were my orders. As a Marine infantry officer, I was trained to follow the chain of command and to respect the orders of my superiors, even when I disagreed with them.

On Twitter, McSwain reiterated his reluctance to pass on voter fraud allegations to Shapiro, the state attorney general who is now a Democratic candidate for governor. "On principle, I disagreed with referring ANY election cases to AG Shapiro because he was conflicted, having declared BEFORE the Presidential election that the result was preordained. Only a fake prosecutor says something like that."

McSwain is referring to a tweet Shapiro sent on Oct. 31 responding to a Philadelphia Inquirer story about Trump in campaign speeches sowing doubt about the upcoming election by making "baseless claims of election fraud."

"If all the votes are added up in PA, Trump is going to lose," Shapiro wrote.

Despite McSwain's concerns about Shapiro, a spokesman for McSwain insists the former federal prosecutor sent along allegations of voter fraud to Shapiro's office.

A spokesperson for Shapiro said his office isn't aware of McSwain having passed along any such cases for investigation.

"We received and sent multiple referrals to local, state, and federal law enforcement but received no direct referrals from Mr. McSwain's office," Shapiro spokesperson Jacklin Rhoads told the Philadelphia Inquirer. "This personal note to President Trump sent seven months after the election is the first our office has heard of Mr. McSwain's concerns. If he was aware of allegations of voter fraud, Mr. McSwain had a duty to report and, as he knows, our office investigates every referral and credible allegation it receives."

Barr also pushed back against McSwain's claims in interviews with the Philadelphia Inquirer, Politico, and the Washington Post.

"It's written to make it seem like I gave him a directive," Barr told Politico. "I never told him not to investigate anything."

Barr said he called McSwain on July 12 after hearing about the letter.

"It's very cutely written," Barr said of McSwain's letter. "He said he was going to try to thread the needle. … He said to me he didn't want to say anything that would advance the president's stolen election narrative, but by the same token, he was going to try to thread the needle by saying some things that were literally, technically accurate."

Barr has found himself in Trump's rhetorical crosshairs since announcing in a Dec. 1 interview that the Department of Justice and FBI "have not seen fraud on a scale that could have affected a different outcome in the election."

Barr said he warned McSwain that his letter gave the false impression that allegations of voter fraud were not fully investigated.

Barr noted that he issued a memo on Nov. 9, six days after the election, authorizing federal prosecutors to "pursue substantial allegations of voting and vote tabulation irregularities."

In that memo, Barr added: "While it is imperative that credible allegations be addressed in a timely and effective manner, it is equally imperative that Department personnel exercise appropriate caution and maintain the Department's absolute commitment to fairness, neutrality, and non-partisanship." He cautioned prosecutors to "exercise great care and judgment in addressing allegations of voting and vote tabulation irregularities" and warned that "specious, speculative, fanciful or far-fetched claims should not be a basis for initiating federal inquiries."

Politico reported that it spoke to "one former official, who spoke on condition of anonymity" who said, "McSwain's office did aggressively investigate several election-related fraud claims and was given no 'stand-down' order from Washington."

Barr told the Washington Post that when he spoke to McSwain earlier this week, McSwain told him the "directive" to pass along serious allegations to the state attorney general involved a single allegation of "irregularities" in Delaware County, Pennsylvania.

Politico reported that the Delaware County allegation came from a Navy veteran who claimed: "47 USB drives went missing during the election process in Delaware County, Pa." The man, a poll watcher, claimed the drives could have held up to 120,000 votes.

We at FactCheck.org wrote about this claim back in December and found that it was not credible.

Delaware County officials explained to us that the vCards are used to transfer data from the paper-ballot scanning machines at each precinct to the central vote tabulating system. Adrienne Marofsky, the county's spokeswoman, also told us, "the report of 47 'missing' vCards is false."

It's not uncommon for some vCards to be delivered after Election Day, she said.

"Within a day or so after Election Day, the vCards that had not been returned on election night were accounted for," Marofsky said. "A number of them were simply left in the scanners by the local election board and were recovered when the scanners (which were put in sealed rolling carts called 'cages' at the end of the day on Election Day) were returned to the voting machine warehouse."

Marofsky also noted that there are two fail-safes if a vCard were to be lost — the vote scanners' hard drives hold the original data, and the paper ballots are held in sealed, numbered bags in case they need to be rescanned.

Nonetheless, Barr said it wasn't him but rather Richard Donoghue, who was then the principal associate deputy attorney general, who told McSwain to share that case with Shapiro's office.

Politico noted that Donoghue issued a statement responding to McSwain's letter saying, "While I was made aware of allegations relating to conduct in Delaware County, I did not preclude DOJ personnel in Pennsylvania from investigating allegations of criminal misconduct relating to the 2020 elections or direct that any such allegations be handled exclusively by state authorities."

"Allegations of election fraud were handled by both federal and state authorities throughout the 2020 election cycle," Donoghue told the Washington Post. "Which authority or authorities reviewed a particular allegation turned largely on the nature of the allegation itself."

Barr told the Philadelphia Inquirer that McSwain told him he had to write the letter to Trump "because he was under pressure from Trump and for him to have a viable candidacy, he couldn't have Trump attacking him."

But Barr said the letter "is written in a very deceptive way that is intended to convey an impression, it's a false one, that he was restrained from looking into election fraud."

"Any suggestion that McSwain was told to stand down from investigating allegations of election fraud is false," Barr told the Washington Post. "It's just false." McSwain's claims, Barr added, "appeared to have been made to mollify President Trump to gain his support for McSwain's planned run for governor."

McSwain responded to Barr's comments with a tweet saying that "everything" in his letter to Trump "is 100% true."

"If Bill Barr wants to run to WaPo to complain about me telling the truth, that's OK – it doesn't bother me," McSwain said, adding in a second tweet, "I have more important things to be concerned about than Bill Barr's feelings."

There are obviously competing versions regarding what McSwain was told about investigating serious allegations of voter fraud following the 2020 election.

But let's take a close look at the two critical sentences in McSwain's letter.

In his letter, McSwain says Barr "instructed me not to make any public statements or put out any press releases regarding possible election irregularities." Two anonymous sources "familiar with the matter," told the Philadelphia Inquirer that after the election, McSwain wanted to hold a press conference making a general complaint about how Pennsylvania administered its election without making any specific charges related to voter fraud. Barr acknowledged to the Inquirer that he put a stop to that.

"He wanted to not do the business of the department, which is to investigate cases, but instead go out and flap his gums about what he didn't like about the election overall," Barr said.

McSwain followed that sentence with a passive one that claims, "I was also given a directive to pass along serious allegations to the State Attorney General for investigation." Note that he does not say Barr directly told him to pass along those allegations. If it was Donoghue he was referring to, as we noted above, Donoghue said that "state and federal authorities referred matters to one another" but that "did not preclude DOJ personnel in Pennsylvania from investigating allegations of criminal misconduct relating to the 2020 elections or direct that any such allegations be handled exclusively by state authorities."

And if McSwain's complaint about turning over allegations to the state attorney general related just to the Delaware County case — as Barr says McSwain told him — that allegation turned out not to be credible.

SPECIAL Agent ROTH- Fake media was the election fraud, not voting machines. Barr should never have said that.

FAKE MEDIA always said the same thing in an hour. Obviously, Fake Media was coordinating with each other. Did the FBI investigate this? Of course not.

Carl Bernstein Just Explained Why the Trump Russia Scandal Is 'Worse Than Watergate'

Brandon Gage

Aug. 03, 2018

Veteran investigative journalist Carl Bernstein issued a warning to the American public during a CNN interview on Thursday, emphasizing that the deepening scandal surrounding President Donald Trump's alleged entanglements with Russia is "worse than Watergate."

As Bernstein tweeted on Friday:

In 1972, Bernstein and colleague Bob Woodward wrote an explosive report in the Washington Post documenting a break-in at the Democratic National Committee's offices inside Watergate Hotel in Washington D.C.

That story led to an investigation that found Nixon not only knew about the crime but willingly participated in its coverup. Nixon won reelection in 1972 and then resigned in 1974 under the threat of impeachment. He was pardoned by President Gerald Ford shortly thereafter.

Blitzer asked Bernstein if President Richard Nixon was as "anxious publicly" during the Watergate investigation as Trump appears to be amid the probe into his alleged ties to Russia.

"First, I think we're seeing more than anxiety on the part of Donald Trump," Bernstein told host Wolf Blitzer. "We are seeing a president who is behaving and acting unhinged."

."Nixon did not really publicly act unhinged," he recalled. Bernstein added that "the system worked" during Watergate, noting: "Nixon did not publicly declare the press an enemy of the people." Bernstein then said Trump "whipped up a kind of hysteria unlike any other president in our history."

I think it's time to recognize that what we are watching in the Trump presidency is worse than Watergate.

Bernstein blasted today's Republicans for "doing almost everything they can to impede and undermine a legitimate investigation."

"The heroes of Watergate were Republicans who demanded the president be held accountable," Bernstein said, "who demanded he be transparent, who demanded 'what did the president know and when did he know it,'" and who worked with Democrats to uncover the truth about "what Nixon had done."

The segment concludes with a blistering takedown of Trump, with Bernstein calling him a "demonstrable authoritarian in terms of his rhetoric... Nixon did not do anything similar to that."

Twitter users overwhelmingly sided with Bernstein, echoing his assessment of Trump and his dictatorial behavior.

"No sh*t." Same.

Published *January 4, 2021, 10:22 pm EST*

Carl Bernstein was mocked for claiming every Trump controversy is 'worse than Watergate'

Bernstein made a comparison following a leaked call between Trump and Georgia secretary of state

By **Joseph A. Wulfsohn | Fox News**

Sen. Perdue doubles down on call for Raffensperger's resignation.

Veteran journalist Carl Bernstein, one of the media's go-to experts on Watergate as he and Bob Woodward were the famed Washington Post journalists who broke the story that led to President Nixon's resignation, has formed quite a different reputation in the era of President Trump.

On Sunday, Bernstein offered his reaction to the breaking news of the leaked recording of a heated phone conversation between Trump and Georgia Secretary of State Brad Raffensperger over the state's election results that were certified for President-elect Biden.

TRUMP CALLS CARL BERNSTEIN A 'TOTAL NUT JOB' AFTER WATERGATE LEGEND CALLS PRESIDENT 'HOMICIDAL'

"It's not déjà vu; this was something far worse than occurred in Watergate," Bernstein said on CNN. "We have both a criminal president of the United States in Donald Trump and a subversive president of the United States at the same time with this one person, subverting the very basis of our democracy and willing to act criminally in that subversion."

While such comments from Bernstein could ring quite chilling from the journalist whose reporting torpedoed Nixon's presidency, the comments could also ring quite familiar as the now-CNN political analyst has repeatedly invoked Watergate over and over and over again during the Trump presidency.

CNN'S CARL BERNSTEIN COMPARES TRUMP-UKRAINE STORY TO WATERGATE

Back in September, as Bob Woodward released his audio tapes of Trump speaking candidly about the severity of the coronavirus outbreak in the early months of the pandemic, Bernstein declared them the "smoking gun of his negligence."

"It's a dereliction of duty, recorded as no other presidential dereliction of duty has been, even more so than the Nixon tapes in this instance," Bernstein said. "The last time this happened during the end of Nixon's presidency, the Republican leadership... went to the White House and told Nixon he had to resign. And the facts here are even graver than in Watergate."

During CNN's coverage of the Ukraine scandal, Bernstein claimed that there were "echoes" of Watergate and later indicated that it was "perhaps worse in some regards."

Back in 2018, amid the Russia investigation headed by special counsel Robert Mueller, Bernstein deemed the entire Trump presidency "worse than Watergate."

SEN. RON JOHNSON CALLS OUT NBC'S CHUCK TODD FOR IGNORING HUNTER BIDEN DURING THE ELECTION ON 'MEET THE PRESS

"What we are watching in the Trump presidency is worse than Watergate. It's worse than Watergate, as I say, because the system worked in Watergate," Bernstein explained. "The heroes in Watergate were Republicans who demanded that the president be held accountable, who demanded that he be transparent, who demanded to know what did the president know and when did he know it, and who conducted a bipartisan investigation that led, in fact, to understanding and finding out what Nixon had done, whereas the Republicans on Capitol Hill thus far have done almost everything they can to impede and undermine the legitimate investigation. So it's a totally different and much more dangerous situation."

Bernstein also invoked Watergate while knocking Trump's chumminess with Russian President Vladimir Putin during the 2018 joint press conference in Helsinki, referred to the 2017 firing of FBI Director James Comey as "potentially more dangerous" than Watergate, and he even made Nixon comparisons before Trump took office, claiming in December 2016 that "Richard Nixon was nothing, in terms of lying, compared to what we have seen from Donald Trump."

CNN'S JAKE TAPPER CALLS GOP LAWMAKERS PUSHING ELECTION CHALLENGE 'SEDITION CAUCUS'

However, during the 2016 election, Bernstein did sing a different tune, only to fact-check Trump's claim that Hillary Clinton's email scandal was "bigger than Watergate," saying that "no way" was the comparison accurate.

"Watergate was about a criminal president of the United States who presided over a criminal administration from the day he took office to the day he left**," Bernstein said during a panel discussion in October 2016, though later stressing that Clinton's conduct was still "reckless."**

Following Trump's leaked phone call, critics on social media pointed out Bernstein's repetitious claims.

"Is there anything that's NOT worse than Watergate to this guy?" commentary writer Drew Holden asked, estimating more than a dozen Watergate comparisons in a lengthy Twitter thread.

Lol, you can't make this stuff up," The Federalist contributor Benjamin Weingarten reacted.

"Carl Bernstein literally calls everything worse than Watergate," GOP strategist Chris Barron wrote.

Joseph A. Wulfsohn is a media reporter for Fox News Digital. Story tips can be sent to joseph.wulfsohn@fox.com and on Twitter: @JosephWulfsohn.

Special Agent Roth- Carl, you were a brilliant and tenacious

investigator. We can't believe you fell for Hillary's B_____t.

George Will's startling assessment of Donald Trump

Analysis by Chris Cillizza, CNN Editor-at-large

Updated 8:20 PM EDT, Mon July 15, 2019

In an interview with The New York Times Book Review podcast, longtime conservative commentator George Will offered a stirring and stark assessment of what Donald Trump's presidency will mean for our politics and our culture.

Here's the key bit:

"I believe that what this president has done to our culture, to our civic discourse ... you cannot unring these bells, and you cannot unsay what he has said, and you cannot change that he has now, in a very short time made it seem normal for schoolboy taunts and obvious lies to be spun out in a constant stream. I think this will do more lasting damage than Richard Nixon's surreptitious burglaries did."

Special Agents Roth

That's George Will, folks. Not Rachel Maddow. And it's George Will saying that what Trump is doing, has done, and will do to – and with – the presidency is more destructive than the actions of a president who was forced to resign in order to keep from being impeached.

Sit with *all of that* for a minute.

Will's broader argument is that Nixon's coordinated burglaries at the Democratic National Committee were secret and, once revealed, broadly condemned by the public and the two political parties. What Trump is doing is happening right in front of our faces – and with the tacit assent of the Republican Party that Will left in 2016.

"What Donald Trump's revolutionary effect has been [is] to make things acceptable that were unthinkable until recently," Will said on the Times podcast, asking host Pamela Paul if she could even conceive of past presidents like John Kennedy or Dwight Eisenhower uttering any of the many things Trump has said in the office.

The words of Will that run truest to me were these: "You cannot unring these bells." I think he is 100% right on that. The idea that once Trump leaves the White House – whether involuntarily in January 2021 or voluntarily-ish in January 2025 – the impacts and reverberations of what he has done to the presidency (and to the way in which the presidency is covered) will disappear is a fallacy.

Politics is a copycat game. Always has been. What Trump has taught politicians is that telling the truth isn't all that important – especially if you have your own bullhorn (in Trump's case Twitter + Fox News) to make your own "alternative facts." And that presidential norms and the idea of "being presidential" is a meaningless construct. And a lot more "lessons" that will be destructive to the way in which people run for president and act once they get elected.

His imprint on the office is deep and wide. The Point: What Will knows is that Trump has already changed the presidency – and our culture – in profound ways that will not simply "snap back" once he leaves office.

CLARENCE THOMAS Pennsylvania Case

Thomas himself seemed to acknowledge that allegations of fraud were not part of the Pennsylvania case. Rather the question before the justices turned on whether the state supreme court had erred by allowing the extended deadline for ballots to stand.

Alito and Gorsuch wrote a separate dissent that did not raise fraud.

READ: Clarence Thomas' dissent in Pennsylvania election decision

Updated 12:33 PM ET, Mon February 22, 2021

(CNN) The Supreme Court on Monday denied an appeal from Republicans challenging a Pennsylvania Supreme Court decision that allowed ballots received up to three days after Election Day to be counted to accommodate challenges by the coronavirus pandemic.

Justice Clarence Thomas wrote a forceful dissent.

Part Ten

January 6 Capitol Incident

The Main Issue.

Special Agent Roth-Whatever was said or not said By President Donald Trump or whether or not it was the truth is immaterial compared to the "Big Lie" perpetrated By Hillary Clinton, her campaign staff, and her lawyers.

Her selfish statement had an immense negative impact on the United States of America and its Constitution and Democracy.

Hillary's statement had no basis whatsoever in truth. The statement caused a great divide among American citizens.

This divide has escalated ever since she made the statement and cost the American citizens millions of their hard-earned tax dollars in false investigations.

House Committee Describes Weapons Trump Supporters Had on Jan. 6, Including AR-15s

In a bombshell hearing about the Capitol attack, witness Cassidy Hutchinson said Donald Trump knew about his supporters carrying weapons on Jan 6.

Sarah Ruiz-Grossman

Jun 28, 2022, 03:05 PM EDT

In a surprise hearing of the House Jan. 6 committee, lawmakers played police radio transmissions identifying weapons — including AR-15s — that supporters of former President Donald Trump had with them on Jan. 6, 2021, the day of Trump's rally and the attack on the U.S. Capitol.

In Tuesday's hearing, Rep. Liz Cheney (R-Wyo.) — vice chair of the House select committee investigating the Capitol attack — played police transmissions that described people carrying firearms near the Ellipse in Washington, D.C., where Trump held his rally the morning of Jan. 6.

"Three men are walking down the street in fatigues carrying AR-15s... at 14th and Independence," a voice says in one transmission.

"White male... stock of an AR-15," someone can be heard saying in another recording. "Green fatigues... Glock-style pistols in their waistband."

"Elevated threat in the trees... American flag face mask... weapon on the right-side hip," a third transmission says.

Cheney noted that among the supporters who chose to pass through metal detectors so they could get closer to Trump, security screened weapons and equipment, including pepper spray, knives, batons, and gas masks. Several thousand more people did not go through metal detectors and watched from the nearBy Washington Monument lawn.

The committee also showed a report sent by the Secret Service at 11 a.m. that day warning of a man with a rifle near the Ellipse, where Trump was speaking.

126

In her surprise testimony Tuesday, Cassidy Hutchinson, a top aide to Trump's chief of staff Mark Meadows, said that Tony Ornato — who oversaw Secret Service movements — said he told Trump there were people armed with weapons attending his rally on Jan. 6.

In videotaped testimony, Hutchinson recalled a meeting around 10 a.m. on Jan. 6 with Meadows and Ornato. At that meeting, she said, Ornato described people carrying knives, pistols, rifles, bear spray, body armor, spears, and flagpoles. "Mark said, have you talked to the president?" Hutchinson said in her video testimony. "And Tony said yes."

Later in her video testimony, Hutchinson said that Trump was angry about the crowd size. He wanted more people in the area where he was speaking, and he blamed the metal detectors, she said.

"I don't f-ing care that they have weapons," Trump said, per Hutchinson. "They're not here to hurt me ... Take the f-ing mags away... Let my people in; they can march to the Capitol from here."

Last year, Trump told Fox News that "there were no guns whatsoever" in the crowd on Jan. 6.

Special Agent Roth- This information must be carefully dissected.

There are two places in question. Number one was the rally when Trump was speaking.

Number two is the Capitol Building.

An armed mob of Trump supporters stormed the U.S. Capitol that day as lawmakers gathered to certify the 2020 presidential election, which Joe Biden won. Before the riot, Trump incited the crowd at his nearby rally by falsely claiming the election had been stolen. Five people died in the ensuing mayhem and its aftermath, including a U.S. Capitol Police officer.

Special Agents Roth- There were no demonstrators in the Capitol that

had guns. Nobody was shot at the Capitol except one Trump supporter who was

shot By Capitol police. The Capitol police officer died from natural causes. The other

people who died were not shot By armed demonstrators.

Sarah Ruiz-Grossman

Reporter, HuffPost

Trump Knew His Supporters Had Guns as He Targeted US Capitol, Jan. 6 Panel Told

Steven T. Dennis - Tuesday

(Bloomberg) -- Former President **Donald Trump knew some of his supporters were armed when he told them to head to march on the US Capitol**, a former top aide to then-White House Chief of Staff Mark Meadows testified Tuesday.

Cassidy Hutchinson told the House Jan. 6 committee that Trump, ahead of his rally that day, was unhappy that some of his supporters weren't able to get in and blamed magnetometers set up by the Secret Service.

"Take the f'ing mags away," she quoted Trump as saying, adding he said he didn't care if they were armed. "They aren't here to hurt me," she quoted him saying. "They can march to the Capitol after the rally's over."

Hutchinson said that another staff member had earlier told Meadows that Trump had been briefed on weapons in the crowd on the morning of Jan. 6.

She also said that Trump wanted to personally head to the Capitol, where Congress was certifying the Electoral College votes, and there was even a discussion of him going to the House chamber. She said she was told Trump was irate after his speech when staffers refused to take him to the Capitol.

DISINFORMATION FROM DEMOCRATS

Capitol Police Officer Brian Sicknick, who suffered a stroke in the immediate aftermath of the riot, died of natural causes, according to a medical examiner

(CNN) The police officer who died after a mob of President Trump's supporters invaded the US Capitol on Wednesday was a New Jersey native who had served in the National Guard.

https://www.cnn.com/2021/01/09/us/officer-crushed-capitol-riot-video/index.html

Disturbing video shows an officer crushed against the door by a mob storming the Capitol

Capitol Police Officer Brian D. Sicknick died Thursday night "due to injuries sustained while on duty," Capitol Police said in a statement. He was one of five people who died in the violence.

Sicknick was injured while physically engaging with the rioters and collapsed after returning to his division office, the statement said.

"He was taken to a local hospital where he succumbed to his injuries," the Capitol Police statement said.

Prosecutors in the US Attorney's office plan to open a federal murder investigation into Sicknick's death, a law enforcement official told CNN.

Officer Sicknick joined the USCP in July 2008 and most recently served in the Department's First Responder's Unit.

"The entire USCP Department expresses its deepest sympathies to Officer Sicknick's family and friends on their loss and mourns the loss of a friend and colleague," Capitol Police said.

'Brian is a hero,' his brother says

Americans watched the Capitol riot in 'horror' and 'disgust.' Here's what they told us.

Sicknick was originally from South River, New Jersey, and the youngest of three sons, according to a statement issued by his brother, Ken Sicknick, on behalf of his family.

Sicknick's family was "very proud" of his service to his country, Ken Sicknick said.

"Brian is a hero, and that is what we would like people to remember," he said.

Sicknick "wanted to be a police officer his entire life" and joined the New Jersey National Guard in his pursuit of that goal, Ken Sicknick said.

According to a statement from New Jersey Gov. Phil Murphy's office, Sicknick was a staff sergeant for the New Jersey National Guard.

He served as a fire team member and a leader of the 108th Security Force Squadron, 108th Wing, at Joint Base McGuire-Dix-Lakehurst, Murphy's statement said.

Sicknick's service included two deployments -- one as part of Operation Southern Watch and another as part of Operation Enduring Freedom, Murphy said.

"Officer Sicknick gave his life protecting the United States Capitol, and by extension, our very democracy, from violent insurrection," Murphy said.

Pelosi orders Capitol flags lowered to half-staff

House Speaker Nancy Pelosi said she ordered the flags at the Capitol lowered to half-staff in Sicknick's honor.

"The sacrifice of Officer Sicknick reminds us of our obligation to those we serve: to protect our country from all threats, foreign and domestic. May it is a comfort to Officer Sicknick's family that so many mourn with and pray for them at this sad time," they said in a statement.

Vice President Mike Pence tweeted that he and the second lady were "deeply saddened to learn of the passing of US Capitol Police Officer Brian D. Sicknick and send our deepest sympathies and prayers to his family, friends, and fellow officers."

Pence goes on to write that Sicknick was an "American hero who gave his life defending our Capitol."

CNN's Eric Levenson, Amir Vera, and Mallika Kallingal contributed to this report.

Hiion' after mob storms Capitol

Lawmakers were evacuated during the counting of Electoral College votes after supporters descended on the Capitol at Trump's urging.

District of Columbia National Guard stands outside the Capitol on Wednesday night. John Minchillo / AP

Jan. 6, 2021, 6:07 AM EST / Updated Jan. 7, 2021, 11:45 AM EST

By NBC News

President Donald Trump, early on Thursday, committed to "an orderly transition" of power soon after Congress confirmed President-elect Joe Biden's election win and following the storming of the Capitol by a mob of violent Trump supporters.

In a statement released by the White House, the president again made false claims about the outcome of the election. Twitter suspended Trump's account for 12 hours Wednesday after he continued to push conspiracy theories about the election after the chaos at the Capitol.

Overnight, Congress reconvened and counted the electoral votes for Biden's victory. After some objections, the count of Biden's 306 votes to President Donald Trump's 232 was finished in proceedings that lasted until 3:40 a.m.

D.C. Mayor declines National Guard

In this daily series, Newsweek explores the steps that led to the January 6 Capitol Riot.

On Thursday, **December 31**, says the currently accepted narrative, the District of Columbia mayor rang an alarm about protests at the Joint Session of Congress. In fact, the opposite is true. What the mayor did, was ask for a minimal number of National Guardsmen and women to help out the Metropolitan Police Department, and she warned that those troops should be unarmed and not directly involve themselves in any protests.

Mayor Muriel Bowser sent a letter on New Year's Eve to Maj. Gen. William Walker, commanding general of the District of Columbia National Guard, requested support on January 5 through 6. She said Guard personnel would support the MPD and the District Fire and Emergency Medical Services. "[N]o DCNG personnel shall be armed during this mission, and at no time will DCNG personnel or assets be engaged in domestic surveillance, searches, or seizures of [U.S.] persons," she wrote.

A follow-up letter from Christopher Rodriguez, director of the District's Homeland Security and Emergency Management Agency, said that the DCNG's primary mission would be "crowd management and assistance with blocking vehicles at traffic posts [traffic control points or TCPs]." He specifically requested six National Guard crowd management teams at 30 TCPs and six specific Metro stations to prevent overcrowded platforms.

Mark Esper and Army Gen. Mark Milley, chairman of the Joint Chiefs of Staff. Milley was wearing a combat uniform. Esper and Milley would both later apologize for their presence and their appearance in involving the military in partisan politics. But beyond the two defense leaders, there was also the question of the DC National Guard and the presence of active-duty military troops.

Guard troops were present at Lafayette Square, and a Guard UH-72 helicopter hovered over protestors. Social media went bananas. "The optics of the past 72 hours are putting people inside the halls of the Pentagon on edge as images of U.S. troops on the streets of the nation's capital dominate airwaves across the globe," Politico wrote. The Pentagon would later pile on the public apologies and explanations, but the damage was done.

Commanding General District of Columbia National Guard Major General William J. Walker testifies before the Senate Homeland Security and Governmental Affairs/Rules and Administration hearing to examine the January 6, 2021 attack on the US Capitol on Capitol Hill; March 3, 2021, in Washington, DC.

In emails sent after the January 2 meeting, McCarthy reiterated that he was not inclined to provide support unless the District of Columbia government had exhausted all resources. Gen. Milley stressed the need for a lead Federal agency (normally the Secret Service) to make the requests and decisions—that the Department of Defense should be the last resort.

The assistant secretary of defense for "homeland defense" wrote to the federal law enforcement agencies to see if they had any concerns that the Pentagon should be tracking. According to the IG report, "The [*deleted* FBI Washington Field Office] responded that they had no specific concerns. The DHS [Department of Homeland Security] representative stated that they were not increasing their posture and were not tracking any threats to Federal facilities. The USMS [U.S. Marshal Service] representative stated that they were not responding to protests on January 5 and 6, 2021, and did not require DoD support."

Trump authorizes National Guard to Capitol protests

519d ago / 3:40 PM EST

Virginia National Guard state troopers are heading to the Capitol

Jane C. Timm

519d ago / 3:37 PM EST

Virginia Gov. Ralph Northam announced this afternoon that the state National Guard and 200 state troopers are heading to the Capitol to help police the protests and rioting happening there.

The sun will set shortly in Washington, and the city has ordered a 6 p.m. curfew.

1 person was shot inside Capitol, law enforcement officials confirm

Pete Williams, Tom Winter, and Doha Madani

519d ago / 3:37 PM EST

One person was shot, and several others were injured amid the frenzy at the Capitol, law enforcement officials confirmed to NBC News Wednesday.

Police did not know details regarding the circumstances of the shooting, who fired the shot, or the nature of the person's injuries. That person is in critical condition, according to D.C. Fire and EMS.

A woman was seen on video being treated for an unknown injury as paramedics moved her on a stretcher out of the Capitol Wednesday. The building remains on lockdown.

Five people have been transported to the hospital, including one officer, according to the city's emergency medical services.

JAN. 6, 202101:19

McCarthy says he heard police say 'shots fired' inside Capitol

Adam Edelman

131

House Minority Leader Kevin McCarthy, R-Calif., said on Fox News on Wednesday that they overheard police saying there were shots fired inside Capitol.

"People are being hurt. People are being; people are being hurt, there have been shots, this is unacceptable," McCarthy said.

Asked whether he could confirm "that shots have been fired inside the capitol or outside," McCarthy said he was with Capitol Police officers and that he "heard on the radio, 'shots fired.'"

McCarthy came moments after a bleeding woman was rushed from the Capitol on a stretcher with medical personnel tending to her. It's unclear how the woman was injured.

3:32 PM EST

A supporter of President Donald Trump sits at a desk after invading the Capitol Building on Jan. 6, 2021.

Georgia election official: 'This is an insurrection.'

Jane C. Timm

519d ago / 3:26 PM EST

Gabriel Sterling, an election official in Georgia who has spent weeks condemning the false attacks on the validity of the U.S. election as dangerous and inflammatory, called the chaotic mob of pro-Trump protesters who breached the U.S. Capitol an "insurrection."

He laid the blame squarely on the president's shoulders: "I said several weeks ago that the words and actions of the President were going to get someone shot, hurt, or killed. Shots were just fired in the U.S. Capitol. Let that sink in for a moment."

One person was shot this afternoon inside the U.S. Capitol building by a member of law enforcement, several law enforcement officials said. No other details are known, including what law enforcement officer fired the shot, the circumstances of the shooting, or the nature of the person's injuries.

SPECIAL AGENT ROTH- Was Mr. Sterling at the Capitol?

Pelosi, Washington Mayor, calls for National Guard help

519d ago / 3:09 PM EST

The Senate floor

Frank Thorp V

519d ago / 3:08 PM EST

Photos: Protesters breach the Capitol

519d ago / 3:08 PM EST

Capitol Police try to hold back protesters outside the east doors to the House side of the Capitol on Jan 6, 2021. Andrew Harnik / APSupporters of President Donald Trump entered the Capitol on Jan. 6, 2021. Saul Loeb / AFP - Getty ImagesA protesters held a Trump flag inside the Capitol Building near the Senate Chamber on Jan. 6, 2021.Win McNamee / Getty ImagesProtesters gesture to Capitol Police in the hallway outside of the Senate chamber at the Capitol on Jan. 6, 2021, near the Ohio Clock. Manuel Balce Ceneta / APMembers of Congress run for cover as protesters try to enter the House Chamber during a joint session on Jan. 6, 2021. Drew Angerer / Getty ImagesLaw enforcement officers point their guns at a door that was vandalized in the House

Doha Madani

519d ago / 3:05 PM EST

Police with guns drawn to watch as protesters try to break into the House Chamber on Jan. 6, 2021.J. Scott Applewhite / AP

Pro-Trump supporters have entered the Senate chamber as others are in a standoff at the door of the House chamber.

A protester who was able to get into the Senate chamber stood on the dais and yelled, "Trump won that election," according to a press pool reporter inside the room. Officers are also in an armed standoff with protesters at the House chamber door, which was barricaded.

The gallery door in the House was broken, and members have been evacuated. Members that are up top in the gallery area above the floor with the press were sheltering as the door was barricaded.

D.C. Mayor Bowser imposes a 6 p.m. curfew

Doha Madani

519d ago / 2:57 PM EST

District of Columbia Mayor Muriel Bowser ordered a curfew on the city as protesters stormed the Capitol building during the Electoral College certification Wednesday.

The 12-hour curfew will begin at 6 p.m. and continue into Thursday morning after hundreds of President Donald Trump's supporters stormed the building as members of both congressional chambers debated the certification of Arizona's electoral votes.

"During the hours of the curfew, no person, other than persons designated by the mayor, shall walk, bike, run, loiter, stand, or motor by car or another mode of transport upon any street, alley, park, or another public place within the district," Bowser's press release said.

Mayor Bowser announces curfew and condemns 'shameful, unpatriotic' protests at the Capitol

Members of the Proud Boys march to the Capitol on Wednesday. A self-described "Western chauvinist" organization, the Proud Boys, is considered a violent, nationalistic, Islamophobic, transphobic, and misogynistic hate group, according to the Anti-Defamation League, a nonprofit organization that tracks extremist groups. Leah Millis / Reuters

SPECIAL AGENT ROTH- WHO IS THE ANTI-DEFAMATION LEAGUE?

WHAT AUTHORITY DOES THIS ORGANIZATION HAVE TO LABEL FELLOW AMERICANS?

A U.S. Capitol Police officer who shot and killed Ashli Babbitt, an unarmed protester climbing through a broken window in a hallway of the U.S. Capitol on January 6, has remained anonymous.

Though his name was known to U.S. Capitol Police, congressional staffers, and federal investigations, no one would divulge it. The secrecy fueled months of online speculation.

Babbitt's family alleged a coverup.

"The U.S. Congress wants to protect this man. He's got friends in high places, and they want to protect him," said Maryland attorney Terry Roberts, who represents the family. "And they've done a pretty good job of it. ... I don't think it's a proud moment for the U.S. Capitol Police or the U.S. Congress."

Roberts told Zenger Wednesday night that the shooter was "Lieutenant Michael Leroy Byrd."

Byrd's attorney, Mark Schamel, did not dispute the positive identification. It adds to information from other sources who told Zenger in recent months that Byrd was the January 6 shooter. None of them would say so on the record.

Byrd is a controversial figure with a record of mishandling firearms, including once leaving a loaded pistol in a Congressional Visitor Center bathroom. Roberts said Byrd's decision to fire his weapon on January 6 indicated his unfitness for duty.

"If I was a congressman, I'd be very concerned about him carrying a gun around me," he said.

How Many Died as a Result of Capitol Riot?

By Robert Farley

Posted on November 1, 2021, | Updated on March 21, 2022

In a tweet on Oct. 24, Rep. Alexandria Ocasio-Cortez referred to the Capitol riot on Jan. 6 as "a terror attack," which she said resulted in "almost 10 dead." She called for "any member of Congress who helped plot" it to be "expelled."

Journalist Glenn Greenwald commented on Twitter that the claim of "'almost 10 dead' from the 1/6 riot is deceitful in the extreme. Four people died on 1/6: all Trump supporters."

There is reasoned debate about the number who died as a result of the Capitol riot. Ocasio-Cortez includes law enforcement officials who responded to the Capitol that day and committed suicide in the days and months afterward. None of them have been officially designated as "line of duty" deaths, though there is some congressional support for it.

Ocasio-Cortez's tally also includes two rally participants who died of heart failure — including one who died before other protesters had breached the Capitol. It includes a rallygoer who was initially believed to have been trampled to death in the mayhem that day but was later determined to have died of an accidental overdose.

We take no position in the debate over whom to include in the deaths from the riots. But here, we lay out what is publicly known about the circumstances surrounding the deaths of the nine people included in Ocasio-Cortez's tally.

Two heart attacks: According to an April release from the Washington, D.C., medical examiner's office, "Stop the Steal" protesters Kevin Greeson, 55, and Benjamin Phillips, 50, both died of cardiovascular disease, and the manner of death was deemed "natural."

According to a ProPublica profile, Greeson, of Athens, Alabama, was participating in the protest outside the Capitol when he suffered a heart attack and died minutes before the first rioters breached the Capitol. The article notes that a Metropolitan Police Department incident report at the time states that Greeson "was in the area of the United States Capitol in attendance of first amendment activities" when he had a heart attack.

Once a supporter of President Barack Obama, Greeson had over the years become an ardent supporter of President Donald Trump and was convinced that the election had been stolen. While Greeson had posted social media messages in the weeks before the rally, such as "Let's take this f—ing Country BACK!! Load your guns and take to the streets!" his family insisted to the *New York Times* the day after his death that "he was not there to participate in violence or rioting, nor did he condone such actions."

In a written statement provided to the media after his death, Greeson's wife, Kristi, stated that her husband "had a history of high blood pressure, and in the midst of the excitement, suffered a heart attack."

The day after the riot, a D.C. Police Department statement said that Philips, a computer programmer from Ringtown, Pennsylvania, had died due to a "medical emergency." Like Greeson, the D.C. medical examiner later determined that Philips died naturally of "hypertensive atherosclerotic cardiovascular disease" — heart failure due to high blood pressure.

A *Philadelphia Inquirer* story said Philips had organized a caravan of Trump supporters to attend the rally in Washington, but the story states, "There's no indication Philips himself participated in the raid on the Capitol."

An accidental overdose: D.C. police also said on the day after the riot that Rosanne Boyland, 34, of Kennisaw, Georgia, suffered a "medical emergency." The *New York Times* reported on Jan. 15 that Boyland died "in a crush of fellow rioters during their attempt to fight through a police line, according to videos reviewed by The Times." That narrative was furthered by prosecutors pressing criminal cases against some of the rioters who said that as rioters clashed with police, Boyland "was dying after being trampled by the mob."

But a month later, the D.C. medical examiner's office released its conclusion that Boyland had died accidentally of "acute amphetamine intoxication." According to the *Washington Post*, "The drug cited in Boyland's death is addictive and can be prescribed to treat attention-deficit disorder and narcolepsy."

Boyland's sister told the Associated Press that a police detective told the family that Boyland — an avid Trump supporter who subscribed to Q Anon conspiracy theories — had collapsed while standing off to the side in the Capitol rotunda.

A shooting death: Ashli Babbitt, 35, of San Diego and an Air Force veteran, died on the day of the riot after being shot in the shoulder by a Capitol Police officer as she attempted to force her way into the House chamber where members of Congress were sheltering in place, according to a Jan. 7 statement from then-U.S. Capitol Police Chief Steven Sund.

In April, the Department of Justice announced that it would not pursue any charges against the Capitol Police officer who shot Babbitt.

According to the Justice Department release, "As members of the mob continued to strike the glass doors" outside an entrance that leads to the chamber of the U.S. House of Representatives, "Ms. Babbitt attempted to climb through one of the doors where the glass was broken out. An officer inside the Speaker's Lobby fired one round from his service pistol, striking Ms. Babbitt in the left shoulder, causing her to fall back from the doorway and onto the floor."

The press release said the Justice Department's investigation "revealed no evidence to establish that, at the time the officer fired a single shot at Ms. Babbitt, the officer did not reasonably believe that it was necessary to do so in self-defense or in defense of the Members of Congress and others evacuating the House Chamber."

In August, U.S. Capitol Police said an internal investigation also cleared the officer who shot Babbitt of any wrongdoing.

Law Enforcement

Ocasio-Cortez's statement that the Capitol attack resulted in "almost 10 dead" includes five police officers, none of whom died at the scene on Jan. 6.

A stroke victim: A Capitol Police release the day after the riots said that USCP Officer Brian Sicknick "passed away due to injuries sustained while on duty." The report stated that Sicknick "was injured while physically engaging with protesters. He returned to his division office and collapsed."

The *New York Times*, citing unnamed law enforcement officials, initially reported that Sicknick was struck by a fire extinguisher but later updated its story to say that medical experts said he did not die of blunt force trauma.

As they storm the U.S. Capitol, Trump supporters clash with police and security forces in Washington, D.C., on Jan. 6, 2021. Credit: Roberto Schmidt/AFP via Getty Images.

The *Washington Post* reported on April 19 that District of Columbia Chief Medical Examiner Francisco J. Diaz found that Sicknick suffered two strokes nearly eight hours after being sprayed with a chemical irritant during the riot.

Diaz told the *Post* that Sicknick died of natural causes, but "all that transpired played a role in his condition."

That day, US. Capitol Police released a statement that read: "The USCP accepts the findings from the District of Columbia's Office of the Chief Medical Examiner that Officer Brian Sicknick died of natural causes. This does not change the fact Officer Sicknick died in the line of duty, courageously defending Congress and the Capitol."

Four suicides: Four other police officers committed suicide in the days and months after the riot.

The first was U.S. Capitol Police Officer Howard Liebengood, 51, who had been guarding the Capitol for 15 years and was on duty at the Capitol on Jan. 6. He took his own life three days after the riots.

The following day, Trump ordered flags at the White House to be lowered to half-staff in honor of both Sicknick and Liebengood.

Several days later, D.C. Police Officer Jeffrey Smith, 35, who was injured in the riots on Jan. 6, also committed suicide.

Smith's wife, Erin, told the *Washington Post* her husband related to her the fear and panic he experienced the day of the assault on the Capitol and that he was afraid he might die.

In defending the Capitol, Smith was struck on the helmet by a metal pole thrown by rioters. Later that night, his wife said he went to the police medical clinic, where he was prescribed pain medication and put on sick leave.

Smith's wife said he "wasn't the same" in the days after the riot and seemed to be in constant pain. After visiting a police clinic on Jan. 14 and being ordered back to work, Smith shot himself on the way to work, the *Post* reported.

The families of Liebengood and Smith both sought to have them recognized as "line of duty" deaths, which would afford their families enhanced benefits.

In a letter sent to Rep. Jennifer Wexton of Virginia, Liebengood's widow wrote, "After assisting riot control at the Capitol on January 6th, USCP scheduled Howie to work lengthy shifts in the immediate days following. He was home for very few hours over the course of four days. Although he was severely sleep-deprived, he remained on duty- as he was directed- practically around the clock from January 6th through the 9th. On the evening of the 9th, he took his life at our home."

In the letter, reported by CNN, Serena Liebengood concluded, "The Liebengood family wants Howie's death to not have been in vain. Recognition of the cause of his death, much like the critical examination of the riot itself, will remain central to how we make right those tragedies and help avoid their repetition."

The Lieben good family later provided a statement to CNN, "Howie dedicated 15 years of his life to protecting these elected officials, as well as millions of visitors at the U.S. Capitol each year. Officials on both sides of the aisle witnessed firsthand the catastrophic events of January 6. We are certain they recognize that this tragedy led to Howie's death."

As part of a lawsuit brought by Smith's widow to have her husband's suicide ruled "in the line of duty," Jonathan L. Arden, the former chief medical examiner of the District of Columbia, provided a declaration that stated "there is hard and reliable evidence that Jeffrey Smith changed after the physical and emotional trauma he experiences on January 6, 2021, as he became withdrawn and upset. These facts, together with the timing of the suicide (nine days after the trauma), strongly support causality."

"The acute, precipitating event that caused the death of Officer Smith was his occupational exposure to the traumatic events he suffered on January 6, 2021," Arden wrote.

However, "line of duty" benefits are not typically granted to those who commit suicide, and the cases for both Liebengood and Smith are still pending. Smith's case, because he was a D.C. police officer, is before the D.C. Police and Firefighters' Retirement and Relief Board. According to D.C. law, survivor benefits are only provided when a death is the "sole and direct result of a personal injury sustained" while performing duty as an officer and was not caused by "his intention to bring about his own death."

But Sens. Tim Kaine and Mark Warner and Reps. Don Beyer and Jennifer Wexton wrote in a letter to D.C. Mayor Muriel Bowser that an exception for Smith ought to be made "both as a legal and a practical matter."

"As a legal matter, Officer Smith's symptoms were clearly the 'sole and direct result of a personal injury since he had never experienced these symptoms prior to being attacked on January 6," the letter states. "He cannot have had intent to bring about his own death if he was not in control of his actions due to severe brain trauma, any more than someone who suffers a medical emergency while driving and inadvertently crashes can be said to have had intent to bring about their own death."

Kaine told NBC News that if the board did not make an exception for Smith, he would consider legislation that would include suicide as a line-of-duty death.

Since he was a member of the Capitol Police, Liebengood's case is pending before the federal Office of Workers' Compensation Programs. The families of Liebengood and Smith may also be eligible for additional federal benefits if their deaths are determined to have been "in the line of duty."

Other elected officials have also lobbied for Smith and Liebengood to get the "line of duty" designation, and legislation was introduced in May to extend federal benefits to "public safety officers who are diagnosed with post-traumatic stress disorder or acute stress disorder following a stressful situation while on duty." The legislation has not progressed out of committee.

In May, House Speaker Nancy Pelosi introduced legislation to award congressional gold medals to the U.S. Capitol Police and the D.C. Metropolitan Police Department for their efforts in protecting the Capitol on Jan. 6. The text of the legislation specifically notes the "sacrifice of heroes, including Capitol Police Officers Brian Sicknick and Howard Liebengood, Metropolitan Police Department Officer Jeffrey Smith."

The legislation passed the House 406-21 (most of the "no" votes were from Republicans who objected to the use of the term "insurrection" to describe the events on Jan. 6), and it passed by unanimous consent in the Senate. It was signed into law by President Joe Biden on Aug. 5.

In July, six months after the riot at the Capitol, two Metropolitan Police Department officers who responded to the Capitol on Jan. 6 committed suicide.

According to *People* magazine, Kyle DeFreytag, 26, was not involved in the clashes with rioters during the breach of the Capitol but was deployed to the Capitol to help enforce the curfew put in place after the mob had been cleared from the building.

The same day the Metropolitan Police Department announced DeFreytag's death, it confirmed that another officer, Gunther Hashida, had also committed suicide.

Metropolitan Police Department spokesperson Kristen Metzger told CNN that Hashida was assigned to the emergency response team within the special operations division and had helped secure the Capitol on Jan. 6.

On Aug. 2, the *Washington Post* reported: "Authorities drew no connection between the riot and his death. An official familiar with the investigation said Hashida had struggles beyond Jan. 6 that could have played a role."

Robert J. Contee III, the chief of the Metropolitan Police Department, said "that he could not say whether the riot was the cause of the suicides," the *New York Times* reported.

At the start of a press briefing on Aug. 3, White House Press Secretary Jen Psaki honored the two officers.

"I wanted to take a moment to recognize the passing of Metropolitan Police Officer Gunther Hashida and Officer Kyle DeFreytag — two officers who bravely defended the Capitol, both during and after the insurrection on January 6th," Psaki said. "Their deaths are a sad reminder of that shameful day in our country's history and of the physical and mental scars left on the officers who risked their lives to protect our Capitol and our democracy."

Update, March 21, 2022: On March 7, the District of Columbia's Police and Firefighters' Retirement and Relief Board declared that Metropolitan Police Officer Jeffrey Smith's suicide in the days after the Jan. 6 riot was a line-of-duty death. The board concluded "that Officer Smith sustained a personal injury on January 6, 2021, while performing his duties and that his injury was the sole and direct cause of his death." As a result, Smith's widow, Erin Smith, will receive an annuity equal to 100% of her husband's salary.

The January 6 insurrection wasn't explicitly billed as a Second Amendment event. But the specter of guns was everywhere: on the flags flown by rioters, in the insurrectionist theory they espoused, and the tactical gear they donned. And in some cases, despite Washington, D.C.'s unusually strict gun laws, which require firearms to be registered with local police, the Trump supporters who gathered at the U.S. Capitol were armed.

As of now, at least 13 people have been hit with illegal gun possession charges stemming from the riot, according to an analysis of arrest records and court documents. Two of them were detained after police noticed a bulge under their clothing. Three people were arrested the night before the riot. Another person, Proud Boys' leader Enrique Tarrio, was found in possession of two large-capacity magazines when police arrested him for another crime on January 4. Because Tarrio planned on going to the rally, we included him in our tally.

But these are only the people who were caught with guns that day. We'll never know how many people brought weapons with them to President Trump's speech and onward to the Capitol. Perhaps cognizant of the penalty for carrying a gun without a license in the District — up to five years in prison — only a few felt comfortable enough to display them. One rioter flashed his handgun at a group of journalists, a moment captured by a Vice reporter.

More gun charges may be coming. We'll be tracking them here.

Jennifer Mascia
Jennifer Mascia is a news writer and a founding staffer at The Trace. She previously covered gun violence at *The New York Times*.

Fact check: Claim about FBI official who said bureau recovered no guns at Capitol riot is missing context

Rick Rouan

The claim: Jill Sanborn, assistant director of the FBI's counterterrorism division, told a Senate committee that the FBI did not recover any guns at the Jan. 6 Capitol riot

Rioters who stormed the U.S. Capitol on Jan. 6 to try to prevent Congress from counting electoral votes that would declare President Joe Biden the winner of the 2020 election carried baseball bats, brought zip cuffs, and used flagpoles to break into the building.

Law enforcement officials have said some also had guns.

After a March 3 meeting of a joint oversight Senate committee investigating the riot, some outlets seized on testimony from the FBI counterterrorism division's assistant director that the bureau had not recovered any guns during the incident.

Sen. Ron Johnson, R-Wis., asked Jill Sanborn, assistant director of the FBI's counterterrorism division, how many guns the FBI had confiscated in the Capitol or on its grounds on Jan. 6.

"To my knowledge, none," Sanborn is quoted as saying in several outlets, including The Epoch Times. At least one other outlet quoted The Epoch Times coverage.

But that leaves out the first part of Sanborn's response when she declined to speak for the D.C. Metropolitan Police Department or U.S. Capitol Police.

The U.S. Department of Justice has charged at least three people on gun charges stemming from the Jan. 6 riot, including one whom prosecutors said Metro police found carrying a loaded handgun with an extra magazine.

The Epoch Times did not immediately respond to a request for comment.

What did Sanborn say?

Johnson already has questioned whether it's fair to call the U.S. Capitol riot an "armed insurrection," as House Speaker Nancy Pelosi, D-Calif., and others have.

The Milwaukee Journal Sentinel reported last month that Johnson told a radio station, "This didn't seem like an armed insurrection to me."

"I mean 'armed,' when you hear 'armed,' don't you think of firearms?" Johnson said. "Here are the questions I would have liked to ask. How many firearms were confiscated? How many shots were fired? I'm only aware of one, and I'll defend that law enforcement officer for taking that shot. It was a tragedy, OK? But I think there was only one."

Johnson asked Sanborn those questions at the March 3 joint oversight committee hearing investigating the riot.

Asked how many firearms were confiscated in the Capitol or on its grounds on Jan. 6, Sanborn said, "To my knowledge, we have not recovered any on that day from any of the arrests at the scene at this point. But I don't want to speak on behalf of Metro and Capitol police but to my knowledge, none."

Sanborn later noted that investigators found a firearm in search of a vehicle that also had Molotov cocktails. The only shots fired that day, she said, were from an officer who shot and killed a woman inside the Capitol.

Gun charges related to Capitol riot

So far, at least three people have been charged in federal court in the District of Columbia with gun crimes related to the Capitol riot, according to the U.S. Department of Justice.

Christopher Alberts of Maryland was charged with unlawful possession of a firearm on Capitol grounds or buildings, carrying a pistol without a license, and possession of a large capacity ammunition feeding device. A Metro police officer said Alberts, who was wearing a bulletproof vest, had a "bulge" on his right hip that turned out to be a loaded handgun with a spare 12-round magazine.

Federal prosecutors also have charged Lonnie Coffman, of Alabama, with possession of an unregistered firearm and carrying a pistol without a license. A Capitol police officer swore in an affidavit that Coffman had a black handgun on the seat of his pickup truck and an assault rifle and magazines in the bed near where explosive devices had been reported at the National Republican Club and the Democratic National Committee headquarters.

A bomb squad also recovered 11 Molotov cocktails from Coffman's truck, according to the affidavit, and Coffman also was carrying two handguns.

On Jan. 7, the day after the riot, the FBI investigated a text message that Cleveland Meredith of Georgia allegedly sent claiming that he was considering going to Pelosi's speech "and putting a bullet in her noggin on Live TV." Meredith told the FBI that he arrived from Colorado in Washington too late for the Capitol riot.

FBI agents discovered a pistol, assault rifle "and approximately hundreds of rounds of ammunition" during a search of Meredith's trailer, according to an arrest complaint. He was charged with possession of unregistered firearms and unregistered ammunition, possession of large capacity ammunition feeding devices, and making threats against Pelosi.

The claim that the FBI's assistant director over the counterterrorism division told a Senate committee that the bureau did not recover any guns at the Jan. 6 Capitol riot is MISSING CONTEXT. While Jill Sanborn did say, the FBI had recovered no firearms at the riot, outlets quoting her have removed the first part of her quote when she notes that she cannot speak for other law enforcement agencies that were present at the riot. The U.S. Department of Justice has levied gun charges against two men law enforcement officials say were at the Capitol riot and a third who arrived too late.

The Cambridge Dictionary defines "insurrection" as: "an organized attempt by a group of people to defeat their government and take control of their country, usually by violence."

By that definition, there was no "insurrection" at the United States Capitol on Jan. 6, according to the FBI. *Reuters* reports:

141

The FBI has found scant evidence that the Jan. 6 attack on the U.S. Capitol was the result of an organized plot to overturn the presidential election result, according to four current and former law enforcement officials.

…

"Ninety to ninety-five percent of these are one-off cases," said a former senior law enforcement official with knowledge of the investigation. "Then you have five percent, maybe, of these militia groups that were more closely organized. But there was no grand scheme with Roger Stone and Alex Jones and all of these people to storm the Capitol and take hostages."

This report is a devastating blow to President Joe Biden and Democrats, who have attempted to make the existence of an "insurrection" on Jan. 6 a key issue in the 2022 midterm elections. *Reuters* does note that some "cells of protesters," including members of the Oath Keepers and Proud Boys, did coordinate to "break into the Capitol," but the FBI found "no evidence that the groups had serious plans about what to do if they made it inside."

None of this excuses the violent riot that happened on Jan. 6. The FBI has arrested 570 rioters, and each and every one of them should be prosecuted to the full extent of the law.

But that is what the event was: a riot, just like so many other riots. Trying to politicize it and turn it into something it wasn't won't make the Capitol any safer.

Is the Jan. 6 committee ready for primetime?

TOM LOBIANCO

June 8, 2022, 11:40 AM

After five years of investigations, House lawmakers seem to have learned the hard lesson that when it comes to making a case against former President Donald Trump, a scandal simply isn't enough to keep the public's attention — even when it comes to the Jan. 6, 2021, attack on the U.S. Capitol.

On Thursday, the House's select committee investigating the insurrection will take its first crack at telling the sweeping story of Trump's attempt to overthrow the 2020 election results and the resulting riot. The first of a series of public hearings, scheduled for 8 p.m. ET, is expected to have all the hallmarks of a traditional network primetime event.

House investigators are reportedly planning to use a mix of live witnesses, pre-taped interviews, and never-before-seen video footage from the Capitol on Jan. 6 to weave a compelling narrative of the day and the events that led up to it. They've even hired a veteran TV news producer to advise on the first hearing, according to an Axios report published Monday morning.

"We humans process information through stories. We need a hero, a villain, a victim, some conflict, then resolution. It seems to me the crimes of Jan. 6 have all of those elements," longtime Democratic strategist Paul Begala told Yahoo News. "This is no academic exercise; it could be life or death for our democracy. I'll be watching."

Many of the details of the Jan. 6 attack and the efforts by Trump and his advisers to throw out the voting results after he lost the White House have dotted the national discussion since the November 2020 election.

Protesters clashed with Capitol Police on Jan. 6, 2021. (Kent Nishimura/Los Angeles Times via Getty Images)

But House investigators promise there will be more to reveal starting Thursday night.

"The select committee has found evidence about a lot more than incitement here, and we're gonna be laying out the evidence about all of the actors who were pivotal to what took place on Jan. 6," Rep. Jamie Raskin, D-Md., and a top member on the committee, told the Washington Post Monday.

The lessons of stagecraft

Lawmakers have plenty of experience with wild Trump scandals, smoking guns indicating corruption, and a circus-like media frenzy with each stunning scoop. And they all seemed to end in public confusion, and limited action as Trump and his team of Republicans muddied the debates with conspiracy theories and misinformation.

Trump and his former aides had plenty to work with, with a litany of mistakes by the press covering the Steele dossier, the Hunter Biden laptop, and other items that seemed to vindicate the former president's grievances.

This time around, investigators may have the goods

The select committee has conducted more than 1,000 witness interviews and obtained over 140,000 documents that, the panel's members argue, paint a picture of a plot by Trump and his allies to subvert the outcome of a presidential election, which culminated in the deadly assault on the Capitol.

While some of the key players in that effort have chosen to stonewall the committee, many more have agreed to play ball, both voluntarily and in response to subpoenas. The public hearings are expected to feature both live and taped testimony from Trump administration insiders who can shed light on the White House's role in the campaign to overturn the 2020 election results, as well as its response to the violence on Jan. 6.

Among the former Trump officials who've reportedly been invited to appear at the public hearings are members of former Vice President Mike Pence's inner circle, including Greg Jacobs, who served as chief counsel, and J. Michael Luttig, a former federal judge who advised Pence in the lead-up to Jan. 6, when Pence faced intense pressure from Trump to block Congress's certification of the Electoral College vote. Pence's former chief of staff, Marc Short, is also expected to appear.

Other potential witnesses include Cassidy Hutchinson, a former White House aide who worked under then-chief of staff Mark Meadows and whose closed-door depositions have already been cited as the source of multiple key details about the goings-on inside the White House during this time, as well as former Justice Department officials who resisted efforts by Trump and his allies to use the DOJ to sow doubt about the 2020 election results after the FBI said it did not find evidence of widespread voter fraud.

There has also been speculation that the panel could show clips of taped interviews with Trump's daughter Ivanka and son-in-law Jared Kushner, both of whom also served as senior advisers to the former president.

Overall, one of the committee's reported goals for the public hearings is to connect the dots between Trump's bid to prevent Congress from certifying Joe Biden's electoral victory on Jan. 6 and the violence at the Capitol that ultimately delayed the certification from taking place.

On Tuesday, the committee announced that one of the first witnesses who will testify live during Thursday's hearing is Nick Quested, a British documentarian who, prior to and during the riot on Jan. 6, was filming members of the far-right Proud Boys, one of the extremist groups that have been accused of coordinating the violent attack on the Capitol. Also scheduled to appear Thursday is Capitol Police Officer Caroline Edwards, who was the first law enforcement official injured by rioters while defending the Capitol.

Pro-Trump Republicans also face a new challenge

House Minority Leader Kevin McCarthy, flanked by fellow Republican congressmen, speaks during a news conference on Speaker Nancy Pelosi's decision to reject two of McCarthy's selected members from serving on the committee investigating the insurrection in July 2021. (Kent Nishimura/Los Angeles Times via Getty Images)

Trump and his supporters will face a new series of hurdles as they attempt to sway public opinion their way in the face of the mountain of evidence promised by the committee.

Throughout the Trump-Russia investigation and both impeachments of the ex-president, his Republican allies were able to coordinate closely with Trump and his teams and make their case on their respective committees.

After a spat between House Speaker Nancy Pelosi and House Minority Leader Kevin McCarthy over who should be allowed to serve on the Jan. 6 committee — Pelosi blocked the appointments of Reps. Jim Jordan, R-Ohio, and Jim Banks, R-Ind., because they supported efforts to overthrow the election results — Trump's allies were largely boxed out of this investigation.

And the core of Trump's election lie — baseless allegations of vote-rigging and fraud — has been kept off even far-right outlets in large part by legal action from voting machine manufacturer Dominion and kept off the airwaves of hard-right outlets including Fox News, NewsMax, and OAN.

And, of course, Trump himself no longer controls the White House and the ability to shift public attention, speaking (or tweeting) as the most powerful politician on earth.

But Trump's allies, led by McCarthy and top Republicans in his leadership team, including Banks, Jordan, and House Republican Conference Chairwoman Elise Stefanik of New York, will be pushing back against the investigation in interviews and appearances. House Republicans are also planning to host a press conference Wednesday to make their case, according to one person familiar with the planning.

The Republican National Committee is also coordinating a messaging strategy to paint the House investigation as a "partisan" attack on Trump, according to a memo obtained by Vox.

The country seems to have moved on for now

The battles between Trump's supporters and lawmakers investigating him, which dominated much of Trump's four years in office, might not matter much for either side in the end, despite the historic nature of the hearings.

Then-President Donald Trump addresses the crowd at the Jan. 6 rally prior to the attack on the Capitol. (Eric Lee/Bloomberg via Getty Images)

Democratic and progressive activists trying to drum up interest are hosting watch parties across the country, including an open-air screening near the Capitol. Fox News won't be carrying the hearing live, though it still plans to cover the event throughout the evening, according to The Hill.

A new NBC poll found that less than half the country believes Trump was responsible for the Jan. 6 attack. And surveys of Republican voters have routinely found they broadly believe Trump's election lies.

But surveys of GOP voters in primary contests across the country have also found that Jan. 6 and Trump's stolen election lie are not motivating issues. Instead, concerns about inflation, the prices of gas and milk, COVID-19, the upcoming abortion decision from the Supreme Court, schooling, and the recent spate of mass shootings are driving voters' decisions.

Jan. 6 committee's long-awaited hearings promise revelations. Will a divided US want to hear them?

BART JANSEN, USA TODAY
June 5, 2022, 12:24 PM

WASHINGTON – The House committee investigating last year's attack on the Capitol hopes to explain what happened minute-by-minute on Jan. 6, 2021, in public hearings starting Thursday, but the challenge is whether the tick-tock sets off alarms or the viewing public simply hits the snooze button.

Plenty of dramatic revelations have hinted at what the committee has found. Court records described the debunked legal strategy behind former President Donald Trump's effort to reject votes in closely contested states. Texts illustrated panic about the violence among Trump's relatives and aides as Republican lawmakers discussed martial law. Closed-door testimony described Trump's inaction for hours after the Capitol was breached.

A year and a half after the attack, the question is whether the public will stay tuned. Several members of the committee acknowledged it is crucial to make the hearings interesting for a national audience.

Former Trump aide indicted: Peter Navarro, former Trump aide, charged with contempt of Congress for defying Jan. 6 subpoena

"Our job is, to tell the truth; it's not to create the next Marvel movie," said one committee member, Rep. Pete Aguilar, D-Calif. "Our job is to organize this in a way that people understand, that we hold their attention if they're watching, and it's our hope that people will understand that we want to fight for democracy, that this was an attempt to thwart a peaceful transfer of power. And that our job is to tell a story about that day."

Aguilar and other lawmakers on the panel said more revelations are coming. More important, lawmakers said, the hearings will connect the dots of what is publicly known and provide a comprehensive description of what happened.

Rep. Jamie Raskin, D-Md., acknowledged the risk in overselling the hearings. During a program at Georgetown University in April, he promised they would "blow the roof off the House."

"The proof will be in the pudding," Raskin said. "I do believe that we are going to tell this story of perhaps the greatest political crime or attempted political crime in American history. We have voluminous detail that is helping us put the whole story together."

Raskin said he didn't know who leaked information about the committee's investigation, but he argued the leaks promoted rather than dampened interest in the probe.

"They are definitely whetting the public's appetite for the hearings because we are going to tell a far more systematic and coherent story than the narrow leaks that are getting out," Raskin said. "The leaks obviously contain just a small proportion of information that is out."

Report: Jan. 6 committee was told that Trump spoke approvingly of calls to 'Hang Mike Pence'

Another committee member, Rep. Elaine Luria, D-Va., said her goal through the hearings is to paint a thorough picture of what led up to and what happened that day.

"People have gotten information in snippets over the course of a year plus, but the fact is that we're going to tell the story in a coherent thread through the hearings," Luria said.

Americans remain divided over the attack

The committee will present its findings Thursday to a country split over the attack and the panel itself.

More than half the country (53%) said storming the Capitol was an attack on democracy that should never be forgotten, while 44% of respondents said too much was made of the attack and it was time to move on, according to a Quinnipiac University poll released in January.

The Quinnipiac poll found Americans supported the congressional investigation nearly 2-1 (61% to 33%), but results were starkly divided by party: 83% of Democrats backed the probe, and 60% of Republicans opposed it.

A Pew Research Center poll conducted in the same month found nearly two-thirds of Republicans (65%) said too much attention was paid to the attack, and 79% said they had little or no confidence in the fairness of the committee's investigation. About half of Democrats (48%) said too little attention had been paid, and about two-thirds (65%) were at least somewhat confident the investigation would be fair and reasonable.

Former Defense Secretary Robert Gates told CBS "Face the Nation" on May 22 that the hearings are important because people need to understand what happened on Jan. 6, 2021.

'The elephant in the room': Police grapple with charges against officers on Jan. 6 Capitol attack

"My worry is that everybody will retreat to their ideological corner, and so nobody will listen," Gates said. "I think maybe the best thing to do is just to rerun the videos."

Robert Gibbs, who was press secretary for President Barack Obama, told the "Hacks on Tap" podcast Tuesday that Democrats could stoke interest in the midterm elections with hearings about the Capitol attack while debating gun control and abortion rights. Gibbs said those issues might get drowned out by concerns over the scarcity of baby formula and the high price of gas.

"You hope that energizes the base a bit more," Gibbs said. "But I don't know that it's in any way going to trump – no pun intended – gas prices or inflation."

Thousands of Donald Trump supporters storm the U.S. Capitol after a "Stop the Steal" rally on Jan. 6, 2021, in Washington. The protesters broke windows and clashed with police.

The committee plans eight hearings. A coalition of 150 advocacy groups announced Tuesday they would organize watch parties for the hearings in Arizona, Florida, Georgia, Michigan, New Hampshire, North Carolina, Pennsylvania, Texas, and Wisconsin.

"This is a criminal conspiracy that has been unfolding for more than a year, not just another blip in the news cycle," Lisa Gilbert, executive vice president of Public Citizen, said in a statement. "It's a top story that includes the fragility of our democracy and the ongoing threats to its integrity."

Though lawmakers haven't outlined what each hearing will focus on, the first session will provide an overview of hearings that delve into specific subjects. A final report is expected in the fall.

"The first hearing will lay the case and talk about the path ahead to the next seven," Aguilar said. One likely theme of the hearings will be Trump's responsibility. The Capitol attack, when 140 police officers were injured as a mob ransacked the building, temporarily halted Congress from counting Electoral College votes certifying Joe Biden's victory over Trump in the 2020 presidential election.

Trump argued he was fighting election fraud by challenging the results of the election, urging his supporters on Jan. 6 to march on the Capitol and "fight like hell." Rioters cited Trump's invitation to Washington and his rally speech that day to justify their actions. The Justice Department found no evidence of fraud, and several courts rejected the claims as baseless.

The hearings will probably lack the marquee witness: Trump. The committee chairman, Rep. Bennie Thompson, D-Miss., said the panel doesn't expect to call Trump because of uncertainty he would provide more information than what it's collected.

"I think the concern is whether or not he would add any more value with his testimony," Thompson said.

The committee continues discussions with former Vice President Mike Pence, who has distanced himself from Trump, though he might not be called because of cooperation from his advisers, Thompson said.

Other witnesses likely to miss the hearings are five Republican House members who spoke with Trump or his chief of staff in the days leading up to and on Jan. 6, 2021. The committee subpoenaed them, but each said he would fight the investigation they all called partisan.

The lawmakers are House Minority Leader Kevin McCarthy of California, who spoke with Trump on Jan. 6, and Reps. Andy Biggs of Arizona, who helped plan to bring protesters to Washington; Mo Brooks of Alabama, who spoke at Trump's rally; Jim Jordan of Ohio, who spoke with Trump on Jan. 6; and Scott Perry of Pennsylvania, who discussed replacing the attorney general with Trump's chief of staff.

Even without key players, the committee hopes to shine a spotlight on the three hours between Trump's speech at 1:10 p.m. and his tweeted video urging rioters to go home at 4:17 p.m. Live television that day showed the crowd surrounding the Capitol, battling police and breaching the building at 2:13 p.m.

Rep. Liz Cheney, R-Wyo., the committee's vice chair, said Trump's silence spoke volumes. The panel has firsthand testimony that Trump watched the attack on television in the dining room next to the Oval Office without acting, she said.

"While the attack was underway, President Trump knew it was happening" and "took no immediate action to stop it," Cheney said on the House floor. "This appears to be a supreme dereliction of duty by President Trump, and we are evaluating whether our criminal laws should be enhanced to supply additional and more severe consequences for this type of behavior."

Jan. 6 committee: Panel got a boost from a ruling on a confidential memo. What's next?

Trump's silence will be contrasted at the hearings with officials who took action.

Pence, in his role as Senate president, refused to reject electors from contested states, as one of Trump's lawyers, John Eastman, urged during an Oval Office meeting on Jan. 4, according to court records. Eastman continued sending messages on Jan. 6 to Pence's counsel, Greg Jacob, who concluded the legal reasoning was "essentially entirely made up," according to court records.

Trump considered ousting acting Attorney General Jeffrey Rosen during his final weeks in office to replace him with someone who would contest the election results. Trump relented after top Justice Department officials threatened to resign as a group if Rosen were removed.

Luria said the hearings will show who took the right action leading up to and including Jan. 6. She said what stood out for her was Trump's duty under a clause in the Constitution that says the president "shall take Care that the Laws be faithfully executed."

"It essentially says that the president must ensure that the laws are faithfully executed," said Luria, a former Navy commander. "To me, that is something that can be woven through all of this because the president has an explicit duty in the Constitution."

The Jan 6. Committee bet big with Cassidy Hutchinson. Did it pay off?

For months, the House committee investigating the Jan. 6, 2021, attack on the U.S. Capitol meticulously gathered evidence, carefully wrote and rewrote scripts, and painstakingly assembled video testimony to present at its televised hearings.

Then came Monday, when that pattern of extreme caution yielded to a scramble. With less than 24 hours' notice, the committee announced there would be a hearing the following afternoon with a single live witness: 25-year-old Cassidy Hutchinson, a former junior White House aide.

The result was the most explosive day of testimony to date in a string of revelation-rich hearings. Hutchinson testified that former president Donald Trump knew his supporters were carrying weapons that day but urged them to the Capitol anyway. She also recounted deputy chief of staff Anthony Ornato telling her that Trump had lunged in rage at a Secret Service agent after the president was informed he could not accompany the rioters as they marched from the Ellipse.

Numerous people close to the committee's work say the abrupt decision to go public with Hutchinson's testimony, which surprised even some of its top aides and which involved presenting the world with details the committee itself had learned only days earlier, was necessary to prevent her account from leaking. With evidence that Trump allies were trying to influence her decision to talk, some members also worried she might back out if they waited any longer.

By rolling the dice, the committee attracted the attention it has sought for its message that Trump's role in precipitating the Jan. 6 attack was illegal, unconstitutional, and disqualifying for any future bid for public office.

Hutchinson describes Trump throwing food at the wall

Hutchinson's account of cleaning Trump-strewn ketchup off White House walls and pleading with her onetime boss, former chief of staff Mark Meadows, to get off his phone and help quell the Capitol riot was watched by more viewers than all but one of the NBA Finals games this year.

But by rushing Hutchinson onto the witness stand, the committee has also exposed itself to criticism that it failed to thoroughly vet her claims.

Hutchinson has come under intense scrutiny from Trump and his allies, who have accused her of lying or derided her for relaying hearsay that would not hold up in a criminal proceeding.

So far, no one has publicly corroborated her account of a struggle between Trump and the Secret Service in his presidential SUV, but nor is anyone known to have disputed it under oath. Officials have said anonymously that the Secret Service agents involved are prepared to contradict Hutchinson in sworn testimony, although they do not appear to have done so.

One person familiar with the investigation which, like others, spoke on the condition of anonymity to address sensitive matters, called the story of Trump lunging at a Secret Service agent an "unforced error" that amounted to a colorful aside when the main point, not in dispute, was that Trump was furious at being barred from proceeding to the Capitol.

"The reality is that Cassidy told the truth about a conversation that was relayed to her, and I can't see an incentive for her to lie about it," the person said. "But the reality is also that the committee has to be perfect. They probably shouldn't have brought it there. I think we know Secret Service agents get very protective of their details."

Others, however, supported the decision to move as expeditiously as possible in making Hutchinson's testimony public.

"It was exactly the right call," said Ted Boutrous, a prominent Democratic lawyer and donor. "They had a super-credible witness with no reason not to be telling the truth. There are reasons why she wouldn't have wanted to step forward. She relayed the facts very precisely as to what she was told."

Nick Akerman, a former federal prosecutor who investigated the Watergate scandal, noted that it is irrelevant that Hutchinson's testimony might not hold up in a criminal proceeding. The House committee is trying to persuade Americans that Trump should never again hold power, he said — and is doing so effectively by creating a dramatic, digestible storyline.

"She was very well-prepared," Akerman said. "And they minimized the risk by doing snippets on tape. You don't get to do this as a prosecutor, where you put your witness on and do your summation at the same time. The public is learning the full scope of what happened here."

A committee aide called Hutchinson's testimony "a landmark moment in the committee's work to uphold the rule of law and protect American democracy. Anyone who questions the gravity and impact of that hearing either didn't watch it, doesn't understand the committee's body of evidence or has another agenda."

Public polling released in recent days offers little hint of whether the hearings have begun to change minds. A survey released Thursday by the Associated Press-NORC Center for Public Affairs Research at the University of Chicago shows that 49 percent of those surveyed say Trump bears responsibility for the Capitol attack, within the margin of error of the result in January 46 percent.

Those numbers may not reflect the impact of Hutchinson's testimony on Tuesday, which drew the largest audiences of any of the daytime hearings so far. The committee's first hearing, which aired in prime time on June 9, drew more than 20 million viewers across a dozen outlets. Tuesday's Hutchinson hearing garnered 13 million viewers, according to Nielsen, a remarkable figure for daytime television.

Fox News, which did not air the prime time debut, has televised the panel's daytime work, and one of its most recognizable personalities has even praised it. "This testimony is stunning," Bret Baier, host of the network's 6 p.m. news show, said Tuesday during a break in Hutchinson's appearance.

Later, after the hearing concluded, Baier belittled Trump's attempts to deny her charges, noting that the former president was making his comments on his own social media platform and Hutchinson was "under oath on Capitol Hill."

The hearings have broken through with Trump voters in ways many inside-the-Beltway obsessions don't, according to Sarah Longwell, an anti-Trump Republican strategist who co-hosts the Bulwark's "Focus Group" podcast. In three groups conducted with Trump voters since the hearings began, participants reported being aware of the hearings or watching parts of them.

"This is not a technical term, but I would describe their engagement as 'hate-watching' some of it," Longwell said. "They say, 'Oh, I turned it off; it's so partisan, they're just trying to get Trump.' But at the end of the day, they're still following it."

Trump surrogates initially tried to dismiss the hearings and point to other subjects, such as gas prices. But that failed, Longwell said, because of how effectively the committee used Trump's own aides and other well-known Republicans as witnesses.

Trump's allies have been forced to respond, driving headlines and leading Fox News to dedicate coverage time to rebuttals. Trump has also been issuing a running commentary of the hearings on his Truth Social platform, marked by frequent denials.

"Her Fake story … is 'sick' and fraudulent," Trump wrote Tuesday of Hutchinson, calling the committee a "Kangaroo Court."

So far, however, the committee has avoided having to make any retractions, a possible reflection of the overall caution with which it has proceeded.

The panel twice announced delays because members said they needed to be careful not to make any mistakes in their preparation. On June 15, the third planned hearing was postponed to avoid holding three proceedings in a single week and risking errors.

"It's just technical issues. The staff putting together all the videos, you know, doing 1, 2, 3 — it was overwhelming," Rep. Zoe Lofgren (D-Calif.), a committee member, told reporters that day in the Capitol. "So we're trying to give them a little room to get their work done."

A week later, as the rest of Congress headed toward a 17-day break, the committee dropped plans to hold one or more hearings during the Independence Day recess for similar reasons: An avalanche of new material needed to be carefully digested and reviewed before it could be put on display before a nationally televised audience.

Lawmakers and committee aides have described a process in which their teams scour depositions, both written and video, to collect the most revealing details and package them together. Then the team goes back into the depositions and video to see what the witnesses said just before and after the selected clips to protect against any suggestion from Trump-friendly witnesses that they were quoted out of context.

By taking the time to check the details, committee members said they hoped to avoid giving Trump and his allies ammunition to discredit their work.

"There's been a deluge of new evidence since we got started. And we just need to catch our breath, go through the new evidence, and then incorporate it into the hearings we have planned," Rep. Jamie Raskin (D-Md.) told reporters on June 22.

But Hutchinson's disclosures triggered a change of plans.

Hutchinson gave her first of four closed-door depositions to the committee in February. Some of the most compelling details from Tuesday's hearing, however, did not emerge until the last of those sessions, during the week of June 20. Afterward, committee members agreed that they needed to question Hutchinson at a live hearing as soon as possible.

If not, they feared the details would leak out, drip by drip, undermining the drama of a highly scripted televised hearing. Members also worried that pro-Trump forces would attempt, perhaps successfully, to intimidate Hutchinson into changing her story or refusing to testify in public.

The young woman's willingness to risk her career and subject herself to an onslaught of abuse from Trump supporters presented an additional potential benefit, according to several people with knowledge of the committee's deliberations: It would contrast sharply with the reluctance of several high-ranking Trump aides, notably former White House counsel Pat Cipollone, to come before the committee.

With Hutchinson's appearance, the committee was "absolutely" hoping to shame other witnesses into coming forward or saying more than they already have, one of the individuals said. Since Hutchinson's testimony, Cipollone has been subpoenaed and continues to correspond with the committee about potential testimony, multiple people confirmed.

The attack: The Jan. 6 siege of the U.S. Capitol was neither a spontaneous act nor an isolated event Most members of the committee did not know exactly what Hutchinson planned to say until Tuesday morning, one individual with knowledge of the hearings said. Members were asked not to do any television or media before the hearing began but were told it would be a big moment and to plan for a "robust TV schedule" afterward. The committee promised to connect members with television bookers to appear across the airwaves Tuesday afternoon.

"There will be no information outside of the fact that we have a hearing tomorrow announced," a committee spokeswoman told staffers on Monday. Later in an email, she reiterated: "We will not be giving out any information."

How Hutchinson's testimony influences the remainder of the committee's work is still unclear. Tentative plans to hold the committee's final two hearings the week of July 11 — including a prime time proceeding on July 14 focused primarily on Trump — are in flux, according to multiple members.

Much of Hutchinson's testimony Tuesday was originally planned to be featured in that final hearing, which must now be reworked. The committee is also hoping that, as more witnesses step forward, more information can be presented to the public.

To some close observers, the Hutchinson gamble has already paid off.

"For those that argue it was a mistake or an unforced error, we'll find out, but that ignores the committee's very capable march up until now," said Norm Eisen, who served as special counsel to the House Judiciary Committee during its first impeachment of Trump. "After all you've seen and perhaps the greatest congressional hearings ever — maybe surpassing Watergate — do you really think that they screwed it up? I sure don't think so."

Isaac Arnsdorf and Scott Clement contributed to this report.

Hutchinson said in her testimony that she overheard Trump reacting to news that protesters had weapons, and he said he did not care.

"I overheard the president say something to the effect of 'I don't f-ing care that they have weapons. They're not here to hurt me. Take the f-ing mags away. Let my people in; they can march to the Capitol from here. Let the people in, take the f-ing mags away."

Hutchinson testified that Trump was enraged that he was being driven back to the White House after his "Stop the Steal" rally, where he told protesters to "fight like hell." She said he lunged for the steering wheel to grab it from a Secret Service agent.

"I'm the effing president," Hutchinson heard Trump say, according to her testimony.

Hutchinson further said that when Meadows learned about violence at the Capitol, he "almost had a lack of reaction."

Hutchinson Recounted Her inside Look at the White House as an Intern under Trump & Said Her Goal Was to Be a Leader 'in the Fight to Secure the American Dream'

Hutchinson told her student newspaper in 2018 about the behind-the-scenes look she was granted through her internship during her junior year of college.

"I attended numerous events hosted by the president, such as signing ceremonies, celebrations, and presidential announcements, and frequently watched Marine One depart the South Lawn from my office window," she said at the time. "My small contribution to the quest to maintain American prosperity and excellence is a memory I will hold as one of the honors of my life."

She said at the time that she planned to return to Capitol Hill to continue her career in politics.

"I'm keeping every opportunity at my fingertips and am open to any job that comes my way," she told the newspaper. "I am confident I will be an effective leader in the fight to secure the American dream for future generations, so they too will have the bountiful opportunities and freedoms that make the United States great."

THE BIG LIE

Democrats say that THE BIG LIE is Donald Trump's claim of a" Rigged Election."
Republicans say that THE BIG LIE is Hillary Clinton's "Collusion between Trump and Russia."
The Hillary Clinton lie has been debunked.
Time will tell of the alleged Trump Lie.

How Americans evaluate the likelihood of dire political scenarios

Taylor Orth | Senior Survey Data Journalist

September 07, 2022, 4:40 PM GMT-4

Two in five Americans believe a civil war is at least somewhat likely in the U.S. within the next decade, according to recent polling by the Economist and YouGov. But what exactly do Americans think a second American civil war would look like? Among 15 potential future scenarios involving instability or political violence, the one that most Americans consider likely in the next decade is that the U.S. ceases to be a global superpower (50% say this), followed by a total collapse of the U.S. economy (47%). Each of the 15 dire scenarios is considered somewhat or very likely in the next decade by at least 20% of Americans.

We arrived at the list of 15 scenarios with a follow-up question to the Economist finding on a separate poll, asking people who earlier in the poll said they think a civil war is likely to tell us in their own words what they think it means for the country to engage in one. Based on responses to this question, we developed the list of 15 specific future scenarios and included it in another poll asking how likely each is to occur in the coming years.

When asked broadly about the chances of a civil war in the next decade, without specifying what kind, 37% of Americans say one is at least somewhat likely to occur. However, expectations vary across five possible scenarios:

- 40% think a civil war is likely — at least either very or somewhat likely — between Republicans and Democrats

- 32% think it's likely between red and blue states

- 30% think it's likely between the rich and poor

- 29% think it's likely between people of different races

- 20% think it's likely between people living in cities and rural areas

After an end to the U.S.'s global-superpower status and economic collapse, the next most likely scenario is that the U.S. will cease to be a democracy (39% say this is likely within the next decade). Slightly more say it's likely the U.S. will become a fascist dictatorship (31%) than say it will become a communist dictatorship (21%). (The poll didn't ask whether people believe a given scenario has already occurred, so some people who believe this probably are included among those who said each scenario is likely.)

Republicans are more likely than Democrats to believe nearly all of the scenarios asked about are likely within the next 10 years. Two-thirds of Republicans (65%) believe that total economic collapse is at least somewhat likely, compared to only 38% of Democrats. Around half of Republicans (48%) say it's likely that the government will confiscate citizens' firearms; only 17% of Democrats say this. Republicans are also more likely than Democrats to believe there will be a total breakdown of law and order (49% vs. 31%) and that the U.S. will be invaded by a foreign country (41% vs. 24%).

While a similar share of Republicans and Democrats believe it's at least somewhat likely that the U.S. will cease to be a democracy in the next decade, there is disagreement as to which type of government is likely to replace it. Democrats are slightly more likely than Republicans to say the U.S. will be a fascist dictatorship (37% vs. 32%). Republicans, on the other hand, are three times as likely as Democrats to say it will be a communist dictatorship (31% vs. 13%).

In terms of the possibility of a civil war, Republicans are likelier than Democrats to believe there will be one between members of each party (45% vs. 35%) or between people from red and blue states (36% vs. 30%). Democrats are slightly more likely than Republicans to believe there will be a war between the poor and rich (37% vs. 25%) or between cities and rural areas (23% vs. 20%). Democrats and Republicans are equally likely (31%) to expect a civil war between racial groups.

The open-ended question we asked to identify the civil-war-like scenarios to poll about elicited a wide range of responses about what Americans who expect a civil war in the next decade envision one looking like. Some imagined a great deal of violence between neighbors, while others had in mind economic instability or the deterioration of democratic norms.

What do you think it would mean for the country to have a civil war?

Among Americans who say a civil war is at least somewhat likely in the U.S. in the next decade:

"I see the country splitting in two, each side having a place for their own like-minded people."

"It would mean people on different sides of the political spectrum fighting for what they want, and maybe even having certain states trying to secede."

"It would mean the further erosion of the laws, norms, and values that most of us thought came with living in a democracy."

"Life for many people may not change as much as we think it would. There would be a small percentage of militants, but most people would probably simply have a harder time economically."

"Ugly. Not civil at all. Not like the first Civil War. This will be neighbor vs neighbor, rather than state vs state."

"We would lose our standing in the world, China would become the de facto superpower, and democracy would be under threat worldwide."

Note: Selected quotes were edited for grammar and may not be representative of the full range of responses.

August 31 – September 4, 2022

Do Americans differentiate between the possibility of civil war and other destabilizing outcomes in the next 10 years compared to say, the next 50? To test this, we split respondents into two groups, half of whom were asked to evaluate dire scenarios in the next 10 years, and the other half who were asked about the next 50 years. Overall, we find few differences between the two contexts: Americans evaluate the chances of most events similarly regardless of whether they're asked about the next decade or the next five decades.

Would a civil war be good or bad for the country? The vast majority of Americans (69%) say a civil war within the next decade would overall be a bad thing; 6% say it would be good, 8% say it wouldn't be good or bad, and 17% aren't sure or preferred not to say. Democrats and Republicans are equally likely to say a civil war would be a bad thing.

How similar would a new civil war be to the original one? Two-thirds of Americans (67%) say a civil war occurring in the next 10 years would be very or somewhat different from the first civil war that occurred in the 1860s. Only 16% say it would be very or somewhat similar to the first civil war, and 17% are unsure.

Would the government be able to defend itself against an armed citizen uprising? Americans are twice as likely to believe the military and law enforcement would prevail against armed rebels (51%) as they are to say they would fail (26%). While Republicans and Independents have similar expectations on the matter, Democrats are far more optimistic about the government's prospects: 68% say the military and law enforcement are at least somewhat likely to succeed, relative to 44% of Republicans and Independents.

How concerned are Americans about different types of extremism? The largest share (43%) say they're very concerned about white-supremacist extremism. This is followed by high concern over right-wing extremism (39%) and left-wing extremism (34%). Slightly fewer are very concerned about Christian extremism (31%), Muslim extremism (29%), or racial-minority extremism (28%). Democrats and Republicans have vastly different concerns when it comes to extremism. Democrats are most likely to be very concerned about extremism among white-supremacists (68%), right-wing groups (60%), and Christians (48%). The greatest share of Republicans are very concerned about extremism among left-wing groups (62%), Muslims (36%), and racial minorities (31%).

In recent weeks, a number of people associated with the far-right anti-government militia group known as the Oath Keepers have faced charges stemming from their involvement in the January 6 Capitol attack. Our latest poll finds that 9% of Americans know someone (including themselves, a family member, a friend, or an acquaintance) who is a member of a militia group.

Younger Americans are especially likely to be familiar with someone affiliated with a militia group: One in four adults under 30 (26%) say they know a person in a militia group compared to only 5% of people who are 45 and older. Another factor linked to knowing someone involved in a militia is whether a person shares a home with a gun-owner: One in four Americans (26%) who say someone in their household owns a gun

(Other than themselves) also say they know someone in a militia group. There are no significant differences between Republicans and Democrats in terms of their familiarity with militia-group members.

— Carl Bialik and Allen Houston contributed to this article

See crosstabs **and** toplines **for this poll.**

Methodology: *This survey was conducted by YouGov using a nationally representative sample of 1,000 U.S. adult citizens interviewed online from September 1 - 4, 2022. This sample was weighted according to gender, age, race, and education based on the 2018 American Community Survey, conducted by the U.S. Census Bureau, as well as 2016 and 2020 Presidential votes (or non-votes). Respondents were selected from YouGov's opt-in panel to be representative of all U.S. citizens. The margin of error is approximately 3% for the entire sample. Responses to open-ended questions mentioned in this article come from a separate poll with the same methodology, fielded starting a day earlier (August 31 - September 4).*

Part Eleven

Special Prosecutor John Durham Appointment

Information; Sussmann Trial

Published *May 31, 2022, 10:51pm EDT*

McCarthy: Was the FBI a dupe, or are they a willing collaborator? McCarthy says they weren't fooled at all By it.

Tuesday's "Special Report" panelists discussed the jury's decision to find Hillary Clinton's campaign lawyer Michael Sussmann, not guilty of lying to the FBI and what to expect next in the Durham probe.

ANDY MCCARTHY: *In order to figure out this case, I think you really have to make up your mind about what the FBI is. Are they a dupe, or are they willing collaborators? Durham has staked his investigation on the notion that they're a dupe. You have to prove for materiality purposes in a false statements trial that the duped party actually was fooled. And I think the evidence here was pretty strong; even though what Sussman told them was false, it was factually untrue. They weren't fooled at all by it. They fully knew that they were getting political information from a partisan source. And a lot of what they did was designed to conceal the fact that they knew that.*

GUY BENSON: *Well, it was a setback because this was an acquittal. There's no debating that. But the piece that you just quoted also makes a decent point, which is the public learned a lot more about what happened on the whole Russia matter and Hillary Clinton's personal involvement in greenlighting some of this oppo research being peddled around that turned out to be f+alse. And we learned that from her campaign manager. There were a few of her donors on this jury in a very blue jurisdiction. I know some people are pointing to that as a factor here, but I defer more to Andy's legal judgment about why this became such a difficult case for the prosecution to argue and win, given the behavior, the actions of the FBI itself, and how it handled the information they got from Mr. Sussmann.*

Hillary Clinton on Durham report: 'Trump & Fox are desperately spinning up a fake scandal.'

Former Secretary of State Hillary Clinton reacted to Special Counsel John Durham's latest filing, criticizing former President Trump and Fox News for "desperately spinning up a fake scandal to distract from his real ones."

The former 2016 Democratic presidential nominee tweeted Wednesday, in her first public statement reacting to Durham's Feb. 11 federal court filing, which Fox News first reported Saturday.

Durham's filing alleged a "Tech Executive-1," now identified as Rodney Joffe, and his associates, including a lawyer for her presidential campaign, Michael Sussmann, "exploited" internet traffic pertaining to a "particular healthcare provider," Trump Tower, Trump's Central Park West apartment building, and the Executive Office of the President of the United States in order to "establish 'an inference' and 'narrative'" to then bring to federal government agencies tying Trump to Russia.

CLINTON CAMPAIGN LAWYER SUSSMANN ASKS COURT TO 'STRIKE' DURHAM'S 'FACTUAL BACKGROUND' FROM LATEST FILING

"Trump & Fox are desperately spinning up a fake scandal to distract from his real ones," Clinton tweeted Wednesday. So it's a day that ends in Y."

"The more his misdeeds are exposed, the more they lie," Clinton tweeted, linking out to a piece published in Vanity Fair "for those interested in reality," which she says is a "good debunking of their latest nonsense."

Clinton's tweet comes days after Durham filed the motion, which focused on potential conflicts of interest related to the representation of former Clinton campaign lawyer Michael Sussmann, who has been charged with making a false statement to a federal agent. Sussmann has pleaded not guilty.

The indictment against Sussmann says he told then-FBI General Counsel James Baker in September 2016, less than two months before the 2016 presidential election, that he was not doing work "for any client" when he requested and held a meeting in which he presented "purported data and 'white papers' that allegedly demonstrated a covert communications channel" between the Trump Organization and Alfa Bank, which has ties to the Kremlin.

But Durham's filing on Feb. 11, in a section titled "Factual Background," reveals that Sussmann "had assembled and conveyed the allegations to the FBI on behalf of at least two specific clients, including a technology executive (Tech Executive 1) at a U.S.-based internet company (Internet Company 1) and the Clinton campaign."

Durham's filing said Sussmann's "billing records reflect" that he "repeatedly billed the Clinton Campaign for his work on the Russian Bank-1 allegations."

Sussmann and his legal team, on Monday, though, demanded that the court "strike" the "factual background" section of Durham's filing, arguing it will "taint the jury pool."

DURHAM PROBE: 'TECH EXECUTIVE-1' SAYS ALLEGATIONS TYING TRUMP TO RUSSIA SHARED WITH CIA

"Unfortunately, the Special Counsel has done more than simply file a document identifying potential conflicts of interest," Sussmann's attorneys wrote. "Rather, the Special Counsel has again made a filing in this case that unnecessarily includes prejudicial—and false—allegations that are irrelevant to his Motion and to the charged offense, and are plainly intended to politicize this case, inflame media coverage, and taint the jury pool."

Sussmann's attorneys added: "Sadly, the Special Counsel seems to be succeeding in his effort to instigate unfair and prejudicial media coverage of Mr. Sussmann's case."

Sussmann's legal team called for the court to "strike the Factual Background portion of the Special Counsel's motion pursuant to the Court's inherent power to 'fashion an appropriate sanction for conduct which abuses the judicial process.'"

The "factual background" section of Durham's filing alleged that Sussmann and the Tech Executive had met and communicated with another law partner, who was serving as General Counsel to the Clinton campaign. Sources told Fox News that the lawyer is Marc Elias, who worked at the law firm Perkins Coie.

Durham's filing states that in July 2016, the tech executive worked with Sussmann, a U.S. investigative firm retained by Law Firm 1 on behalf of the Clinton campaign, numerous cyber researchers, and employees at multiple internet companies to "assemble the purported data and white papers."

"In connection with these efforts, Tech Executive-1 exploited his access to non-public and/or proprietary Internet data," the filing states. "Tech Executive-1 also enlisted the assistance of researchers at a U.S.-based university who were receiving and analyzing large amounts of Internet data in connection with a pending federal government cybersecurity research contract."

"Tech Executive-1 tasked these researchers to mine Internet data to establish 'an inference' and 'narrative' tying then-candidate Trump to Russia," Durham states. "In doing so, Tech Executive-1 indicated that he was seeking to please certain 'VIPs,' referring to individuals at Law Firm-1 and the Clinton campaign."

CLINTON CAMPAIGN PAID TO INFILTRATE TRUMP TOWER, WHITE HOUSE SERVERS TO LINK TRUMP TO RUSSIA, DURHAM FINDS

Durham also writes that during Sussmann's trial, the government will establish that among the Internet data Tech Executive-1 and his associates exploited was domain name system (DNS) internet traffic pertaining to "(i) a particular healthcare provider, (ii) Trump Tower, (iii) Donald Trump's Central Park West apartment building, and (iv) the Executive Office of the President of the United States (EOP)."

Durham states that the internet company that Tech Executive-1 worked for "had come to access and maintain dedicated servers" for the Executive Office of the President as "part of a sensitive arrangement whereby it provided DNS resolution services to the EOP."

"Tech Executive-1 and his associates exploited this arrangement by mining the EOP's DNS traffic and other data for the purpose of gathering derogatory information about Donald Trump," Durham states.

A spokesperson for Tech Executive-1, Joffe, defended his work on Tuesday.

"Contrary to the allegations in this recent filing, Mr. Joffe is an apolitical internet security expert with decades of service to the U.S. Government who has never worked for a political party and who legally provided access to DNS data obtained from a private client that separately was providing DNS services to the Executive Office of the President (EOP)," Joffe's spokesperson said in a statement Tuesday.

"Under the terms of the contract, the data could be accessed to identify and analyze any security breaches or threats," Joffe's spokesperson continued. "As a result of the hacks of EOP and DNC servers in 2015 and 2016, respectively, there were serious and legitimate national security concerns about Russian attempts to infiltrate the 2016 election."

Durham's filing also alleges that Sussmann provided "an updated set of allegations," including the Russian bank data and additional allegations relating to Trump "to a second agency of the U.S. government" in 2017.

Durham says the allegations "relied, in part, on the purported DNS traffic" that Tech Executive-1 and others "had assembled pertaining to Trump Tower, Donald Trump's New York City apartment building, the EOP, and the aforementioned healthcare provider."

Joffe's spokesperson suggested that the second federal government agency was "the CIA."

"Upon identifying DNS queries from Russian-made Yota phones in proximity to the Trump campaign and the EOP, respected cyber-security researchers were deeply concerned about the anomalies they found in the data and prepared a report of their findings, which was subsequently shared with the CIA," Joffe's spokesperson said.

In Sussmann's meeting with the second U.S. government agency, Durham says he "provided data which he claimed reflected purportedly suspicious DNS lookups by these entities of internet protocol (IP) addresses affiliated with a Russian mobile phone provider" and claimed that the lookups "demonstrated Trump and/or his associates were using supposedly rare, Russian-made wireless phones in the vicinity of the White House and other locations."

"The Special Counsel's Office has identified no support for these allegations," Durham wrote, adding that the "lookups were far from rare in the United States."

"For example, the more complete data that Tech Executive-1 and his associates gathered--but did not provide to Agency 2--reflected that between approximately 2014 and 2017, there were a total of more than 3 million lookups of Russian Phone-Prover 1 IP addresses that originated with U.S.-based IP addresses," Durham wrote. "Fewer than 1,000 of these lookups originated with IP addresses affiliated with Trump Tower."

TRUMP SAYS DURHAM PROBE EXPOSING 'THE CRIME OF THE CENTURY,' PREDICTS IT'S 'JUST THE BEGINNING'

Durham added that data collected by Tech Executive-1 also found that lookups began as early as 2014, during the Obama administration and years before Trump took office, which he said is "another fact which the allegations omitted."

"In his meeting with Agency-2 employees, the defendant also made a substantially similar false statement as he made to the FBI General Counsel," Durham wrote. "In particular, the defendant asserted that he was not representing a particular client in conveying the above allegations."

"In truth and in fact, the defendant was representing Tech Executive-1--a fact the defendant subsequently acknowledged under oath in December 2017 testimony before Congress, without identifying the client by name," Durham wrote.

A spokesperson for the CIA did not immediately respond to Fox News' request for comment.

At this point, Durham has indicted three people as part of his investigation: Sussmann in September 2021, Igor Danchenko on Nov. 4, 2021, and Kevin Clinesmith in August 2020.

Danchenko was charged with making a false statement and is accused of lying to the FBI about the source of information that he provided to Christopher Steele for the anti-Trump dossier.

Kevin Clinesmith was also charged with making a false statement. Clinesmith had been referred for potential prosecution by the Justice Department's inspector general's office, which conducted its own review of the Russia investigation.

Specifically, the inspector general accused Clinesmith, though not by name, of altering an email about Page to say that he was "not a source" for another government agency. The page has said he was a source for the CIA. The DOJ relied on that assertion as it submitted a third and final renewal application in 2017 to eavesdrop on Trump campaign aide Carter Page under the Foreign Intelligence Surveillance Act (FISA).

Brooke Singman is a Fox News Digital politics reporter. You can reach her at Brooke.Singman@Fox.com or @BrookeSingman on Twitter.

Hillary Clinton feeds 2024 buzz with red-meat speech, rejects the charge of spying on Trump

By Susan Ferrechio - *The Washington Times - Thursday, February 17, 2022*

Former Secretary of State Hillary Clinton pledged Thursday to help Democratic candidates on midterm election ballots in a speech to New York Democrats that took aim at former President Donald Trump, Republican lawmakers, and Fox News.

Mrs. Clinton promised Democrats that she would play an active role in their campaigns in the coming months amid speculation that she might launch a political comeback if President Biden, 79, decided not to run for a second term.

In the address before the New York State Democratic Convention in New York City, she characterized as a right-wing attack a recent federal court filing that implicated her 2016 presidential campaign in spying on Mr. Trump.

"It's funny: The more trouble Trump gets into, the wilder the charges and conspiracy theories about me seem to get," Mrs. Clinton said.

Her party is girding for a tough campaign season.

House and Senate Democrats face an increasing chance that Republicans will take over the majority in both chambers in November. Voters have become increasingly frustrated with the way Mr. Biden and Democratic officials have handled the economy and the COVID-19 pandemic. Rising inflation and gas prices, as well as unpopular COVID-19 mandates, have contributed to the discontent, polls show.

Mrs. Clinton, 74, said in her keynote address that a Republican majority would not govern for the working class and would continue to embrace Mr. Trump, 75.

"They will do nothing to invest in our schools or make college more affordable. They'll ban books but do nothing about guns. They'll make it harder for people to vote but easier for big corporations to bust unions. They'll let polluters trash our environment and let Donald Trump trash our democracy," Mrs. Clinton said. "That's why I intend to work my heart out to elect Democrats up and down the ticket this November."

The convention was held to nominate Gov. Kathy Hochul for a four-year term in November. Mrs. Hochul became governor after Andrew Cuomo was forced to resign because of a sexual harassment scandal.

Before introducing Mrs. Hochul, Mrs. Clinton accused Fox News of "getting awfully close to actual malice" in the network's coverage of a court filing that says her 2016 campaign paid for spying on Mr. Trump.

Special counsel John Durham, who filed the charges, said he has evidence that the Clinton campaign paid for a technology expert to access Mr. Trump's email communications at his New York City residences and later at the White House to look for damaging information linking him to Russia.

Mr. Durham is investigating the origins of the FBI's probe of Trump-Russia collusion to meddle in the 2016 election.

Mrs. Clinton said conservatives are trying to protect Mr. Trump from his legal problems, including the New York attorney general's investigation of his businesses and finances.

Republicans, she said, "have been coming after me again lately."

She said the attacks are intended to deflect attention from the House committee investigation into the Jan. 6. 2021 riot at the U.S. Capitol. Democrats leading the investigation are focusing on House Republicans and Trump administration officials who they accuse of instigating and helping facilitate the riot.

Republicans say the Democratic-run committee is politically motivated and designed to smear Mr. Trump and other Republicans during the midterm campaigns.

On Thursday, Mrs. Clinton accused Republicans of engaging in "a cover-up" of the attack at the Capitol. She also dismissed "the latest culture war nonsense" that Republicans have highlighted as parents at school board meetings across the country rebel against COVID-19 restrictions and liberal curricula such as critical race theory and the promotion of LGBTQ lifestyles.

She said Mr. Trump continues to divide the country even though he is no longer in office. The recent revelation that his accounting firm dropped him over unreliable financial statements is among the reasons Fox News is reporting on the spying accusations, and she told the convention crowd.

"Investigations draw closer to him, and right on cue, the noise machine gets turned up, doesn't it?" Mrs. Clinton said. "Fox leads the charge with accusations against me, counting on their audience to fall for it again and again."

• *Susan Ferrechio can be reached at sferrechio@washingtontimes.com.*

Strzok claims ignorance of FBI mistakes in launching Alfa-Bank investigation

by Jerry Dunleavy, Justice Department Reporter |
June 07, 2022, 09:45 AM

Peter Strzok claimed ignorance of the FBI's mistakes in the opening of an investigation into discredited Alfa-Bank claims in 2016, as the fired bureau agent renewed his criticism of special counsel John Durham's investigation into the Trump-Russia investigators.

Last week, a jury found Democratic cybersecurity lawyer Michael Sussmann not guilty on charges of concealing his two clients from FBI General Counsel James Baker when he pushed debunked allegations of a secret line of communication between the Trump Organization and Russia's Alfa-Bank in 2016.

Strzok made his remarks on the *In Lieu of Fun* webcast hosted by Ben Wittes of the Brookings Institution on Friday. Wittes is a friend of fired FBI James Comey and of Baker, who had worked at Brookings after his time as FBI general counsel. Some texts between Baker and Wittes were entered into evidence during the Sussmann trial, and Wittes describes Baker as a "personal friend."

He was visibly frustrated throughout parts of the discussion, especially when discussing Durham and former Attorney General William Barr. Strzok said he had learned "a couple of things" from the Sussmann trial.

SUSSMANN'S COZY RELATIONSHIP WITH THE FBI REVEALED

"First, I was not aware that Chicago, in this case, who had opened the case, was unaware of where the information came from," Strzok said. "You know, they put in the EC [electronic communication], and I guess they, you know, the opening communication to the case, that it had come from the Department of Justice, which is incorrect. … And they put it in their closing EC, and that was obviously correct [sic]."

Strzok was fired after the discovery of anti-Trump texts with then-FBI lawyer Lisa Page, with whom he was having an affair. He played a key role in opening the Crossfire Hurricane investigation. Sussmann relied in part on a legal analysis by Strzok in his failed attempt to convince the judge to dismiss the case.

A number of top FBI officials were copied on the flawed launch document By the Chicago field office, including Strzok, who was Deputy Assistant Director for the Counterintelligence Division, Deputy Assistant Director Jonathan Moffa, and agent Joseph Pientka. The opening document was approved By other FBI officials.

Strzok has said he took the Alfa-Bank allegations from Baker and then handed them off for FBI cyber experts to examine.

The electronic communication marking the opening of a full counterintelligence investigation wrongly cited a nonexistent "referral" from the Justice Department rather than correctly saying the Alfa-Bank allegations came from a lawyer for Clinton's campaign. The opening communication was authored by FBI agents Curtis Heide and Allison Sands, who both testified, and the investigation was initiated on Sept. 23, 2016, four days after Sussmann's meeting with Baker.

Sands and Heide both referred to the glaring errors as "typos." The closing communication in January 2017 also wrongly claimed the Alfa-Bank allegations were referred to the bureau by the Justice Department rather than from Sussmann.

Strzok also said, "One of the agents who were there testifying made some mention of the fact that you know, a colleague of mine, a partner of mine for a long time as well as then, that partner and I had been at some meeting where he said, you know, to keep it close hold, specifically to the source. I remember broadly all of these things being very close hold."

FBI agent Ryan Gaynor testified that FBI headquarters leadership "made the decision not to share the identity of Mr. Sussmann with the field." He repeatedly described what he believed he'd been told was a "close hold," preventing the disclosure of Sussmann's identity.

Sussmann's defense team tried to poke holes in that, but Strzok seems to have confirmed it. Gaynor said Moffa told him senior FBI leadership had put a "close hold" on the fact that the information came from Sussmann and that he, Moffa, and Strzok talked about a close hold at some point.

Sussmann's defense team accused Gaynor of concealing Sussmann's identity, but Gaynor testified, "The leadership did not allow me to share the information with the Chicago field office." Gaynor said the close-hold order "must have come down from" Baker. "I was told that it came from above, so above Pete Strzok," he said.

Heide said, "We may have been conflating the Department of Justice and the Office of General Counsel."

Strzok authored the opening electronic communication for Crossfire Hurricane in July 2016. Heide was working on the part of that Trump-Russia investigation, too.

Strzok also said Friday: "I was not aware that, you know, they had made, it turns out, repeated attempts to — or made repeated requests to interview some of the people, whether it was Sussmann or Rodney Joffe."

"We had asked numerous times" who the source was, **"and we elevated to headquarters,"** Sands testified. **"We were told that headquarters was working on it, that they were aware, and that we should at the division level focus on the technical analysis."**

Heide said he said he never learned who the anonymous source was.

Strzok also attacked Durham during the discussion, saying that "the behavior, in this case, I found not be honorable." He said he no longer believed Durham was excellent nor well respected and added Attorney General Merrick Garland or Deputy Attorney General Lisa Monaco should force Durham to finish his investigation, saying, "I would hope that DOJ is insisting that he get the report in this summer."

Garland told lawmakers in October 2021 that Durham had the freedom to continue his investigation and said, "You would know if he weren't continuing to do his work." Garland also noted his support for Durham making his report public.

Strzok also attempted to revive the debunked Alfa-Bank claims.

"What I was told and what we were told is that this was looked at, and it was dismissed, and it didn't appear to be anything, and from what I heard at trial, I don't know that's accurate," Strzok said, citing unnamed "non-government computer scientists who really know what they're talking about in this field that I've spoken to in the past year or two."

Special counsel Robert Mueller, the FBI, the CIA, and a bipartisan Senate Intelligence Committee investigation cast doubt on or rejected the Alfa-Bank claims touted by the Clinton campaign in the closing days of the 2016 election. Baker said the final conclusion of the FBI was that "there was nothing there."

SPECIAL AGENT ROTH- Again and again, there was no interview with the person who provided false information. Hillary Clinton's case should have been closed after the communication from the FBI Chicago Field Office.

"We had asked numerous times" who the source was, "and we elevated to headquarters," Sands testified. "We were told that headquarters was working on it, that they were aware, and that we should at the division level focus on the technical analysis."

Heide said he said he never learned who the anonymous source was.

Sussman was never interviewed.

Former Clinton campaign manager RobBy Mook testified Friday that Hillary Clinton approved of leaking Trump-Russia allegations to the media.

The Washington Post was accused of bias on Monday after publishing a piece that claimed there is "no evidence" Hillary Clinton triggered the Russian probe despite her former campaign manager testifying that she approved distributing materials alleging a secret communications channel between the Trump Organization and Russia's Alfa Bank to the media, despite not being "totally confident" in the legitimacy of the data.

On Friday, ex-Clinton campaign manager Robby Mook testified that his former boss approved the move when grilled during the trial of ex-Clinton campaign lawyer Michael Sussmann, who has been charged with making a false statement to the FBI. Mook was called to the stand for testimony by Sussmann's defense, and during cross-examination, he was asked about the campaign's understanding of the Alfa Bank allegations against Trump and whether they planned to release the data to the media.

Mook said the campaign was not totally confident in the legitimacy of the data but eventually admitted Clinton herself approved "the dissemination" of the information to the media.

"She agreed," Mook testified. "All I remember is that she agreed with the decision."

NO EVIDENCE THAT HILLARY CLINTON TRIGGERED THE RUSSIAN PROBE

MSNBC, ABC, NBC, and CBS are among the mainstream news outlets that have completely ignored the bombshell testimony, but Washington Post nation correspondent Phillip Bump took a different strategy and provided cover for Clinton.

The Post's piece headlined, "Again: there's no evidence Hillary Clinton triggered the Russian probe," began by criticizing a Wall Street Journal editorial board column that condemned the 2016 Democratic nominee for harming the country by pushing the narrative that Trump's campaign colluded with Russia.

"The editorial is titled: 'Hillary Clinton Did It,'" Bump wrote of the Journal's piece. "A fiery, furious bit of rhetoric. Also, rhetoric is indefensible given the evidence. It is rhetoric aimed at scratching a long-frustrating itch rather than accurately informing readers."

Bump declared Mook's testimony was the "trigger" for the editorial to be written before defending the 2016 presidential runner-up at all costs.

"Mook told the jury that Clinton had approved the leak of an allegation tying Donald Trump's private business to a Russian bank as the election neared. This, the Journal argues, is what Clinton 'did,'" Bump wrote. "The criminal trial centers on whether the attorney, Michael Sussmann, was working for the Clinton campaign when he brought the rumored digital link between Alfa Bank and the Trump Organization to the FBI and, if so, whether he failed to disclose that relationship to the bureau. Special counsel John Durham — appointed by Trump Attorney General William P. Barr to investigate the origins of the Russia probe, which so annoyed the then-president — appears to be hoping to bolster the idea elevated by the Journal: that Clinton was a primary trigger for allegations about Trump and Russia."

Bump informed Washington Post readers that Trump's alleged ties to the Alfa bank were quickly debunked and that nothing suspicious or election-related was involved.

Bump went on to claim that "a community of fervent conspiracy theorists" thought Trump and Russia had some sort of strange relationship well before Clinton got involved.

"Why was there already so much chatter about Trump and Russia? Because so many things had emerged to draw attention to the unusual nature of the candidate's approach to that country," Bump wrote before listing examples of Trump's rumored ties to Russia.

SUSSMANN TRIAL: MSNBC, ABC, CBS, AND NBC IGNORE TESTIMONY THAT CLINTON OK'D LEAKING OF TRUMP-RUSSIAN ALLEGATIONS

Bump attempted to make the case that things including WikiLeaks publishing Democratic National Committee emails, George Will pondering why Trump wouldn't release his taxes, and ex-campaign manager Paul Manafort all helped the public believe there could have been more to the Trump-Russia story.

"Law enforcement also understood that Russia was continuing to try to influence the election, publishing a warning in early October about possible threats to state elections systems. By that point, a federal probe of possible campaign-Russia ties was already underway," Bump wrote.

Essentially, the Post's national correspondent feels Clinton couldn't have triggered the Russian probe, despite Mook's damning testimony, because people were already curious about the collusion narrative.

"The Clinton campaign was following the conversation to undercut its opponent, not leading it," Bump wrote. "Put another way: Hillary Clinton didn't do it."

The House Judiciary Committee's Republicans are among the critics of the liberal newspaper's framing.

"Can't make up the bias sometimes," the House Judiciary GOP tweeted.

Fox News' Brooke Singman contributed to this report.

Brian Flood is a media reporter for Fox News Digital. Story tips can be sent to brian.flood@fox.com and on Twitter: @briansflood.

Published *May 19, 2022 12:40pm EDT*

FBI concerns about the media getting ahold of the Trump-Russia story

Baker said that during the meeting, Sussmann warned him that a "major" news outlet would be publishing a story on the allegations by the end of the week.

"Articles coming out revealing any part of what might be happening between the Trump Organization and Russia was of concern to me in terms of the impact on the investigation and ability to conduct it without the other side knowing," Baker said, adding that the FBI had to act "quickly" because if the story on the allegations were reported, the communication could "disappear" and make it "much harder" for the FBI to investigate.

"I know from my prior experience in this field that if a news organization were to publish something about an alleged surreptitious communications channel, it is likely that as soon as it came out, the communications channel would disappear and make it that much harder for the FBI to investigate the existence of such a channel," Baker said, noting that the users could begin to do "something different," and that the information, then, "wouldn't be as much use to the bureau."

Baker added that because of the potential involvement of news media, investigating the allegations of a channel between the Trump Organization and Alfa Bank was "time sensitive."

"If the FBI wanted to investigate this in the counterintelligence world, really in any part of criminal investigations, but especially in the counterintelligence world, you don't want the bad guys to know that you're looking at them," Baker said. "You want to be able to investigate without them being aware you're looking at them."

He added: "It is critically important."

Baker testified that days after the meeting with Sussmann at the FBI on Sept. 19, 2016, the two spoke by phone.

"The point of the phone call was to ask Michael the identity of the reporter he had identified in the meeting with me so that we could ask the reporter to slow down on publishing the article," Baker said, noting that the FBI wanted to "delay publication of this article so the FBI could conduct its investigation into the alleged secret surreptitious communications channel."

The government presented a text message from Sussmann to Baker on Sept. 21, 2016:

168

"Jim, Sorry I have been unable to respond sooner. Travel and person availability were not ideal this afternoon and evening. I am working on your request and expect to have an answer for you by 9:00 am tomorrow- and I'm hoping for a positive response," Sussmann texted Baker.

Baker testified Thursday that he interpreted that text to mean that Sussmann was "working hard to respond to my request about getting the identity of that reporter, but that he had not been able to contact the people he needed to contact yet."

MARC ELIAS SAYS HE BRIEFED CLINTON CAMPAIGN OFFICIALS ON FUSION GPS OPPO AGAINST TRUMP

"But it seemed that everything was going in the direction that we, at the FBI, had hoped for," Baker said, noting they were "optimistic about the possibility of getting the identity of that reporter."

The reporter in question was New York Times reporter Eric Lichtblau.

FBI finds no 'surreptitious communications channel' after weeks of investigation

Baker said he eventually had a meeting with Priestap and the head of FBI's public affairs with Lichtblau to convince him to slow down the publication of the story. Baker testified that Lichtblau eventually agreed.

"My recollection is he was trying to understand how seriously we were taking this allegation and the extent to which we thought there was some kind of nefarious activity between the Trump Organization and Russia," Baker said. "He was asking us a series of probing questions, most of which we rebuffed because we didn't want to disclose what we were up to."

Baker added that Lichblau seemed "frustrated with the conversation to some degree."

Baker, though, said the New York Times did not seem to be "persuaded yet either about whether this material actually showed there was a surreptitious communications channel."

"They weren't yet convinced and weren't ready to publish and were doing additional research to test the material, validate the material, and make sure they understood the material," Baker said, adding that the FBI notified the reporter that the bureau was "still working on it and needed more time to investigate it fully."

Meanwhile, testimony from FBI Special Agent Scott Hellman on Tuesday afternoon said that the data revealing the alleged covert communications channel between Trump and Russia that Sussmann brought to the FBI turned out to be untrue and said he did not agree with the narrative.

Hellman testified that whoever drafted the narrative describing the DNS data was "5150" and clarified on the stand that meant he believed the individual who came to the conclusions was "was suffering from some mental disability."

Baker testified Thursday that the FBI's investigation "did not reveal there was some kind of surreptitious communications channel."

"We concluded there was no substance. We couldn't confirm it. We could not confirm there was a surreptitious communications channel," Baker said, noting the investigation was "several weeks, maybe a month, maybe a month and a half."

"There was nothing there," he said.

SPECIAL AGENT ROTH – Yes, there was something there. FBI should have interviewed Sussman about where he obtained this information. Again, if the FBI followed up on this case, it would be an end to the trump-Russian fake collusion story and the pedaling of misinformation. The conspirators should have been charged

With violation title 18, section 1001making a false statement to a federal agent.

Sussmann has pleaded not guilty to making a false statement to the FBI

By Brooke Singman | Fox News

Prosecutors set to call former FBI officials to the stand as week two of the Sussmann trial begins

WASHINGTON, D.C.—Week two of former Clinton campaign lawyer Michael Sussmann's trial will begin Monday morning, with prosecutors from Special Counsel John Durham's team set to call former FBI officials to the stand for testimony.

The government is set to call the former FBI assistant director for counterintelligence, Bill Priestap, and the FBI's former deputy general counsel for national security, Trisha Anderson, to testify.

Prosecutors could also call Justice Department Inspector General Michael Horowitz to the stand as a witness.

Sussmann has been charged with making a false statement to the FBI during a meeting he had in September 2016 with then-FBI General Counsel James Baker. Sussmann, during that meeting less than two months before the presidential election, brought "purported data and 'white papers' that allegedly demonstrated a covert communications channel" between the Trump Organization and Russia's Alfa Bank, which has ties to the Kremlin.

Sussmann, during that meeting, told Baker he was not doing work "for any client" but rather bringing the allegations to the FBI as a citizen concerned with national security.

Durham's team alleges that Sussmann was, in fact, doing work for two clients: the Hillary Clinton campaign and a technology executive, Rodney Joffe. Following the meeting with Baker, Durham claims Sussmann billed the Hillary Clinton campaign for his work.

Sussmann has pleaded not guilty to the charge.

Baker did not take handwritten notes on his meeting with Sussmann on Sept. 19, 2016—something Sussmann's defense attorneys criticized Baker for—but prosecutors have repeatedly referenced handwritten notes from both Priestap and Anderson as evidence, as they both wrote that Sussmann was not bringing the allegations to the FBI on behalf of any specific client, but on his own.

Baker testified last week that the FBI began an investigation into the Trump-Alfa Bank allegations, which lasted "several weeks, maybe a month, maybe a month and a half."

"We concluded there was no substance," Baker testified. "We couldn't confirm it. We could not confirm there was a surreptitious communications channel."

Baker added: "There was nothing there."

Clinton OK'd leak to a reporter about alleged Trump-Russia tie, her campaign manager says

MARK HOSENBALL

May 20, 2022, 4:07 PM

Hillary Clinton personally approved leaking to the media information alleging a connection between Donald Trump and a Russian bank in 2016, which the campaign itself had not fully confirmed, according to testimony Friday by Clinton's campaign manager.

Robby Mook, Clinton's campaign chief, said in federal court that as the campaign against Trump heated up in the late summer and early fall of 2016, Marc Elias, who was then a lawyer with the Perkins Coie law firm and served as the campaign's top legal adviser, told Mook that "people with expertise" in cyberactivity had briefed the campaign on data alleging links between the Trump Organization and Alfa Bank, a Russian financial institution with ties to the Kremlin.

Mook's testimony, for the first time, puts Clinton in the middle of a leak to the news media that ultimately blew up in the campaign's face. The FBI quickly determined that the purported connection between the Russian bank and the Trump Organization was implausible, and Michael Sussmann, Elias's then law partner who brought the claims to the FBI, has since been indicted by Justice Department special counsel John Durham on charges he lied to the bureau's general counsel to hide his connection to the Clinton campaign.

The account from Mook came on the fourth day of the trial of Sussmann, a cyber and national security law expert who worked at Perkins Coie in 2016. The closely watched case is widely seen as a major test for Durham, the longtime U.S. attorney in Connecticut who had been initially appointed by Trump's attorney general, William Barr, to investigate alleged wrongdoing by the FBI and other federal agencies in the course of their investigation into alleged Trump-Russia ties.

Even though Durham's prosecutors have yet to rest their case, the judge presiding over the trial, Christopher Cooper, permitted the defense to call Mook early since he was slated to leave the country for a previously scheduled trip. But the immediate impact of Mook's testimony on the charge against Sussmann is unclear.

After learning about the Alfa Bank allegations, the source of which Mook said was unknown to him; Mook said his "recollection is we decided to give it to a reporter so the reporter could pin it down more." He said the Clinton campaign itself did not have sufficient data or expertise to confirm the accuracy of the information itself.

After consulting with Clinton campaign chairman John Podesta, Mook said he told Clinton that the campaign wanted to share the Alfa Bank information with the media, and "she agreed to that." One of the main purposes of giving the data to the media was so that a reporter could investigate and try to confirm it, Mook said.

The campaign subsequently did make the information available to Eric Lichtblau, then with the New York Times, as well as a reporter for the online magazine Slate. Mook, though, was vague about precisely who in the campaign's "press department" did the leaking.

On Oct. 31, 2016, days before the election, Slate published a lengthy story about the purported Alfa Bank/Trump link under the headline "Was a Trump Server Communicating With Russia?" That same day, the New York Times published a story by Lichtblau and another journalist claiming that for much of the summer of 2016, the FBI had been pursuing a "widening investigation" of possible Trump links to Russia that included chasing a lead regarding a possible Trump/Alfa Bank communications link.

The Times, however, noted that the FBI "ultimately concluded that there could be an innocuous explanation" for the Trump/Alfa computer link.

Despite this apparent caveat, Hillary Clinton that day tweeted that "Computer scientists have apparently uncovered a covert server linking the Trump Organization to a Russian-based bank." Campaign adviser Jake Sullivan also released a statement declaring, "This could be the most direct link yet between Donald Trump and Moscow."

But while Mook's testimony clearly established the Clinton campaign's role in spreading the unsubstantiated Alfa Bank allegations, Mook may also have bolstered Sussmann's defense that he approached James Baker, then the general counsel of the FBI, about the Alfa material on his own — and not as a lawyer for the Clinton campaign.

Mook said he had no knowledge that Sussmann had any involvement in commissioning, producing, or circulating the Trump/Alfa Bank allegations. Elias, the general counsel for the campaign, had previously testified that he had no knowledge beforehand that Sussmann was taking the Alfa Bank material to the FBI and never approved his doing so.

In trial testimony on Friday afternoon, a retired CIA counterintelligence official identified only as Kevin P. testified that he and another CIA official met with Sussmann at CIA headquarters in February 2017 to discuss the Alfa Bank allegations.

He said Sussmann "said he was not representing a client" and also "made it clear" that although other lawyers at Perkins Coie did represent the Democratic National Committee and the Clinton campaign, "such work was unrelated to his reasons for contacting the CIA."

He said Sussmann had reached out to the CIA's general counsel in September 2016 but that nobody got back to him, so he went through third parties, including a former CIA official, to arrange the February meeting. The CIA official said Sussmann told him he had previously contacted Baker at the FBI about similar but unrelated information.

The former CIA official said that at the meeting, Sussmann was told by the CIA officials that it was likely the information he provided would be passed on to the FBI.

FBI Special Agent Scott Hellman also testified last week, saying the data from Sussmann turned out to be untrue and stressed that he did not agree with the narrative.

Hellman testified that whoever drafted the narrative describing the DNS data was "5150" and clarified on the stand that meant he believed the individual who came to the conclusions "was suffering from some mental disability."

HILLARY CLINTON APPROVED DISSEMINATION OF TRUMP-RUSSIAN BANK ALLEGATIONS TO MEDIA, CAMPAIGN MANAGER TESTIFIES

Meanwhile, former Clinton campaign manager Robby Mook testified last week that Hillary Clinton herself approved the dissemination of those allegations tying Trump to the Kremlin-linked bank to the media ahead of the 2016 election.

Mook testified that former Clinton campaign officials John Podesta, Jennifer Palmieri, and Jake Sullivan (who now serves as White House National Security Advisor) were also involved in the plan to share the allegations with the media.

The government, in its opening statement last week, argued that Sussmann's delivery of the Trump-Alfa Bank allegations to the FBI was part of the Clinton campaign's plan to create an "October surprise" against then-candidate Donald Trump.

Brooke Singman is a Fox News Digital politics reporter. You can reach her at Brooke.Singman@Fox.com or @BrookeSingman on Twitter.

Trial evidence shows 'internet phone book' used to get to Trump-Russia tale

By Ben Feuerherd, Jack Morphet and Bruce Golding

May 18, 2022 2:20pm

Updated

WASHINGTON, D.C. — They let their cyber fingers do the walking.

Opposition research that found a since-debunked back channel between Donald Trump and Russia got started with a simple search of the name Trump in the "phone book of the internet."

The misguided origin of the purported Russia-Trump cyber connection was revealed in a document entered into evidence at the trial of former Hillary Clinton campaign lawyer Michael Sussmann.

The eight-page report, titled "White Paper #1 — Auditable V3," claims that on July 28, 2016, a search of the global Domain Name System — also known as the "phonebook of the internet" — yielded 1,933 results containing the word "Trump."

Another search turned up 3,352 domains registered by the Trump Organization, including "trump-email.com," which was then linked to an email server named "mail1.trump-email.com" that showed "anomalous data," according to the document.

Special counsel John Durham, whom Attorney General William Barr appointed in 2019 to probe the origins of the Trump-Russia investigation.Ron Sachs – CNP

The white paper further asserted that between May 4 and Sept. 4, 2016, the majority of online lookups for mail1.trump-email.com came from IP addresses registered or linked to Russia's Alfa-Bank, including an "unusually configured server" run by the Spectrum Health system in Grand Rapids, Michigan.

"The only plausible explanation for this server configuration is that it shows the Trump Organization and Alfa Bank to be using multiple layers of protection in order to obfuscate their considerable recent email traffic," according to the report's "findings."

Sussmann, 57, is charged with lying to the government by denying that he wasn't "acting on behalf of any client" when he gave White Paper #1 and other material to then-FBI general counsel James Baker on Sept. 19, 2016, according to an indictment obtained last year by special counsel John Durham.

During opening statements in DC federal court Tuesday, prosecutor Deborah Brittain Shaw accused Sussmann of engaging in "a plan to create an October surprise on the eve of the presidential election."

Shaw also told jurors that an FBI investigation of the material Sussmann gave Baker found it merely involved a "spam email server" used for marketing purposes.

FBI agent Scott Hellmann testified Monday that he disagreed with the conclusions in White Paper #1, saying they "were not supported by the technical data."

Hellman was also questioned by the defense about an electronic message in which he told an FBI colleague that the report "feels a little 51-50ish," using a slang term that refers to mental illness.

"I thought perhaps the person who drafted this document was suffering from a mental disability," Hellman said.

Who's who in the case

Michael Sussmann: Cybersecurity lawyer who worked for Hillary Clinton's 2016 campaign; charged with lying to the FBI

Rodney Joffee: Former tech executive and Sussmann client who told him about a purported cyber back channel between the Trump Organization and Russia's Alfa-Bank

Christopher Steele: British ex-spy hired by Fusion GPS; compiled the infamous "Steele dossier" of reports on Trump and Russia

John Durham: Special counsel investigating potential criminality in the government investigations of former President Donald Trump's purported ties to Russia

James A. Baker: Former FBI general counsel; received Alfa-Bank information from Sussmann

Marc Elias: Clinton campaign general counsel, former partner of Sussmann's at Perkins Coie law firm

Judge Christopher Cooper: Presiding over Sussman's trial in Washington, DC, a federal court

Peter Fritsch and Glenn Simpson: Former Wall Street Journal reporters who co-founded the Fusion GPS research company; worked for Clinton's campaign

Andrew McCabe: Former FBI deputy director; allegedly contradicted the basis for the charge against Sussmann during a 2017 briefing

It's unclear from the exhibit who wrote White Paper #1, but the underlying data was "assembled" by April Lorenzen, a data scientist and founder of the ZETAlytics company based in Rhode Island, according to court papers.

Lorenzen, a registered Democrat, last week declined to comment through a woman who identified herself as her spouse when The Post visited their home in North Kingstown, Rhode Island.

"She will not talk to you. Do not waste your time or breath," the woman said.

A woman claiming to be the partner of April Lorenzen outside their home.David McGlynn for NY Post

The woman also used a cellphone to take a picture of a Post photographer after emerging from the house to smoke a cigarette.

Last year, Lorenzen's lawyer told the New York Times that she's "dedicated her life to the critical work of thwarting dangerous cyberattacks on our country."

Published May 18, 2022 8:32pm EDT

FBI lawyer James Baker testifies he's 'not out to get' Sussmann: 'This is not my investigation, it's yours'

Sussmann is charged with making a false statement to the FBI in his meeting with Baker about the information on Trump in Sept. 2016. He has pleaded not guilty

By Brooke Singman, Jake Gibson, David Spunt | Fox News

WASHINGTON, D.C. — Former FBI General Counsel James Baker took the stand in the trial of Michael Sussmann on Wednesday afternoon, declaring that he is "not out to get Michael" but is simply cooperating as part of Special Counsel John Durham's investigation.

Baker falls at the center of the trial. Sussmann has been charged with making a false statement to the FBI when he told Baker in September 2016, less than two months before the presidential election, that he was not doing work "for any client" when he requested and attended a meeting where he presented "purported data and 'white papers' that allegedly demonstrated a covert communicates channel" between the Trump Organization and Alfa Bank, which has ties to the Kremlin.

SUSSMANN-DURHAM TRIAL: MARC ELIAS SAYS HE BRIEFED CLINTON CAMPAIGN OFFICIALS ON FUSION GPS OPPO AGAINST TRUMP

Durham's team alleges Sussmann was, in fact, doing work for two clients: the Hillary Clinton campaign and a technology executive, Rodney Joffe. Following the meeting with Baker, Sussmann billed the Hillary Clinton campaign for his work.

Sussmann has pleaded not guilty to the charge.

Baker, during testimony Wednesday, explained that the 2016 meeting was initially requested by Sussmann via text message to his personal phone on Sept. 18, 2016.

Durham, in a filing in the weeks leading up to the trial, referenced these text messages, saying, "the night before the defendant met with the general counsel, the defendant conveyed the same lie in writing and sent the following text message to the general counsel's personal cellphone."

Baker testified that he had forgotten about the text conversation and found it in response to a request from the government earlier this year. Baker said that in March, Durham asked him to "look for" emails and other communications he may have had with Sussmann.

SUSSMANN-DURHAM TRIAL: PROSECUTION SAYS CLINTON LAWYER USED FBI TO CREATE AN 'OCTOBER SURPRISE' AGAINST TRUMP

"I'm not out to get Michael, and this is not my investigation; it's yours," Baker said to the prosecution. "Nobody had asked me to go look for this material before that."

Baker testified that upon finding the text messages, he notified the government through his attorney "as quickly as I could" and said that same afternoon, FBI agents "came to my house."

Baker explained his relationship with Sussmann, saying the two were "friends" who had kept in contact but testified that he was "a bit surprised" to receive the texts.

"I was a bit surprised to get it from Michael, kind of wondered how he got my personal cell number, but Michael is a friend, so it didn't really freak me out," Baker testified. "I trust Michael, it seemed to me at the time it was very important, and so I thought I should meet with him right away."

The government presented the text messages to the jury for consideration Wednesday.

DURHAM-SUSSMANN TRIAL: JUDGE 'NOT INCLINED' TO DECLARE MISTRIAL, DESPITE ATTEMPT FROM DEFENSE

The text message stated: "Jim — it's Michael Sussmann. I have something time-sensitive (and sensitive) I need to discuss," the text message stated, according to Durham. "Do you have availability for a short meeting tomorrow? I'm coming on my own — not on behalf of a client or company — want to help the Bureau. Thanks."

Baker replied, "OK. I will find a time. What might work for you?"

Sussmann replied: "Any time but lunchtime, you name it."

"2:00 pm in my office? Do you have a badge, or do you need help getting into the building?" Baker responded.

"I have a badge. Please remind me of your room #," Sussmann said.

Baker on Wednesday explained he thought Sussmann could have a badge to admit him into the FBI Headquarters due to the work he often did with clients and law enforcement.

Baker is expected to continue their testimony on Thursday.

Brooke Singman is a Fox News Digital politics reporter. You can reach her at Brooke.Singman@Fox.com or @BrookeSingman on Twitter.

DURHAM PROBE

Published *May 18, 2022, 5:53pm EDT*

Sussmann-Durham trial: Marc Elias says he briefed Clinton campaign officials on Fusion GPS oppo against Trump

The former Clinton campaign lawyer says he never directed Michael Sussmann to take opposition research on Trump to the FBI

By Brooke Singman, Jake Gibson, David Spunt | Fox News

WASHINGTON, D.C. — Former Clinton campaign lawyer Marc Elias testified for more than three hours on Wednesday as part of the trial of Michael Sussmann, confirming that he hired Fusion GPS to run opposition research for Hillary For America during the 2016 election cycle and revealing that he would share "the fruits of their work" with senior Clinton campaign officials.

Elias, a former partner at law firm Perkins Coie and the former general counsel for the 2016 Clinton campaign, testified he hired opposition research firm Fusion GPS in April 2016, saying he retained the firm on behalf of the Clinton campaign at "about the time that Donald Trump looked like he was going to be the nominee."

Elias also said that Fusion GPS, at the time, was doing work for the Democratic National Committee related to its work for the Clinton campaign.

Elias went on to testify that Clinton campaign officials, including campaign manager Robby Mook, campaign chairman John Podesta, policy director Jake Sullivan — who now serves as White House National Security advisor in the Biden administration — and communications official Jennifer Palmieri, were aware of the opposition research Fusion GPS was conducting against Trump.

Elias said that if he had gathered information from Fusion GPS that he thought would "help the campaign," he would pass it to officials in either their communications division or the research team.

Elias said Fusion GPS was researching a "broad" range of issues related to then-candidate Trump and said he was regularly briefed by Fusion GPS employees Glenn Simpson and Peter Fritsch in his office.

Fusion GPS is the opposition firm that commissioned the now-infamous anti-Trump dossier, which contained allegations of purported coordination between Trump and the Russian government. The dossier was authored by Christopher Steele, an ex-British intelligence officer.

The Clinton campaign and the DNC funded the dossier through the law firm Perkins Coie, where both Elias and Sussmann were employed at the time.

The government called Elias to the stand Wednesday as part of the trial of Michael Sussmann — the first trial out of Special Counsel John Durham's years-long investigation into the origins of the Trump-Russia probe.

Sussmann is charged with making a false statement to the FBI when he told former FBI General Counsel James Baker in September 2016 — less than two months before the presidential election — that he was not doing work "for any client" when he requested and attended a meeting with Baker where he presented "purported data and 'white papers' that allegedly demonstrated a covert communicates channel" between the Trump Organization and Alfa Bank, which has ties to the Kremlin.

Durham's team alleges Sussmann was, in fact, doing work for two clients: the Hillary Clinton campaign and a technology executive, Rodney Joffe. Following the meeting with Baker, Sussmann billed the Hillary Clinton campaign for his work.

Sussmann has pleaded not guilty to the charge.

With regard to the Alfa Bank allegations against Trump, Elias testified that he did not specifically recall who on the campaign he briefed on that research but said, "it would have been Robby, it would have been John... Jake would make sense; Palmieri would make sense."

As to whether the campaign had put out any public statements about the Alfa Bank allegations, Elias said they had, shortly before the election. Elias went on to say that he did not remember if the communication was put out to the public via Twitter.

On Oct. 31, 2016, Hillary Clinton tweeted: "Computer scientists have apparently uncovered a covert server linking the Trump Organization to a Russian-based bank."

Clinton also shared a statement from Jake Sullivan, which stated: "This could be the most direct link yet between Donald Trump and Moscow. Computer scientists have uncovered a covert server linking the Trump Organization to a Russian-based bank."

Sullivan said the "secret hotline may be the key to unlocking the mystery of Trump's ties to Russia."

"This line of communication may help explain Trump's bizarre adoration of Vladimir Putin and endorsement of so many pro-Kremlin positions throughout this campaign," Sullivan's 2016 statement continued. "It raises even more troubling questions in light of Russia's masterminding of hacking efforts that are clearly intended to hurt Hillary Clinton's campaign."

Sullivan added that they "can only assume federal authorities will now explore this direct connection between Trump and Russia as part of their existing probe into Russia's meddling in our elections."

Durham, in a filing in early April, motioned to admit the Clinton campaign tweet from Oct. 31, 2016, as evidence, but U.S. District Judge Christopher Cooper, who is presiding over the trial, ruled that the court would exclude the tweet as hearsay.

FBI Special Agent Scott Hellman testified on Tuesday afternoon that the data revealing the alleged covert communications channel between Trump and Russia that Sussmann brought to the FBI turned out to be untrue and said he did not agree with the narrative. Hellman testified that whoever drafted the narrative describing the DNS data was "5150" and clarified on the stand that meant he believed the individual who came to the conclusions was "was suffering from some mental disability."

Meanwhile, much of Elias' testimony Wednesday centered around billing records and how Perkins Coie traditionally billed its clients.

Durham's team insists that Sussmann billed the Clinton campaign directly after his meeting at the FBI in September 2016 — a claim that is central to their argument in proving Sussmann's allegedly false statement.

One specific billing record was shown to the courtroom Wednesday, dated Sept. 17, 2016. The billing record revealed Sussmann had billed the Clinton campaign for nearly five hours of work.

The record states that work consisted of "multiple telephone conferences and other communications with experts, media; communication with M. Elias."

Elias could not recall what Sussmann could have been billing for but said that he had occasional check-ins with him during that timeframe about the Alfa Bank allegations.

During cross-examination, the defense asked Elias if he, or anyone from the Clinton campaign, had directed or authorized Sussmann to bring the Alfa Bank allegations to the FBI.

"No," Elias testified.

As for the government's argument that the data was brought to the FBI as part of an effort to create an alleged "October Surprise" ahead of the 2016 presidential election, Elias quipped: "An October surprise comes in October."

Sussmann's meeting at the FBI was on Sept. 19, 2016.

"What makes an October surprise useful is not just that it comes in October, but essentially, that it comes too late in the campaign process to un-do it," Elias said. "Usually, something comes in the second half of October where the media is landing something that is both explosive and effectively too late to rebut."

Brooke Singman is a Fox News Digital politics reporter. You can reach her at Brooke.Singman@Fox.com or @BrookeSingman on Twitter.

FBI agent mocked Trump-Russia tale pushed By Clinton camp as '51-50ish.'

By **Ben Feuerherd and Bruce Golding**

May 17, 2022, 7:46pm
 Updated
The prosecutors told the jury
FBI agent testifies about red flags in Trump-Russia data from ex-Clinton campaign lawyer

WASHINGTON — A research paper that Hillary Clinton campaign lawyer Michael Sussmann told the FBI would show ties between then-candidate Donald Trump and Russia was so weak that an agent joked it must have been written by a nutjob.

On cross-examination Tuesday at Sussmann's trial for allegedly lying to the feds, FBI supervisory agent Scott Hellman was confronted with an electronic message he sent a colleague the same day he received the paper and two thumb drives of data that Sussmann also gave then-FBI general counsel James Baker.

"It feels a little 51-50ish," Hellman wrote.

Defense lawyer Sean Berkowitz then asked Hellman what the message meant.

"I thought perhaps the person who drafted this document was suffering from a mental disability," Hellman answered.

Section 5150 of California's Welfare and Institutions Code allows authorities to involuntarily hospitalize mentally ill people for up to 72 hours and has been widely adopted as slang to refer to someone who's crazy.

An FBI agent at the trial of Hillary Clinton lawyer Michael Sussman mocked a document he had sent to the bureau as insane. FBI agent Scott Hellman testified that he was hoping that a document that Sussman alleged proved former President Donald Trump had ties to Russia was written by someone with a mental disorder.

In 1986, it was notably used as the title for Van Halen's first album to feature "I Can't Drive 55" singer Sammy Hagar, who's said he thinks he was abducted by aliens.

Hellman was the second witness called by special counsel John Durham's team following opening statements Tuesday at Sussmann's trial for allegedly lying to the FBI by denying he was "acting on behalf of any client" when he met with Baker on Sept. 19, 2016.

During direct examination by prosecutor Andrew DeFilippis, Hellman said the since-debunked material Sussmann gave Baker — which purportedly showed a secret back channel between a Trump Organization computer server and Russia's Alfa Bank — was marked by numerous red flags.

The most obvious was the Internet domain name assigned to the server, which Hellman described as a dead giveaway that nothing nefarious was going on.

"The name 'Trump' was in the name. It did not suggest secret communications," he testified.

"We believe Russia would have a much more technical capability to hide organizations. It wouldn't be so overt and direct."

Hellman also said he "did not agree with the conclusion in the paper" he reviewed.

"I felt that whoever had written that paper had jumped to some conclusions that were not supported by the technical data," he said.

179

"I did not feel they were objective in the conclusions they came to. The assumption is so far-reaching it just didn't make any sense."

Hellman speculated that whoever authored the report simply searched for "Trump" on a dataset of email servers to make the since-debunked connection.

Hellman also recalled being stymied when he tried to determine the source of the data.

"I do remember I was frustrated at not being able to ID who had provided these thumb drives to Mr. Baker. He was not willing to tell me," Hellman told prosecutor Andrew DeFilippis.

Hellman said he tried to establish the official "chain of custody" for the thumb drives when he received them in September 2016.

Hellman said the incomplete record shows that Baker passed the drives to then-agent Peter Strzok, who initially led the "Crossfire Hurricane" Trump-Russia probe.

Strzok was later removed from former special counsel Robert Mueller's investigation after text messages surfaced showing that Strzok and then-FBI lawyer Lisa Page bashed Trump while carrying on an affair.

Hellman said that Strzok gave Sussmann's material to another agent, who gave it to him.

After Hellman reviewed the material with FBI unit chief Nate Batty, they wrote a report on their findings and sent the material to the bureau's Chicago field office, Hellman testified.

Durham also alleges that Sussmann, in February 2017, provided an "updated set of allegations," including the Alfa Bank claims and additional allegations related to Trump, to a second U.S. government agency, which Fox News has confirmed was the CIA.

With regard to the data, Bosworth said Sussmann brought the information first to the New York Times, but when it appeared the story would be imminently published, Sussmann took the initiative to reach out to the FBI so that the bureau would not be caught "by surprise."

"Sussmann said there might be smoke, they look, and said, no fire," Bosworth said of the FBI's investigation into the data allegedly showing a connection between Trump and the Kremlin-tied bank. "Which is what they do with tips they get a day, after day, after day. That's what the FBI does."

Bombshell testimony that Hillary Clinton personally authorized giving a reporter since-debunked data about Donald Trump and Russia was part of a chess-like maneuver to "protect the queen," a former US Justice Department official told The Post.

Jim Trusty said former Clinton campaign manager Robby Mook's revelation Friday, which he quickly tried to walk back, actually meshed with other testimony in which Mook and former campaign general counsel Marc Elias both said they were unaware campaign lawyer Michael Sussmann planned to also provide the information to the FBI.

Both men said they would have objected to the move if they'd known.

"The strategy here is Protect the Queen!" Trusty said in an email.

"The Knights (lawyers for the campaign, the campaign manager) have drawn the line – admitting what they have to admit."

Meanwhile, Mook and Elias also suggested that Clinton "was shocked, shocked by Sussmann going to the FBI," said Trusty, now a Washington, DC, lawyer.

"Legal representation simply does not work that way. You don't 'free-lance' a visit to the FBI while billing your client for the time," he said.

"The defense is basically trying to provide a fig leaf to any partisan jurors who want to acquit."

Former FBI agent Thomas J. Baker also told The Post, "Whether Sussmann is found guilty or innocent or otherwise, [special counsel John] Durham has already laid out, in my opinion, what these people were up to and what was going on.

"It paints a picture of Sussmann colluding with other people to drag the FBI into an investigation and besmirch a presidential candidate," he said.

Sussmann is on trial in DC on a single count of lying to the government when he met with then-FBI general counsel James Baker on Sept. 19, 2016, and handed over material that purportedly showed a cyber backchannel between a Trump Organization server and Russia's Alfa Bank.

He's accused of falsely denying that he was acting on behalf of a client, with Durham alleging that Sussmann was actually working for both the Clinton campaign and Rodney Joffe, a tech executive who told him about the data.

Thomas Baker suggested that the case against Sussmann would be stronger if not for changes instituted by former FBI Director Robert Mueller following the Sept. 11 terror attacks.

"Moving away from being a law enforcement agency to an intelligence agency changed the culture," he said.

"Part of it is they got rid of agent-executives and replaced them with so-called professionals, like James Baker."

Thomas Baker said that if James Baker had been an FBI agent, he would have immediately summoned another agent to participate in the meeting with Sussmann and prepare an official report known as a "302."

Former FBI general counsel James A. Baker, who received Alfa-Bank information from Michael Sussmann, departs United States District Court. Ron Sachs – CNP

Instead, James Baker didn't take any notes and left what Sussmann said open to question, he said.

In a recent column for The Post, former Manhattan federal prosecutor Andrew McCarthy said Durham "appears to have built a case of historic consequence" that "portrays the Clinton campaign as guilty of perhaps the worst dirty trick in the history of American presidential elections."

"The problem for Durham is that, because he hasn't charged the big scheme, Judge [Christopher] Cooper is restricting what he can tell the jury about it," McCarthy wrote.

"On the other hand, to the extent Sussmann directly participated in the scheme, the court is inclined to let Durham prove it."

A different view was put forward on Thursday by US Rep. Matt Gaetz (R-Fla.), who tweeted: "I do not believe that the Durham trial of Michael Sussmann is about convicting Michael Sussmann at all."

"I think the entire purpose of this trial is to inoculate the FBI and the DOJ against the charge that they were in on the Russia Hoax," he said.

Sussmann's trial is set to resume Monday. If convicted as charged, he'd face a maximum sentence of five years in prison.

Jurors hear contrasting stories about FBI handling of Trump-Russia secret server claims

Agents detail their role in the probe prompted by attorney Michael Sussmann, who is on trial over an alleged false statement to the FBI.

By Josh Gerstein and Kyle Cheney

05/23/2022 02:27 PM EDT

Updated: 05/23/2022 05:39 PM EDT

An FBI agent involved in the investigation of links between Donald Trump and Russia told a colleague weeks before the 2016 election that top FBI brass were "fired up" about since-discredited allegations of a secret communications channel between Trump and a Russian bank with close ties to Vladimir Putin.

"People on 7th floor to include Director are fired up about this server," FBI agent Joseph Pientka wrote in an internal instant message to another agent working on the issue, Curtis Heide, on Sept. 21, 2016. "Reach out and put tools on… it's [sic] not an option — we must do it."

But Pientka's comment, revealed in courtroom testimony Monday, was part of a conflicting narrative presented to jurors about the secrecy and urgency with which the FBI treated allegations related to the Putin-linked Alfa Bank. Those claims arrived at the bureau via Michael Sussmann, a cybersecurity attorney who represented the Democratic National Committee and the Hillary Clinton campaign, in the final weeks of the 2016 contest.

Special Counsel John Durham has charged Sussmann with falsely telling the bureau he had brought the Alfa Bank tip in his personal capacity, not on behalf of any of his clients — potentially affecting the FBI's handling of the tip. But Sussmann's defense team has emphasized that the bureau was well aware of Sussmann's ties to the Democratic Party and that the circumstances of the tip were irrelevant to the FBI's decision to pursue it and ultimately deem it unsubstantiated.

The ongoing trial is the first courtroom test of Durham's long-running investigation into the origins of the FBI's Trump-Russia investigation, and he's used the Sussmann prosecution to publicly disclose a broad swath of his case. Sussmann's team, though, has cast doubt on the allegations, describing them as a desperate effort to shoehorn salacious and misleading evidence into the public record.

So far, Sussmann's trial has featured testimony from a series of high-profile witnesses, including Democratic Party attorney Marc Elias, former Clinton campaign manager Robby Mook, and former senior FBI officials.

Despite Pientka's messages, other witnesses described the bureau's reaction to the Alfa Bank tip as relatively modest — a limited offshoot of a much broader and more urgent investigation of Russia's interference in the 2016 election and any evidence of the Trump campaign's involvement.

Indeed, current and former FBI witnesses seemed to have hazy memories of aspects of the Alfa Bank episode and indicated their recollections were heavily influenced by notes, emails, and messages they exchanged at the time, which have been unearthed by Durham's team.

Bill Priestap, who led the FBI's counterintelligence division in 2016, said he recalled regular briefings about the broader Trump-Russia investigation, known as Crossfire Hurricane, but that he didn't recall similar briefings on Alfa Bank.

"It was not something I was regularly briefed on, and if I recall correctly, at the end of the day, it didn't amount to much," said Priestap, who is now retired from the law enforcement agency. "It fizzled out."

Asked about Pientka's assessment that the leadership was "fired up," Priestap said he didn't recall that reaction from FBI leadership or from FBI Director James Comey, specifically.

Perhaps more significantly, the description of the FBI's handling of the Alfa Bank tip allowed Sussmann's attorneys to remind the jury about the significant alarm within the bureau about

182

connections between the Trump campaign and Russia, which were the subject of FBI and special counsel investigations for nearly three years.

Jurors saw an internal FBI intelligence report Monday that indicated the FBI viewed Alfa Bank as closely connected to Putin.

"As of 1998, Putin was on Alfa Bank's payroll," the report said, in addition to detailing other alleged links between the bank, its owners, and Putin.

Witnesses at Sussmann's trial continued to provide murky accounts of how FBI personnel were told to handle the issue of the DNC-connected cybersecurity lawyer when pursuing the allegations he had relayed.

Agent Ryan Gaynor said he was told that Sussmann's identity was considered "close-hold," but he did not recall being told why.

"If I was given any reason at the time, I do not remember what that was," Gaynor said.

Gaynor became the focal point of the Sussmann defense team's effort Monday to poke holes in the prosecution's case.

Gaynor provided two important pieces of evidence for prosecutors: claiming the existence of the "close hold" — which he says prevented him from sharing Sussmann's identity with the Chicago-based agents leading the investigation — and testifying that if he had been aware of Sussmann's potential motivations for lodging the allegations, he wouldn't have devoted his attention to the case, diverting from other matters.

But Sussmann's attorney Michael Bosworth hammered away at Gaynor's credibility, noting that the FBI agent's story shifted throughout multiple interviews with Durham's team, ultimately ending with the most incriminating version of the story that prosecutors deployed against Sussmann.

Bosworth noted that the account Gaynor gave during an October 2020 interview with Durham's prosecutors led to them warning him that he was no longer merely a witness in their probe but was now a subject of the investigation–meaning that he could face criminal charges.

"I was in significant peril," Gaynor said. "It is very concerning as a DOJ employee that now the Department of Justice is looking at you."

Gaynor said he was told his status was "in jeopardy" after he said he didn't recall any direction to other agents that they couldn't contact the person who delivered the server allegations to the FBI.

Gaynor said that after his interview, he re-read records related to the case and recalled that he had told others at the FBI about the "close hold" designation. Bosworth suggested that Gaynor changed his account to please prosecutors, but the agent said his recollections were refreshed by looking at his own notes.

Former FBI General Counsel James Baker testified last week that while he didn't widely share the details of Sussmann's role with others at the FBI, he did tell Priestap, who wrote it down. Baker said he didn't recall refusing to disclose the name to others at the FBI.

Heide and other agents in Chicago seeking to verify the claims asked if they could be told who provided the data and accompanying analytical white papers to the bureau.

"We really want to interview the source of this information. Any way we can track down who this guy is and how we're getting this information?" Heide wrote to Gaynor in an Oct. 3, 2016, email.

Testifying for the prosecution, Gaynor said he felt that revealing the source wasn't necessary at that point because agents were still trying to trace the alleged data links. He said they were ultimately determined to be spam email messages sent by a marketing server.

The FBI did reach out "discreetly" to a cybersecurity firm, Mandiant, and learned that the company looked into the allegations and found them to be without merit, Gaynor said. However, he testified that the FBI avoided other steps like interviewing outside technology experts because they feared that doing so would lead to reports, just prior to the presidential election, that the FBI was investigating the issue.

"The decision was made that doing an overt interview so close to the election could inadvertently impact the election," Gaynor said. "I believed that in a politically-charged environment that the ones and zeroes would answer the question of whether or not there was a national security threat." Gaynor said officials also had concerns that the FBI openly investigating might also discourage those who brought the matter to the FBI from going to the media.

"We're not supposed to engage in overt activities that could be interpreted to be dissuading people from engaging in First Amendment-protected speech," he said.

Sussmann's defense also spent considerable effort raising questions about Gaynor's credibility, questioning his memory of the events in question.

Defense attorney Michael Bosworth suggested that Gaynor's memory had evolved over time, particularly about the central issue in the case: whether Sussmann said he was bringing the so-called secret server allegations forward independent of the Clinton campaign or the DNC. Gaynor said he remembers having the impression during another conversation at the FBI in 2016 that the server information came from a lawyer who worked for the DNC but said he was bringing forward the information on his own.

Bosworth said the records of Gaynor's interviews by Durham's team, and of his grand jury testimony show Gaynor never mentioned that until he was in a meeting with prosecutors ten days ago.

"I don't believe that came up in an interview," Gaynor acknowledged.

"Never once?" Bosworth asked skeptically.

"Correct," said Gaynor.

Jurors also heard from a former FBI agent in Chicago, Allison Sands, who prepared a memo formally opening a counterintelligence investigation into the Alfa Bank server claims days after Sussmann brought them to Baker.

Under questioning by the prosecution, Sands said not knowing who the information came from or whether political partisans produced it may have led to the Bureau taking it more seriously than it should have.

"There wasn't even an opportunity for us to even do a sanity check on: Does it make sense for us to use more time and engagement?" she said.

However, Sands said she'd only been on the job for a little more than three months when she was instructed by a supervisor to open the investigation in the case, which she was told had "headquarters interest." As a result, the investigation was going to be opened regardless of what she thought, and briefings on developments were conducted twice a day, she said.

"Especially as a new agent, this was my most important thing," she said.

Sands also said both the opening and closing records for the investigation say the information came from the Department of Justice. That appears to be an error, perhaps garbling the fact that Sussmann was once a DOJ prosecutor.

"I still don't know 100 percent at all," Sands said.

Sands acknowledged that some cybersecurity agents within the FBI dismissed the alleged evidence from near the outset of the probe, with one saying in an instant message to her: "What a waste of time ... but a fun exercise."

As the trial entered its second week Monday, a dispute is also brewing over potential testimony by former New York Times reporter Eric Lichtblau. Witnesses have heard that the FBI sought to slow down a story Lichtblau was working on in the fall of 2016 about the alleged server links.

Sussmann's defense wants to call Lichtblau and has waived the confidentiality of any discussions Sussmann had with the journalist.

The defense has agreed not to delve into other matters, but Durham's prosecutors are not a party to that agreement and are arguing that they should be permitted to question Lichtblau about the full range of his reporting on the issue, including his interactions with other sources or experts such as a private investigation firm that looked into the subject for the Democrats, Fusion GPS.

"We think it's fair game to probe Mr. Lichtblau on the exact substance of that," Assistant Special Counsel Andrew DeFilippis told Judge Christopher Cooper before the jury was brought into the courtroom Monday. "These communications are highly probative."

Lichtblau's attorneys have argued that his testimony should be limited to his interactions with Sussmann.

Cooper signaled doubts Monday about whether prosecutors had done all they could to obtain such information or testimony without getting it from the reporter.

After DeFilippis noted that some of the people involved declined to speak with prosecutors, Cooper noted that the government could have forced them to do so by getting orders guaranteeing that their testimony wouldn't be held against them.

"You could've immunized them," the judge said.

Durham-Sussmann trial: Baker briefed Comey, and McCabe on alleged covert communications between Trump Org, Russia

Baker says the FBI was "already conducting an investigation" into alleged connections between the Trump campaign and Russia at the time of the Sussmann meeting in September 2016.

By Brooke Singman, Jake Gibson, David Spunt | Fox News

Fox News Flash top headlines for May 19

WASHINGTON, D.C. — Former FBI General Counsel James Baker on Thursday testified that he briefed then-FBI Director James Comey and Deputy Director Andy McCabe on allegations brought to him by Clinton campaign lawyer Michael Sussmann in September 2016, claiming a covert communications channel between the Trump Organization and a Kremlin-linked bank and confirmed that the FBI was "already conducting an investigation" into possible ties between Russia and then-candidate Donald Trump at the time of the Sussmann meeting.

During questioning by federal prosecutors Thursday morning, Baker repeatedly stressed that he believed Sussmann when he said he was acting as a concerned citizen in bringing the Trump-Russia allegations to the FBI and "not on behalf of any client."

Baker testified that upon receiving the information from Sussmann during their meeting on Sept. 19, 2016, which alleged what Baker described as a "surreptitious" communications channel between the Trump Organization and Russian-based Alfa Bank.

"The FBI was already conducting an investigation into alleged connections between the Trump campaign and Russians at this point in time, so that was a matter of great concern to all of us," Baker said.

Baker later testified that after the FBI investigated the allegations of a connection between the Trump Organization and Alfa Bank, they found that "there was nothing there."

Following Sept. 19, 2016, meeting with Sussmann, Baker said he immediately notified then-FBI Assistant Director for Counterintelligence Bill Priestap and later briefed Comey and McCabe.

"Here was another type of information between Trump and Russia that had come to me," Baker said, describing it as "concerning" and "time sensitive."

"It seemed to me of great urgency and great seriousness that I would want to make my bosses aware of this information," Baker said. "I think they were quite concerned about it."

"Trump, at the time, was a candidate for the office of the president of the United States, so the FBI is investigating allegations related to his potential interactions, and those people on his campaign, with the government of the Russian Federation," Baker said.

He added: "And that was of high, high importance to the FBI at this point in time."

Sussmann has been charged with making a false statement to the FBI when he told Baker in September 2016, less than two months before the presidential election, that he was not doing work "for any client" when he requested and attended a meeting where he presented "purported data and 'white papers' that allegedly demonstrated a covert communicates channel" between the Trump Organization and Alfa Bank, which has ties to the Kremlin.

Durham's team alleges Sussmann was, in fact, doing work for two clients: the Hillary Clinton campaign and a technology executive, Rodney Joffe. Following the meeting with Baker, Sussmann billed the Hillary Clinton campaign for his work.

Sussmann has pleaded not guilty to the charge.

Meanwhile, Baker testified that he was aware that Sussmann represented the Clinton campaign and the Democratic National Committee but stressed that he believed that he was not working "on behalf of any client." Baker said that he understood Sussmann to be bringing allegations to him from "serious cyber" people and was something separate from those Democratic entities.

When asked why he believed that, Baker testified: "Because he said he wasn't. He told me in his statement to me he wasn't there on behalf of any client."

DURHAM PROBE

Dem lawyer found not guilty of lying to FBI over alleged Trump-Russia link

MARK HOSENBALL

May 31, 2022, 11:51 AM

A federal jury on Tuesday found Michael Sussmann, a former lawyer at a firm that represented Hillary Clinton's campaign and the Democratic National Committee during the 2016 presidential campaign, not guilty of lying to a top FBI official over an alleged link between Donald Trump and a Russian bank linked to the Kremlin.

A jury foreperson told D.C. District Court Judge Christopher Cooper that jurors unanimously agreed to acquit Sussmann of the criminal charge. The courtroom reacted quietly to the announcement, and the judge then dismissed the jury.

The jury acquitted Sussmann of lying to the FBI about who he was representing when he presented the agency's lawyer with data and documents raising questions about alleged dealings between the Trump Organization and Russia's Alfa Bank.

In brief remarks to reporters while leaving the courthouse, Sussmann welcomed the verdict. "I told the truth to the FBI, and the jury clearly recognized that with their unanimous verdict," he said, adding that he was "relieved that justice ultimately prevailed in this case."

"I'm looking forward to getting back to work that I love," Sussmann said.

The verdict is a major setback for John Durham, the special prosecutor appointed by William Barr, Trump's attorney general, to look into the origins of federal investigations into alleged Russian interference in U.S. politics.

Durham, who sat in the courtroom during the trial, left the courthouse Tuesday without commenting to reporters. In a statement released by the Justice Department, he said: "While we are disappointed in the outcome, we respect the jury's decision and thank them for their service. I also want to recognize and thank the investigators and the prosecution team for their dedicated efforts in seeking truth and justice in this case."

The case, which is the first Durham brought to trial, presented dueling narratives about the early months of the FBI's investigation into Trump's ties to Russia and the role that Hillary Clinton's campaign played in feeding allegations — some of them unsubstantiated or since discredited — to the bureau.

According to prosecutors, Sussmann, a cybersecurity lawyer for the Clinton campaign, brought claims in September 2016 about a supposed pattern of computer messages between the Alfa Bank and the Trump Organization to the bureau's chief counsel in an effort to gin up an FBI probe that would serve as an "October surprise" that would damage Trump.

Prosecutors said Sussmann deliberately lied that he was not acting on behalf of any client when he was actually serving the interests of the Clinton campaign and another law firm client, cybersecurity researcher Rodney Joffe.

But the defense insisted that Sussmann went to the FBI as a public-spirited citizen who was genuinely concerned about the national security implications of potential communications between the Russians and Trump's business. (The FBI concluded that there was nothing nefarious about the alleged pattern of messages and that they may have been nothing more than computer spam.)

The key witness for Durham's prosecution team was James Baker, a longtime personal friend of Sussmann's who, during the run-up to the 2016 presidential election, was serving as the FBI's general counselor chief lawyer. Baker testified at the trial that Sussmann told him about the allegations during a meeting in September 2016 at FBI headquarters.

During the meeting, Sussmann handed Baker memory sticks and printed materials purportedly documenting the link between the Trump Organization and Alfa Bank. Baker testified, however, that he was "100% confident" that at the meeting, Sussmann told him he was not presenting the allegations on behalf of a law firm client.

Arguing that Sussmann actually was acting on behalf of Clinton's campaign and his private cybersecurity client, prosecutors presented the jury with records from Perkins Coie, the law firm where Sussmann worked in 2016, which showed that the firm billed the Clinton campaign for meetings and other communications involving Sussmann during the summer and fall of 2016 that were related to what the billing records described as a "confidential project."

Baker and prosecutors did not produce any written notes of the meeting, which is the focus of Durham's indictment. In a conversation after the meeting with Bill Priestap, the FBI's counterintelligence chief, Baker testified that he told Priestap that the issue Sussmann had raised was urgent and that Sussmann was not representing a particular client.

Notes of the conversation taken by Priestap, which were entered into evidence, stated that, on the one hand, Sussmann told Priestap that he was "not doing this for any client." But Priestap then went on to note that Sussmann "represents DNC, Clinton Foundation, etc."

In the wake of Sussmann's meeting and Baker's conversation with Priestap, the FBI soon opened a full-scale investigation of the allegations Sussmann had presented to Baker, in which an FBI cyber squad based in Chicago played a major role. The field agents looking into the allegations concluded fairly quickly that the allegations of a serious link between the Trump Organization and the Russian bank lacked backup evidence.

Some witnesses said that if the FBI had known that the principal and original sources of the allegations had connections to the Clinton campaign or the Democratic National Committee, the bureau might have been more hesitant to launch a full-scale investigation.

Defense lawyers at one point indicated to Cooper, the judge, that Sussmann was considering testifying in the case, but ultimately he did not appear on the witness stand.

Durham's team told the jury that less than 12 hours after meeting with Baker, Sussmann recorded 4.5 hours of work on written material and a confidential project. But a prosecutor said that two months later, Sussmann moved to revise the billing records to show he billed the Clinton campaign for 3.3 hours of work that day.

The defense team told the jury that Sussmann had told Baker to take whatever action he thought was appropriate. "There is a difference between having a client and going somewhere on their behalf," defense lawyer Sean Berkowitz argued.

In his instructions to the jury, Cooper said that in order to convict Sussmann of the offense, the jury must have been convinced by the evidence that he knowingly and willingly made a fraudulent or fictitious statement to Baker intended to deceive the FBI and that the statement was "material" to the FBI investigation.

Marc Elias, a Perkins Coie lawyer who was the top attorney for Clinton's campaign and was called as a prosecution witness, told the jury that he did not authorize or instruct Sussmann to take the Alfa Bank allegations to the FBI. Clinton's 2016 campaign manager Robbie Mook, who testified for the defense, also said he had not authorized Sussmann to tell the FBI about Alfa Bank and Trump.

Last year, Kevin Clinesmith, a onetime FBI lawyer, pleaded guilty after Durham charged him with doctoring an email that other officials used to justify spying on a Trump campaign adviser. Clinesmith was sentenced to only a year of probation.

A false statement indictment brought by Durham is still pending against Igor Danchenko, a Russian who was a source for some of the allegations against Trump, including allegations related to Russia, which were laid out in a controversial anti-Trump "dossier" prepared for the Clinton campaign operatives in 2016 by former British intelligence officer Christopher Steele.

Published *May 19, 2022 12:40pm EDT*

Second Scandal Hillary Clinton

What Hillary Clinton's email scandal is really about

By Alvin Chang@alv9nalvin@vox.com *Updated Oct 28, 2016, 1:14pm EDT*

The FBI announced Friday it was **renewing their investigation** into Hillary Clinton's use of private email servers after deciding not to press charges in September after their first round of investigation. For months, the "email scandal" has haunted Clinton's campaign, and conservatives have used it to feed into a larger message: that Clinton can't be trusted.

Just look at all the stories Breitbart puts under the "**Hillary Clinton Email Scandal**" tag. It's a mishmash of stories — including ones about her hiding health problems, which have nothing to do with email. All the articles together weave a storyline that seems more egregious than the individual parts that make it up.

But at the core of it, there really are problems. And we should be able to talk about those problems with clarity. **Vox's Jeff Stein created a concise framework** about the scandal, so we made a cartoon that pinpoints the primary issues at play.

First, let's walk through what actually happened

To understand what exactly it was that Clinton did, we need to understand what an email server is. It's the technical underpinning of the controversy.

It's basically like a post office. It's a computer connected to the internet that sorts through letters and delivers them.

And much like a post office, the server has three jobs:

Don't let intruders see your mail.

Verify senders are who they are they are.

Make sure it gets delivered to the recipient, not other people.

So that means the person in charge of this digital post office — a postmaster, if you will — has an important job. This person has to implement security features to make sure the server can do its job well. This person also has control of the messages coming in and out.

Normally for the secretary of state, this responsibility would've belonged to people in the federal government who have the expertise to maintain email systems.

But when Clinton was offered an email address on State Department servers, her staff refused. Instead, they **used a server in Clinton's home**, maintained part-time by two staffers.

We don't know why Clinton used a private server. **She says** it's because she only wanted to carry one mobile device — and since State Department devices only allowed for State Department email addresses to be added to the phone, she chose to use her personal device and her personal email. But this is what led to multiple problems — and multiple storylines around those problems.

Problem 1: Clinton made herself vulnerable to hackers

Clinton's private server had **several potential points of vulnerability**, so it was possible for spies to hack into the system — both to view messages or to reroute messages.

There was no evidence that Clinton's server was breached, but hackers are good at covering their tracks, and the **FBI hints that it thinks** a hack was likely.

On her servers, an FBI investigation in July 2016 found **81 email chains** that ranged from confidential to top secret, but intelligence agencies overuse these labels, so it's unclear if revealing these emails would've actually threatened national security.

There was **"gross negligence,"** as the FBI points out.

Eventually, Clinton's staff hired a private company to run their email servers in Secaucus, New Jersey. This was a more secure option but still not ideal. In fact, if we're talking about pure security, it's unclear what the best option would've been.

Even if Clinton used the State Department mail servers, it wouldn't have been foolproof. The State Department has been **accused of having poor institutional security**, which manifested in a **2015 hack of its unclassified email system**.

Problem 2: Clinton may have been trying to skirt transparency laws

Email servers are physical computers — and the person who controls those servers has your data. When Congress was investigating the terrorist attacks in Benghazi, it asked the State Department for Clinton's emails. But the department **only turned over eight emails**. That's because Clinton's emails were on her own server, not theirs.

That said, Republicans have insisted Clinton did this to avoid having her emails released or subject to the Freedom of Information Act. In other words, the accusation is that she did it so the public couldn't see her communication. This goes to motive, which means it's difficult to prove either way, and anyone who claims otherwise is speculating.

But the idea that she is actively trying to hide her communication feeds into a more absurd accusation that we should dismiss: that Clinton tried to delete emails from her server during the House's Benghazi investigation. Vox's Jeff Stein has a good timeline showing why **this theory makes no sense**.

What has been lumped into this storyline: the idea that Clinton is compromised

There is another completely separate case that has to do with emails but gets thrown into the "Clinton email scandal" bin as well. The right-wing transparency group Judicial Watch obtained emails between top officials at the State Department and the Clinton Foundation.

Some think it shows that people who donated to the Clinton Foundation received preference from the secretary of state's office. There is no evidence to back this up, and this storyline has nothing to do with her private server. It's another story, like the one about her health, that is woven into the larger narrative that Clinton can't be trusted.

What we should actually take away from this

There are two primary problems with Clinton's decision to use a private email server.

The first is cybersecurity. The FBI concluded that Clinton and her staff were not fully aware of the threat they exposed themselves to. It points to a larger problem with government, where public servants outside the intelligence agencies often treat cybersecurity as an afterthought. Last year, Congress did **pass a law** that allows private companies to work with the government to improve cybersecurity, and this year President Barack Obama created a **commission on cyber defense**. But there are still massive **political** and **bureaucratic** problems that the next executive has to deal with.

The second issue is transparency. The Obama administration has been among the **"least transparent"** in recent history, even though Obama promised greater transparency during his 2008 campaign. The administration has kept entire **government programs secret, stonewalled public records requests**, and viciously **gone after those who leak information**.

An Associated Press investigation found that the backlog of public records requests **grew 55 percent** under Obama. So whatever Clinton's motive was for the private server, it brings up concerns about whether the public's right to know will continue to erode under the next administration. And Donald Trump **hasn't exactly been the model** for transparency either, though he has **tried to create the illusion of it**.

Both of these are massive, nuanced issues that raise real questions about how Clinton or Trump would govern. It touches on two increasingly relevant issues about our data — how we should protect it and who should be able to see it. But they've been reframed into this amorphous narrative about trust.

Correction: A previous version of this story said Clinton's server contained 81 emails ranging from "classified to top secret," but it should read "confidential to top secret." There are **three levels of classified information**: confidential, secret, and top secret.

The Washington Times - Friday, October 28, 2016
The FBI has renewed its investigation into Hillary Clinton's secret emails, Director James Comey told Congress in a new letter Friday, heightening the stakes for the Democratic presidential nominee with less than two weeks before Election Day.

Mr. Comey said his agents learned of new emails "pertinent" to their probe while working on an unrelated case. He said his agents need to review those messages to see whether they contain classified information and whether they affect his previous decision.

In July, Mr. Comey announced that while he determined Mrs. Clinton did mishandle classified information, she was too inept to know the risks she was running, so he couldn't prove she did it intentionally — undercutting a criminal case.

Washington Times
Clinton e-mails Comey
"Director Comey's letter refers to emails that have come to light in an unrelated case, but we have no idea what those emails are, and the Director himself notes they may not even be significant," he said.

"It is extraordinary that we would see something like this just 11 days out from a presidential election."

Mrs. Clinton's running mate, Sen. Tim Kaine of Virginia, said Mr. Comey owes the campaign and the public a "clearer accounting" of the new information.

"When you do this 11 days before a presidential election, and you don't provide many details — but details apparently are being given by the FBI to the press — this is very, very troubling," Mr. Kaine told VICE News. "We hope that the director, and we really think that he should, give a clearer accounting of exactly what's going on right now."

Mr. Podesta predicted the FBI would come to the same conclusion this time as it did in July, and he pointedly noted that the letter was sent to eight Republican committee chairmen in Congress. But it was also carbon-copied to the ranking Democrats.

Mr. Comey did not explain in his letter what information the new emails contain, how long it will take to evaluate them, nor how they were obtained.

The New York Times reported Friday that the emails were snagged as part of an investigation into former Rep. Anthony Weiner and allegations he sent illicit messages through text and social media applications to a 15-year-old North Carolina girl. The paper reported that law enforcement officials seized at least one device shared by Mr. Weiner and his now estranged wife, Huma Abedin — a top personal aide to Mrs. Clinton. The couple announced they were separating in August amid Mr. Weiner's involvement in another sexting scandal, but before the 15-year-old girl's allegations surfaced.

As Mrs. Clinton's top personal aide, Ms. Abedin also had an account on the secret Clinton email server and exchanged classified information with her boss.

Mr. Comey said he was briefed on the new emails on Thursday and felt it was important to promptly alert Congress of investigators' latest efforts.

Republican leaders who were among the eight recipients of the letter called for further disclosures by the FBI director, with Sen. Richard C. Shelby urging him to provide additional information before voters go to the polls on Nov. 8.

"While I am pleased that the FBI is re-opening this case in light of new information, it is imperative that the Bureau immediately evaluate the material to complete this investigation," said Mr. Shelby, chairman of the Appropriations Subcommittee on Commerce, Justice, Science, and Related Agencies. "The American people are electing their next Commander-in-Chief only days from now, and they deserve to know the conclusion of your review prior to Election Day."

Sen. Charles E. Grassley, who as chairman of the Senate Judiciary Committee was one of the letter's recipients, said Mr. Comey owes the country more of an explanation about what he's found.

"The letter from Director Comey was unsolicited and, quite honestly, surprising. But it's left a lot more questions than answers for both the FBI and Secretary Clinton," the Iowa Republican said.

GOP presidential nominee Donald Trump, campaigning in Manchester, New Hampshire, said he respected the FBI for reversing itself.

"Perhaps, finally, justice will be done," he said.

For her part Mrs. Clinton, campaigning in Cedar Rapids, Iowa, did not address the issue, instead sticking doggedly to her stump speech of attacks on Mr. Trump mixed with a plea to voters to focus on issues.

President Obama, who has been saddled by association with Mrs. Clinton, who was serving him during the time she maintained her secret email server, did not respond to questions shouted by reporters Friday afternoon as he left the White House on a campaign trip to Florida to stump for Mrs. Clinton and Democratic Senate candidate Patrick Murphy.

Briefing reporters on Air Force One, deputy press Secretary Eric Schultz said Mr. Obama President Obama expects the FBI to "follow the facts wherever they lead" and to act "irrespective of politics."

Mr. Schultz said the new email development does not affect Mr. Obama's support of Mrs. Clinton.

Libertarian candidate Gary Johnson said on CNN, "Obviously, the FBI didn't do this lightly. There has to be something there."

He lamented the prospect of "a president-elect under criminal investigation."

"That's what's going to now be the case if she is elected," he said. "She will control those jobs [in the Justice Department] that control how this issue moves forward, which points to a special prosecutor. This is a mess. It's a mess. I think Trump is toast, so is Hillary moving forward as president-elect? Four years of this? Ugh."

Congressional Republicans, who have been at odds with Mr. Trump on many issues, found common ground with their nominee in attacking Mrs. Clinton.

"This decision, long overdue, is the result of her reckless use of a private email server and her refusal to be forthcoming with federal investigators," said House Speaker Paul D. Ryan.

He again called for the Obama administration to suspend the classified intelligence briefings Mrs. Clinton is getting as the Democratic nominee.

And Sen. John Cornyn, Texas Republican, wondered whether the Justice Department would now convene a grand jury to pursue the case.

He said the FBI had already cleared Mrs. Clinton of mishandling classified information, so to reopen the case suggests either potential new evidence of intent to mishandle secrets or other potential criminal questions.

"Originally, FBI focused on 'classification rules' and not broader issues related to government records/obstruction of justice. Will they now?" Mr. Cornyn tweeted.

An FBI spokesman declined Friday to comment on the reopening of the investigation.

The revelation that the investigation is continuing comes too late to affect the 16 million voters who have already cast ballots in absentee or in-person voting.

Republicans have said Mrs. Clinton appeared to mislead Congress in her sworn testimony to the Benghazi probe in 2015.

The staggering reversal by Mr. Comey comes as Mrs. Clinton is reeling from another electronic scandal — the revelations from emails obtained and posted by WikiLeaks from Mr. Podesta's personal email address.

Mrs. Clinton refused to use an official state.gov email account during her four years as secretary, instead setting up an account on a server she kept at her home in New York. That arrangement shielded her emails from public disclosure for six years, thwarting open-records laws.

She belatedly turned over some 30,000 messages she deemed government-related, but the FBI recovered thousands of others she didn't — including some that contained classified information His new announcement Friday threatened to upend the presidential campaign.

John Podesta, Mrs. Clinton's campaign chairman, demanded Mr. Comey explain what new information he's found and blamed Republicans for "browbeating" the FBI into Friday's decision.

• *Andrea Noble and Dave Boyer contributed to this article.*

• *Stephen Dinan can be reached at sdinan@washingtontimes.com.*

Part Twelve

Conflicts of Interest FBI Officials

Terry McAuliffe's PAC donated to campaign of FBI official's wife Jill McCabe
By Julia Boccagno
OCTOBER 24, 2016 / 1:01 PM / CBS NEWS

Virginia Gov. Terry McAuliffe's political action committee donated nearly $500,000 to the election campaign of Dr. Jill McCabe--the wife of an FBI official who helped oversee the investigation into Hillary Clinton's use of a private email server while secretary of state, the Wall Street Journal first reported.

And the Virginia Democratic Party, a group over which the governor has considerable influence, contributed an additional $207,778 in the form of mailers, the campaign finance records indicate. The WSJ noted that this put donations from entities directly under McAuliffe or influenced by him at nearly $700,000, which was about a third of McCabe's total campaign fundraising efforts. McAuliffe also reportedly recruited McCabe for the race.

Spokespeople for McAuliffe and the FBI told the WSJ that there weren't any ties between McCabe's state senate run--which she ultimately lost to incumbent Republican Dick Black--and the promotion of her husband, Andrew McCabe, to deputy director at the FBI months after Jill McCabe's campaign ended. McAuliffe's spokesperson told the WSJ that "any insinuation that his support was tied to anything over than his desire to elect candidates who would help pass his agenda is ridiculous."

STROZK Wife Assistant Director SEC

Melissa Hodgman Named Associate Director in SEC Enforcement Division
FOR IMMEDIATE RELEASE
2016-217

Special Agent Roth- Note the Date Oct.14, 2016, which is right in the middle of the Trump-Russia Collusion operation by the FBI.

Washington *D.C., Oct. 14, 2016* —The Securities and Exchange Commission today announced that Melissa Hodgman had been named Associate Director in the SEC's Enforcement Division. Ms. Hodgman succeeds Stephen L. Cohen, who left the SEC in June.

Ms. Hodgman began working in the Enforcement Division in 2008 as a staff attorney. She joined the Market Abuse Unit in 2010 and was promoted to Assistant Director in 2012.
EXECUTIVE LEADERSHIP
SABINA MENSCHEL
PARTNER, PRESIDENT & CHIEF OPERATING OFFICER
Our People/Sabina Menschel
Sabina Menschel is Partner, President, and Chief Operating Officer of Nardello & Co. and is based in Washington, DC. A graduate of Harvard College and Harvard Business School, Sabina has more than 20 years of experience leading domestic and international due diligence, litigation support, fraud, and global asset recovery investigations on behalf of financial institutions, law firms, and multinational corporations. In addition to leading complex investigations for clients, she works with the firm's executive committee to manage the firm's operations globally.
EXPERIENCE PRIOR TO NARDELLO & CO.
REPRESENTATIVE MATTERS

- Sabina helped lead Nardello & Co.'s assignment as the independent investigator pursuing a settlement between the State of New York and leading tobacco manufacturers. The mandate was to assess and review the information provided by the interested parties and carry out an independent review to determine the number of Native American tribal cigarette packs sold to New York consumers on which the state did not collect excise tax. The assessment and investigation included open-source research, surveillance, and source inquiries, as well as econometric analysis and considered evidence provided by the tobacco manufacturers and New York State. Nardello & Co.'s findings determined the credit to which each tobacco company was entitled toward their payments to the State of New York under the 1998 Tobacco Master Settlement Agreement.
- Sabina led investigations into proxy slates submitted by dissident shareholders. This work included: exposing integrity issues, identifying undisclosed liabilities such as regulatory issues and significant litigation matters, documenting misrepresentations, misstatements, or material omissions in securities filings; uncovering conflicts of interest; and identifying undisclosed relationships and affiliations to establish that adverse parties were acting in concert.

JUST THE FACTS

Education
- MBA, Harvard Business School
- AB, Harvard College

Awards
- 2018 Women in Investigations, Global Investigations Review

Professional Affiliations
- Charina Endowment Fund, director
- Goddard Riverside Community Center, board member
- Only Make Believe, the DC regional board member

Behind Every Deep State Puppet Is A Powerful Woman

The Deep State

has thrust the "feminazi" movement on America. The Deep State practices what they preach. The Deep State seems to have a gender equality clause in the performance of their anti-government duties.

Behind some Deep State puppets, who are all male, lies their Deep State wives, who have considerably more power than their spouses.

Look at the facts of Supreme Court nominee Brett Kavanaugh, Deputy Attorney General Rod Rosenstein's wife,

Lisa Barsoomian,

Assistant Head of FBI Counterintelligence, Bill Priestap's wife, who is the Associate Director of the SEC and now the wife of

Peter Strzok,

Melissa Hodgson... we have a pattern in which the publicly known figure, a male, has a more powerful spouse who operates in the shadows.

All of them have direct links back to the criminal behaviors of either the Clintons or the Bush family.

Think about this reality... America has become an intended monarchy in which the royal families are the Bush and Clinton, families.

President of the United States: George H. W. Bush 1988-1992

President of the United States: Bill Clinton 1992-2000

President of the United States: George W. Bush 2000-2008

Of course, we had a brief respite when we had Obama, or whoever he really is from 2008-2016, with Hillary Clinton, Secretary of State from 2008-2012.

Hillary Clinton was to be coronated President and serve from 2016-2024, but that didn't happen the way they planned.

When we look at the Bush/Clinton dynasty and their puppet, Obama, we were to have 36 years of fascist, totalitarian, and anti-American rule.

This would have been enough to sink the country. Fortunately, the bulk of the American voters woke up long enough to elect Donald Trump, and now the Deep State and their controllers are in a state of panic.

The point of this article is to shine light upon powerful males who are Deep State minions with their wives, causing more damage to America in the background. For anyone who doubts the veracity, power, and true existence of a Deep State, this article should help you understand in to expose this undeniable reality.

Brett Kavanaugh-Supreme Court Nominee

Here's a brief recitation of the relationship between Kavanaugh's wife and the Bush family with a little Bush family criminal background mixed in:

- Prescott Bush was found guilty of violating the Trading with the Enemies Act in WWII. Because he was the head of the USO, he was given a pass because of the potential damage done to service personnel morale

- George Bush and 9/11 and the Presidential order that led to the concealment of physical evidence after the investigation was concluded. This is what LBJ did with the JFK assassination evidence.

- George H. W. Bush was the director of the CIA and, according to most researchers, was involved in the assassination of JFK. He was the first to label the New World Order and predicted its success.

- Neil Bush was involved in a dirty bank scandal in Colorado. President George H. W. Bush closed Fitzsimmons Army Hospital and Lowry AFB in retaliation for Colorado legal authorities pursuing Neil Bush.

- The Bush crime family syndicate were major players in the growth of the private prison system, which has ripped off all 50 states and their taxpayers billions of dollars.

This is only a small sample of the Bush family corruption. The Kavanaughs were and remained very close allies. The Bush family attended the Kavanaugh's wedding. They remain close personal friends to this day.

Rod Rosenstein's Wife, Lisa Barsoomian:

Lisa Barsoomian is the poster child for the Deep State. Sometimes, the best clues are the ones hiding in plain sight, as evidenced by this tweet.

"Enter Lisa Barsoomian, wife of Rod Rosenstein...an attorney who has represented...Bill Clinton 40 times, and Hillary Clinton 17 times"

#ReleaseTheMemo

Mueller, Rosenstein, and Comey: The Three Amigos from the Deep State | Roger Stone - Stone Cold Truth

Mueller, Rosenstein, and Comey: The Three Amigos from th...
By Roger Stone There is a longtime and incestuous relationship between the fixers who have been tasked with taking down President Trump, under the fake narrative of enforcing the law.
stonecoldtruth.com

4:52 PM - 1 Feb 2018

1,709 Retweets 1,688 Likes

96   1.7K   1.7K

In organized crime terminology, we could categorize at least some of Barsoomian's duties as that being the "cleaner".

The cleaner is called to the scene of the crime and erases all the evidence. She has certainly served in that capacity. She is the ultimate shot blocker as she has also served as the guardian of the Deep State secrets gate.

In the days of Janet Reno's tenure as the Attorney General, privacy activists' requests for information about the FBI Carnivore email surveillance system were received and ignored by the FBI.

It took court action to partially release a small part of the program, which showed that the system erased 4th Amendment protections for all Americans.

Representing the FBI and their resistance to the FOIA requests… was Lisa Barsoomian.

Along with her boss, R. Craig Lawrence, Barsoomian is the go-to attorney for the Democratic establishment in D.C. She's made her living defending the swamp and preventing the public from gaining access to information about the Obama administration that they are entitled to under the Freedom of Information Act.

Rosenstein & atty./wife Lisa Barsoomian

Lisa has represented the FBI in blocking FOIA requests filed by Judicial Watch. She's also represented the CIA in blocking requests.

Barsoomian also represented Bill Clinton in a lawsuit in '98

— Jenna (@jenn_mallory) December 14, 2017

"But more importantly, she's the **wife of Rod Rosenstein,** the **man who appointed Robert Mueller.**

Rosenstein supervises Mueller and has to approve all of his subpoenas, his depositions, and his indictments." This is a case of who is watching the watcher.

Because Barsoomian represents what strongly appears to be Deep State interests, the relationship between Rosenstein and Mueller is inappropriate because of the personal conflict of interest. This is not only unethical; it is illegal in the world of special prosecutors.

The Assistant Attorney General, Rod Rosenstein, is supposed to be non-partisan and impartial, but in reality, he has deep family and financial connections to the Clintons, Obama, and the Democratic Party, as expressed through his wife, Lisa Barsoomian.

Look at this graphic:

This

Assistant Attorney General Rod Rosenstein's wife, Lisa Barsoomian, represented Bill Clinton
Original lawsuit: *Hamburg v. Clinton,* 98-cv-01459-TPJ
Appeal: 99-5053: *Hamburg, Al v. Clinton, William J.,* Case No. 99-5053
Note: **All court filings are removed from court dockets**

1:98-cv-01459-TPJ HAMBURG v. CLINTON
Thomas Penfield Jackson, presiding
Date filed: 06/11/1998
Date terminated: 01/25/1999
Date of last filing: 08/17/1999

Plaintiff: AL HAMBURG
Defendant: WILLIAM J. CLINTON represented by Lisa Barsoomian Email:Lisa.Barsoomian@nih.gov

WILLIAM J. CLINTON
President of the United States

Added: 06/11/1998
(Defendant)

represented by

Lisa Barsoomian
**See Ms. Barsoomian file
Lisa.Barsoomian@nih.gov
Assigned: 08/28/1998
LEAD ATTORNEY
ATTORNEY TO BE NOTICED

graphic illustrates the duplicity of the Deep State and what a major player Lisa Barsoomian has become to that interest.

Rosenstein's wife represented Bill Clinton in 1998—**court records are missing—ethics rules required his recusal**

"Lisa H. Barsoomian, U.S. Attorney, wife of Assistant Attorney General Rod J. Rosenstein. Graduated from Georgetown Law. Protégé of James B. Comey and Robert S. Mueller. Represented Bill Clinton in 1998.

Researchers say **the Internet has been cleansed of information about Barsoomian,** which is a telltale sign of a protected rogue Deep State C.I.A. operative.

She has specialized in opposing Freedom of Information Act requests on behalf of the intelligence community.

Rod J. Rosenstein has no business being involved at all in the Hillary Clinton/DNC-triggered Russia investigation, much less the selection of his mentor Robert S. Mueller, III as special counsel.

This is because Rosenstein's wife, Lisa H.Barsoomian represented Bill Clinton in 1998 with her boss, R. Craig Lawrence (6,459 cases, 321 pgs. 10 MB).

Lawrence also represented Mueller (3 times), Comey (5 times), Obama (45 times), Kathleen Sebelius (56 times), Bill (40 times), and Hillary (17 times) between 1991-2017.

Barsoomian has herself represented the FBI (at least 5 times). Barsoomian's loyalties are clearly tainted. How could such "pillow talk" not have influenced Rosenstein?

This clearly violates the "appearance of impropriety" lawyer rules. It's obvious they owe their careers as U.S. Attorneys to Comey, Mueller, Obama, Bush, and the Clintons and CAN NOT, therefore, be impartial.

The other odd situation is Barsoomian's NIH (National Institute of Health) email address, even though she's been involved in 100's of cases representing the D.C. Office of the U.S. Attorney.

Is she on loan from the C.I.A.? The C.I.A. often uses another organization as "cover" for their activities."

Bill Priestap-Assistant Director of Counterintelligence of the FBI (Peter Strzok's boss). In an article that received absolutely no attention, Patriots for Truth uncovered stunning accounts of Priestap's wife and her role in the Deep State:

On Dec. 21, 2015, then FBI Director James B. Comey appointed William E. "Bill" Priestap as Assistant Director of the Counterintelligence Division at the FBI.

Priestap is embroiled in the current cover-up of the FBI's lies and disinformation to Senate and House Judiciary, Intelligence, and Homeland Security Committees.

Investigations into Priestap's background reveal some new clues about his Deep State mission at the FBI.

Priestap's biographies are uniformly **missing the name(s) of the universities where he claims to have received education and business degrees.**

Clearly, the identities of those schools are being intentionally withheld. What is Mr. Priestap and the FBI hiding?

Sabina Menschel, Priestap's spouse, has a suspiciously successful intelligence resume for a 1999 Harvard College graduate, then a 2005 Harvard MBA grad. Menschel IMMEDIATELY became a Special Advisor at the FBI (Jul. 2005)—a truly magical rise.

Sabina Menschel—one of the world's most feared private spies, wife of FBI Counterintelligence Chief E.W. "Bill" Priestap, and billionaire heiress to Goldman Sachs fortune.

Sabina attended Harvard Business School during the tenure of Lawrence "Larry" Summers as President, where his chief of staff was Marne L. Levine (Deutch).

Levine (Deutch) is related to Bill Clinton's disgraced and pardoned (with fraudster Marc Rich) C.I.A. Director Philip J. Deutch. She later was senior advisor to Hillary Clinton (2009), then became a **vice president at Facebook.**

She is now a **chief operating officer at Instagram** (owned by Facebook)—another truly magical rise. (Editor's Note: Instagram has begun to practice the extreme censorship of Google, its puppet Youtube, Facebook, and Twitter. Once again, the spouse is more interesting than the Deep State puppet husband).

Note that Facebook Boy King Mark Zuckerberg started attending Harvard in 2001, along with Sabina—another amazing coincidence.

Sabina's father, Richard L. Menschel, funded Harvard X in 2013—one of the primary M.O.O.C. ("Massive Open Online Course.") platforms for the takeover of higher education by the Deep State shadow government. (It's essentially Common Core for higher education…..)

Given the Deep State's intensive anti-Trump virtue signaling, the control of Priestap and his family over M.O.O.C. renders him hopelessly compromised.

These relationships alone prove that **Bill Priestep cannot be impartial in the Trump-Russia investigation.**

It's beginning to look like Facebook's Mark Zuckerberg is no more than a Harvard (Deep State) groomed cutout designed to control the reach of the Independent Media.

Rhetorical question: Has anyone taken a serious look at the background of Mark Zuckerberg's wife?

Melissa Hodgman: Peter Strzok's Betrayed Wife:

Peter Strzok is a disgraced FBI counterintelligence traitor. A lot of focus has fallen on disgraced FBI agent Peter Strzok, but who his wife is is an even more important question.

Her name is Melissa Hodgman. Here's what one investigation reported about Hodgman.

Melissa Hodgman is an impressive person, professionally speaking. She presently holds the position of the Associate Director of the Enforcement Division of the Securities Exchange Commission, and she has held that position since October 14, 2016. In total, Hodgman has been with the SEC for a total of 10 years, and she is the wife of the traitor, Peter Strzok. The couple met while both were attending college at Georgetown University.

Just like Lisa Barsoomian, Hodgman is likely a CIA undercover agent as she graduated from the School of Foreign Service at Georgetown, which has served as a fertile recruiting ground for various US intelligence agencies.

And just like Lisa Barsoomian, Hodgman provided partial cover for Hillary Clinton during the FBI"s so-called investigation into the scandalous and illegal emails Hillary Clinton.

What a nice, tight, little circle the Deep State is. This is classic Deep State persona, and Strzok's wife is clearly a CIA cut-out with direct ties to Clinton.

If this were a movie, nobody would believe it. This is a case of the modern-day Stepford Wives, but the roles are reversed. The men are controlled by the more powerful women in the background. With Kavanaugh and Rosenstein's wives, we had an interesting coincidence. But, with the addition of Strzok's and Priestap's wives, we have a VERY clear pattern.

Were these marriages of convenience designed by the intelligence apparatuses of the Deep State? It looks like it very much. This clearly demonstrates just how "deep" the Deep State swamp really is.

ABOUT THE AUTHOR

Steve Allen

About the Author: I'm just another voice crying out for truth in a society that seems content to stay asleep. My name is Steve Allen, and I'm the publisher of ThinkAboutIt.news and ThinkAboutIt.online. The controversial opinions in this article are either mine alone or a guest author and do not necessarily reflect the views of the websites where my work is republished. This article may contain opinions on political matters, but it is not intended to promote the candidacy of any particular political candidate. The material contained in this article is for general information purposes only. Those responding to this article by making comments are solely responsible for their viewpoints, and those viewpoints do not necessarily represent the viewpoints of Steve Allen or the operators of the websites where my work is republished. Follow me on social media, Facebook, and Twitter, and any way that you can share these articles with others is a great help. Thank you, Steve

BRUCE OHR Wife worked for GPS
Wife of demoted Justice Department official worked for 'dossier' firm
By David K. Li
December 11, 2017 10:40pm
 Updated
AP

The wife of a Justice Department official who was demoted for failing to disclose his meeting with the Trump "dossier" author worked for the opposition research firm behind the document, according to a published report Monday.

Bruce Ohr, who lost his senior-level post as associate deputy attorney general, is the husband of Nellie Ohr — an employee during the 2016 election for Fusion GPS, which compiled the anti-Trump document, officials told Fox News Channel.

It wasn't immediately clear what Nellie Ohr did for Fusion GPS or if she had any ties to the salacious document. In public biographies, Nellie Ohr has been listed as a Russia expert, according to Fox.

Bruce Ohr had two titles until last week, as director of the Organized Crime Drug Enforcement Task Force but more significantly as associate deputy attorney general — a top post that put him just four office doors away from his boss, Deputy AG Rod Rosenstein.

But he lost the bigger gig after it was disclosed that he had secret meetings with Fusion GPS founder Glenn Simpson and former British spy Christopher Steele, who penned the dossier, according to FNC.

Republican lawmakers want to know if Fusion GPS — funded by the Democratic National Committee and the Hillary Clinton campaign — played any role in FBI surveillance of Carter Page, a Trump campaign adviser.

Age made contradictory statements on his connections to Russians during the campaign before invoking his Fifth Amendment rights to House Intelligence Committee investigators in November.

Twitter hires former FBI lawyer James Baker to join the legal team
Twitter hires former top FBI lawyer involved in Trump campaign investigation
At Twitter, Baker is likely to be heavily involved in defending the company's protections under Section 230 of the Communications Decency Act
By **Tyler Olson FOXBusiness**

Twitter has brought on the former FBI attorney who was at the center of some of the controversies in the investigation into the Trump campaign during the 2016 presidential election, including the decision to surveil then-campaign aide Carter Page 2016.

Sean Edgett, Twitter's general counsel, announced Monday evening that former FBI counsel James Baker would join the social media company as a deputy general counsel. The hiring comes as the social media company is under fire for alleged bias against conservatives. The company was specifically called out by the Trump administration in an executive order ostensibly aimed at stymieing "censorship" from social media platforms.

"Thrilled to welcome @thejimbaker to @Twitter as Deputy General Counsel," Edgett tweeted Monday. "Jim is committed to our core principles of an open internet and freedom of expression and brings experience navigating complex, global issues with a principled approach."

Baker replied that he is happy to join the social media company.

"Thanks @edgett!! I'm very excited to join such a great team @Twitter doing such important work," he said. 'Glad to be on board."

Perhaps the most notable element of Baker's involvement in the Russia investigation was his work on the Foreign Intelligence Surveillance Act (FISA) warrant application against Page, which relied largely on an unverified anti-Trump dossier compiled by former British spy Christopher Steele.

That warrant application has been the subject of multiple investigations relating to the Russia probe, including a DOJ inspector general review, which revealed no political bias in the launch of the investigation but found at least 17 "significant inaccuracies and omissions" in the Page applications.

Baker even drew a reference in a Trump tweet in January 2019 after he told House investigators he was involved in the Page FISA application.

Whoops! We couldn't access this Tweet.

"Former FBI top lawyer James Baker just admitted involvement in FISA Warrant and further admitted there were IRREGULARITIES in the way the Russia probe was handled," Trump said. "They relied heavily on the unverified Trump 'Dossier' paid for by the DNC & Clinton Campaign."

SOCIAL MEDIA COMPANIES DISTRUSTED BY MOST AMERICANS ON CONTENT DECISIONS: POLL

Now U.S. Attorney John Durham is running a criminal probe into alleged federal surveillance abuses, and Attorney General William Barr told Fox News last week he is "very troubled" by what Durham has found about "familiar names."

At Twitter, Baker is likely to be heavily involved in defending the company's protections under Section 230 of the Communications Decency Act, which limits liability for platforms like Twitter that allows anyone to publish content.

Trump and some Republicans had argued that because they remove and modify content in an allegedly politically biased way -- like when Twitter flagged multiple Trump tweets with warning labels -- Twitter and other social media platforms that take similar actions should lose their Section 230 protections.

But some have argued that such a move would do more harm than good, particularly for the Republicans complaining about censorship.

"Without Section 230, companies would be forced to choose between heavily restricted access and completely open access. In the latter case, content moderators would no longer be able to remove objectionable content like pornography, violence, terrorist propaganda from Facebook, Twitter, or YouTube," Patrick Hedger recently argued in The Bulwark, an anti-Trump conservative publication.

He added: "Eliminating Section 230 would reinvigorate the dominant media gatekeepers that conservatives have long accused of shutting out their viewpoints. For web services focused on user-created content that do manage to survive, content-moderation practices would be significantly tightened—and ultimately enforced by the same people being accused of anti-conservative bias today."

News' Adam Shaw, Brooke Singman, Bret Baier, and Ronn Blitzer contributed to this report.

PART
TRUMP TAX

TRUMP MANHATTAN TAX CHARGES
CRIME FEB. 24, 2022

What Really Happened to the Criminal Investigation of Trump?
By Ankush Khardori

The Manhattan district attorney's office's criminal investigation into Donald Trump's financial dealings has been thrown into disarray following the news Wednesday that the two prosecutors leading the investigation had abruptly resigned. A rough account already seems to have taken shape in the press — two well-respected lawyers in New York's white-collar legal circles were stymied by a newly elected DA who has been distracted by a barrage of bad press since taking office — but there remain considerable reasons to maintain a healthy degree of caution about this version of events as we get our first glimpses behind the scenes of a very consequential mess.

A lively evening newsletter about everything that just happened.

The prosecutors who quit, Carey Dunne and Mark Pomerantz, were frustrated that after the previous DA, Cyrus Vance Jr., "authorized them to seek an indictment against the former president, the new district attorney appeared uninterested," according to the Washington *Post*, which quoted a spokesperson who said the investigation is "ongoing." (Some disclosures: I used to work at the same firm as Pomerantz but did not know him well; I interned for Bragg in law school and have maintained a cordial relationship with him since.)

A source familiar with the investigation provided an account to me that is broadly consistent with what has been reported elsewhere but sheds greater light on the breakup. Vance had repeatedly said last year that he was going to make final charging decisions before leaving office at the end of December, reiterating it to the *Financial Times* in late September. Around that time, Vance was disinclined to move forward against Trump, skeptical about the strength of the proposed case Dunne and Pomerantz had put together. By early December, though, Dunne and Pomerantz persuaded him there was a chargeable case. At that point, Vance authorized the two to move forward with their investigation with an eye toward indicting Trump after Bragg took over on January 1, using the second of two grand juries that had been empaneled over the course of the investigation.

The charges that might have been brought against Trump were not entirely clear, according to the source, who says prosecutors were considering some combination of charges based on falsifying business records (which can either be a misdemeanor or the lowest-level felony offense in New York), conspiring to falsify Trump's financial condition (in relation, perhaps, to lenders, tax authorities, or insurers), or committing criminal fraud such as grand larceny, which sounds dramatic but can also be charged at a variety of felony levels.

After Bragg took over, Dunne and Pomerantz briefed him on the investigation both in writing and in a series of meetings. The *Post* reported that Bragg "appeared not to be focused on the case," taking his time to engage with the duo and their work, and the two prosecutors decided to stop presenting evidence to the grand jury once they realized a case against Trump was not a foregone conclusion. According to the source, things finally reached a breaking point when Bragg recently told the two that he did not think they had sufficient evidence to indict Trump — at least not yet — and that they should instead wait to see if they could develop or obtain additional evidence. Trump, for instance, might opt not to invoke his right against self-incrimination and could provide testimony to the New York State Attorney General's Office in its civil probe that could be used against him in the DA's criminal case. Another possibility was Trump Organization CFO Allen Weisselberg, who was indicted last summer for tax fraud along with the company, might decide to cooperate if he were ultimately convicted.

At that point, Dunne and Pomerantz concluded they were at an impasse. They believed they had a provable case against Trump — not a slam dunk, necessarily, but a case that was worthy of being brought right now, according to the source familiar with their thinking. Bragg disagreed, and Dunne and Pomerantz did not want to wait longer since there did not appear to be any dramatic breakthroughs on the horizon of the sort Bragg felt were necessary. Weisselberg, for instance, is currently scheduled to go on trial in late summer, but that could be pushed back.

It is worth taking a very big step back in order to consider a wider range of possibilities than the one many members of the media and legal commentariat appear to have been quick to adopt. Within hours of the first report of Dunne and Pomerantz's departure, the editor-in-chief of *Rolling Stone* tweeted that a "source" had told him, "Bragg appeared to back away from the politically-sensitive probe after the D.A.'s 'day 1' memo got so much blowback," but the source's claim makes little sense. If the knock on Bragg is that he is too soft on crime, then charging Trump would provide powerful evidence to the contrary, and indeed, anyone who had followed the DA's race even cursorily last year knows Bragg campaigned on the increase in white-collar criminal enforcement. Some of the many legal pundits who became prominent during the Trump years — people whose entire public profile depends on the existence of Trump and his legal troubles — also quickly weighed in with dubious and occasionally offensive innuendo. On Wednesday evening, George Conway resurfaced an unrelated and unconfirmed allegation of misconduct against Bragg. Harry Litman, a former federal prosecutor and columnist for the Los Angeles *Times* who repeatedly and incorrectly assured people that a criminal fraud prosecution against Trump "would be easy," referred to Dunne and Pomerantz as "top dogs" and urged his followers to "remember that Bragg has very little experience with and feel for state corruption cases," a claim he later had to walk back in a "correction of sorts" because it is false.

Bragg has, after all, worked as a line prosecutor and as a supervisor on complex investigations both as a federal prosecutor and in the New York State Attorney General's Office. There is no reason to doubt that his strictly professional judgment is just as reliable as that of Dunne or Pomerantz, even if he happens not to fit the profile of the mostly white, well-to-do lawyers in the elite legal circles of New York and Washington, D.C., who seem to more easily attain the status of being "very seasoned and respected" (as Litman described Pomerantz), despite Bragg managing the considerable feat of becoming the first Black DA in Manhattan.

In fact, so far as we can tell, based on the public record, there are some considerable reasons to doubt the strength of the case that Dunne and Pomerantz were able to build against Trump and that they may have presented to Bragg. This was always going to be a challenging case: Any complex financial fraud is hard to prosecute, particularly one that involves lawyers, accountants, or other advisers, all of whom can complicate the ability of investigators to establish that any particular person — much less the head of the relevant enterprise — intended to defraud third parties. The fact that the real estate and hospitality industries appear to have more flexible and debatable methodologies of financial appraisal and valuation would make things harder.

Of course, Trump's longtime accountants at Mazars recently disclaimed responsibility for a decade's worth of Trump's financial statements, but that development was not as clear-cut as many in the media sought to portray it. In any suspected financial fraud scheme involving records that went through an accountant or auditors, there are, very broadly speaking, two possibilities: The advisers were either lied to, or they were in on the scheme. Mazars clearly wanted to dissociate itself from that second possibility, but even so, the firm carefully noted that it had "not concluded that the various financial statements, as a whole, contain material discrepancies" — not exactly a ringing endorsement of a criminal fraud theory.

Then there is the question of key witnesses against Trump. Having evidently tried and failed to flip Weisselberg, Dunne and Pomerantz's best potential cooperator against Trump appears to have been Michael Cohen, and the source familiar with the prosecutors' thinking argued Cohen would have been a viable cooperator. But it would be extremely risky to use Cohen — a serial liar who did not fully cooperate with federal prosecutors in Manhattan and who has undercut his own value as a witness by spending much of the past two years railing against Trump in cable-news interviews and on his own podcast — as the key witness in a case against Trump without many other credible sources of independent corroboration.

How about other documentary evidence? Trump, of course, famously does not use email and loves destroying hard copies of documents. This would not foreclose the possibility of a criminal case based in large part on paper since prosecutors could try to establish Trump's knowledge of misrepresentations in his various financial submissions by establishing that he had been apprised of the truth at around the same time as misrepresentations were delivered to third parties he signed off on, but this is one more very real evidentiary challenge in any prosecution of Trump.

If this was roughly the state of the investigation, it is not hard to see how reasonable and experienced prosecutors might come to different conclusions about the merits of pushing forward. By themselves, any one of the issues noted above would be significant but potentially manageable; all of them together would make for a serious uphill battle. In any long-term investigation, the sunk-cost fallacy — the tendency to push forward after a significant investment of time and resources even when it makes little sense — is a major problem, and that is one reason it can be helpful for someone who is clear-eyed and who has less of a mental and emotional stake in the proceedings to make an independent judgment about the strength of the evidence and the merits of moving full speed ahead.

In this case, it appears that person may have ended up being Bragg himself — the man who would ultimately bear the risk and responsibility of an unprecedented criminal prosecution against a former president.

Part Thirteen

The Deep State Is Real

Exposing the 'deep state' is one of Trump's greatest achievements

Eddie Scarry *12/21/2020*
More Than 50 Former Intel Officials Say Hunter Biden Smear Smells Like Russia

Spies who lie: 51 'intelligence' experts refuse to apologize for discrediting true Hunter Biden story

Here Are the 51 Senior Intelligence Officials Who LIED About the Hunter Biden Laptop from Hell

By Daniel - 2 weeks ago

Now that the "paper of record" (the New York Times) has FINALLY confirmed what the rest of us have known for the last two years, the New York Post is having a field day.

You see, the New York Post is the news source that first published the truth about Hunter Biden's laptop from hell.

But 51 members of the intelligence community wrote and signed a letter saying that the story was false.

They called it "Russian misinformation."

Do the officials who tried to flip the 2020 election feel any regret for their actions? The Post reached out to those who signed the letter. Most would not answer the question. A few doubled-down, including Clapper. No remorse. No shame. And no apologies:

Mike Hayden, former CIA director, now an analyst for CNN: Didn't respond.

Jim Clapper, former director of national intelligence, now CNN pundit: "Yes, I stand by the statement made AT THE TIME, and would call attention to its 5th paragraph. I think sounding such a cautionary note AT THE TIME was appropriate."

Leon Panetta, former CIA director, and defense secretary, now runs a public policy institute at California State University: Declined comment.

Special Agent Roth- I always had great respect for Leon Panetta.

John Brennan, former CIA director, now analyst for NBC and MSNBC: Didn't respond.

Thomas Fingar, former National Intelligence Council chair who now teaches at Stanford University: Didn't respond.

Rick Ledgett, former National Security Agency deputy director, now a director at M&T Bank: Didn't respond.

John McLaughlin, former CIA acting director who now teaches at Johns Hopkins University: Didn't respond.

Michael Morell, former CIA acting director, now at George Mason University: Didn't respond.

Mike Vickers, former defense undersecretary for intelligence, now on board of BAE Systems: Didn't respond.

Doug Wise, former Defense Intelligence Agency deputy director who teaches at the University of New Mexico: Didn't respond.

Nick Rasmussen, former National Counterterrorism Center director, now executive director, Global Internet Forum to Counter Terrorism: Didn't respond.

Russ Travers, former National Counterterrorism Center acting director: "The letter explicitly stated that we didn't know if the emails were genuine, but that we were concerned about Russian disinformation efforts. I spent 25 years as a Soviet/Russian analyst. Given the context of what the Russians were doing at the time (and continue to do — Ukraine is just the latest example), I considered the cautionary warning to be prudent."

Andy Liepman, former National Counterterrorism Center deputy director: "As far as I know, I do [stand by the statement], but I'm kind of busy right now."

John Moseman, former CIA chief of staff: Didn't respond.

Larry Pfeiffer, former CIA chief of staff, now senior advisor to The Chertoff Group: Didn't respond.

Jeremy Bash, former CIA chief of staff, now an analyst for NBC and MSNBC: Didn't respond.

Rodney Snyder, former CIA chief of staff: Didn't respond.

Glenn Gerstell, former National Security Agency general counsel: Didn't respond.

David Priess, former CIA analyst, and manager: "Thank you for reaching out. I have no further comment at this time."

Pam Purcilly, former CIA deputy director of analysis: Didn't respond.

Marc Polymeropoulos, former CIA senior operations officer: Didn't respond.

Chris Savos, former CIA senior operations officer: Didn't respond.

John Tullius, former CIA senior intelligence officer: Didn't respond.

David A. Vanell, former CIA senior operations officer: Didn't respond.

Kristin Wood, former CIA senior intelligence officer, now non-resident fellow, Harvard: Didn't respond.

David Buckley, former CIA inspector general: Didn't respond.

Nada Bakos, former CIA analyst, and targeting officer, now senior fellow, Foreign Policy Research Institute: Didn't respond.

Patty Brandmaier, former CIA senior intelligence officer: Didn't respond.

James B. Bruce, former CIA senior intelligence office: Didn't respond.

David Cariens, former CIA intelligence analyst: Didn't respond.

Janice Cariens, former CIA operational support officer: Didn't respond.

Paul Kolbe, former CIA senior operations officer: Didn't respond.

Peter Corsell, former CIA analyst: Didn't respond.

Brett Davis, former CIA senior intelligence officer: Didn't respond.

Roger Zane George, former national intelligence officer: Didn't respond.

Steven L. Hall, former CIA senior intelligence officer: Didn't respond.

Kent Harrington, former national intelligence officer: Didn't respond.

Don Hepburn, former national security executive, now president of Boanerges Solutions LLC: "My position has not changed any. I believe the Russians made a huge effort to alter the course of the election . . . The Russians are masters of blending truth and fiction and making something feel incredibly real when it's not. Nothing I have seen really changes my opinion. I can't tell you what part is real and what part is fake, but the thesis still stands for me, that it was a media influence hit job."

Timothy D. Kilbourn, former dean of CIA's Kent School of Intelligence Analysis: Didn't respond.

Ron Marks, former CIA officer: Didn't respond.

Jonna Hiestand Mendez, former CIA technical operations officer, is now on board the International Spy Museum: "I don't have any comment. I would need a little more information."

Emile Nakhleh, former director of CIA's Political Islam Strategic Analysis Program, now at the University of New Mexico: "I have not seen any information since then that would alter the decision behind signing the letter. That's all I can go into. The whole issue was highly politicized, and I don't want to deal with that. I still stand by that letter."

Gerald A. O'Shea, former CIA senior operations officer: Didn't respond.

Nick Shapiro, former CIA deputy chief of staff and senior adviser to the director: Didn't respond.

John Sipher, former CIA senior operations officer: Declined to comment.

Stephen Slick, former National Security Council senior director for intelligence programs: Didn't respond.

Cynthia Strand, former CIA deputy assistant director for global issues: Didn't respond.

Greg Tarbell, former CIA deputy executive director: Didn't respond.

David Terry, former National Intelligence Collection Board chairman: Couldn't be reached.

Greg Treverton, former National Intelligence Council chair, now a senior adviser at the Center for Strategic and International Studies: "I'll pass. I haven't followed the case recently."

Winston Wiley, former CIA director of analysis: Couldn't be reached.

I don't know about you, but to me, this sounds like a coordinated cover-up by the Deep State.

They did everything they could to make sure Donald Trump could be re-elected, so they plotted behind his back.

SPECIAL AGENT ROTH. *Boys and Girls of the CIA. Didn't you review the receipt from the computer repair shop? The receipt had an FBI case number on it, not a KGB case number. The case number listed the United States federal criminal classification: money laundering, not a Russian criminal classification. Did you have the certainty that it was a "slam dunk" like the Saddam Hussein weapons of mass destruction in Iraq that the CIA reported in Iraq?* If the CIA can't find the information regarding an FBI case number, how can they find information regarding highly sophisticated covert enemy operations?

MSNBC's Beschloss, former CIA director Hayden 'suggest' Trump be executed for having nuclear documents

Hayden and Beschloss reacted to a report that Trump may have retained nuclear documents after his term

By Gabriel Hays

MSNBC contributor and historian Michael Beschloss posted a tweet on Thursday evening recounting historical figures who had been executed for sharing U.S. nuclear secrets with foreign governments, and a former CIA chief shared the post with his own approving tweet.

Conservative commentator Jerry Dunleavy accused Beschloss of "suggesting that Trump should be executed," considering it was posted just after the Washington Post piece speculating that the FBI had raided Trump's Mar-a-Lago estate to find missing nuclear documents.

The Washington Post exclusive from Thursday afternoon attempted to offer more details as to what the FBI was searching for at Mar-a-Lago on Monday, as Attorney General Merrick Garland remained tight-lipped about it in his address to the nation.

The report cited sources speaking "on the condition of anonymity," claiming, "Classified documents relating to nuclear weapons were among the items FBI agents sought in a search of former President Donald Trump's Florida residence on Monday, according to people familiar with the investigation."

FBI RAID ON TRUMP LATEST PROOF OF DEMOCRAT WAR ON RULE OF LAW

The claim sent shock waves through social media and became a top Twitter trend. Several hours after the claim in the exclusive report, Beschloss provided some historical context as to what happens to those who illegally retain and pass off nuclear information to non-U.S. entities. Tweeting out an image of Soviet spies Julius and Ethel Rosenburg, he wrote, "Rosenbergs were convicted for giving U.S. nuclear secrets to Moscow and were executed June 1953."

The tweet caught the attention of the former director of both the National Security Agency and the CIA, Michael Hayden. Hayden, who is also a retired four-star Air Force general and whose tenure in the intelligence agencies happened under former Presidents Barack Obama, George W. Bush and Bill Clinton, commented on Beschloss's post.

"Sounds about right," the ex-CIA head tweeted.

Washington Examiner reporter Jerry Dunleavy slammed Hayden's comment and accused the retired general and former NSA director of "suggesting that Trump should be executed."

Dunleavy wrote, "NBD [no big deal] just a former NSA & CIA Director (who also was among the dozens of ex-intel officials who signed the infamous October 2020 Hunter Biden laptop letter) out here suggesting that Trump should be executed."

SUSSMAN TRIAL

Bombshell testimony that Hillary Clinton personally authorized giving a reporter since-debunked data about Donald Trump and Russia was part of a chess-like maneuver to "protect the queen," a former US Justice Department official told The Post.

Jim Trusty said former Clinton campaign manager Robby Mook's revelation Friday, which he quickly tried to walk back, actually meshed with other testimony in which Mook and former campaign general counsel Marc Elias both said they were unaware campaign lawyer Michael Sussmann planned to also provide the information to the FBI.

Both men said they would have objected to the move if they'd known.

"The strategy here is Protect the Queen!" Trusty said in an email.

"The Knights (lawyers for the campaign, the campaign manager) have drawn the line – admitting what they have to admit."

Meanwhile, Mook and Elias also suggested that Clinton "was shocked, shocked by Sussmann going to the FBI," said Trusty, now a Washington, DC, lawyer.

"Legal representation simply does not work that way. You don't 'free-lance' a visit to the FBI while billing your client for the time," he said.

"The defense is basically trying to provide a fig leaf to any partisan jurors who want to acquit."

Former FBI agent Thomas J. Baker also told The Post, "Whether Sussmann is found guilty or innocent or otherwise, [special counsel John] Durham has already laid out, in my opinion, what these people were up to and what was going on.

"It paints a picture of Sussmann colluding with other people to drag the FBI into an investigation and besmirch a presidential candidate," he said.

Sussmann is on trial in DC on a single count of lying to the government when he met with then-FBI general counsel James Baker on Sept. 19, 2016 and handed over material that purportedly showed a cyber backchannel between a Trump Organization server and Russia's Alfa Bank.

He's accused of falsely denying that he was acting on behalf of a client, with Durham alleging that Sussmann was actually working for both the Clinton campaign and Rodney Joffe, a tech executive who told him about the data.

Thomas Baker suggested that the case against Sussmann would be stronger if not for changes instituted by former FBI Director Robert Mueller following the Sept. 11 terror attacks.

"Moving away from being a law enforcement agency to an intelligence agency changed the culture," he said.

"Part of it is they got rid of agent-executives and replaced them with so-called professionals, like James Baker."

Thomas Baker said that if James Baker had been an FBI agent, he would have immediately summoned another agent to participate in the meeting with Sussmann and prepare an official report known as a "302."

Former FBI general counsel James A. Baker, who received Alfa-Bank information from Michael Sussmann, departs United States District Court. Ron Sachs – CNP

Instead, James Baker didn't take any notes and left what Sussmann said open to question, he said.

In a recent column for The Post, former Manhattan federal prosecutor Andrew McCarthy said Durham "appears to have built a case of historic consequence" that "portrays the Clinton campaign as guilty of perhaps the worst dirty trick in the history of American presidential elections."

"The problem for Durham is that, because he hasn't charged the big scheme, Judge [Christopher] Cooper is restricting what he can tell the jury about it," McCarthy wrote.

"On the other hand, to the extent Sussmann directly participated in the scheme, the court is inclined to let Durham prove it."

A different view was put forward on Thursday by US Rep. Matt Gaetz (R-Fla.), who tweeted: "I do not believe that the Durham trial of Michael Sussmann is about convicting Michael Sussmann at all."

"I think the entire purpose of this trial is to inoculate the FBI and the DOJ against the charge that they were in on the Russia Hoax," he said.

Sussmann's trial is set to resume Monday. If convicted as charged, he'd face a maximum sentence of five years in prison.

Jurors hear contrasting stories about FBI handling of Trump-Russia secret server claims

Agents detail their role in the probe prompted by attorney Michael Sussmann, who is on trial over an alleged false statement to the FBI.

By Josh Gerstein And Kyle Cheney
05/23/2022 02:27 PM EDT
Updated: 05/23/2022 05:39 PM EDT

An FBI agent involved in the investigation of links between Donald Trump and Russia told a colleague weeks before the 2016 election that top FBI brass were "fired up" about since-discredited allegations of a secret communications channel between Trump and a Russian bank with close ties to Vladimir Putin.

"People on 7th floor to include Director are fired up about this server," FBI agent Joseph Pientka wrote in an internal instant message to another agent working on the issue, Curtis Heide, on Sept. 21, 2016. "Reach out and put tools on… it is [sic] not an option — we must do it."

But Pientka's comment, revealed in courtroom testimony Monday, was part of a conflicting narrative presented to jurors about the secrecy and urgency with which the FBI treated allegations related to the Putin-linked Alfa Bank. Those claims arrived at the bureau via Michael Sussmann, a cybersecurity attorney who represented the Democratic National Committee and the Hillary Clinton campaign, in the final weeks of the 2016 contest.

Special Counsel John Durham has charged Sussmann with falsely telling the bureau he had brought the Alfa Bank tip in his personal capacity, not on behalf of any of his clients — potentially affecting the FBI's handling of the tip. But Sussmann's defense team has emphasized that the bureau was well aware of Sussmann's ties to the Democratic Party and that the circumstances of the tip were irrelevant to the FBI's decision to pursue it and ultimately deem it unsubstantiated.

The ongoing trial is the first courtroom test of Durham's long-running investigation into the origins of the FBI's Trump-Russia investigation, and he's used the Sussmann prosecution to publicly disclose a broad swath of his case. Sussmann's team, though, has cast doubt on the allegations, describing them as a desperate effort to shoehorn salacious and misleading evidence into the public record.

So far, Sussmann's trial has featured testimony from a series of high-profile witnesses, including Democratic Party attorney Marc Elias, former Clinton campaign manager Robby Mook, and former senior FBI officials.

Despite Pientka's messages, other witnesses described the bureau's reaction to the Alfa Bank tip as relatively modest — a limited offshoot of a much broader and more urgent investigation of Russia's interference in the 2016 election and any evidence of the Trump campaign's involvement.

Indeed, current and former FBI witnesses seemed to have hazy memories of aspects of the Alfa Bank episode and indicated their recollections were heavily influenced by notes, emails, and messages they exchanged at the time, which have been unearthed by Durham's team.

Bill Priestap, who led the FBI's counterintelligence division in 2016, said he recalled regular briefings about the broader Trump-Russia investigation, known as Crossfire Hurricane, but that he didn't recall similar briefings on Alfa Bank.

"It was not something I was regularly briefed on, and if I recall correctly, at the end of the day, it didn't amount to much," said Priestap, who is now retired from the law enforcement agency. "It fizzled out."

Asked about Pientka's assessment that the leadership was "fired up," Priestap said he didn't recall that reaction from FBI leadership or from FBI Director James Comey, specifically.

Perhaps more significantly, the description of the FBI's handling of the Alfa Bank tip allowed Sussmann's attorneys to remind the jury about the significant alarm within the bureau about connections between the Trump campaign and Russia, which were the subject of FBI and special counsel investigations for nearly three years.

Jurors saw an internal FBI intelligence report Monday that indicated the FBI viewed Alfa Bank as closely connected to Putin.

"As of 1998, Putin was on Alfa Bank's payroll," the report said, in addition to detailing other alleged links between the bank, its owners, and Putin.

Witnesses at Sussmann's trial continued to provide murky accounts of how FBI personnel were told to handle the issue of the DNC-connected cybersecurity lawyer when pursuing the allegations he had relayed.

Agent Ryan Gaynor said he was told that Sussmann's identity was considered "close-hold," but he did not recall being told why.

"If I was given any reason at the time, I do not remember what that was," Gaynor said.

Gaynor became the focal point of the Sussmann defense team's effort Monday to poke holes in the prosecution's case.

Gaynor provided two important pieces of evidence for prosecutors: claiming the existence of the "close hold" — which he says prevented him from sharing Sussmann's identity with the Chicago-based agents leading the investigation — and testifying that if he had been aware of Sussmann's potential motivations for lodging the allegations, he wouldn't have devoted his attention to the case, diverting from other matters.

But Sussmann's attorney Michael Bosworth hammered away at Gaynor's credibility, noting that the FBI agent's story shifted throughout multiple interviews with Durham's team, ultimately ending with the most incriminating version of the story that prosecutors deployed against Sussmann.

Bosworth noted that the account Gaynor gave during an October 2020 interview with Durham's prosecutors led to them warning him that he was no longer merely a witness in their probe but was now a subject of the investigation–meaning that he could face criminal charges.

"I was in significant peril," Gaynor said. "It is very concerning as a DOJ employee that now the Department of Justice is looking at you."

Gaynor said he was told his status was "in jeopardy" after he said he didn't recall any direction to other agents that they couldn't contact the person who delivered the server allegations to the FBI.

Gaynor said that after his interview, he re-read records related to the case and recalled that he had told others at the FBI about the "close hold" designation. Bosworth suggested that Gaynor changed his account to please prosecutors, but the agent said his recollections were refreshed by looking at his own notes.

Former FBI General Counsel James Baker testified last week that while he didn't widely share the details of Sussmann's role with others at the FBI, he did tell Priestap, who wrote it down. Baker said he didn't recall refusing to disclose the name to others at the FBI.

Heide and other agents in Chicago seeking to verify the claims asked if they could be told who provided the data and accompanying analytical white papers to the bureau.

"We really want to interview the source of this information. Any way we can track down who this guy is and how we're getting this information?" Heide wrote to Gaynor in an Oct. 3, 2016, email.

Testifying for the prosecution, Gaynor said he felt that revealing the source wasn't necessary at that point because agents were still trying to trace the alleged data links. He said they were ultimately determined to be spam email messages sent by a marketing server.

The FBI did reach out "discreetly" to a cybersecurity firm, Mandiant, and learned that the company looked into the allegations and found them to be without merit, Gaynor said. However, he testified that the FBI avoided other steps like interviewing outside technology experts because they feared that doing so would lead to reports, just prior to the presidential election, that the FBI was investigating the issue.

"The decision was made that doing an overt interview so close to the election could inadvertently impact the election," Gaynor said. "I believed that in a politically-charged environment that the ones and zeroes would answer the question of whether or not there was a national security threat."

Gaynor said officials also had concerns that the FBI openly investigating might also discourage those who brought the matter to the FBI from going to the media.

"We're not supposed to engage in overt activities that could be interpreted to be dissuading people from engaging in First Amendment-protected speech," he said.

Sussmann's defense also spent considerable effort raising questions about Gaynor's credibility, questioning his memory of the events in question.

Defense attorney Michael Bosworth suggested that Gaynor's memory had evolved over time, particularly about the central issue in the case: whether Sussmann said he was bringing the so-called secret server allegations forward independent of the Clinton campaign or the DNC. Gaynor said he remembers having the impression during another conversation at the FBI in 2016 that the server information came from a lawyer who worked for the DNC but said he was bringing forward the information on his own.

Bosworth said the records of Gaynor's interviews by Durham's team, and of his grand jury testimony show Gaynor never mentioned that until he was in a meeting with prosecutors ten days ago.

"I don't believe that came up in an interview," Gaynor acknowledged.

"Never once?" Bosworth asked skeptically.

"Correct," said Gaynor.

Jurors also heard from a former FBI agent in Chicago, Allison Sands, who prepared a memo formally opening a counterintelligence investigation into the Alfa Bank server claims days after Sussmann brought them to Baker.

Under questioning by the prosecution, Sands said not knowing who the information came from or whether political partisans produced it may have led to the Bureau taking it more seriously than it should have.

"There wasn't even an opportunity for us to even do a sanity check on: Does it make sense for us to use more time and engagement?" she said.

However, Sands said she'd only been on the job for a little more than three months when she was instructed by a supervisor to open the investigation in the case, which she was told had "headquarters interest." As a result, the investigation was going to be opened regardless of what she thought, and briefings on developments were conducted twice a day, she said.

"Especially as a new agent, this was my most important thing," she said.

Sands also said both the opening and closing records for the investigation say the information came from the Department of Justice. That appears to be an error, perhaps garbling the fact that Sussmann was once a DOJ prosecutor.

"I still don't know 100 percent at all," Sands said.

Sands acknowledged that some cybersecurity agents within the FBI dismissed the alleged evidence from near the outset of the probe, with one saying in an instant message to her: "What a waste of time ... but a fun exercise."

As the trial entered its second week Monday, a dispute is also brewing over potential testimony by former New York Times reporter Eric Lichtblau. Witnesses have heard that the FBI sought to slow down a story Lichtblau was working on in the fall of 2016 about the alleged server links.

Sussmann's defense wants to call Lichtblau and has waived the confidentiality of any discussions Sussmann had with the journalist.

The defense has agreed not to delve into other matters, but Durham.'s prosecutors are not a party to that agreement and are arguing that they should be permitted to question Lichtblau about the full range of his reporting on the issue, including his interactions with other sources or experts such as a private investigation firm that looked into the subject for the Democrats, Fusion GPS.

"We think it's fair game to probe Mr. Lichtblau on the exact substance of that," Assistant Special Counsel Andrew DeFilippis told Judge Christopher Cooper before the jury was brought into the courtroom Monday. "These communications are highly probative."

Lichtblau's attorneys have argued that his testimony should be limited to his interactions with Sussmann.

Cooper signaled doubts Monday about whether prosecutors had done all they could to obtain such information or testimony without getting it from the reporter.

After DeFilippis noted that some of the people involved declined to speak with prosecutors, Cooper noted that the government could have forced them to do so by getting orders guaranteeing that their testimony wouldn't be held against them.

"You could've immunized them," the judge said.

Durham-Sussmann trial: Baker briefed Comey, and McCabe on alleged covert communications between Trump Org, Russia

Baker says the FBI was "already conducting an investigation" into alleged connections between the Trump campaign and Russia at the time of the Sussmann meeting in September 2016.

By Brooke Singman, Jake Gibson, David Spunt | Fox News

WASHINGTON, D.C. — Former FBI General Counsel James Baker on Thursday testified that he briefed then-FBI Director James Comey and Deputy Director Andy McCabe on allegations brought to him by Clinton campaign lawyer Michael Sussmann in September 2016, claiming a covert communications channel between the Trump Organization and a Kremlin-linked bank, and confirmed that the FBI was "already conducting an investigation" into possible ties between Russia and then-candidate Donald Trump at the time of the Sussmann meeting.

During questioning by federal prosecutors Thursday morning, Baker repeatedly stressed that he believed Sussmann when he said he was acting as a concerned citizen in bringing the Trump-Russia allegations to the FBI and "not on behalf of any client."

Baker testified that upon receiving the information from Sussmann during their meeting on Sept. 19, 2016, which alleged what Baker described as a "surreptitious" communications channel between the Trump Organization and Russian-based Alfa Bank.

"The FBI was already conducting an investigation into alleged connections between the Trump campaign and Russians at this point in time, so that was a matter of great concern to all of us," Baker said.

Baker later testified that after the FBI investigated the allegations of a connection between the Trump Organization and Alfa Bank, they found that "there was nothing there."

Following Sept. 19, 2016, meeting with Sussmann, Baker said he immediately notified then-FBI Assistant Director for Counterintelligence Bill Priestap and later briefed Comey and McCabe.

Former FBI Deputy Director Andrew McCabe and former FBI Director James Comey are among those whose conduct is being reviewed in Justice Department Inspector General Michael Horowitz's report. (Reuters)

"Here was another type of information between Trump and Russia that had come to me," Baker said, describing it as "concerning" and "time sensitive."

"It seemed to me of great urgency and great seriousness that I would want to make my bosses aware of this information," Baker said. "I think they were quite concerned about it."

"Trump, at the time, was a candidate for the office of the president of the United States, so the FBI is investigating allegations related to his potential interactions, and those people on his campaign, with the government of the Russian Federation," Baker said.

He added: "And that was of high, high importance to the FBI at this point in time."

Sussmann has been charged with making a false statement to the FBI when he told Baker in September 2016, less than two months before the presidential election, that he was not doing work "for any client" when he requested and attended a meeting where he presented "purported data and 'white papers' that allegedly demonstrated a covert communicates channel" between the Trump Organization and Alfa Bank, which has ties to the Kremlin.

Durham's team alleges Sussmann was, in fact, doing work for two clients: the Hillary Clinton campaign and a technology executive, Rodney Joffe. Following the meeting with Baker, Sussmann billed the Hillary Clinton campaign for his work.

Sussmann has pleaded not guilty to the charge.

Meanwhile, Baker testified that he was aware that Sussmann represented the Clinton campaign and the Democratic National Committee but stressed that he believed that he was not working "on behalf of any client." Baker said that he understood Sussmann to be bringing allegations to him from "serious cyber" people and was something separate from those Democratic entities.

When asked why he believed that Baker testified: "Because he said he wasn't. He told me in his statement to me he wasn't there on behalf of any client."

Dem lawyer found not guilty of lying to FBI over alleged Trump-Russia link

Mark Hosenball

May 31, 2022, 11:51 AM

A federal jury on Tuesday found Michael Sussmann, a former lawyer at a firm that represented Hillary Clinton's campaign and the Democratic National Committee during the 2016 presidential campaign, not guilty of lying to a top FBI official over an alleged link between Donald Trump and a Russian bank linked to the Kremlin.

A jury foreperson told D.C. District Court Judge Christopher Cooper that jurors unanimously agreed to acquit Sussmann of the criminal charge. The courtroom reacted quietly to the announcement, and the judge then dismissed the jury. The jury acquitted Sussmann of lying to the FBI about who he was representing when he presented the agency's lawyer with data and documents raising questions about alleged dealings between the Trump Organization and Russia's Alfa Bank.

In brief remarks to reporters while leaving the courthouse, Sussmann welcomed the verdict. "I told the truth to the FBI, and the jury clearly recognized that with their unanimous verdict," he said, adding that he was "relieved that justice ultimately prevailed in this case."

"I'm looking forward to getting back to work that I love," Sussmann said.

The verdict is a major setback for John Durham, the special prosecutor appointed by William Barr, Trump's attorney general, to look into the origins of federal investigations into alleged Russian interference in U.S. politics.

Durham, who sat in the courtroom during the trial, left the courthouse Tuesday without commenting to reporters. In a statement released by the Justice Department, he said: "While we are disappointed in the outcome, we respect the jury's decision and thank them for their service. I also want to recognize and thank the investigators and the prosecution team for their dedicated efforts in seeking truth and justice in this case."

The case, which is the first Durham brought to trial, presented dueling narratives about the early months of the FBI's investigation into Trump's ties to Russia and the role that Hillary Clinton's campaign played in feeding allegations — some of them unsubstantiated or since discredited — to the bureau.

According to prosecutors, Sussmann, a cybersecurity lawyer for the Clinton campaign, brought claims in September 2016 about a supposed pattern of computer messages between the Alfa Bank and the Trump Organization to the bureau's chief counsel in an effort to gin up an FBI probe that would serve as an "October surprise" that would damage Trump.

Prosecutors said Sussmann deliberately lied that he was not acting on behalf of any client when he was actually serving the interests of the Clinton campaign and another law firm client, cybersecurity researcher Rodney Joffe.

But the defense insisted that Sussmann went to the FBI as a public-spirited citizen who was genuinely concerned about the national security implications of potential communications between the Russians and Trump's business. (The FBI concluded that there was nothing nefarious about the alleged pattern of messages and that they may have been nothing more than computer spam.)

The key witness for Durham's prosecution team was James Baker, a longtime personal friend of Sussmann's who, during the run-up to the 2016 presidential election, was serving as the FBI's general counsel or chief lawyer. Baker testified at the trial that Sussmann told him about the allegations during a meeting in September 2016 at FBI headquarters.

During the meeting, Sussmann handed Baker memory sticks and printed materials purportedly documenting the link between the Trump Organization and Alfa Bank. Baker testified, however, that he was "100% confident" that at the meeting, Sussmann told him he was not presenting the allegations on behalf of a law firm client.

Arguing that Sussmann actually was acting on behalf of Clinton's campaign and his private cybersecurity client, prosecutors presented the jury with records from Perkins Coie, the law firm where Sussmann worked in 2016, which showed that the firm billed the Clinton campaign for meetings and other communications involving Sussmann during the summer and fall of 2016 that were related to what the billing records described as a "confidential project."

Baker and prosecutors did not produce any written notes of the meeting, which is the focus of Durham's indictment. In a conversation after the meeting with Bill Priestap, the FBI's counterintelligence chief, Baker testified that he told Priestap that the issue Sussmann had raised was urgent and that Sussmann was not representing a particular client.

Notes of the conversation taken by Priestap, which were entered into evidence, stated that, on the one hand, Sussmann told Priestap that he was "not doing this for any client." But Priestap then went on to note that Sussmann "represents DNC, Clinton Foundation, etc."

In the wake of Sussmann's meeting and Baker's conversation with Priestap, the FBI soon opened a full-scale investigation of the allegations Sussmann had presented to Baker, in which an FBI cyber squad based in Chicago played a major role. The field agents looking into the allegations concluded fairly quickly that the allegations of a serious link between the Trump Organization and the Russian bank lacked backup evidence.

Some witnesses said that if the FBI had known that the principal and original sources of the allegations had connections to the Clinton campaign or the Democratic National Committee, the bureau might have been more hesitant to launch a full-scale investigation.

Defense lawyers at one point indicated to Cooper, the judge, that Sussmann was considering testifying in the case, but ultimately, he did not appear on the witness stand.

Durham's team told the jury that less than 12 hours after meeting with Baker, Sussmann recorded 4.5 hours of work on written material and a confidential project. But a prosecutor said that two months later, Sussmann moved to revise the billing records to show he billed the Clinton campaign for 3.3 hours of work that day.

The defense team told the jury that Sussmann had told Baker to take whatever action he thought was appropriate. "There is a difference between having a client and going somewhere on their behalf," defense lawyer Sean Berkowitz argued.

In his instructions to the jury, Cooper said that in order to convict Sussmann of the offense, the jury must have been convinced by the evidence that he knowingly and willingly made a fraudulent or fictitious statement to Baker intended to deceive the FBI and that the statement was "material" to the FBI investigation.

Marc Elias, a Perkins Coie lawyer who was the top attorney for Clinton's campaign and was called as a prosecution witness, told the jury that he did not authorize or instruct Sussmann to take the Alfa Bank allegations to the FBI. Clinton's 2016 campaign manager Robbie Mook, who testified for the defense, also said he had not authorized Sussmann to tell the FBI about Alfa Bank and Trump.

Last year, Kevin Clinesmith, a onetime FBI lawyer, pleaded guilty after Durham charged him with doctoring an email that other official used to justify spying on a Trump campaign adviser. Clinesmith was sentenced to only a year of probation.

A false statement indictment brought by Durham is still pending against Igor Danchenko, a Russian who was a source for some of the allegations against Trump, including allegations related to Russia, which were laid out in a controversial anti-Trump "dossier" prepared for the Clinton campaign operatives in 2016 by former British intelligence officer Christopher Steele.

 Published *May 19, 2022 12:40pm EDT*

Published May 27, 2022, 11:41 am EDT

Special Counsel, John Durham's team, says evidence has 'proven' Sussmann is guilty

Sussmann has been charged with one count of making a false statement to the FBI

By Brooke Singman, David Spunt | Fox News

The problem for Durham in the Sussmann trial

WASHINGTON, D.C. – Special Counsel, John Durham's team, delivered its closing argument in the trial of Michael Sussmann Friday morning, saying the evidence has "proven beyond a reasonable doubt" that Sussmann made a false statement to the FBI. Sussman had said he was not bringing the debunked allegations of a covert communications channel between the Trump Organization and a Russian bank to the bureau on behalf of any client when he, in fact, billed Hillary Clinton's presidential campaign for his time and worked on the matter.

Federal prosecutor Jonathan Algor delivered the government's closing argument Friday morning, presenting their final case to the jury.

Sussmann has been charged with one count of making a false statement to the FBI when he met with then-FBI General Counsel James Baker on Sept. 19, 2016. The government alleges Sussmann told Baker that he was not bringing allegations tying then-candidate Donald Trump to the Kremlin-linked Alfa Bank on behalf of any client but rather as a citizen concerned with national security. Sussmann has pleaded not guilty to the charge.

But the government argued that billing records, testimony, and other written evidence prove that Sussmann was charging the Clinton campaign for his work on the matter and has said throughout the trial that he billed the Clinton campaign for the FBI meeting.

"The evidence has proven beyond a reasonable doubt that the defendant Michael Sussmann made a false statement to the FBI," Algor said. "The defendant used his privilege as a high-powered Washington lawyer, a former DOJ prosecutor... to bypass normal channels and expedite a meeting with the FBI general counsel."

"He knew he had to conceal his connection to the Clinton campaign and to Rodney Joffe," Algor said. "He knew if he told Baker he was there on behalf of the Clinton campaign, the chances of an FBI investigation would be diminished."

Algor went on to stress that the allegations were "not about national security" but "about opposition research against candidate Donald Trump."

Algor laid out the false statement charge, alleging that Sussmann's statement to Baker during the meeting was a false statement, saying the evidence shows the statement was "untrue when it was made, and he knew it was untrue."

HILLARY CLINTON APPROVED DISSEMINATION OF TRUMP-RUSSIAN BANK ALLEGATIONS TO MEDIA, CAMPAIGN MANAGER TESTIFIES

Algor referenced the "materiality" of the false statement, saying that jurors are required to decide on whether Sussmann's false statement was capable of influencing the FBI.

"The government is not required to prove that the statement influenced the FBI but only that it could have influenced the FBI," Algor told jurors.

"How do we know it mattered?" Algor asked. "Baker said he doesn't know if he would have taken the meeting had he known [Sussmann was representing the Clinton campaign]."

Algor pointed to Baker's testimony, in which he said he would have paused the investigation, consulted with FBI leadership, and would have invited others to participate in the meeting with Sussmann on Sept. 19, 2016, due to the fact that it took place "a month and a half before the presidential election."

Algor reminded the jury that a government witness, former FBI agent Allison Sands, also raised concerns, saying she would have wanted to know about "motivations."

Video

Algor presented a number of billing records and emails to the jury Friday, beginning on July 29, 2016, and through October 2016, revealing Sussmann repeatedly billed the Clinton campaign for work on the Alfa Bank opposition research against Trump.

The government also reminded jurors of a key text message Sussmann sent to Baker on the night before his FBI meeting on Sept. 19, 2016. Durham's team alleges Sussmann put his "lie in writing" in his Sept. 18, 2016, text to Baker.

SUSSMANN-DURHAM TRIAL: MARC ELIAS SAYS HE BRIEFED CLINTON CAMPAIGN OFFICIALS ON FUSION GPS OPPO AGAINST TRUMP

The text message stated: "Jim — it's Michael Sussmann. I have something time-sensitive (and sensitive) I need to discuss," the text message stated, according to Durham. "Do you have availability for a short meeting tomorrow? I'm coming on my own — not on behalf of a client or company — want to help the Bureau. Thanks."

Baker replied, "OK. I will find a time. What might work for you?"

Algor, on Friday, said that the text message had "43 words" and said "20" of those words were "a lie."

"The defendant's own words, own actions, are overwhelming," Algor said. "The evidence has proven beyond a reasonable doubt that Sussmann made a false statement to the FBI."

"You should return the only verdict supported by the evidence in this case – guilty," Algor closed.

Sussmann decided not to testify in his defense, and his defense began delivering its closing argument Friday morning.

Brooke Singman is a Fox News Digital politics reporter. You can reach her at Brooke.Singman@Fox.com or @BrookeSingman on Twitter

Sussmann's defense faults FBI probe of Trump-Russia server claims

The Durham case should wrap up later this week.

Michael Sussmann, a prominent cybersecurity attorney and former federal prosecutor, was charged with lying to the FBI during the Trump-Russia investigation. | Jose Luis Magana/AP Photo

By Josh Gerstein and Kelly Hooper

05/24/2022 05:56 PM EDT

Updated: 05/24/2022 07:38 PM EDT

The defense for a Democratic attorney accused of lying to the FBI hammered away Tuesday at the prosecution, arguing that the FBI probe the lawyer triggered with his Trump-Russia allegations was so shoddy and haphazard that any falsehood uttered by the attorney would not have affected the Russia investigation.

Lawyers for former Perkins Coie partner Michael Sussmann maintain he did not lie to the FBI when he allegedly claimed he wasn't acting on behalf of any client while giving the FBI data and reports suggesting that a secret server connected to Donald Trump was in communication with another computer controlled by a Russian bank.

At the jury trial in U.S. District Court in Washington, prosecutors have argued that Sussmann's obfuscation of the fact that the allegations came from experts working for or supporting Hillary Clinton's campaign affected the way the FBI investigated the matter.

However, Sussmann's defense suggested that miscommunication, hesitation, and internal bureaucracy led to FBI agents failing to try to find the information they easily could have discovered about the source of the allegations.

To get a conviction in the case, prosecutors have to show beyond a reasonable doubt not only that Sussmann lied but that any false statement could have been expected to impact the FBI's investigation. Sussmann's defense suggested there were so many loose ends and internal roadblocks that prosecutors couldn't make that case.

FBI agent Curtis Heide testified that he and another agent tasked with running down the so-called secret server claims repeatedly asked officials at FBI headquarters for permission to interview the source of the data and "white papers" that spurred the investigation. However, those requests were rebuffed, he said.

"That made your investigation incomplete, did it not?" defense attorney Sean Berkowitz asked.

"Yes," Heide replied.

SPECIAL AGENTS ROTH- The Most Important Criticism That He has of The FBI Is the Failure of the FBI HEADQUARTERS TO ALLOW THE STREET AGENTS TO INTERVIEW THE SOURCE OF THE DATA.

Berkowitz highlighted that the FBI made a probationary agent Heide was supervising, Allison Sands, the lead agent on the investigation, even though she'd never opened a case before. The defense attorney also pointed out errors in the FBI's official opening and closing memoranda for the probe, including saying that the information about the alleged secret server came from the Justice Department.

At least a half dozen FBI employees were involved in drafting or approving the memos containing those errors, which Heide referred to as "typos."

"Not a lot of attention to detail, I take it?" Berkowitz said.

"There were a couple of mistakes, yes," Heide responded.

Heide said he and Sands, based in Chicago, were also kept out of the loop on where officials at FBI Headquarters were getting other tips or data relevant to the probe.

"It appears that we were getting more and more information from people who were anonymous, and headquarters was not giving us the ability to go interview them," said Heide.

"Fair to say that was pretty frustrating for you?" Berkowitz asked.

"Yes, sir," the FBI agent said.

Sussmann, a prominent cybersecurity attorney and former federal prosecutor, was indicted last year by a grand jury at the request of Special Counsel John Durham. Durham was appointed in 2019 by Attorney General William Barr to examine the origins of the FBI's investigation into ties between Russia and President Donald Trump.

Michael Sussmann, a cybersecurity lawyer who represented the Hillary Clinton presidential campaign in 2016, arrives at the E. Barrett Prettyman Federal Courthouse Monday, May 16, 2022, in Washington, D.C. | Evan Vucci/AP Photo

While Sussmann's team kept reminding the jury Tuesday about slip-ups in the FBI probe, Durham's team underscored the flimsiness of the allegations.

Heide said the research done by FBI agents and computer experts concluded that the allegations about the secret server lacked merit. "Our investigation was unable to substantiate any of the allegations in the white paper," he said.

On Tuesday, Judge Christopher Cooper rejected another request by prosecutors to introduce evidence that the experts and researchers who worked on the server issue had doubts about the accuracy of their own work.

However, jurors did see an email tech executive Rodney Joffe sent to associates in September 2016 saying his goal in preparing one such white paper was "NOT to be able to say that this is, without doubt, fact, but to merely be plausible."

Heide said he would have liked to have known that because the email suggests the accompanying document "appears to be fabricated."

Sussmann's trial, now in its second week, kept to an established pattern Tuesday of offering up disclosures not directly related to the charge against the cybersecurity attorney. While on the witness stand, Heide said he and others at the FBI are the subjects of an internal investigation into whether they intentionally suppressed information from a court application under the Foreign Intelligence Surveillance Act.

The probe appears to be an outcropping of a 2018 Justice Department Inspector General investigation that found errors and omissions in FISA application related to former Trump campaign adviser Carter Page. Heide said he did not deliberately withhold any information, and the internal investigation by the FBI's Inspection Division has not made a finding of wrongdoing.

Testimony for the day finished up with Jared Novick, a business associate of Joffe and the former CEO of BitVoyant, a cyber defense, and intelligence company that is now called BlueVoyant. Novick testified that he received an "extremely uncommon" request from Joffe to research data ties between Trump and Russia.

Novick recalled receiving a "very nondescript PDF" that included the names of individuals, spouse information, Russian companies and affiliations, and email addresses of people connected to Trump.

"Immediately, I knew it was a political request," Novick said.

Novick said the task made him "extremely uncomfortable" because it could be opposition research, so he kept the project small. He gave it the name "Crimson Rhino" because the "last thing I wanted was Donald Trump's name" on company whiteboards.

During cross-examination, Berkowitz highlighted the strained relationship between Novick and Joffe. He also questioned Novick's credibility in assessing the data that the company researched in relation to Trump and Russia.

In one exchange, Novick incorrectly identified the meaning of the acronym DNS, saying he thought it stood for domain name service.

"Would it surprise you to know it actually stands for domain name system?" Berkowitz said.

"It would surprise me, yes. But I'm not a cyber expert," Novick said.

Novick admitted that he argues at times with Joffe — conceding that in 2016, he had a "challenging time" with the tech executive.

On redirect, prosecutor Jonathan Algor asked Novick whom the intended audience was of the information his company compiled for the project: "It was to go to an attorney," Novick said.

The prosecution will rest its case Wednesday, with Durham paralegal Kori Arsenault serving as its summary witness. Once the defense begins arguments — on Thursday morning at the latest — Berkowitz said he plans on calling to the stand former New York Times reporter Eric Lichtblau, FBI agent Tom Grasso, attorney Tashina Gauhar and "some character witnesses."

Prosecution, defense spar over bill allegedly proving Sussmann charged Clinton campaign for 2016 FBI meeting
John Durham claims Sussmann's billing records prove he lied to the FBI

By **Brooke Singman, Jake Gibson, David Spunt | Fox News**

WASHINGTON, D.C. – Government prosecutors on Wednesday presented the jury with Michael Sussmann's billing records, which they say prove he charged the Hillary Clinton campaign for his meeting with then-FBI General Counsel James Baker, where he shared allegations of a covert communications channel between the Trump Organization and Russia's Alfa Bank.

The prosecution's final witness was Kori Arsenault, a paralegal with Special Counsel John Durham's office. Arsenault worked on much of the government's exhibits and helped to explain the records to the jury.

The prosecution on Wednesday morning produced the record from Perkins Coie that they say proves the law firm billed "Hillary for America" for the meeting Sussmann had with Baker at FBI headquarters on Sept. 19, 2016.

On the bill, also dated Sept. 19, 2016, the Clinton campaign is listed as the client, the time is listed as 3.3 hours, and the memo states: "work and communications regarding the confidential project." Other testimony revealed that Sussmann charged approximately $800 per hour.

SPECIAL COUNSEL JOHN DURHAM'S PROSECUTION OF MICHAEL SUSSMANN: EVERYTHING YOU NEED TO KNOW

Hillary Clinton and Michael Sussmann (Getty Images | CSPAN)
Durham's team also produced a receipt from a Staples near Perkins Coie in Washington, D.C., from Sept. 13, 2016. On the receipt was a two-pack of flash drives.

The prosecution alleged the receipt was included in an expense report from Sussmann, and the billing code on the report connects the expense to the Clinton campaign as the client.

During his meeting with Baker on Sept. 19, 2016, Sussmann brought two thumb drives of data and white papers alleging the Trump Organization was using a secret back channel to communicate with Kremlin-linked Alfa Bank in the weeks leading up to the presidential election.

Special Counsel John Durham departs the U.S. federal courthouse after opening arguments in the trial of attorney Michael Sussmann. (Reuters/Julia Nikhinson)
Sussmann is charged with making a false statement to the FBI.

Durham's team aims to convince the jury that the records revealing Sussmann billed the Clinton campaign to prove Sussmann lied when he allegedly told Baker on Sept. 19, 2016, that he was not bringing the allegations on behalf of any specific client but rather as a citizen concerned with national security.

DURHAM-SUSSMANN TRIAL: BAKER BRIEFED COMEY, MCCABE ON ALLEGED COVERT COMMUNICATIONS BETWEEN TRUMP ORG, RUSSIA

But during cross-examination Wednesday, defense attorney Michael Bosworth noted that in meetings Sussmann had at the FBI in years prior, he would specifically make reference to the FBI in the bill's "memo" section.

Bosworth noted that on Sept. 19, 2016, the bill only specifies "work and communication regarding the confidential project."

FBI LEADERSHIP WAS 'FIRED UP' ABOUT ALLEGED SECRET CHANNEL BETWEEN TRUMP-RUSSIAN BANK: SUSSMANN TRIAL

"There's no reference to the FBI in that entry, is there?" Bosworth asked Arsenault.

"There is not," Arsenault answered.

The prosecution rested Wednesday morning after questioning witnesses for almost eight days straight.

The defense will begin calling their witnesses to the stand for questioning.

It was not immediately clear whether Sussmann would testify in his own defense.

Brooke Singman is a Fox News Digital politics reporter. You can reach her at Brooke.Singman@Fox.com or @BrookeSingman on Twitter.

Sussmann told the CIA a similar 'client' lie in 2017; Durham says

by Jerry Dunleavy, Justice Department Reporter |

May 20, 2022, 09:23 PM

Just In...

Michael Sussmann told the CIA he was "not representing a client" when he pushed debunked Trump-Russia collusion allegations in early 2017, a former agency officer testified Friday.

Kevin P., who retired from the CIA a few years ago after more than 32 years of service, testified Friday about Feb. 9, 2017, meeting Sussmann had requested and obtained with the CIA and said, "He said he was not representing a client."

The comments are similar to the lie special counsel John Durham accuses Sussmann of making to the FBI in 2016.

Sussmann was indicted last September for allegedly concealing his clients, Hillary Clinton's 2016 presidential campaign, and Rodney Joffe, from FBI general counsel James Baker in September 2016 after pushing claims of a secret back channel between the Trump Organization and Russia's Alfa-Bank.

Durham says Sussmann similarly concealed his client, Joffe, when he pushed further collusion claims to the CIA in February 2017.

The special counsel said Sussmann pushed the Russian bank allegations and also claimed data he had access to "demonstrated that Trump and/or his associates were using supposedly rare, Russian-made wireless phones," called YotaPhones, "in the vicinity of the White House and other locations." Durham found "no support for these allegations" and revealed the CIA "concluded in early 2017" that the Alfa-Bank and YotaPhone information was not "technically plausible."

HILLARY CLINTON SIGNED OFF ON SHARING ALFA-BANK CLAIMS WITH THE MEDIA

A senior officer in counterintelligence missions at the time, Kevin P., said Sussmann told him other lawyers at Perkins Coie represented Clinton and the Democratic National Committee, but "he made it clear that he did not have any connection with that." He noted that "he had contacts that provided him the information" related to the Alfa Bank allegations, as well as what the CIA veteran referred to as "secondary information" on "another technical security threat."

Sussmann provided the CIA with thumb drives and white papers, similar to what he had done with the FBI. Kevin P. said, "In the meeting, I said to Mr. Sussmann that it was likely this information would be forwarded to the FBI."

After the meeting, Steve M., a CIA employee who was also at the meeting, sent a draft memo to Kevin P. that day. A final version of that memo, corrected by Kevin P., reads, "Mr. Sussmann advised that he was not representing a particular client and the information he was volunteering to us was not privileged. His contacts wished to provide information to the [U.S. government] through Mr. Sussmann, preferring anonymity citing a potential threat from the Russian Intelligence Services."

Kevin P. stressed Friday that Sussmann "did not refer to them as clients in the meeting — he referred to them as contacts." The retired officer said he had used his contemporaneous notes to refresh his recollection back in 2017 when editing the memorandum.

Another witness Friday, Mark Chadason, also a former CIA employee, said he was asked by a friend to meet with Sussmann, meeting on Jan. 31, 2017, for breakfast at a hotel in northern Virginia. He said he took notes of the meeting and typed it up into a memorandum the same day.

At that meeting, Chadason testified that Sussmann told him he had a client and that his client would go to the *New York Times* if the CIA wouldn't meet with Sussmann.

Chadason's memorandum stated, "Sussmann said that he represents a CLIENT who does not want to be known, but who had some interesting information."

Chadason wrote that Sussmann would not provide the client's identity but that he "was able to elicit that the CLIENT is an engineer with a number of patents, and is most likely a contractor to the [intelligence community]" and that "Sussmann also said that [the] CLIENT is a Republican."

Joffe was a confidential human source for the FBI at the time but was cut off in 2021 due to revelations in Durham's investigation, although the judge said the jury could not be told about his termination. Shortly after Clinton's loss to former President Donald Trump in November 2016, Joffe said in an email, "I was tentatively offered the top [cybersecurity] job by the Democrats when it looked like they'd win. I definitely would not take the job under Trump." The jury is not allowed to see that email either.

Chadason sent an email to CIA employees that day, writing, "Please remember this guy is a partisan lawyer who works closely with DNC. So I am not sure what the real story here is — but I am sure you guys will figure it out."

He also sent the CIA his memo about the Sussmann meeting.

Kevin P. testified Friday that he didn't recall reading that particular memo before meeting Sussmann himself but said he would've expected the lawyer to say he was representing a client if he had read the emails stating that he was.

Defense attorney Sean Berkowitz asked Kevin P. whether he had read Chadason's memo, which used the word "CLIENT" over a dozen times, prior to meeting with Sussmann, and he replied, "I do not recall reading it, but I may have read it." Berkowitz also pointed to a Jan. 31, 2017, email from Chadason that labeled Sussmann a "prominent lawyer who is representing a client."

Kevin P. said he didn't recall reading that email beforehand but insisted again that Sussmann told him he was not there for a client.

The FBI, CIA, special counsel Robert Mueller, a bipartisan Senate Intelligence Committee investigation, and Durham's team have all cast doubt on or shot down the Alfa-Bank claims.

Baker testified this week that the final conclusion of the FBI was that "there was nothing there." The CIA said Sussmann told them he had met with Baker "on a similar, though unrelated, matter." But Durham said that was "misleading" because information regarding the Alfa-Bank allegations that he had pushed to the FBI was among the materials Sussmann provided to the CIA. Sussmann denies wrongdoing and has pleaded not guilty.

DOJ 'referral' of Trump-Russia material a 'mistake' By FBI, agent says

By **Ben Feuerherd**

May 24, 2022, 2:16pm

Updated

An FBI agent testified during the trial of Michael Sussmann, a lawyer who represented the Hillary Clinton presidential campaign, that he mistakenly indicated that the probe into an alleged link between Donald Trump and a Russian bank was sparked by the DOJ. AP

An FBI agent already under scrutiny over claims he withheld key information in the "Crossfire Hurricane" investigation admitted Tuesday to a screwup that led other agents to believe the probe of Trump-Russia links was spurred by the Justice Department — rather than a lawyer for Hillary Clinton's presidential campaign.

FBI agent Curtis Heide was asked by prosecutors about a communication drafted by him and fellow agent Allison Sands on Sept. 23, 2016, that stated, "THE DEPARTMENT OF JUSTICE provided the FBI with a white paper that was produced by an anonymous third party."

"According to the white paper, a U.S.-based server that is owned by the TRUMP ORGANIZATION has been communicating with the Russian-based ALFA BANK organization in Moscow, Russia," added the document, which functioned as confirmation that an investigation had been opened into the since-debunked allegation.

Prosecutors say Sussman was acting for the campaign of Hillary Clinton when he turned over data to the FBI, purportedly tying candidate Donald Trump to a Russian bank.REUTERS

"That's a mistake in our paperwork," Heide said of the DOJ reference.

Asked by prosecutor Jonathan Algor how such a mistake could have been made, Heide answered, "I honestly don't know" before adding that he and Sands may have conflated the department with the office of then-FBI general counsel Jim Baker.

The "white paper" had been passed to Baker on Sept. 19, 2016, by Michael Sussmann, who is accused of lying to Baker by claiming he was not turning over the document on behalf of any client.

The purpose of Sussmann's alleged information leak to the feds was to establish a connection between Donald Trump's campaign and Russia's Alfa-Bank. AP

Prosecutors led by special counsel John Durham say Sussmann was, in fact, acting for both the Clinton campaign and an internet executive, Rodney Joffe.

The disclosure by Heide comes one day after another FBI agent, Ryan Gaynor, testified that bureau brass shielded Sussmann's identity from investigating agents as part of a longstanding practice known as a "close hold."

Referring to Sussmann only as an "anonymous third party" appeared to frustrate investigators, according to emails introduced by prosecutors Monday.

In one message from Oct. 3, 2016, Heide wrote to Gaynor, "We really want to interview the source of all this information. Any way we can track down who this guy is and how we're getting this information?"

Gaynor responded that it was being discussed at headquarters but did not provide the identity of the source.

At the beginning of his testimony, Heide also revealed that he is being investigated in an FBI administrative inquiry for "not identifying exculpatory information as it pertained to one of the Crossfire Hurricane Investigations." He allegedly left the information off a warrant application to the Foreign Intelligence Surveillance Court.

When Algor asked Heide if he intentionally withheld information from the Crossfire Hurricane case team, the G-man replied, "No."

Defense attorney Sean Berkowitz raised the investigation into Heide's alleged conduct during cross-examination.

"That's a serious allegation, right?" Berkowitz asked Heide at one point, suggesting it could have a serious "consequence on your career."

Heide acknowledged it could but reiterated that the case is "still pending."

Sussmann's defense is laughable — or he's just a terrible lawyer

By Andrew McCarthy

May 24, 2022 11:44pm

 Updated

Attorney Michael Sussmann is accused of insisting that he was not representing any client in September 2016 when he peddled to the FBI bogus evidence of a supposed communications backchannel between Donald Trump and the Kremlin.REUTERS/Julia Nikhinson

- Eric Adams for president? Not so fast, Mr. Mayor!
- FBI brass were 'fired up' about now-debunked Trump-Russia ties: texts, testimony
- DOJ 'referral' of Trump-Russia material a 'mistake' by FBI, agent says
- FBI wrongly told its agents Trump-Russia collusion claims had come from DOJ, bombshell document reveals

Defense attorneys for Clinton campaign lawyer Michael Sussmann have portrayed their client as the paragon of patriotic professionalism.

Yet to believe his defense to the felony false-statement charge brought by Russiagate special counsel John Durham, you'd have to conclude that Sussmann is the most unethical lawyer in Washington, DC.

Sussmann is accused of insisting that he was not representing any client in September 2016 — the stretch run of the heated presidential campaign — when he peddled to the FBI bogus evidence of a supposed communications backchannel between Donald Trump and the Kremlin. Sussmann was bringing the information only because he wanted to "help the bureau" protect the country, he told the FBI's then-general counsel, James Baker, in a text message.

Sussmann has no real defense to the charge. The evidence is so overwhelming that he was representing the Clinton campaign at the time of his meeting with Baker that Sussmann does not challenge it. Moreover, the information he provided to the FBI — Internet data explained by white papers — was compiled by another client, tech executive Rodney Joffe, who was hoping for a cybersecurity job in the anticipated Hillary Clinton administration. Joffe worked on the materials in conjunction with Fusion GPS; the information outfit retained to dig up dirt on Trump by top Clinton campaign counsel Marc Elias, who was then Sussmann's law partner.

Sussmann told Former FBI general counsel James A. Baker in a text that wanted to "help the bureau" protect the country. Ron Sachs – CNP

Truth is obvious

It's obvious that Sussmann was representing the Clinton campaign and Joffe when he said he wasn't representing anyone. For conviction, prosecutors must show that a statement was not only false but also material. On this, though, the evidence is also irrefutable.

For obvious reasons, the FBI needs to know the motivations of people who proffer information. As a former longtime Justice Department lawyer, Sussmann knew this. Indeed, he lied precisely because he knew that if he had honestly told Baker the information was partisan opposition research he was providing to the FBI on behalf of the Clinton campaign, his gambit would have been dismissed as a ploy to enmesh the bureau in electoral politics.

So what is Sussmann's defense?

Though he was working for Hillary Clinton's campaign, Sussmann claims his actions with the FBI were not connected to the presidential hopeful. Cindy Ord/Getty Images

He claims that, although he may technically have been representing the Clinton campaign during that time frame, he was not really representing the campaign in connection with the FBI meeting.

He insists that campaign officials would have been opposed to his bringing the Trump-Russia information to the bureau because they wanted it to be promoted by the media — a strategy Hillary Clinton personally approved. Going to the FBI, on this rationalization, would have been counterproductive because the bureau would lean on the press to delay publishing until agents had time to investigate.

Consequently, we're to believe that Sussmann went to the FBI against his client's interests because of his own patriotic concerns for national security.

Sussmann is on trial in federal court in Washington, DC, for one count of lying to the FBI in September 2016.AP/Manuel Balce Ceneta

This is a laughable defense. Enticing the FBI into investigating the Trump-Russia allegations would have made the story more attractive to the media and more explosive for the "October surprise" objective of the Clinton campaign — an election-eve story that the FBI suspected Trump of being a Putin plant.

But put that aside. Under professional ethics standards, a lawyer has a duty of fealty to his client. Thus, as the American Bar Association's rules put it, "the lawyer's own interests should not be permitted to have an adverse effect on the representation of a client."

If Sussmann truly believed that his visit to the FBI, purportedly motivated by his own selfless patriotism, was against the Clinton campaign's interests, then his ethical obligation was to disclose his intention to his client and obtain a waiver allowing him to go ahead with the meeting.

No campaign waiver

Of course, Sussmann didn't seek permission, and he didn't obtain a waiver from the Clinton campaign. To believe Sussmann's defense, then, you'd have to believe he is without scruples — precisely the opposite of the image his attorneys have projected.

We shouldn't puzzle long over this. It is utter nonsense.

Sussmann didn't violate the ethics rules because his visit to the FBI was absolutely in the Clinton campaign's interests. That's why Sussmann billed the campaign for his visit to Baker. And it's why, eight days before the election, Hillary and her then-adviser (and now- Biden national security adviser) Jake Sullivan tweeted: "We can only assume that federal authorities will now explore this direct connection between Trump and Russia."

If Sussmann is acquitted, it will be because he lucked into being tried in Washington, DC, where the jury pool runneth over with partisan Democrats. He's got nothing else.

FBI DIRECTORS

J. Edgar Hoover JFK
L. Patrick Gray WATERGATE
Louis Freeh $100,000 HUNTER BIDEN
JAMES COMEY, HILLARY CLINTON

FBI leadership during Russiagate makes Durham's job in the Sussman trial very tricky

Opinion by **Andrew McCarthy** - *Yesterday 6:04 PM*

Key government witness testifies in Michael Sussmann trial
"Making a false statement." What a nice, clean, uncomplicated world it would be for prosecutors, such as Justice Department Special Counsel John Durham if that were the crime on the federal books.
All you'd have to do is prove that a person made a false statement like Democratic lawyer Michael Sussmann. He said he was not representing a client when in fact, he was representing the Clinton campaign. There's no doubt he said it. There's no doubt it wasn't true. Case closed.
Except, down here on Planet Earth, it's never that simple. The crime is not "making a false statement." It is making a false statement *to the FBI*.

SPECIAL COUNSEL JOHN DURHAM'S PROSECUTION OF MICHAEL SUSSMANN: EVERYTHING YOU NEED TO KNOW
That is not a small additional detail because the law further requires that the false statement be *material*. That is, the false statement cannot be about a trifling detail. It has to have made a difference in how the FBI evaluated the information in connection with its investigation. It has to have mattered.
This is a big problem for Durham. In Russiagate, it turns out that the FBI was not the impartial, just-the-facts-ma'am investigator we expect it to be. At the headquarters level, the FBI had a rooting interest. It was invested in the proposition that Donald Trump was a corrupt, clandestine agent of Russia. And it wasn't willing to drop the idea even if the evidence didn't pan out.
That meant headquarters was willing to mislead its frontline agents.

FBI LEADERSHIP WAS 'FIRED UP' ABOUT ALLEGED SECRET CHANNEL BETWEEN TRUMP-RUSSIAN BANK: SUSSMANN TRIAL

Those agents diligently did their investigative work and determined that there was nothing to the allegation made by Clinton lawyer Sussmann to FBI general counsel James Baker that Trump and the Kremlin had established communications back channel through a Trump email domain and servers at Russia's Alfa Bank. But headquarters wouldn't take "no" for an answer and wouldn't share basic facts that would have shown how unreliable the allegation was.

Hence the problem for Durham: How does he prove that Sussmann's false statement mattered when the agents were also being misled by their own bosses?

FBI agent being investigated for potentially withholding exculpatory info in Trump-Russia probe

This week, we were treated to the startling revelation that the FBI's "EC" – the electronic communication by which the bureau formally opens investigations – contained a false statement, claiming that the predicate for the probe was information referred to the bureau by "the US DEPARTMENT OF JUSTICE." Of course, the information came from *Sussmann*, not the Justice Department.

How could a false statement get into a critical FBI document … *in a false-statement case*? Embarrassingly, none of the FBI officials who've been asked about it, including the agents who drafted the EC, has been able – or at least willing – to answer that question. But we know the gist of how it must have happened.

Baker, the FBI general counsel who took the information (internet data and white-paper analyses) from Sussmann, immediately alerted his chain of command – FBI Director James Comey, Deputy Director Andrew McCabe, and counterintelligence agent Bill Priestap. Whatever happened in those consultations, headquarters made a decision to treat Sussmann as if he were a confidential informant and thus *conceal his identity* from the agents who would be tasked to assess Sussmann's information.

DURHAM-SUSSMANN TRIAL: BAKER BRIEFED COMEY, MCCABE ON ALLEGED COVERT COMMUNICATIONS BETWEEN TRUMP ORG, RUSSIA

Why did they do that? Baker suggested that it was to protect Sussmann. But there is no indication that Sussmann asked for his identity to be concealed from Bureau investigators – *he came to the FBI quite intentionally*. There was no threat to him from publicity – he was part of a Hillary Clinton campaign effort that *wanted the information to go public*.

Baker rationalized that Sussmann's identity should be shielded from professional investigators because Baker believed Sussmann's story about coming to the Bureau strictly as a patriotic American, not as a lawyer representing a client.

Call me cynical, but I'm not buying it. The FBI was not protecting Sussmann. The FBI was protecting itself – guarding its reputation, which has been the top headquarters priority throughout the agency's history.

The FBI had already bought into the Trump-Russia collusion narrative. Even as Baker met with Sussmann, the Bureau was preparing to seek surveillance warrants from the FISA court based on the Steele dossier – another compendium of bogus anti-Trump information sourced to the Clinton campaign.

Baker was not a babe in the woods. He knew Sussmann represented top Democrats – Sussmann had been the DNC's lawyer when its servers got hacked. Baker and his bosses knew the FBI was taking a big risk accepting derogatory information about Trump about six weeks before Election Day from a top Democratic Party lawyer who refused to say who had given it to him.

Knowing they were playing with fire, headquarters officials hedged their bets. They uncritically accepted Sussmann's dubious story that he wasn't representing a client and rationalized treating him as a confidential informant. But it wasn't to protect Sussmann's safety; it was to avoid leaving a paper trail identifying him. It was to avoid recording that headquarters had accepted anti-Trump opposition research from a highly partisan source in the stretch-run of a presidential campaign.

This concealment of Sussmann's identity caused confusion and frustration for the Chicago cyber-crime agents who were called on to assess the information. Whatever headquarters told the field, the message got garbled (or worse) into a claim that the information came from the Justice Department. Headquarters would not tell them the source, a rudimentary piece of information that any investigator would want for purposes of assessing reliability.

And even when the agents concluded the data provided by "the Justice Department" was deeply flawed, headquarters would not permit the investigation to be shut down. Unable to establish a cybercrime, Chicago agents were told they had to open a counterintelligence investigation because "People on 7th floor to include Director are fired up about this server," as agent Joe Pientka, assigned to headquarters and deeply involved in the Trump-Russia investigation, put it.

The 7th floor, FBI headquarters, has given Sussmann his defense: Sussmann didn't lie to the FBI investigators; *their headquarters lied to them.* Susmman may have misled Baker in claiming not to represent a client, but Baker wasn't fooled – headquarters officials fully understood the political nature of the information; that's precisely why they concealed it from the agents doing the actual investigating. And in the end, what did it matter? After all, even when the information turned out to be nonsense, the FBI nevertheless continued pursuing the Trump-Russia collusion narrative.

Durham has banked his case on the premise that the FBI was a dupe rather than a willing, though cagey participant in the Russiagate farce. That turns what looks like a slam-dunk false statement into a very tough case for prosecutors.

Published May 31, 2022, 9:59 am EDT

Miranda Devine: The Trump-Russia collusion hoax was a 'dirty trick' sanctioned By Hillary Clinton

Fox News contributor slammed Hillary Clinton for creating the Russian collusion hoax

Miranda Devine joined "Fox & Friends" to discuss the ongoing Michael Sussmann trial and the consequences of former presidential candidate Hillary Clinton fabricating allegations of Russian collusion against former President Trump.

SUSSMANN TRIAL PROVES HILLARY CLINTON PERPETRATED 'MASSIVE FRAUD', SHOULD BE 'BANNED FROM TWITTER': TAIBBI

MIRANDA DEVINE: *If he's convicted of lying to the FBI, Michael Sussmann faces a maximum of five years in jail. But it's not really just about him. He is just the first of the trials to come out of the Durham probe into the Trump-Russia collusion hoax. And we have gleaned some really valuable insights into that dirty tricks game by the Clinton campaign. Chiefly, I think, out of this trial, that Hillary Clinton was behind it, that she sanctioned this dirty trick, this attempt to go to the FBI and pretend Michael Sussmann was just a concerned citizen, concerned about national security. They passed off bogus opposition research, which claimed that Donald Trump was in bed with Vladimir Putin. Now, the ramifications of that were extreme. It crippled the Trump presidency. And to this day, we're seeing that there are national security implications for America's relationship with Russia and with Vladimir Putin.*

Hunter Biden

MONEY LAUNDERING

What is money laundering?

With few exceptions, criminals are motivated by one thing-profit. Greed drives the criminal, and the end result is that illegally gained money must be introduced into the nation's legitimate financial systems. Money laundering involves disguising financial assets so they can be used without detection of the illegal activity that produced them. Through money laundering, the criminal transforms the monetary proceeds derived from criminal activity into funds from an apparently legal source.

This process has devastating social consequences. For one thing, money laundering provides the fuel for drug dealers, terrorists, arms dealers, and other criminals to operate and expand their criminal enterprises.

We know that criminals manipulate financial systems in the United States and abroad to further a wide range of illicit activities. Left unchecked, money laundering can erode the integrity of our nation's financial institutions.

U.S. Congress passed the Money Laundering Control Act in 1986 to combat any attempt to obscure the source of criminal funds or evade reporting requirements. From a general standpoint, this act prohibits any person from conducting financial transactions with the money, proceeds, or property of various criminal activities. In order to gain a deeper understanding of this federal offense, the following sections will explore money laundering, qualifying criminal activities, and the use of criminal funds.

What are the U.S. Federal Laws Against Money Laundering?

18 U.S. Code Section 1956 is the main federal statute that defines, prohibits, and penalizes money laundering. In order to qualify as money laundering, a person must conduct or attempt to conduct a financial transaction with the intent to:

Promote the performance of a specified unlawful activity;

Engage in tax evasion or fraud under the Internal Revenue Code;

Conceal or disguise the proceeds of a specified unlawful activity; or

Avoid financial reporting requirements under U.S. federal or state law.

Essentially, Section 1956 prohibits the use of financial transactions to further a criminal act, referred to as specified unlawful activity and defined in the next section. Furthermore, money laundering occurs whenever a person attempts to obscure the source of the funds or avoid reporting requirements. Taken as a whole, Section 1956 makes it illegal to conduct financial transactions with money or property derived from criminal activity.

'Doesn't look good': Hunter Biden reportedly raked in $11M from overseas biz deals

By Joshuwa Rhett Miller and Bruce Golding

May 19, 2022, 01:50pm

Updated

Hunter Biden and a company he ran raked in around $11 million from his controversial business dealings while his dad served as vice president and shortly thereafter, according to new scrutiny of the first son.

President Biden's scandal-scarred son also burned through cash at a rate of more than $200,000 a month from October 2017 through February 2018, spending it on luxury hotel rooms, payments on a Porsche sports car, and dental work, as well as making unexplained bank withdrawals, an NBC News report found.

The eye-popping figures emerged from an analysis of information stored on the first son's laptop — the contents of which were first reported by The Post in 2020 — and documents released by Senate Republicans, the network said.

His river of income flowed from 2013 through 2018 as a result of ties to a Ukrainian natural gas company suspected of bribery and a since-vanished Chinese tycoon accused of bribery and fraud, NBC said.

"This is an enormous amount of money for Hunter Biden, whom I don't believe is an experienced corporate transactional attorney," former White House chief ethics lawyer Richard Painter told The Post.

Hunter Biden's income flowed from 2013 through 2018 as a result of ties to Burisma. Sergey Dolzhenko/EPA

"All I know is I wouldn't be pulling that kind of money, and I've been a securities law expert for almost 30 years. There's no way I'd be pulling down that kind of money."

Painter, now a University of Minnesota law professor and Democratic candidate for Congress, also said, "If Hunter Biden cared about protecting the family's reputation, he would disclose everything."

"The whole thing doesn't look good," he added.

CEFC China Energy is accused of bribery and fraud. Yang jin/Imaginechina via AP

NBC's report came more than 18 months after The Post first revealed emails from the laptop that detailed Hunter Biden's business dealings with Ukraine's Burisma Holdings and Ye Jianming, former chairman of the CEFC China Energy conglomerate.

The mainstream media largely ignored The Post's October 2020 reports or suggested they were the product of Russian disinformation efforts ahead of the 2020 presidential election.

But both the New York Times and the Washington Post recently authenticated for themselves some of the emails amid a federal grand jury probe in Wilmington, Delaware, that's reportedly focused on possible tax fraud, money laundering, and violations of lobbying laws by Hunter Biden. Hunter Biden's laptop contained emails detailing business dealings with Ye Jianming, former chairman of the CEFC China Energy conglomerate. China Energy Fund Committee Congressional Republicans have also vowed to launch investigations next year if they regain control of the House and Senate, with some polls giving the GOP an edge amid surging inflation and President Biden's low approval ratings.

NBC didn't detail the sources of the entire $11 million but cited previously reported payments totaling $4.8 million to Owasco PC, a company controlled by Hunter Biden, from a joint venture funded by CEFC and Ye.

The network also cited a previously reported $1 million attorney engagement letter between Hunter Biden and CEFC exec Chi Ping Patrick Ho, who was later sentenced to three years in prison in the US for a pair of bribery schemes involving government officials in Africa.

Hunter Biden's defense lawyer, Chris Clark, declined to discuss NBC's analysis on the record, the network said.

The Post has reported that Hunter Biden made as much as $1 million a year by serving on the Burisma board of directors, but that the amount was slashed by 50% in March 2017, two months after his dad stopped serving as vice president.

Critics, including Sen. Ron Johnson (R-Wisconsin), have accused Hunter Biden of profiting off his father's influence.

A federal grand jury probe in Wilmington, Delaware, is reportedly focused on possible tax fraud, money laundering, and violations of lobbying laws by Hunter Biden. Andy Wong/Pool/EPA

Shortly after The Post first revealed his son's emails, Joe Biden angrily denied the accusation, calling it "garbage" and "a last-ditch effort in this desperate campaign to smear my family and me."

"Ron should be ashamed of himself," he added during an interview with Milwaukee TV station WISN.

Former FBI assistant director for counterintelligence Frank Figliuzzi told NBC that national security could be put at risk when foreign powers like China see an opportunity to get close to someone like Hunter Biden.

President Biden has said that he is "confident that his son didn't break the law."

"It's all about access and influence, and if you can compromise someone with both access and influence, that's even better," said Figliuzzi, an NBC News contributor who often appears on MSNBC.

"Better still if that target has already compromised himself."

Walter Shaub, a former director of the US Office of Government Ethics, also told NBC that although government ethics rules don't apply to Hunter Biden, "it's imperative that no one at [the Justice Department and no one at the White House interfere with the criminal investigation in Delaware."

Hunter Biden has denied any wrongdoing and last year told CBS News that he was "being completely cooperative" with the federal investigation in his family's hometown.

Former FBI assistant director for counterintelligence Frank Figliuzzi told NBC that national security could be put at risk when foreign powers like China see an opportunity to get close to someone like Hunter Biden.

President Biden has said that he is "confident that his son didn't break the law."Image from Hunter Biden's laptop

"It's all about access and influence, and if you can compromise someone with both access and influence, that's even better," said Figliuzzi, an NBC News contributor who often appears on MSNBC.

"Better still if that target has already compromised himself."

Walter Shaub, a former director of the US Office of Government Ethics, also told NBC that although government ethics rules don't apply to Hunter Biden, "it's imperative that no one at [the Justice Department and no one at the White House interfere with the criminal investigation in Delaware."

Hunter Biden has denied any wrongdoing and last year told CBS News that he was "being completely cooperative" with the federal investigation in his family's hometown.

Part Fourteen

Political Criticism By Democrats

Harris says she's concerned about 'integrity' of Supreme Court

September 9, 2022, 4:33 PM

Vice President Harris on Friday said she is concerned about the integrity of the Supreme Court in the wake of the decision to strike down Roe v. Wade, which had protected a woman's right to an abortion for decades.

"I think this is an activist court," Harris told NBC's "Meet the Press" when asked about her confidence in the court.

"It means that we had an established right for almost half a century, which is the right of women to make decisions about their own body, as an extension of what we have decided to be, the privacy rights to which all people are entitled," Harris continued. "And this court took that constitutional right away. And we are suffering as a nation, because of it."

"That causes me great concern about the integrity of the Court overall," Harris added, calling it a "very different court" from the one served by Justices Earl Warren, Thurgood Marshall and Sandra Day O'Connor.

Harris has taken a leading role in the Biden administration in pushing back on the Supreme Court's decision to reverse Roe v. Wade. The vice president, who is the first woman to hold the role, has met with health care providers and activists in recent months to voice support for abortion access and reproductive health.

Democrats have ridden the wave of outrage over the court decision to wins at the ballot box, including in Kansas where voters rejected a referendum that would have stripped abortion protections from the state constitution.

The court has a 6-3 conservative majority, even with the confirmation of Justice Ketanji Brown Jackson, who joined the court in July upon the retirement of Stephen Breyer.

An Associated Press poll released in late July found 43 percent of Americans don't have any confidence in the Supreme Court, an increase of 16 percentage points since April.

Maxine Waters on SCOTUS abortion ruling: 'The hell with the Supreme Court'

By **Caroline Vakil** - *06/24/22 10:34 PM ET*

Rep. Maxine Waters (D-Calif.) declared "the hell with the Supreme Court" after its justices ruled on Friday to eliminate federal-level abortion protections, overturning a 50-year precedent.

"This turnout here?" asked Waters, who stood near fencing that was installed in front of the high court. "You ain't seen nothing yet. Women are going to control their bodies no matter how they try and stop [us]. The hell with the Supreme Court. We will defy them."

"Women will be in control of their bodies, and if they think Black women are intimidated or afraid, they got another thought coming," she continued. "Black women will be out in droves. We will be out by the thousands. We will be out by the millions. We're going to make sure we fight for the right to control our own bodies."

The Supreme Court issued its most consequential decision of its term on Friday when it overturned Roe v. Wade.

The decision was mourned by Democrats, fearful of how it could impact abortion access in states across the country, including those with so-called trigger laws already on the books, while Republicans celebrated the move.

Some prosecutors have already said they do not plan on enforcing abortion bans, while a group of West Coast states announced a commitment to protecting abortion access.

Meanwhile, a group of states has already started the process of officially ending abortion access or severely restricting it in states like Missouri, Louisiana, South Dakota, and Arkansas.

Special Agent Roth- These statements By Maxine Waters, Chuck Schumer and Kamala Harris are far worse than anything that Donald Trump said.

Schumer, the Supreme Court, and the Mob

U.S. Senate Democratic Leader Chuck Schumer speaks about impeachment to reporters after a weekly policy lunch on Capitol Hill in Washington, U.S., January 7, 2020. (REUTERS/Leah Millis)

By **Andrew C. Mccarthy**

March 5, 2020, 2:39 PM

The senator treats the Court like a political body — which it is.

Should Chuck Schumer be censured? Of course, he *should*, in the sense that the rule of law, were it actually our cynosure, would cry out for it.

On Wednesday morning, the Democrats' Senate minority leader stirred up the mob outside the Supreme Court, unabashedly threatening Justices Neil Gorsuch and Brett Kavanaugh: "I want to tell you, Gorsuch. I want to tell you, Kavanaugh. You have released the whirlwind and you will pay the price," Schumer inveighed. "You won't know what hit you if you go forward with these awful decisions."

Inside, the justices were then hearing argument on what ought to be a straightforward abortion case (i.e., one in which the "right" invented in *Roe v. Wade* is not up for consideration). When called on his menacing remarks, rather than apologize, Schumer brazenly lied about what he had done. This morning, he was still lying — a tepid apology, offered under pressure while insisting that "in no way was I making a threat."

In a rule-of-law society, that should rate censure. Case closed.

Except it's not closed, because we are not a rule-of-law society. We just pretend to be. In a rule-of-law society, a mob would not gather on the steps of the courthouse in the first place.

Why is the mob out there?

Because nearly a half-century ago, the Supreme Court took on the mantle of super-legislature, weaving from whole cloth a right to terminate the lives of unborn children. In terms of constitutional interpretation and the judiciary's place in our system, *Roe* was so indefensible that it took less than 20 years — the blink of a jurisprudential eye — for its farcical underpinnings to

242

vanish. (In point of fact, *Planned Parenthood v. Casey*, not *Roe*, has been what passes for the law of abortion for almost 30 years.)

With *Roe*, the High Court decisively transformed itself into a political institution. The worst kind of political institution, in fact: One that pretends to be something quite different — an apolitical arbiter of what the law says, an oracle of justice shorn of passion. One that is politically unaccountable to the people whose lives it deeply affects — and affects not as a court deciding the private disputes of litigants, but as a ruler imposing national policy on a heretofore self-determining republic.

The mob is in front of the courthouse because we are inured to the unspoken reality that the Court is innately political. Political entities can be moved by mobs, such as the one that gleefully cheered Senator Schumer on.

There is no mob outside a medical lab. When specimens are submitted, the techs do their tests, and the patients either have whatever condition is suspected or they don't. No one, however, believes any longer that jurists work with such professional detachment and rigor. No one believes they check their political, ideological, and emotional baggage at the door, applying law to facts without fear or favor.

When President Obama nominated Judge Sonia Sotomayor to the Court, it was not for her legal acumen. The salient argument made in her favor, as if there were nothing remarkable about advocating such an attribute as a credential, was that she is a model of "empathy" — a "wise Latina" who would bring a "perspective" outside the ken of your average staid old white guy.

There is, of course, a very appropriate place in our system for a person of such gifts. Justice Sotomayor would make a superb congresswoman. That I wouldn't agree with her about most things is beside the point. In a pluralistic society, the legislature is where we want our diverse interests effectively represented. That's the place where majorities must be persuaded to empathize with other interests if we are to have domestic tranquility.

But that is not what a court is for.

A court is for telling us what the law is, as opposed to what the judges wish it were, or think it had better be if the mob is to be appeased. If a court does its job properly, and the people and their representatives do not like the result, they can try to change the law democratically. No one would blame the judges. They are supposed to be the messengers, not the lawgivers.

That is the system we were bequeathed. It is no longer the system we have.

The Court is a political institution. And Senator Schumer is simply conducting politics the way the Left does politics. It is what the Alinskyites call "direct action." You pretend that you're all about the rule of law — in fact, that you are the very embodiment of the rule of law — until the second the law does not go your way. Then you claim the system is rigged, corrupt, racist, and so on. Then you call in the mob.

The Left does what Senator Schumer did on Wednesday because it works.

Censure? Perish the thought. The demagogues are already telling us he's just passionate about women's health issues (the health of Justices Gorsuch and Kavanaugh is obviously not a concern). The Democrats will close ranks behind him — and use the publicity to raise money based on Schumer's heroic activism in protecting "choice." The left-leaning legacy media will look the other way — there's no reason you need to know that the case at issue is not actually about the enduring legality of abortion, but rather about whether abortionists should have admitting privileges at local hospitals (which actually is a women's health issue), and whether abortion providers — rather than women purportedly harmed by such a requirement — have standing to sue.

No, better for you to be told the lie that Gorsuch and Kavanaugh are scheming to consign women to back-alley quacks, and that Schumer had no choice but to call out the pitchforks. When you're pressuring a political institution, a little extortion can go a long way.

Part Fifteen

Mar-a Logo Search Warrant

SPECIAL AGENT ROTH- The execution of the search warrant at President Trump's home at Mar a Lago, Florida on August 8,2022 has quickly developed into a major conflict between the Department of Justice, the Federal Bureau of Investigation and former President Donald Trump. Legal pundits on each

side are waying in on all legal theories across the spectrum. The Federal Court system has already held hearings and requested motion papers from each side. This is escalating each day with no end in sight.

The Department of Justice apparently has leaked particularly disturbing information that there were

documents related to nuclear weapons found by the F.B.I. agents during the search.

The case will go beyond the midterm elections in November,2022.

These are the main issues.

1) Did President Trump have the authority to remove documents from the White House or other locations and store them in his house?
2) Did President Trump have the authority to declassify these documents?
3) If he did have the authority to declassify these documents, what paperwork did he have to prepare, if any?
4) Did President Trump have to get permission from anybody to declassify these documents.
5) Was a grand jury empaneled on this case.?
6) Did the Department of Justice have the authority to "leak" that is tell the media what Information was in these documents?
7) Is the Trump case similar to the Hillary Clinton e-mail case?

Trump baselessly bashed Obama for transferring records from the White House to Chicago. Here's why Obama was allowed while Trump is under scrutiny by the FBI.

Sep 1, 2022, 5:56

President Barack Obama and President-elect Donald Trump at the inauguration ceremony swearing in Trump as president on January 20, 2017. Carlos Barria/File Photo/Reuters

- Donald Trump invoked Barack Obama while bashing the FBI raid on his Mar-a-Lago home on August 8.
- Trump and Fox News compared his situation to Obama moving records to Chicago after his term.
- The National Archives took it upon itself to dispel Trump's claims.

Former President Donald Trump is no longer satisfied with talking only about Hillary Clinton's emails when it comes to deflecting potential allegations, he mishandled classified documents.

As part of his shifting defense following the FBI search of Mar-a-Lago, the former president and his allies are bringing up completely unrelated claims about former President Barack Obama.

On August 8, the FBI executed an unprecedented search warrant on Trump's Mar-a-Lago home in Palm Beach, Florida. It's now known that federal agents were retrieving sensitive White House documents — some of which were marked highly classified or top secret — and that the Justice Department is investigating whether the former president broke federal laws by keeping them and obstructing the probe by claiming that the files have all been returned.

In the days following the raid, Trump and his allies on Fox News delivered the whataboutism defense of Obama transferring records from the White House to Chicago for his presidential library.

"What happened to the 30 million pages of documents taken from the White House to Chicago by Barack Hussein Obama? He refused to give them back!" Trump wrote in an August 11 post on Truth Social. "What is going on? This act was strongly at odds with NARA. Will they be breaking into Obama's 'mansion' in Martha's Vineyard?"

The former president and his son Donald Trump Jr. cited an opinion piece published by The New York Post in support of their baseless accusations.

But the facts don't align with Trump's statements

Tens of thousands of Obama's documents were transported to Chicago. But these items were shipped to a federal government facility — which is what's supposed to happen with a president's records. Federal law requires that presidents and their administrations keep a detailed collection of emails, documents, and even gifts from their time in office since all of those things are actually the property of the American people.

In Obama's case, the National Archives took legal ownership of Obama's documents and then began the long process of sorting through the material before the public could request it years later. Some of this material was then turned over to Obama's presidential library, which is the standard legal process.

On August 12, the National Archives took it upon itself to further dispel Trump's claims.

"NARA moved approximately 30 million pages of unclassified records to a NARA facility in the Chicago area where they are maintained exclusively by NARA," the archives said in a statement. "Additionally, NARA maintains the classified Obama Presidential records in a NARA facility in the Washington, DC, area. As required by the PRA, former President Obama has no control over where and how NARA stores the Presidential records of his Administration."

Apart from the long processes, Obama's presidential library will break from the precedent in that the Obama Foundation will pay for the unclassified records to be digitized in a bid to democratize access to the documents, in what has been billed to be the "first digital archives for the first digital president," according to The New York Times.

Trump and Trump Jr. also drew on a line from The New York Post column noting that, to date, the records transferred to Obama's presidential library have yet to digitize the materials and make them available to the public — five years since the end of his term and when the record transfer began.

Though the delay has sparked some ire from historians and critics, the process of transferring the records themselves often take years, not to mention the task of digitizing roughly 30 million documents to be made available online.

Trump's lawyer, on the other hand, said the Feds took at least a dozen boxes containing sensitive — and some "top secret" — material from the former president's Mar-a-Lago home, according to The Washington Post. The FBI's search warrant was aimed at finding out if Trump had taken documents home with him that should have been turned over at the end of his term.

Though Trump world can draw similarities between Trump and Obama both taking records from the White House, the significant difference in how they took the documents explains why the former remains under scrutiny by the FBI and the latter is still in the process of setting up a library unbothered by federal law enforcement.

Published September 5, 2022, 11:57am EDT

Federal judge orders appointment of special master to review seized Trump records

Special master will review records seized in FBI raid of Trump's home

By **Brooke Singman , David Spunt , Bill Mears , Tyler Olson** | Fox News

A federal judge ordered Monday that an independent special master be appointed to review the records seized by the FBI during its raid of former President Trump's Mar-a-Lago home and ordered the Justice Department stop its own review of the material for investigative purposes.
U.S. District Judge from the Southern District of Florida Judge Aileen M. Cannon ordered that the special master be appointed to "review the seized property, manage assertions of privilege and make recommendations thereon, and evaluate claims for return of property."

TRUMP FBI RAID: DOJ RELEASES MORE DETAILS ON DOCUMENTS TAKEN FROM MAR-A-LAGO

"The Court hereby authorizes the appointment of a special master to review the seized property for personal items and documents and potentially privileged material subject to claims of attorney-client and/or executive privilege," the order states.

Fox News first reported last month that FBI agents seized boxes containing records covered by attorney-client privilege and potentially executive privilege during the raid.

248

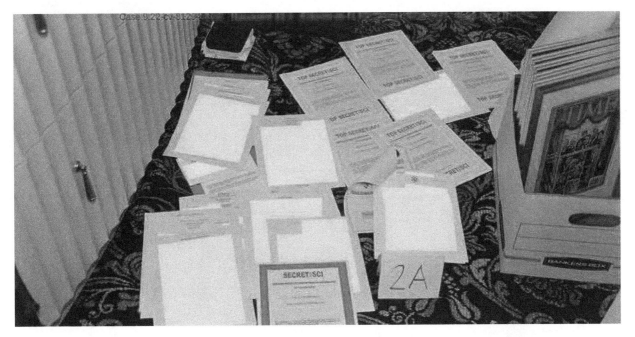

This image contained in a court filing By the Department of Justice on Aug. 30, 2022, and redacted By in part By the FBI, shows a photo of documents seized during the Aug. 8, 2022, search By the FBI of former President Donald Trump's Mar-a-Lago estate in Florida. (Department of Justice via AP)

Attorney-client privilege refers to a legal privilege that keeps communications between an attorney and their client confidential. It is unclear, at this point, if the records include communications between the former president and his private attorneys, White House counsel during the Trump administration or a combination.

A Department of Justice "taint" or "filter" team had been reviewing those documents, but Cannon's Monday order temporarily halts that review.

"Furthermore, in natural conjunction with that appointment, and consistent with the value and sequence of special master procedures, the Court also temporarily enjoins the Government from reviewing and using the seized materials for investigative purposes pending completion of the special master's review or further Court order."

TRUMP FBI RAID: JUDGE DELAYS RULING ON 'SPECIAL MASTER' AFTER KEY HEARING

The order, though, "shall not impede the classification review and/or intelligence assessment by the Office of the Director of National Intelligence ("ODNI") as described in the Government's Notice of Receipt of Preliminary Order."

Former President Donald Trump's Mar-a-Lago resort in Palm Beach, Florida. (Charles Trainor Jr./Miami Herald/Tribune News Service via Getty Images)

Trump's legal team last month asked Cannon to appoint a special master in the wake of the unprecedented search of his property, arguing that the DOJ's "Privilege Review Team" should not be the final arbiter of whether its actions were proper in such a high-profile case and that the review team's scope was too narrow.

"We need to take a deep breath. These are presidential records in the hands of the 45th president at a place which was used frequently for work during his presidency," Trump attorney Christopher Kise said in a hearing Thursday.

Meanwhile, federal prosecutors during the hearing last week argued that appointing a special master would delay their investigation, that Trump didn't have standing for his request and that he didn't have a right to possess the classified documents.

"He is no longer the president, and because he is not … he was unlawfully in possession of them," DOJ attorney Jay Bratt said of the documents the FBI took from Trump's home.
A more detailed list of documents taken from Trump's home revealed that dozens of highly classified documents, and even empty folders with classified markings, were among the items the FBI seized.

JUDGE ANNOUNCES 'PRELIMINARY INTENT TO APPOINT A SPECIAL MASTER' TO REVIEW TRUMP RECORDS SEIZED BY FBI

"Some of those records included the most highly classified records in the U.S. There was no place at that property [Mar-a-Lago] that was authorized for those records," DOJ prosecutor Julie Edelstein said Thursday.

Cannon's ruling came after she declined to rule on the request from the bench at a Thursday hearing over Trump's motion. The judge said then she would announce her ruling "in due course."

Cannon did, however, indicate that she was leaning toward appointing a special master.

Last week, Cannon announced in an order her "preliminary intent" to grant Trump's request. And she seemed skeptical of some of the government's arguments in Thursday's hearing.

"What is the harm of appointing a special master?" she said. "What is your articulation of harm other than the general concern that it would delay a criminal investigation?"

The government conducted the initial search of Trump's home in response to what it believes to be a violation of federal laws: 18 USC 793 — gathering, transmitting or losing defense information; 18 USC 2071 — concealment, removal or mutilation; and 18 USC 1519 — destruction, alteration or falsification of records in Federal investigations.

Attorney General Merrick Garland said he personally approved the search of Trump's home.

Fox News' Jake Gibson contributed to this report.

Brooke Singman is a Fox News Digital politics reporter. You can reach her at Brooke.Singman@Fox.com or @BrookeSingman on Twitter.

William Barr, on Fox, says there's no legitimate reason for classified docs to be at Mar-a-Lago and doubts Trump declassified

By Sonnet Swire, CNN
Updated 10:19 PM ET, Fri September 2, 2022
Veteran takes issue with Marines placed in backdrop of Biden's speech

(CNN) Former Attorney General William Barr appeared on Fox News on Friday to say there is no "legitimate reason" for classified documents to have been at Mar-a-Lago and cast doubt in the idea that they had somehow been declassified.

"No. I can't think of a legitimate reason why they should have been -- could be taken out of government, away from the government if they are classified," Barr said of the documents found at former President Donald Trump's Florida resort.

"I, frankly, am skeptical of the claim that [Trump] declassified everything," Barr added.

"Because frankly, I think it's highly improbable, and second, if in fact he sort of stood over scores of boxes, not really knowing what was in them and said 'I hereby declassify everything in here,' that would be such an abuse and that shows such recklessness, it's almost worse than taking the documents," he said.

Mar-a-Lago search inventory shows documents marked as classified mixed with clothes, gifts, press clippings

Barr also rejected criticism that the FBI search was in the wrong because it was "unprecedented."

"Let me just say, I think the driver on this from the beginning was loads of classified information sitting in Mar-a-Lago. People say this [raid] was unprecedented -- well, it's also unprecedented for a president to take all this classified information and put them in a country club, okay," Barr said.

"And how long is the government going to try to get that back? They jawboned for a year, they were deceived on the voluntary actions taken, they went and got a subpoena, they were deceived on that they feel, and the facts are starting to show that they were being jerked around," he added. "And so how long, you know, how long do they wait?"

Asked about his stance on Trump's request for a special master to review documents pertaining to the FBI raid at Mar-a-Lago, Barr called the idea a "red herring" and "waste of time."

"Well, I think the whole idea of a special master is a bit of a red herring," Barr said, adding, "at this stage, since they have already gone through the documents, I think it's a waste of time."

Trump says he will 'very, very seriously' consider January 6 pardons if he runs and wins in 2024

Barr said there's a "legitimate concern" about protecting documents that could be related to Trump's private lawyer communications, but it does not "appear to be much of it," and noted he's "not sure you need a special master to identify it."

"What people are missing is that all the other documents taken, even if they claim to be executive privilege, either belong to the government because they are government records -- even if they are classified, even if they are subject to executive privilege -- they still belong to the government and go to the Archives," he added.

252

Barr doubled down on the comments in a phone interview Friday with The New York Times, which reported he laughed when asked what he thought of Trump's argument for needing a special master in the case and said that he doesn't think one "is called for."

As more information is revealed, Barr said, "the actions of the department look more understandable."

"It appears that there's been a lot of jerking around of the government," he told the Times. "I'm not sure the department could have gotten it back without taking action."

Classified documents were mingled with magazines and clothes at Trump's Mar-a-Lago club

Bart Jansen, Kevin Johnson and Josh Meyer, USA Today

September 2, 2022, 1:54 PM

A more detailed list of the documents seized from Donald Trump's Florida estate was released Friday by the federal judge overseeing the former president's lawsuit seeking a third-party special master to review the records, which FBI agents found stored in a haphazard way that mingled "top secret" records with magazines and articles of clothing.

Aside from the classified materials, the list appears to show the chaotic nature in which thousands of documents were kept.

Here's what was recovered in the search:

- Overall, the list described 31 confidential documents, 54 "secret" documents and 11 "top secret."
- 48 empty folders with classified banners
- 42 folders marked "return to staff secretary/military aide"
- More than 11,000 government documents or pictures without classification markings
- Nearly 1,673 magazines, newspapers, or press clippings
- 19 articles of clothing or gift items
- 33 books

The comingled contents of the 33 boxes not only highlight a potential security risk posed by the unsecured classified documents but also underscore the chaotic nature of Trump's exit from the White House and his desperate attempts to cling to power, which federal and state prosecutors are reviewing in connection with other criminal investigations.

At about the same time the more detailed list of evidence was made public, Patrick Cipollone, a former Trump White House counsel, arrived at the federal courthouse in Washington, D.C., where he was expected to appear before a grand jury investigating the Capitol attack. Cipollone would be the highest-ranking Trump administration official known to testify so far.

Meanwhile, the thousands of unmarked government records recovered in the Mar-a-Lago search were not specifically identified, and it was unclear whether the volume of the material would factor into the judge's decision on whether to appoint a special master to oversee a document review.

FBI agents searched Mar-a-Lago on Aug. 8 for documents from the Trump administration that may have provided evidence of violations of the Espionage Act or obstruction of justice. Trump filed a lawsuit for a special master to review the documents, to possibly block the Justice

Department from documents related to communications from his lawyers or from administration aides.

U.S. District Judge Aileen Cannon released the list while deciding whether to appoint a special master and potentially limit Justice Department access to the documents.

FBI: Search part of 'active criminal investigation'

In a status report filed with the document list, prosecutors described the inquiry as an "active criminal investigation."

"It is important to note, 'review' of the seized materials is not a single investigative step but an ongoing process in this active criminal investigation," prosecutors said. "That said, the government can confirm for the court that the investigative team has already examined every item seized (other than the materials that remain subject to the filter protocols), even as its investigation and further review continues."

In addition to the criminal investigation, the Justice Department said in court records it is working with the Office of the Director of National Intelligence to assess the potential national security risk posed by the discovery of the unsecured classified documents.

Who is Trump lawyer Christina Bobb?: How Trump lawyer Christina Bobb, an ex-OAN host, took spotlight in Mar-a-Lago case

Empty classified folders

Although the newly unsealed search warrant receipt does not contain enough information to determine what happened to the documents within the empty "classified" folders retrieved by the FBI, one former senior White House information security official said the discrepancy raises serious concerns.

"It's tough to know, but empty folders could raise some alarm bells. Important decision memoranda and other papers often need to be returned from the president to the staff secretary for distribution and implementation by senior aides on the whole range of subjects," said Rajesh De, a White House staff secretary in the Obama administration who was in charge of securing classified documents and managing the paper flow to the president and senior staff.

"As for the empty classified folders, one also has to wonder what became of the contents and what if they fall into the wrong hands?" said De, a former senior Justice Department and National Security Agency official who now chairs the national security practice at law firm Mayer Brown.

Bradley Moss, a national security lawyer, said in a tweet that if empty folders were used to store classified documents, there will be documentation indicating who put the records in that folder and what they were.

House Minority Leader Kevin McCarthy, R-Calif., and Republicans on the House Judiciary Committee sent a letter Friday to Attorney General Merrick Garland and FBI Director Christopher Wray calling for testimony and hearings about the search.

The DOJ's obstruction case against Trump, aides: DOJ mapped out strong obstruction evidence against Trump, aides in filing, experts say

Classified documents were mingled with magazines, clothes, news clippings

At least seven boxes of documents, photographs and other materials were taken from the former president's Mar-a-Lago office and included at least 24 classified documents and an array of emptied folders. Two of them were labeled with directions to "return to staff secretary military aide."

The list describes 15 "secret" documents, seven "top secret" documents and 43 empty folders with "classified" banners from a box retrieved from Trump's office at Mar-a-Lago. Another secret document was found separately in the "45 Office."

The haphazard nature of the storage was revealed in Box 10, recovered from the Mar-a-Lago storage room. The contents included 32 classified documents along with articles of clothing, magazine clippings, a book and a mix of 255 unidentified records and photographs.

Thousands of pictures were found in boxes in the storage room. The list also featured hundreds of magazines, press articles and other documents without classified markings. Several articles of clothing were retrieved from the storage room.

What that Mar-a-Lago evidence photo reveals: What Trump Mar-a-Lago photo shows vs. what we know about handling classified documents

Documents seized after Trump lawyers said in June that all records were turned over

The trove of records was seized after Trump's lawyers certified in June that all records had been turned over to federal authorities in response to a grand jury subpoena seeking any remaining classified material at the property.

Prosecutors cited the prior certification in a scathing assessment of how the records were handled, asserting that the Trump team likely concealed and moved the remaining documents to obstruct the government's investigation.

"That the FBI, in a matter of hours, recovered twice as many documents with classification markings as the 'diligent search' that the former President's counsel and other representatives had weeks to perform calls into serious question the representations made in the June 3 certification and casts doubt on the extent of cooperation in this matter," Justice officials stated in court documents earlier this week.

Judge orders release of detailed list of property seized in Trump FBI search

Melissa Quinn

September 1, 2022, 10:19 AM

West Palm Beach, Florida — A federal judge on Thursday ordered the release of a detailed list of the property seized during the FBI's search at former President Donald Trump's South Florida residence last month, while reserving judgment on whether to appoint an outside party to review the documents.

Federal prosecutors initially submitted a property receipt to the U.S. District Court for the Southern District of Florida on Tuesday, though it was filed under seal. The Justice Department told the court in a separate filing it was prepared to release the receipt to the public given the "extraordinary circumstances" of the case and provide it "immediately" to Trump.

Trump's legal team said they did not oppose unsealing the detailed inventory. It remained sealed as of Thursday afternoon.

Last month, the Justice Department agreed to release a more generalized version of the list, along with the warrant used to justify the search. That inventory revealed that the FBI seized 11 sets of

255

documents containing material marked as classified, including four sets that contained documents marked "top secret," in the Aug. 8 search at Mar-a-Lago, Trump's estate.

U.S. District Judge Aileen Cannon, who is overseeing Trump's lawsuit stemming from the Aug. 8 search, ordered the release of the detailed inventory during a hearing on Thursday. Justice Department lawyers and members of Trump's legal team appeared for arguments over whether the judge should appoint a "special master" to review the documents seized by federal agents.

Cannon did not issue a decision on the special master from the bench but said she will issue a written order "in due course." She seemed potentially inclined to block the Justice Department from accessing the seized materials should she appoint a special master, but appeared open to allowing the Office of the Director of National Intelligence to continue its assessment of the documents for potential national security risks.

During the hearing, federal prosecutors said an FBI filter team, a group of agents responsible for sifting through and setting aside documents that may be privileged, reviewed 520 pages from 64 sets of documents. The records were taken from a storage room at Mar-a-Lago and Trump's office, known as the "45 Office" by the Justice Department, they said.

Jay Bratt, the top counterintelligence official at the Justice Department, and Juan Antonio Gonzalez, the U.S. Attorney in Miami, told Cannon that the "vast majority" of records taken during the search are likely not privileged, but investigators acted out of an "abundance of caution" in separating those that may be.

Bratt also revealed that on the morning after the search, Trump's team asked the Justice Department for the appointment of a special master, which prosecutors declined. Trump's team made "no subsequent request" for a special master until filing their lawsuit, Bratt said, and was advised that the filter team was in place.

Will Trump be indicted over classified documents found at Mar-a-Lago?

David Knowles

September 1, 2022, 4:11 PM

The Justice Department's recent response to a request by Donald Trump's legal team for the appointment of a "special master" to review classified documents discovered during a search of the former president's Florida resort and residence set off a flurry of speculation about whether an indictment would be forthcoming.

Since America's founding, no U.S. president has faced a criminal indictment, but the details revealed in Tuesday's DOJ court filing — including a photo of top-secret documents arrayed on the floor of Trump's office — showed he continued to possess such documents at Mar-a-Lago despite months of negotiations with the National Archives and a signed assurance from his lawyers that all the sensitive documents had been returned.

While Trump and his lawyers initially stated that he had declassified all the documents he brought with him from the White House, their court response to the DOJ's filing gave no mention of that claim.

Based on the filing, some conservative observers said an indictment appeared likely.

"Even a cursory review of the redacted version of the affidavit submitted in support of the government's application for a search warrant at the home of former President reveals that he will soon be indicted by a federal grand jury for three crimes: Removing and concealing national defense information (NDI), giving NDI to those not legally entitled to possess it, and obstruction of justice by failing to return NDI to those who are legally entitled to retrieve it," Andrew Napolitano, Fox News legal analyst and former Superior Court judge, wrote in an opinion piece for the Washington Times.

A redacted FBI photograph of documents and classified cover sheets recovered from a container stored at Donald Trump's Florida estate. (Department of Justice/Handout via Reuters)

Writing at National Review, conservative author Andrew McCarthy agreed that the filing made clear that a Trump indictment is a strong possibility.

"Former president Donald Trump is facing the very serious prospect of being indicted for obstruction of justice and causing false statements to be made to the government," McCarthy wrote. "That is the upshot of a court submission filed by the Justice Department on Tuesday night, in response to the Trump camp's belated motion for the appointment of a special master to review materials seized three weeks ago from the former president's Mar-a-Lago estate."

On Sunday, days before the DOJ laid out its case against appointing a special master, Sen. Lindsey Graham, R-S.C., made headlines when he predicted what would happen if Trump were to be indicted.

"If they try to prosecute President Trump for mishandling classified information after Hillary Clinton set up a server in her basement, there literally will be riots in the street. I worry about our country," he said.

Former Harvard law professor Alan Dershowitz picked up on what Trump and his supporters see as a potential double standard regarding former Secretary of State Clinton's handling of classified material, and, prior to the DOJ filing on Tuesday, confidently predicted that Trump would not face indictment over the documents.

"There is enough evidence here to indict Trump, but Trump will not be indicted, in my view, because the evidence doesn't pass what I call the Nixon-Clinton standards. The Nixon standard is, a case has to be so overwhelmingly strong that even Republicans support it, and the [Hillary] Clinton standard is, why is this case more serious than Clinton's case where there wasn't the criminal prosecution?" Dershowitz said Friday on Fox News.

"So I think the three points are: There was probable cause, they shouldn't have sought a warrant, there is enough for an indictment but there will not be an indictment and should not be an indictment based on what we've seen to now. Maybe once we see it unredacted, we'll have to change our minds."

Bloomberg reported Wednesday that Attorney General Merrick Garland's decision on whether to indict Trump will likely wait until after the midterm elections due to a department policy that prohibits prosecutors from "taking investigative steps or filing charges for the purpose of affecting an election or helping a candidate or party, traditionally 60 days before an election," Bloomberg journalist Chris Strohm wrote.

Of course, that policy did not prevent former FBI Director James Comey from reopening an investigation into Clinton's use of a private computer server only days prior to the 2016 election.

Given the historical significance of a possible criminal indictment of the former president, the Justice Department will not make its decision lightly, most legal analysts agree. That's especially true given that the DOJ will seek to keep the highly classified material at the heart of the case from public view. As Politico's senior legal affairs reporter Josh Gerstein put it, charging Trump would result in likely "the highest-profile criminal case in American history," and one in which a not-guilty verdict would have long-lasting implications for the DOJ while a conviction might result in the unrest Graham predicted.

A Quinnipiac poll released Wednesday found that 50% of Americans believe Trump should face criminal charges over his handling of the classified documents, while 41% do not.

While Trump and his supporters see a plot by the Biden administration to damage his political prospects in 2024, others say his public statements are not helping his case. On Wednesday, for instance, STrump posted a message to Truth Social, his struggling social media platform, that appeared to confirm that he knew he had been in possession of the classified documents in question.

"There seems to be confusion as to the 'picture' where documents were sloppily thrown on the floor and then released photographically for the world to see, as if that's what the FBI found when they broke into my home," Trump wrote. "Wrong! They took them out of cartons and spread them around on the carpet, making it look like a big 'find' for them. They dropped them, not me — Very deceiving ... And remember, we could have NO representative, including lawyers, present during the Raid. They were told to wait outside."

CNN legal analyst Norm Eisen said that message involved "really the last key issue that will determine whether or not Donald Trump is charged ... his personal knowledge that these classified documents were where they were."

"Well, guess what," Eisen continued, "by admitting that he knew they were in the cartons, he just provided the government with more proof that, yes, he was involved in this."

The appearance that the Justice Department may be preparing to indict Trump is not the same, however, as the announcement of an actual indictment.

"It seems to me that it's moving in the direction of warranting criminal charges," David Laufman, former chief of the counterespionage section at the Justice Department's National Security Division, told Politico. "I think [Trump] has significant criminal exposure. Whether they ultimately decide to exercise prosecutorial discretion in favor of prosecuting him is another question."

Jim Trusty, one of Trump's lawyers, argued that in addition to asserting attorney-client privilege over some of the records, the former president is also assserting executive privilege over others.

Exclusive: An Informer Told the FBI What Docs Trump Was Hiding, and Where

BY **William M. Arkin** *ON 8/10/22 AT 10:03 AM EDT*

The raid on Mar-a-Lago was based largely on information from an FBI confidential human source, one who was able to identify what classified documents former President Trump was still hiding and even the location of those documents, two senior government officials told Newsweek.

The officials, who have direct knowledge of the FBI's deliberations and were granted anonymity in order to discuss sensitive matters, said the raid of Donald Trump's Florida residence was deliberately timed to occur when the former president was away.

A confidential informer told the FBI what documents Donald Trump was hiding at Mar-a-Lago, and where. The former president at a rally on August 05, 2022, in Waukesha, Wisconsin.SCOTT OLSON/GETTY IMAGES

FBI decision-makers in Washington and Miami thought that denying the former president a photo opportunity or a platform from which to grandstand (or to attempt to thwart the raid) would lower the profile of the event, says one of the sources, a senior Justice Department official who is a 30-year veteran of the FBI. The effort to keep the raid low-key failed: instead, it prompted a furious response from GOP leaders and Trump supporters. "What a spectacular backfire," says the Justice official.

"I know that there is much speculation out there that this is political persecution, but it is really the best and the worst of the bureaucracy in action," the official says. "They wanted to punctuate the fact that this was a routine law enforcement action, stripped of any political overtones, and yet [they] got exactly the opposite."

Both senior government officials say the raid was scheduled with no political motive, the FBI solely intent on recovering highly classified documents that were illegally removed from the White House. Preparations to conduct such an operation began weeks ago, but in planning the date and time, the FBI Miami Field Office and Washington headquarters were focused on the former president's scheduled return to Florida from his residences in New York and New Jersey.

"They were seeking to avoid any media circus," says the second source, a senior intelligence official who was briefed on the investigation and the operation. "So even though everything made sense bureaucratically and the FBI feared that the documents might be destroyed, they also created the very firestorm they sought to avoid, in ignoring the fallout." A "Florida For Trump" flag being displayed outside Mar-a-Lago following the FBI search.

On Monday at about 9 a.m. EDT, two dozen FBI agents and technicians showed up at Donald Trump's Florida home to execute a search warrant to obtain any government-owned documents that might be in the possession of Trump but are required to be delivered to the Archives under the provisions of the 1978 Presidential Records Act. (In response to the Hillary Clinton email scandal, Trump himself signed a law in 2018 that made it a felony to remove and retain classified documents.)

259

The act establishes that presidential records are the property of the U.S. government and not a president's private property. Put in place after Watergate to avoid the abuses of the Nixon administration, the law imposes strict penalties for failure to comply. "Whoever, having the custody of any such record, proceeding, map, book, document, paper, or other thing, willfully and unlawfully conceals, removes, mutilates, obliterates, falsifies, or destroys the same, shall be fined" $2,000, up to three years in prison or "shall forfeit his office and be disqualified from holding any office under the United States."

The act, and concerns about the illegal possession of classified "national defense information" are the basis for the search warrant, according to the two sources. The raid had nothing to do with the January 6 investigation or any other alleged wrongdoing by the former president.

The road to the raid began a year-and-a-half ago, when in the transition from the Trump administration to that of President Joe Biden, there were immediate questions raised by the National Archives and Records Administration (NARA) as to whether the presidential records turned over to the federal agency for historical preservation were complete or not.

In February, Archivist David Ferriero testified before Congress that his agency began talking with Trump's people right after they left office and that the Trump camp had already returned 15 boxes of documents to the Archives. Ferriero said that in those materials, the Archives discovered items "marked as classified national security information," unleashing further inquiries as to whether Trump continued to possess classified material.

Will Trump Do Time? What It Would Take to Convict the Former President

Will Trump Do Time? What It Would Take to Convict the Former President

The basic outlines of the facts surrounding this timeline have been confirmed by the former president. He has previously said that he was returning any official records to the Archives, labeling any confusion in the matter as "an ordinary and routine process to ensure the preservation of my legacy and in accordance with the Presidential Records Act." He also claimed the Archives "did not 'find' anything" in what he had already been returned, suggesting that there was nothing sensitive. He said the documents had inadvertently shipped to Florida during the six-hour transition period in which his belongings were moved.

According to the Justice Department source, the Archives saw things differently, believing that the former White House was stonewalling and continued to possess unauthorized material. Earlier this year, they asked the Justice Department to investigate.

In late April, the source says, a federal grand jury began deliberating whether there was a violation of the Presidential Records Act or whether President Trump unlawfully possessed national security information. Through the grand jury process, the National Archives provided federal prosecutors with copies of the documents received from former President Trump in January 2022. The grand jury concluded that there had been a violation of the law, according to the Justice Department source.

In the past week, the prosecutor in the case and local Assistant U.S. Attorney went to Florida magistrate Judge Bruce Reinhart in West Palm Beach to seek approval for the search of Donald Trump's private residence. The affidavit to obtain the search warrant, the intelligence source says, contained abundant and persuasive detail that Trump continued to possess the relevant records in violation of federal law, and that investigators had sufficient information to prove that those records were located at Mar-a-Lago—including the detail that they were contained in a specific safe in a specific room.

"In order for the investigators to convince the Florida judge to approve such an unprecedented raid, the information had to be solid, which the FBI claimed," says the intelligence source.

Will GOP Fury Over Trump-FBI Battle Blunt Democrats' Post-Roe Midterm Edge?

Will GOP Fury Over Trump-FBI Battle Blunt Democrats' Post-Roe Midterm Edge?

According to experts familiar with FBI practices, Judge Reinhart reviewed the prosecutor's evidence and asked numerous questions about the sources and the urgency. The judge signed a search warrant allowing the FBI to look for relevant material and the FBI then planned the operation, wanting to conduct the raid while Trump was spending time at his golf club in Bedminster, New Jersey. A Secret Service source who spoke on background said the Secret Service director was given advance warning and was later told the specifics of the raid.

Because the Secret Service is still responsible for protecting the former president, his family, and his property, the FBI had to coordinate with the Secret Service to gain access to the grounds.

A convoy of unmarked black SUVs and a Ryder rental truck filled with about three dozen FBI special agents and technicians entered the gates in the early evening. Heavily armed Secret Service agents were also visibly present at the gates. The Palm Beach Police Department was also present at the scene.

The entire operation, which concluded about 7 p.m., was conducted relatively stealthily. No FBI people were seen in their iconic blue windbreakers announcing the presence of the Bureau. And though local law enforcement was present, the Palm Beach Police Department was careful to tweet on Tuesday that it "was not aware of the existence of a search warrant nor did our department assist the FBI in the execution of a search warrant."

According to news reports, some 10-15 boxes of documents were removed from the premises. Donald Trump said in a statement that the FBI opened his personal safe as part of their search. Trump attorney Lindsey Halligan, who was present during the multi-hour search, says that the FBI targeted three rooms—a bedroom, an office and a storage room. That suggests that the FBI knew specifically where to look.

"This unannounced raid on my home was not necessary or appropriate," former President Trump said in a statement. He called the raid "prosecutorial misconduct, the weaponization of the Justice System, and an attack by Radical Left Democrats who desperately don't want me to run for President in 2024."

Though Trump and his Republican Party allies are portraying the raid as politically motivated, it is likely the unprecedented nature of the raid on the property of a former president will have the greatest reverberation. Even Trump's political rivals have rallied in condemning the FBI.

Former Vice President Mike Pence tweeted that "no former President of the United States has ever been subject to a raid of their personal residence in American history." Mike Pompeo, Trump's Secretary of State and CIA director, tweeted that Attorney General Merrick Garland "must explain why 250 yrs of practice was upended w/ this raid. I served on Benghazi Com[mittee] where we proved Hillary possessed classified info. We didn't raid her home."

The Biden White House says the president was not briefed about the Mar-a-Lago raid and knew nothing about it in advance. "The Justice Department conducts investigations independently and we leave any law enforcement matters to them," Press Secretary Karine Jean-Pierre said Tuesday afternoon. "It would not be appropriate for us to comment on any ongoing investigations."

As U.S. President Joe Biden, appearing via teleconference, looks on, Attorney General Merrick Garland attends a meeting of the Task Force on Reproductive Healthcare Access during an event at the White House complex August 3, 2022 in Washington, DC.

The senior Justice Department source says that Garland was regularly briefed on the Records Act investigation, and that he knew about the grand jury and what material federal prosecutors were seeking.

FBI director Christopher Wray ultimately gave his go-ahead to conduct the raid, the senior Justice official says. "It really is a case of the Bureau misreading the impact."

Correction, 8/11; 10:30 a.m.: The story now clarifies that the raid took place between 9 a.m. and 7 p.m.

6:30 p.m.: A quote that mischaracterized Garland's role was deleted. Newsweek regrets the error.

DNI vows 'assessment' of probable danger in advance of Mar-a-Lago raid as Trump slams 'egregious assault' on democracy

Carl Richardson | 18 hours ago

DOJ releases redacted Mar-a-Lago raid affidavit

Online News 72h' David Spunt, Martha MacCallum and Andy McCarthy present examination and reaction to the release of the redacted affidavit in the FBI raid of previous President Trump's Mar-a-Lago residence

Director of National Intelligence Avril Haines alongside with other officers will give an "evaluation" to major lawmakers about "the potential hazard" to nationwide stability posed by previous President Trump allegedly holding leading top secret files at his Florida home, Online News 72h has learned.

Haines sent a letter to Oversight Committee Chairwoman Carolyn Maloney, D-N.Y. as perfectly as Intelligence Committee Chairman Adam Schiff, D-Calif., and informed them both about the selection.

In a joint assertion, Reps. Maloney and Schiff explained that they are "delighted" by the determination.

"We are delighted that in response to our inquiry, Director Haines has confirmed that the Intelligence Neighborhood and Section of Justice are assessing the destruction triggered by the poor storage of classified files at Mar-a-Lago. The DOJ affidavit, partly unsealed yesterday, affirms our grave issue that amongst the files stored at Mar-a-Lago ended up people that could endanger human resources. It is significant that the IC shift quickly to evaluate and, if vital, to mitigate the harm done—a procedure that really should continue in parallel with DOJ's legal investigation," they wrote.

FEDERAL Decide UNSEALS REDACTED TRUMP RAID AFFIDAVIT THAT FBI Made use of TO Look for MAR-A-LAGO

Director of National Intelligence Avril Haines appears ahead of the Senate Intelligence Committee for a listening to on all over the world threats as Russia continues to attack Ukraine, at the Capitol in Washington, Thursday, March 10, 2022.

The affidavit unsealed on Friday exposed that the FBI experienced "possible lead to to think" that documents that have categorised info, which incorporate National Defense information and facts, would be at Mar-a-Lago, the home of previous President Trump.

The affidavit was closely redacted, with 20 out of the 38 webpages getting with noticeably or entirely redacted.

"A preliminary triage of the paperwork with classification markings unveiled the pursuing approximate figures: 184 distinctive files bearing classification markings, together with 67 paperwork marked as Private, 92 paperwork marked as Secret, and 25 files marked as Top Secret," the affidavit states.

FBI Reported **it** Had 'PROBABLE CAUSE' **to** Feel Additional Classified DOCS REMAINED AT MAR-A-LAGO, AFFIDAVIT Suggests

Trump took to social media on Saturday and identified as the raid performed by the Federal Bureau of Investigations on Aug. 8 "a single of the most egregious assaults on democracy."

"The Raid on my home, Mar-a-Lago, is just one of the most egregious assaults on democracy in the record of our Country which is, by the way, going to areas, in a extremely undesirable way, it has never ever witnessed just before!," Trump explained in a Real truth Social submit.

Trump also requested in a Truth of the matter Social write-up when FBI brokers are likely to say "we are not heading to acquire it anymore."

Previous U.S. President Donald Trump leaves Trump Tower to fulfill with New York Attorney General Letitia James for a civil investigation on Aug. 10, 2022, in New York Metropolis. (James Devaney/GC Pictures)

"When are the great Agents, and some others, in the FBI going to say "we aren't likely to take it any more," a lot as they did when James Comey go through off a checklist of all of Crooked Hillary Clinton's crimes, only to say that no sensible prosecutor would prosecute. The amazing persons of the FBI went certainly "nuts," so Comey experienced to backtrack and do a Bogus INVESTIGATION in get to hold them at bay. The end result, we won in 2016 (and did Significantly better in 2020!). But now the "Still left" has lost their minds!!," Trump reported.

Online News 72h' Brooke Singman contributed to this report.

Adam Sabes is a author for Online News 72h Electronic. Tale strategies can be sent to Adam.Sabes@fox.com and on Twitter @asabes10

Shameless feds leak details of Mar-a-Lago raid but push the court to keep affidavit sealed

By **Jonathan Turley**

August 24, 2022, 6:10pm

 Updated

Federal investigators have claimed the affidavit for raiding former President Donald Trump's Mar-a-Lago estate must remain redacted -- while also leaking information to the press. Robert Miller

This week, a curious scene will play out in a Florida courtroom. A federal magistrate will be asked to uphold what are expected to be extensive redactions of the affidavit supporting the search warrant on Mar-a-Lago. The judge, however, will be able to read an array of the same details at breakfast in newspaper accounts leaked by the government.

The feds have maintained that absolute secrecy is essential to protect their investigation and national security while reportedly leaking some of the very information the affidavit contains. It is an all-too-familiar pattern for some of us who have litigated national-security cases against the government.

The Washington Post and The New York Times have published a series of leaks clearly designed to put Donald Trump and his team on the defense in the media, including claims that he was hiding sensitive nuclear-weapons material and details on how the search was prompted by video surveillance outside the storage room at Mar-a-Lago.

Most recently, a Times report disclosed that the Justice Department recovered more than 300 documents with classified markings, citing multiple sources connected to the investigation. The leak further revealed that the government collected more than 150 documents marked as classified in January and another 150 in June and in the August raid. It also recounted specific meetings and individuals involved in past discussions.
The Washington Post and The New York Times have reported on leaks about the allegedly classified documents taken from Mar-a-Lago.REUTERS/Marco Bello//File Photo

The Times story made the purpose of the leak evident when reporters concluded that the divulged information "suggested to officials that the former president or his aides had been cavalier in handling it, not fully forthcoming with investigators, or both."

This is precisely the type of information the government has refused to release under a claim that any disclosures would materially endanger the investigation and national security.

What did Biden 'really' know about the drive to raid Mar-a-Lago?

In addition, both the Trump team and the National Archives and Records Administration have released accounts of the communications leading up to the raid. NARA put out a letter from May 10 that suggested the Biden White House was involved in the controversy and detailed how Trump sought repeatedly to block the archives from sharing documents taken from Mar-a-Lago with the FBI.

Despite the leaks and these public accounts, the Justice Department is still implausibly insisting that no substantive information can be released in a redacted affidavit. These affidavits commonly have sections on the case background that can be released in redacted form without compromising sources, including confirmation of how the FBI presented facts the Trump team and NARA allege.

There are also common legal sections that discuss the basis for probable cause. The government alleged that Trump was "unlawfully" holding material that he claims to have declassified. It references presidential papers Trump holds, but the ability of presidents to retain documents under the Presidential Records Act remains a matter of intense debate.

On both the legal and factual background, a redacted affidavit could reveal whether this information was presented fairly and accurately. It is a reasonable concern for many in the public given the record of the FBI and the Justice Department in falsifying information or misleading courts on prior Trump investigations. During the Russian-collusion investigation, some of us flagged Justice officials using the presumptively unconstitutional Logan Act.

The legal sections could reveal both the basis and nexus used to establish probable cause of criminal acts. It could well support the government, but there is no reason why such legal arguments cannot be released in part.

Attorney General Merrick Garland has failed to inform the public about the reasoning behind the Mar-a-Lago raid.AP Photo/Susan Walsh

These sections could also shed light on why the court approved a warrant that was ridiculously broad. It allowed the FBI to seize not only any box containing any paper with any classification marking, but then allowed it to take every other box stored with that box. It also allowed the seizure of any paper created during the Trump presidency. It had all the selectivity of a cyclone. The legal section of the affidavit could disclose how such a seemingly limitless warrant was justified under the law.

Some of these sections could also explain how the department justified this extraordinary action very different from how it treated past figures like Hillary Clinton and her associates who resisted inquiries into classified material kept on unsecured servers, including top-secret material. There were also allegations of efforts to influence investigators.

These are legitimate questions that could be answered through the redacted affidavit or simply an independent Justice Department disclosure. Attorney General Merrick Garland has had at least four opportunities to take modest steps to assure the public on the department's motives and means in this controversy. This includes the use of a special master to sort through the documents seized in this overbroad search. Garland failed to take any of these steps as he lashed out at those who question his department's integrity.

It is that affidavits are routinely released after charges to the defense. Though it's certainly less common before charges, this is a unique circumstance that justifies greater transparency while recognizing the need to protect confidential sources and methods. The Justice Department does not deny it can release a redacted affidavit but insists any material would be so limited and disconnected as to be incomprehensible.

That simply doesn't appear to be true. It is plainly implausible that these sections cannot be released in some form without compromising confidential sources or the already publicly known investigation. Garland cannot ignore his department's checkered history in Trump-related investigations or the contrast in treatment with past investigations like Clinton's classified emails.

That does not mean this investigation is baseless or that there were no crimes committed. But with modest disclosures, Garland can earn the trust of the public rather than simply demand it.

Jonathan Turley is an attorney and professor at George Washington University Law School.

Special Agent Roth- The "crazies" are really coming out of the woodwork to comment on the "nuclear weapons." Note that the "crazies" are careful not to say that the "nuclear weapons" story is verified.

We've reached the endgame of Trump's imperial presidency

The Washington Post's report about nuclear secrets at Mar-a-Lago further exposes Trump's attempts to wield presidential power after losing in 2020.

Sept. 7, 2022, 1:46 PM EDT

By **Ja'han Jones**

The Washington Post's report on Tuesday that top secret documents were seized from former President Donald Trump's Mar-a-Lago estate moves us into the MAGA movement's endgame.

The report, which has not been independently verified by MSNBC or NBC News, cites people familiar with the FBI's search who say among the documents seized last month at least one discussed "a foreign government's nuclear-defense readiness."

Every minute Trump evades justice damages the presidency, perhaps irreparably.

Such documents are so sensitive, according to the Post, they were typically kept "under lock and key, almost always in a secure compartmented information facility, with a designated control officer to keep careful tabs on their location." Not, you know, at Trump's tropical "heaven" for spies.

With each new revelation, the story of Trump's apparent mishandling of government-owned records gets more sinister, the need to prosecute him for any and all crimes he may have committed gets more urgent, and the national security implications for failing to do so grow more severe.

In spite of Trump-loving Republicans trotting out desperate excuses for their dear leader, we've reached a point where there is no earnest reading of the situation that shows him in a positive light.

And much like Dr. Strange in "Avengers: Endgame," I've looked forward in time to view all the possible outcomes of this conflict, and the only one that salvages the country is the prosecution and conviction of Donald Trump. The ultimate test of the imperial presidency. The validity of future presidents, and American democracy as a whole, hinges on it.

To be clear: Trump's repeated refusal to hand over the documents he stole would be an issue — and a serious one — if he'd simply taken the White House grocery list. Fundamentally, it's his refusal to surrender the documents — the country's documents — that suggests something sinister was afoot: Trump trying to assume presidential powers he did not have. The risk his reported mishandling of top secret nuclear documents posed to each and every American is almost unfathomable — but will need to be sorted out in a far-reaching national security investigation.

And every minute he evades justice damages the presidency, perhaps irreparably. Because make no mistake: possessing those documents unlawfully, but with impunity, would continue to bolster Trump's portrayal of himself as a dual president of sorts.

Just think about the influence he could wield over global affairs with this information he's alleged to have kept. Of course, we don't yet know for sure why Trump kept classified documents at his golf resort — but the possibilities are endless and alarming. In the same way people feared Russia might try to wield influence over morally bankrupt Trump, the former president could theoretically wield power over other countries — for financial or political gain — simply by showing them he still had the goods on their nuclear program.

Every day Trump faces zero accountability for his actions, he continues to call the shots. And that's a fatal situation for American democracy. His goal is simple: to dismantle the semblance of democracy that existed before him and replace it with an imperial presidency. Trump and his loyal followers, with the help of some judicial hacks he appointed during his term, have tried their damnedest.

Charging him is the only way to end his claims to kingship. We're in the endgame now.

Ja'han Jones

Ja'han Jones is The ReidOut Blog writer. He's a futurist and multimedia producer focused on culture and politics. His previous projects include "Black Hair Defined" and the "Black Obituary Project."

Former FBI assistant director says Trump could have kept hold of a foreign country's nuclear secrets because they had 'the highest price tag' for classified info

Cheryl Teh

Sep 8, 2022, 12:23 AM

Special Agent Roth- Frank, I have given you the respect from one agent to another. But you have

stepped over the line.

Growing Number of FBI Agents Accuse MSNBC Commentator Frank Figliuzzi of Fabricating Passage in His Book on Bureau Ethics

By Allan Lengel

Eight current and former ex-FBI agents who are eyewitnesses tell ticklethewire.com that both an original and revised version of a passage in a book by MSNBC commentator Frank Figliuzzi is fabricated, possibly to justify a controversial decision known in the bureau as "Stripgate."

Figliuzzi is sometimes a go-to guy on MSNBC for breaking news.

 Figliuzzi, a former assistant director of counterintelligence for the FBI, insists it's all factual.

"I stand by my account. Call me a liar in print at your legal peril," he said in an email.

Conversely, agents stand by their story, and say he's not telling the truth when he alleges in his book that an agent mishandled seized drug money.

"Absolutely didn't happen. It's just a complete fabrication," says one of eyewitnesses, retired agent Gary Rizzo, referring to a passage about a 1999 incident in Miami in Fligliuzzi's book: "The FBI Way: Inside the Bureau's Code of Excellence," which was published in January. Rizzo retired in 2018 but now works for the FBI as a firearms instructor at Quantico.

"Frank's statements in his book are untrue," echoes retired agent Michael Anderson, who eventually left Miami and went on to head the Chicago FBI Office. He was a co-case agent on the Miami case in question.

The agents who have come forward expressed concern that Figliuzzi, who retired from the FBI in 2012, is representing the bureau image on TV. It's particularly bothersome, they say, because he fabricated a passage in his book that touts the high standards of the FBI.

NBC, which has helped build Figliuzzi's increasingly popular brand on TV since 2017, ignored repeated requests for comment. The TV appearances have helped him get exposure for his podcast, "The Bureau with Frank Figliuzzi," in which he talks to active agents and specialists "who share their mission, their cases, and their lives."

On June 24, ticklethewire.com published an article in which three FBI agents – two current and one retired – accused Figliuzzi of making up the passage in his book, possibly intended to whitewash a controversial decision Figliuzzi made 22 years ago ordering two agents to be strip-searched because the boxes they were transporting in a Brink's truck with millions of dollars in just-seized Miami drug money weren't sealed according to an operations plan for raids conducted that day. Some have suggested he made up the story in the book about the money being mishandled to cast himself in better light,and justify the controversial strip-search that was frowned upon by many inside the bureau, including some supervisors.

 After publication of the story, five additional eyewitnesses, all retired agents, came forward to tell ticklethewire.com the portion in the book – the original and the revised version in the ebook– was fabricated.

The strip-search in the locker room of the FBI Miami Field Office turned up nothing. The agents were clean. Figliuzzi and his boss subsequently were investigated by the FBI's Office of Professional Responsibility (OPR) for alleged misconduct because they authorized an unprecedented and demeaning strip. Though Figliuzzi writes in his book that he wasn't charged with wrongdoing, the decision was forever known in the bureau as "Stripgate."

Money in the Brink's Truck

Figliuzzi, 58, in his book describes the incident involving FBI agent Stephen Lawrence in 1999 without mentioning his name. Lawrence, who says hundreds of current and former agents know who Figliuzzi is referring to in the book says he was in the back of the Brink's truck with the boxes of money when the doors finally opened.

Figliuzzi was an assistant special agent in charge in Miami and 36 at the time. Lawrence was a 33-year-old agent.

Lawrence, one of the eight agents accusing Figliuzzi of being untruthful, was part of a search team that was raiding properties one day in August 1999 linked to a violent Cuban-American drug cartel that had killed witnesses and bribed jurors. While raiding a Miami home, he found $9 million in boxes in the attic. A Brink's truck was summoned to transport the money.

To maintain a chain of custody, Lawrence stayed in the back of a Brink's truck with the money and an armored truck guard. Another agent sat up front in the passenger seat. A Brink's guard drove, and FBI SWAT agents were in vehicles behind and in front of the truck escorting it back to the Miami Field Office at 16320 N.W. 2nd Ave in North Miami Beach.

Figliuzzi and other agents, including those who escorted the truck back, were standing in the back of the vehicle when it opened. Just before it opened, Lawrence said the Brink's guard who was with him, slipped out of the truck through a side door, leaving him by himself.

According to Figliuzzi's original account in the book, when the door opened:

"Inside the back of the truck on this sweltering sauna of a Miami day, were two very proud and perspiring agents who had just found the most money they had ever seen in their relatively young lives. In fact, they were so happy and eager to show their bosses the fruits of their labor that they were "making it rain" inside that truck. Loose bills were cascading from the agent's hands in a shower onto the floor of the vehicle."

Figliuzzi has a podcast

Figliuzzi writes in his book that he ordered the strip search because the boxes weren't sealed according to the operational plans, and the money was flying around, putting the seizure in legal peril. The agents agree the boxes weren't sealed according to the plan for the day, but that's all they agree about.

Lawrence, who is currently an agent in the FBI Los Angeles Field Office, says the money remained intact and was never thrown around, not one bill.

Lawrence asked the publisher, HarperCollins, to correct and remove the false passage in ebooks and future printings about the mishandling of the money.

Publisher's Response

In March, Beth Neelman Silfin, a lawyer for the publisher, wrote Lawrence's Beverly Hills attorney Neville L. Johnson, offering to remove the phrase "making it rain" in the ebook and future printings to avoid any "frivolous" litigation. But she insisted the description of the tossing of money was accurate. Figliuzzi at the time told ticklethewire.com he agreed with Neelman Silfin's letter, and commented no further.

Last Thursday, ticklethewire.com contacted Figliuzzi to let him know that five more agents, who were eyewitnesses had come forward to say his version about throwing money around was false, and a second story was forthcoming.

"This is irresponsible reporting at its worst," Figliuzzi responded by email. "I will speak to you later this week. But I suggest you cease and desist with the false angles you are portraying."

Subsequently, Figliuzzi wrote to say the passage in the ebook and the audio were being modified "to accommodate (Lawrence) while remaining true to what I witnessed."

The phrase "making it rain" had been removed, but the passage still said Lawrence had improperly grabbed some of the seized money, something agents say, if true, would have created potential discipline problems for Lawrence and evidence issues in court for the FBI and U.S. Attorney's Office. Lawrence was never investigated for any allegations of mishandling money.

The ebook now reads: "On this sweltering sauna of a Miami day, were two very proud and perspiring agents who had just found the most money they had ever seen in their relatively young lives. In fact, they were happy and eager to show their bosses the fruits of their labor. They reached into open boxes and displayed the case in their hands, then let it drop back down."

Lawrence Responds to Revision

Lawrence responded to the change:

"I understand Figliuzzi recently changed his version of events once confronted with the fact there were additional witnesses, but it's still all a lie. Despite his wordsmithing, all of this is still completely false.

"I was the agent in the back of the truck with an armored guard, while the other agent (who also got strip searched) rode in the front of the truck with the driver. While the boxes weren't sealed with evidence tape at the search location by the search team, the boxes were closed and remained closed at all times while in the truck. Let me be crystal clear – no one touched the money in the boxes. Figliuzzi made a horrible judgment call and ordered us to be stripped searched simply because the boxes weren't sealed at the search location, not because anyone touched any money.

"I challenge Figliuzzi to find one credible witness who can corroborate his version. There's only one version of the truth and it never changes. Perhaps he should consider practicing what he's preached – be truthful and accept responsibility."

Figliuzzi on Friday responded with a statement:

"You are falsely assuming that these other 'witnesses' you spoke with saw what I saw at the first moment I saw it. They did not. Not the people who conceded they weren't even there, nor the people you say were 'near' there, nor the people who mistakenly believe they were the first to see, or close enough to see inside the truck."

Neelman Silfin of HarperCollins declined comment late last week, and instead deferred to Figliuzzi.

"At no point was Stephen Lawrence handling money, throwing money or touching money. I was standing right there about six or ten feet away," says Scott Umphlet, one of the five former agents who came forward after the first article. He said he was among a group of SWAT agents who escorted the Brink's truck back to the office and stood outside it when the back door opened with the boxes of money inside.

"I was extremely disappointed how the events were reported later (by Figliuzzi) because that's not what I observed."

Brian Jerome, an agent quoted in the first ticklethewire.com story, says of the ebook revision: "That's baloney. Those guys didn't open the boxes. The boxes were closed. And there was only one agent in the back. He can't even get his story straight."

Retired agent Kevin Olsen, another eyewitness, called the account a "figment of Figliuzzi's imagination. This doesn't surprise me he lied to sell a book."

"He's full of shit," added retired FBI agent Ed Knapp, another eyewitness. "He should have removed the whole section. He should have said, 'I screwed up. I'm sorry.'"

- The former FBI official Frank Figliuzzi has a theory on why Trump kept top-secret nuclear files.
- Figliuzzi said these files held "the greatest value" to interested foreign powers and their enemies.
- He said countries would give "their right arm" to find out what the US knows about their defenses.

A former FBI official said former President Donald Trump may have wanted to keep top-secret documents about a foreign power because of the astronomical price that country — or its adversaries — might pay for such information.

Frank Figliuzzi, a former FBI assistant director, was asked by the MSNBC host Stephanie Ruhle on Wednesday why Trump would have wanted to keep top-secret documents about a foreign country's nuclear program at his Mar-a-Lago home in Florida. The Washington Post reported Tuesday that Trump had such documents at his home.

In response, Figliuzzi posited that the high price of these documents would make them attractive assets.

"If I were to be asked what the highest price tag or highest value might be on what kind of classified US government information, certainly among the top of my answers would be: nuclear-related information," he said.

He added that such information had "potentially the greatest value" if one were to try to "market it and capitalize" on having such files.

"Well, first, a country would give its right arm to learn what the US knew about its nuclear program and capabilities, not only for the obvious reason of, 'Hey, they figured this out,' but also because it would signal what we don't know about their program," Figliuzzi said.

"Secondly, let's move to that country's adversary. They would give their left and right arms to find out what their adversary is doing in terms of nuclear capability," he added.

Aside from the value of the information, Figliuzzi noted that the files were at Mar-a-Lago, which Figliuzzi said had "some of the lowest security you can imagine," with foreign nationals "traipsing in and out."

A representative at Trump's postpresidential office did not immediately respond to a request for comment.

Figliuzzi is not the first FBI official to speculate that foreign nationals may have tried to obtain access to Mar-a-Lago.

The former FBI official Peter Strzok — who has a bitter history with Trump — said in August that "any competent foreign intelligence service" would have tried to gain access to the former president's Florida residence. Strzok cited Russia, China, Iran, and Cuba as countries agents could've come from.

Figliuzzi is also not alone in speculating that Trump may have tried to sell such classified data.

In August, Charles Leerhsen — an author who ghostwrote one of Trump's books — said the former president may have taken White House documents to sell as presidential memorabilia. Separately, the Fox News host Eric Shawn asked during a broadcast whether Trump had tried to "sell or share" these top-secret files "to the Russians" or to "the Saudis."

During the FBI's raid on Mar-a-Lago last month, agents seized 11 sets of classified documents, including some marked "top secret." Some of the documents may have concerned nuclear weapons, The Washington Post reported.

According to the search warrant, the Justice Department is investigating whether Trump broke any of three federal laws — including the Espionage Act — by keeping the documents at his Florida residence.

Last month, Trump dismissed the idea that there were any nuclear documents in his possession.

August 31, 2022

Peter Strzok says Russia might have tried to infiltrate Trump's Mar-a-Lago residence

By **Eric Utter**

During a recent episode of MSNBC's *Katie Phang Show*, Peter Strzok — disgraced former deputy director of the FBI's counterintelligence division — weighed in on his former organization's raid on Mar-a-Lago. Phang asked Strzok if he thought it was possible that Russia had "tried to infiltrate" former president Trump's home to obtain classified data, considering the allegedly "top-secret" documents that were being stored there.

Strzok replied:

Absolutely the Russians, but not just the Russians, any competent foreign intelligence service, whether that's those belonging to China, those belonging to Iran, to Cuba, certainly including Russia, are all — were interested, and are interested in gaining access to Mar-a-Lago.

First off, the documents that the FBI seized during its August 8 raid of Trump's private residence were declassified by then-president Trump — the only person with the ultimate authority to do so. If the commander-in-chief says a document or documents is/are declassified, they are, *ipso facto*, declassified.

Secondly, Strzok is a NeverTrump and was fired from his job for sending anti-Trump messages on his work phone. Like many in the alphabet agencies, he has an acute case of Trump

273

Derangement Syndrome (TDS) and is therefore anything but an objective source. Strzok casting aspersions on Trump would be like a Hatfield saying a McCoy might be up to no good. It's laughable on its face. (And we all remember Strzok's face when he testified during the House Committee's hearing on oversight of the FBI and DOJ — it appeared to some of us that he may well have been possessed by the devil at the time. Perhaps Beelzebub is responsible for TDS, too.)

But anything is *possible*. Maybe the DOJ should send Hunter Biden, Hillary Clinton, and Eric Swalwell to Mar-a-Lago to help investigate. A crack team to get to the bottom of this Chinese puzzle of deception and intrigue! We *know* Hillary and Hunter worked with "foreign agents," so they know what to look for. As previously mentioned, it's *possible* that a foreign agent infiltrated Strzok's *soul*. (Possibly his phone as well?) And a foreign agent named Fang Fang apparently infiltrated *Swalwell's pants*. But I'm sure none of them shared any classified information.

Come to think of it, maybe the feds should send Sandy Berger, too. Berger temporarily stored classified documents in *his* pants. Not very secure. And that was after *stealing* them from the National Archives. Moreover, he also briefly "hid" them under a construction trailer. Again, not very secure! If someone can walk into the Archives, stuff confidential documents down his pants and walk out unchallenged, maybe classified material would be *safer* at Mar-a-Lago.

While there is no evidence that any competent foreign intelligence service infiltrated the former president's home, we know for a fact that *the FBI* did.

Material on foreign nation's nuclear capabilities seized at Trump's Mar-a-Lago

Some seized documents were so closely held, only the president, a Cabinet-level or near-Cabinet level official could authorize others to know

By **Devlin Barrett and Carol D. Leonnig**

Updated September *6, 2022, at 10:36 p.m. EDT* |Published September 6, 2022 at 7:53 p.m. EDT

Pages from an FBI property list of items seized from former president Donald Trump's Mar-a-Lago estate and made public by the Department of Justice. FBI agents who searched the home found empty folders marked with classified banners. The inventory reveals in general terms the contents of the 33 boxes taken during the Aug. 8 search. (Jon Elswick/AP)

A document describing a foreign government's military defenses, including its nuclear capabilities, was found by FBI agents who searched former president Donald Trump's Mar-a-Lago residence and private club last month, according to people familiar with the matter, underscoring concerns among U.S. intelligence officials about classified material stashed in the Florida property.

Some of the seized documents detail top-secret U.S. operations so closely guarded that many senior national security officials are kept in the dark about them. Only the president, some members of his Cabinet or a near-Cabinet-level official could authorize other government officials to know details of these special-access programs, according to people familiar with the search, who spoke on the condition of anonymity to describe sensitive details of an ongoing investigation.

Documents about such highly classified operations require special clearances on a need-to-know basis, not just top-secret clearance. Some special-access programs can have as few as a couple dozen government personnel authorized to know of an operation's existence. Records that deal with such programs are kept under lock and key, almost always in a secure compartmented information facility, with a designated control officer to keep careful tabs on their location.

But such documents were stored at Mar-a-Lago, with uncertain security, more than 18 months after Trump left the White House.

Deep inside busy Mar-a-Lago, a storage room where secrets were kept

After months of trying, according to government court filings, the FBI has recovered more than 300 classified documents from Mar-a-Lago this year: 184 in a set of 15 boxes sent to the National Archives and Records Administration in January, 38 more handed over by a Trump lawyer to investigators in June, and more than 100 additional documents unearthed in a court-approved search on Aug. 8.

National correspondent Philip Bump explains what we can learn from a Justice Department photograph related to the FBI's search of Trump's Mar-a-Lago resort

It was in this last batch of government secrets, the people familiar with the matter said, that the information about a foreign government's nuclear-defense readiness was found. These people did not identify the foreign government in question, say where at Mar-a-Lago the document was found or offer additional details about one of the Justice Department's most sensitive national security investigations.

Christopher Kise, a lawyer for Trump, decried leaks about the case, which he said "continue with no respect for the process nor any regard for the real truth. This does not serve well the interests of justice."

"Moreover, the damage to public confidence in the integrity of the system simply cannot be underestimated. The responsible course of action here would be for someone — anyone — in the Government to exercise leadership and control. The Court has provided a sensible path forward which does not include the selective leak of unverifiable and misleading information. There is no reason to deviate from that path if the goal is, as it should be, to find a rational solution to document storage issues which have needlessly spiraled out of control."

Spokespeople for the Justice Department and FBI declined to comment.

The Office of the Director of National Intelligence is conducting a risk assessment, to determine how much potential harm was posed by the removal from government custody of hundreds of classified documents.

The Washington Post previously reported that FBI agents who searched Trump's home were looking, in part, for any classified documents relating to nuclear weapons. After that story published, Trump compared it on social media to a host of previous government investigations into his conduct. "Nuclear weapons issue is a Hoax, just like Russia, Russia, Russia was a Hoax, two Impeachments were a Hoax, the Mueller investigation was a Hoax, and much more. Same sleazy people involved," he wrote, going on to suggest that FBI agents might have planted evidence against him.

A grand jury subpoena issued May 11 demanded the return of "all documents or writings in the custody or control of Donald J. Trump and/or the Office of Donald J. Trump bearing classification markings," including "Top Secret," and the lesser categories of "Secret" and "Confidential."

The subpoena, issued to Trump's custodian of records, then listed more than two dozen sub-classifications of documents, including "S/FRD," an abbreviation for "Formerly Restricted Data," which is reserved for information that relates primarily to the military use of nuclear weapons. Despite the "formerly" in the title, the term does not mean the information is no longer classified.

One person familiar with the Mar-a-Lago search said the goal of the comprehensive list was to ensure recovery of all classified records on the property, and not just those that investigators had reason to believe might be there.

Investigators grew alarmed, according to one person familiar with the search, as they began to review documents retrieved from the club's storage closet, Trump's residence and his office in August. The team soon came upon records that are extremely restricted, so much so that even some of the senior-most national security officials in the Biden administration weren't authorized to review them. One govenent filing alluded to this information when it noted that counterintelligence FBI agents and prosecutors investigating the Mar-a-Lago documents were not authorized at first to review some of the material seized.

Among the 100-plus classified documents taken in August, some were marked "HCS," a category of highly classified government information that refers to "HUMINT Control Systems," which are systems used to protect intelligence gathered from secret human sources, according to a court filing. A partially unsealed affidavit said documents found in the boxes that were sent to the National Archives in January related to the Foreign Intelligence Surveillance Court. There was also material that was never meant to be shared with foreign nations.

The investigation into possible mishandling of classified information, as well as possible hiding, tampering or destruction of government records, grew even more complex Monday when a federal judge in Florida granted Trump's request to appoint a special master to review the material seized in the Aug. 8 search and weed out documents that may be covered by executive privilege — a legal standard that, as applied to former presidents, is poorly defined.

U.S. District Court Judge Aileen M. Cannon ruled the special master also will sift through all of the nearly 13,000 documents and items the FBI took to identify any that might be protected by attorney-client privilege, even though Justice Department lawyers have said a "filter" team has already completed that task.

Why a special master will review Trump's Mar-a-Lago files

The Post's Perry Stein explains how a special master will identify if any documents seized by the FBI are protected by attorney-client or executive privilege. (Video: The Washington Post)

Cannon's ruling could slow down and complicate the government's criminal probe, particularly if the Justice Department decides to appeal over the unsettled and tricky questions of what executive privilege a former president may have. The judge ruled that investigators cannot "use" the seized material in their investigation until the special master concludes his or her examination.

A special master has yet to be appointed; Cannon has asked Trump and the Justice Department to agree on a list of qualified candidates by Friday. Legal experts noted that the Justice Department can still interview witnesses, use other evidence and present information to a grand jury while the special master examines the seized material.

In her order, Cannon said the appointment of a special master was necessary "to ensure at least the appearance of fairness and integrity under the extraordinary circumstances presented."

Justice Dept. filing points to new legal peril for Trump, his lawyers

She also reasoned that a special master could mitigate potential harm to Trump "by way of improper disclosure of sensitive information to the public," suggesting that knowledge or details of the case were harmful to the former president, and could be lessened by inserting a special master into the document-review process.

Kise, the Trump lawyer, cited that part of the judge's reasoning in his statement Tuesday night in which he denounced leaks in the case.

Trump finishes up his speech during a rally at the Mohegan Sun Arena in Wilkes-Barre Township, Pa., on Sept. 3. (Sean Mckeag/The Citizens' Voice/AP)

Cannon wrote that Trump's position as a former president means "the stigma associated with the subject seizure is in a league of its own" and that a "future indictment, based to any degree on property that ought to be returned, would result in reputational harm of a decidedly different order of magnitude."

While the FBI search has drawn strong condemnation from Trump and his Republican allies, who accuse the Justice Department of acting with political malice against a past president who may seek the office again in 2024, some Republicans have said the action might have been necessary.

In an interview that aired Friday, former Trump attorney general William P. Barr said there is no reason classified documents should have been at Mar-a-Lago after Trump was out of office.

"People say this was unprecedented," Barr told Fox News. "But it's also unprecedented for a president to take all this classified information and put them in a country club, okay?"

Josh Dawsey contributed to this report.

Described foreign govt's nuclear capabilities - Washington Post

September 7, 2022, 5:50 AM

The Post report, which cited people familiar with the matter, did not identify the foreign government discussed in the document, nor did it indicate whether the foreign government was friendly or hostile to the United States.

An FBI spokesperson declined to comment on the report. Trump representatives did not immediately respond to requests for comment.

The FBI recovered more than 11,000 government documents and photographs during its Aug. 8 search at Trump's Mar-a-Lago estate, according to court records.

An aerial view of former President Donald Trump's Mar-a-Lago home. (Marco Bello/Reuters)

According to the Post report, some of the seized documents detail top-secret U.S. operations that require special clearances, not just top-secret clearance.

Some of the documents are so restricted that even some of the Biden administration's senior-most national security officials were not authorized to review them, the Post said.

The U.S. Justice Department is investigating Trump for removing government records from the White House after he departed in January 2021 and storing them at Mar-a-Lago.

On Monday, a federal judge agreed to Trump's request to appoint a special master to review records seized in the FBI search, a move that is likely to delay the Justice Department's criminal investigation.

From The Rachel Maddow Show

Did Donald Trump really bring nuclear secrets to Mar-a-Lago?

Donald Trump spent much of his term mishandling classified information, including nuclear-related information. But now, the story is vastly worse.

Aug. 12, 2022, 8:00 AM EDT

By **Steve Benen**

UPDATE: (Aug. 12, 2022, 2:30 p.m. ET): *NBC News on Friday obtained a copy of the warrant used in the FBI's search of former President Donald Trump's Mar-a-Lago home in Florida, as well as the related property receipt. The FBI recovered 11 sets of classified documents in the search, according to the documents.*

It was late Monday when the public learned, by way of a written statement from Donald Trump, that FBI agents had executed a search warrant at Mar-a-Lago. The next morning, a Republican commentator named Alice Stewart appeared on CNN and argued that federal law enforcement better have been looking for something extremely important.

Unless there were nuclear secrets at stake, Stewart said, the search warrant "is going to hugely backfire on the Biden administration."

Yesterday, Fox News' Dana Perino, another Republican commentator, said effectively the same thing. Unless there were nuclear secrets on the premises, the former White House press secretary said, "I really don't understand how a document could warrant this kind of warrant."

It was against this backdrop that The Washington Post published a truly jaw-dropping report.

Classified documents relating to nuclear weapons were among the items FBI agents sought in a search of former president Donald Trump's Florida residence on Monday, according to people familiar with the investigation. Experts in classified information said the unusual search underscores deep concern among government officials about the types of information they thought could be located at Trump's Mar-a-Lago Club and potentially in danger of falling into the wrong hands.

The article added the newspaper's sources did not shed light on whether the materials in question "involved weapons belonging to the United States or some other nation."

To be sure, Trump has denied the accuracy of the reporting, comparing it to the Russia scandal. The problem, of course, is that the Republican has repeatedly denied the accuracy of reporting that turned out to be correct, and the Russia scandal was entirely legitimate.

For much of the week, much of the political world — including the former president's critics and his allies — has pondered some core questions about the controversy. Just how sensitive were the classified documents Trump inappropriately took to his golf resort? How serious must they have been for FBI agents to show up at Mar-a-Lago?

If you'd asked me to come up with the single worst scenario imaginable — the most profoundly dangerous information he could've inappropriately taken to his golf resort known as a haven for spies — I would've said, "Nuclear secrets."

And here we are.

David Laufman, the former chief of the Justice Department's counterintelligence division, told the Post, "If that is true, it would suggest that material residing unlawfully at Mar-a-Lago may have been classified at the highest classification level. If the FBI and the Department of Justice believed there were top-secret materials still at Mar-a-Lago, that would lend itself to greater 'hair-on-fire' motivation to recover that material as quickly as possible."

Some key caveats are in order. For one thing, the Post's reporting hasn't been independently verified by other news organizations, including MSNBC or NBC News. For another, if the FBI was looking for classified documents related to nuclear weapons, we don't know if they were found or whether the former president took them deliberately.

For that matter, as Joe Cirincione, whose expertise on nuclear matters has few rivals, noted overnight, some nuclear-related documents are sometimes over-classified.

In other words, there are elements of this story that we do not yet know. Some caution is in order.

That said, if the Post's reporting is accurate, it does help the larger series of events make sense. Federal law enforcement realized that executing a search warrant at the home/business of a former president was a dramatic move, and it's one official probably wouldn't have taken if this were simply a matter involving love letters between the Republican and North Korea's dictator.

It becomes easier to understand why these events unfolded the way they did if Trump took national security secrets to his resort — and wouldn't give them back.

House Republican Conference Chair Elise Stefanik declared on Tuesday morning, "If the FBI can raid a U.S. President, imagine what they can do to you." Three days later, the response seems painfully obvious: If any of us took nuclear secrets to a golf club, we should expect the FBI to show up at our door.

What's more, let's also not forget the degree to which this fits into a pattern of indefensible behavior: Trump spent much of his presidency repeatedly mishandling classified information, including nuclear-related information. This pattern makes it nearly impossible to give him the benefit of the doubt.

In 2016, Sen. Marco Rubio repeatedly told Americans that Trump was so "dangerous" that he couldn't be trusted with nuclear secrets. Six years later, it's difficult to think of an issue on which the Florida Republican was more correct.

Steve Benen

Steve Benen is a producer for "The Rachel Maddow Show," the editor of MaddowBlog and an MSNBC political contributor. He's also the bestselling author of "The Impostors: How Republicans Quit Governing and Seized American Politics."

MARA-A LAGO- SEARCH WARRANT

(Aug. 15, 2022) — On the August 14 edition of "Sunday Morning Futures," Department of Defense Chief of Staff Kash Patel under President Trump and former California Congressman Devin Nunes, now CEO of the Trump Media & Technology Group, appeared with host Maria Bartiromo to shed light on the origins of the raid on Trump's Mar-a-Lago home last Monday morning.

Bartiromo recounted that Patel, then an aide to Nunes, had early on refuted the claim that anyone in Trump's 2016 campaign had colluded with the Russian government as put forth by the Hillary Clinton campaign and fueled by the disseminating of a "dossier" compiled by former British intelligence agent Christopher Steele after Clinton commissioned the opposition research. The allegations the dossier made spawned an FBI counterintelligence investigation into the Trump campaign which overshadowed much of the former businessman's presidency.

"What tie does this seize-and-search in President Trump's home have to do with the Russia collusion story?" Bartiromo directed her first question to Patel.

"It starts and ends with Russiagate," he replied. "The corruption and the two-tiered system of justice that Devin and I exposed during Russiagate has been carried out to the Hillary Clinton email investigation scandal to the Hunter Biden laptop to 'Jan. 6' and now to the raid on President Trump's home."

While serving as chairman on the House Permanent Subcommittee on Intelligence, Nunes and other committee Republicans conducted their own investigation into the Trump-Russia "collusion" claims, reporting in a February 2, 2018 memo no evidence of improprieties between the campaign and Russian government. In March 2019, a similar conclusion was reached following a 22-month special counsel investigation costing taxpayers approximately $40 million and bankrupting, jailing or otherwise impoverishing a number of Trump campaign associates.

Democrats, particularly Rep. Adam Schiff (D-CA28), insisted there was tangible evidence of collusion but ultimately never produced it. In May 2020, radio host Michael Berry wrote, "So what price will Schiff pay for the lies he told repeated over the past three years. Nothing. He'll still be invited back on CNN, MSNBC along with the networks and the journalist [sic] will complain why Trump attacks them and why the general public not only doesn't trust them, but bitterly despises them."

While Trump claims he declassified all the documents FBI agents seized last Monday prior to their arrival at Mar-a-Lago, Schiff, now chairman of the House Subcommittee on Intelligence, said Sunday "he hasn't seen any evidence that materials the FBI seized from Donald Trump's home were properly declassified."

Just before the Nunes memo was cleared for release in the midst of the probe led by Special Counsel Robert Mueller, CNN reported, "In recent phone calls, Trump has told friends he believes the memo would expose bias within the FBI's top ranks and make it easier for him to argue the Russia investigations are prejudiced against him, according to two sources."

As the FBI pursued its counterintelligence investigation into the Trump campaign, it obtained a FISA warrant on informal policy adviser Carter Page which was revealed much later as having its basis in false premises, earning a harsh admonishment from the chief judge of the FISA court. Judge Rosemary Collyer's rebuke followed a December 2019 inspector general report itemizing 17 deficiencies on the part of the FBI during its probe and the observation that the agency had depended solely on material from the dossier as justification to seek the Page FISA warrant.

The findings of insufficient evidence of "collusion" from the Mueller investigation prompted then-Attorney General William Barr to appoint a special prosecutor, John Durham, to discover the origins and justification of what the FBI had dubbed "Crossfire Hurricane." Durham's investigation remains ongoing.

Several FBI agents were fired or left voluntarily once their roles in the plot were exposed, including Acting Director Andrew McCabe, now a CNN commentator; Counterintelligence Deputy Assistant Director Peter Strzok, who filed suit against the agency in a case which remains open; former agency attorney Lisa Page, who filed a separate lawsuit alleging privacy violations relating to the release of thousands of text messages she exchanged with Strzok, with whom she was romantically involved at the time; and then-General Counsel James Baker, who was demoted and then voluntarily left the Bureau.

Baker was reported to have leaked the existence of the dossier to a left-leaning reporter prior to the 2016 election.

Thus far, Durham has achieved one plea deal from former FBI attorney Kevin Clinesmith, who admitted to altering an exculpatory email in the Carter Page FISA application. In late May, Perkins Coie attorney Michael Sussmann was acquitted on a single charge of lying to the FBI when making assertions to Baker about communication between a computer at Trump Tower and a Russian bank.

The allegation of Trump-Russia communication via computers proved unfounded.

Patel's reference to "Jan. 6" is to the incursion into the U.S. Capitol resulting in the death of Air Force veteran Ashli Babbitt at the hand of a U.S. Capitol Police officer following a rally, said to have consisted of approximately one million attendees, at which then-President Trump and others spoke, claiming massive election fraud deprived him of a second term.

Another woman who lost her life during the melee was Roseann Boyland, who the media depicted as having been trampled to death, a claim refuted by eyewitnesses.

During his speech in which he alleged significant voter fraud, Trump urged supporters to "peacefully and patriotically make your voices heard" at the Capitol following the rally, when Congress was scheduled to count and certify the electoral votes submitted from the states. Democrats in the House of Representatives used Trump's words and actions as the basis for a second impeachment which failed to garner a conviction in the Senate three weeks after Trump left office.

On February 4, 2021, Time Magazine released a column in which a "conspiracy" to safeguard against "Trump's assault on democracy" was said to have taken place on the part of U.S. corporations and "left-wing activists" in advance of the election. "There was a conspiracy unfolding behind the scenes, one that both curtailed the protests and coordinated the resistance from CEOs," Time's Molly Ball wrote. "Both surprises were the result of an informal alliance between left-wing activists and business titans. The pact was formalized in a terse, little-noticed joint statement of the U.S. Chamber of Commerce and AFL-CIO published on Election Day. Both sides would come to see it as a sort of implicit bargain–inspired by the summer's massive, sometimes destructive racial-justice protests–in which the forces of labor came together with the forces of capital to keep the peace and oppose Trump's assault on democracy…The scenario the shadow campaigners were desperate to stop was not a Trump victory. It was an election so calamitous that no result could be discerned at all, a failure of the central act of democratic self-governance that has been a hallmark of America since its founding."

"Basically," Patel told Bartiromo, "the same corrupt FBI government gangsters, the same agents that were involved in Russiagate, the same counterintelligence agents that were involved in making the bad, false call on Hunter Biden's laptop that you're going to see are the same counterintelligence agents that helped raid or assist in the raid to President Trump's home. And why is that a problem? Because these agents knowingly break or violate their oath of office and the law, get promotions, and we need to demand their names: guys like Auten and Tibble and other guys who also stood up the fake Whitmer prosecution in Michigan."

The "Whitmer" case, in which four men were charged with a plot to kidnap Michigan Gov. Gretchen Whitmer, resulted last April in a hung jury for two of the defendants and an acquittal on all charges for the other two.

A new trial for the remaining defendants is now under way.

In a congressional hearing on August 4, FBI Director Christopher Wray, a Trump appointee, admitted that the Special Agent in Charge of the Detroit Field Office, which reportedly "entrapped" the four original defendants in the Whitmer case, now leads the Washington, DC Field Office, which dispatched agents to Trump's home one week ago.

Wray himself made the appointment, according to the field office's website, of Steven D'Antuono, who spent little more than a year in Detroit.

According to The New York Post, Mar-a-Lago is "closed for the season," with "only a skeleton staff, including groundskeepers" on the premises at the time of the raid.

"When Devin and I first walked down to DOJ to expose the likes of Peter Strzok, they laughed us out of the building, but what happened?" Patel continued. "He was placed on administrative leave because he broke his oath of office, and you're going to find that exactly is what's happening here. And that it is a counterintelligence investigation means it's being run out of FBI headquarters as a national security case by these same select few of corrupt politicians who are acting as FBI agents." [sic]

According to The Washington Examiner on July 27, 2022, "Brian Auten, a supervisory intelligence analyst within the bureau, was referred to the Office of Professional Responsibility following Justice Department Inspector General Michael Horowitz's December 2019 report on the Trump-Russia investigation and its use of FISA surveillance against Trump campaign associate Carter Page. Shortly after the referral, Auten was involved with the bureau's inquiry into the son of now-President Joe Biden, with his Aug. 2020 analysis being used in part to justify the decision to 'shut down investigative activity.'"

Further, the article reported, Auten was assigned to evaluate the veracity of the Steele "dossier." Auten reportedly interviewed one of Steele's sources, Igor Danchenko, who was arrested in November for allegedly "making false statements to the FBI."

Shortly after the Mueller report was released, the U.S. House of Representatives launched impeachment hearings on an allegation by an unnamed "whistleblower" claiming, citing secondhand information, that Trump abused his authority on a phone call with newly-elected Ukrainian president Volodymyr Zelensky by requesting an investigation into the possibility that the Biden family had engaged in corrupt dealings surrounding a Ukrainian energy company, Burisma. Although lacking any experience in the discipline, Burisma had paid the younger Biden tens of thousands of dollars monthly to sit on its board of directors while the elder Biden was vice president.

In early 2018, the elder Biden himself bragged about pressuring then-Ukrainian president Petro Poroshenko to halt an independent investigation into Burisma or forfeit $1.5 billion in U.S. loan guarantees.

On February 5, 2020, Trump was acquitted in the Senate on both impeachment charges.

Ties between the Bidens and Ukrainian, Russian and Chinese government officials have since been illustrated by the material found on Hunter Biden's laptop computer, left in a Delaware repair shop and reported to the FBI in 2019 but not immediately retrieved or acted upon by the Bureau. The revelations, first released by The New York Post and then-Trump personal attorney Rudy Giuliani just weeks before the 2020 election, were blocked by social media platforms and labeled as likely "Russian disinformation" by 51 former intelligence officials.

Giuliani's home and office have been raided by the FBI, and he continues to be the subject of a probe alleging he engaged in unlawful lobbying on behalf of Ukraine. An indictment "appears unlikely," The New York Daily News reported on August 3 to little media fanfare.

In an August 11 article at The Post, the now-former computer repair-shop owner, John Paul Mac Isaac, is quoted as having written in his new book that the FBI agents who finally retrieved the Hunter Biden laptop said to him upon their departure, "It is our experience that nothing ever happens to people that don't talk about these things."

The media has gone as far as to lie about the findings of different official investigations launched into the 2020 election, including in Wisconsin, where a special counsel, Michael Gableman, assigned by Speaker of the state House of Representatives Robin Vos found copious evidence of systemic fraud, including that "Wisconsin Election Officials' Widespread Use of Absentee Ballot Drop Boxes Facially Violated Wisconsin Law" (p. 2).

Early last month, the Wisconsin Supreme Court ruled that outside ballot drop boxes are illegal in the state and cannot be used again, a move CNN opined is "a blow to Democrats."

Another finding of Gableman's was that the Wisconsin Election Commission (WEC), tasked by the legislature with administering elections and reporting results, "unlawfully encouraged evasion of ballot security measures related to 'indefinitely confined' voters at the behest of outside corporations."

Further, Gableman wrote in his March 1, 2022 report, the WEC "unlawfully directed clerks to violate rules protecting nursing home residents, resulting in a 100% voting rate in many nursing homes in 2020, including many ineligible voters," a finding Racine County Sheriff Christopher Schmaling said last fall he would refer to the district attorney.

Late last week, Vos ended the investigation after both he and Gableman were accused in six different lawsuits of mishandling communications related to the investigation. Gableman is also facing a contempt of court finding and possible loss of his law license.

Late last month, Sen. Chuck Grassley (R-IA) disclosed that several FBI and DOJ whistleblowers informed him that FBI agents assigned to assess "evidence" pertaining to Hunter Biden, who is under investigation for possible tax violations, deemed the evidence to be "disinformation" stemming from political bias.

In a July 25 letter to Attorney General Merrick Garland and FBI Director Christopher Wray, Grassley wrote:

The information provided to my office involves concerns about the FBI's receipt and use of derogatory information relating to Hunter Biden, and the FBI's false portrayal of acquired evidence as disinformation. The volume and consistency of these allegations substantiate their credibility and necessitate this letter.

First, it's been alleged that the FBI developed information in 2020 about Hunter Biden's criminal financial and related activity. It is further alleged that in August 2020, FBI Supervisory Intelligence Analyst Brian Auten opened an assessment which was used by a FBI Headquarters ("FBI HQ") team to improperly discredit negative Hunter Biden information as disinformation and caused investigative activity to cease. Based on allegations, verified and verifiable derogatory information on Hunter Biden was falsely labeled as disinformation.

In a press release issued the same day, Grassley wrote:

Multiple FBI whistleblowers, including those in senior positions, are raising the alarm about tampering by senior FBI and Justice Department officials in politically sensitive investigations ranging from election and campaign finance probes across multiple election cycles to investigative activity involving derogatory information on Hunter Biden's financial and foreign business activities. The legally protected disclosures to Senate Judiciary Committee Ranking Member Chuck Grassley (R-Iowa) suggest a political double standard has influenced and infected decisions in matters of paramount public interest.

The real FBI gets its man

By **Kevin R. Brock**, Opinion Contributor - *10/28/18 2:00 Pm Et*

The views expressed by contributors are their own and not the view of the hill

Let me re-introduce you, America, to the real FBI where investigations are run out of field offices by working agents, and not by politically influenced elites of the upper echelons of headquarters. These FBI agents, out on the street, partnered with sister agencies and local police, can focus with awesome intensity and resourcefulness when dangerous prey needs to be caught.

After two years of enduring bi-partisan verbal muggings for the missteps of its former feckless leadership, the real FBI reminded us this week where the important work is done on behalf of the American people.

On Tuesday, a bomb was delivered to the mailbox at George Soros's New York residence. Twelve more followed in the next two days, addressed to prominent Democrats and others perceived to be aligned with the Democratic Party. Just three days later, on Friday, the real FBI made an arrest. Remarkable, and a tremendous relief to us all. FYI, the arrestee's name won't be used in this article out of principle. The weak like their notoriety.

Kevin R. Brock, former assistant director of intelligence for the FBI, was an FBI special agent for 24 years and principal deputy director of the National Counterterrorism Center *(NCTC)*

Election & Campaign Finance Investigations

Whistleblowers allege that Washington Field Office Assistant Special Agent in Charge Timothy Thibault disregarded agency guidelines requiring substantial factual predication to trigger investigations, while declining to move forward with other investigations despite proper predication. Thibault and Richard Pilger, director of the election crimes branch within the FBI's public integrity section, reportedly were instrumental in the opening of an investigation into the Trump campaign and its associates based in substantial part on information from left-aligned organization. Thibault allegedly scrubbed and diluted details of the sources' political bias from a memo seeking the full investigation, which was ultimately approved by FBI Director Chris Wray and Attorney General Merrick Garland.

Although the property receipt of items taken and search warrant on Mar-a-Lago were released Friday afternoon at Trump's urging and the Justice Department's acquiescence, the sworn affidavit has not been made public. The warrant enumerates categories of documents sought while also encompassing "Any government and/or Presidential Records created between January 20, 2017, and January 20, 2021" (p. 4).

Magistrate Judge Bruce E. Reinhart, who recused himself from a lawsuit Trump filed earlier this year against Hillary Clinton; her 2016 campaign manager, Robert Mook; the Democratic National Committee; former Deputy Attorney General Rod Rosenstein and others, signed the warrant, which provided the FBI a two-week window to conduct its search.

Before becoming a magistrate, Reinhart posted an uncomplimentary remark about Trump on Facebook. Reinhart is a donor to Obama and former Florida Gov. Jeb Bush's presidential campaigns.

Despite the urgency claimed by the Justice Department to seize the materials, the FBI waited until Monday to make its descent on the property.

For his part, Nunes told Bartiromo he believes the corruption "actually goes back pre-Russiagate hoax. I think this goes back to the IRS scandal where they targeted conservatives," he said. "I think it goes back to Fast & Furious during the Obama administration where they ran guns and tried to set people up, remember, and innocent Americans ended up getting killed…"

He included in the litany of missteps the September 11, 2012 attack on the U.S. embassy in Benghazi, Libya, which killed four Americans, including Ambassador Christopher Stevens. "They got away with that," Nunes said.

He characterized the 2016 Clinton campaign as having "worked with dirty cops at DOJ and FBI, and the media" to launch the "Russia hoax" which he said "framed an innocent man." That "then led to the Mueller witch hunt," Nunes said. "So all of this stuff is intertwined. And then you just fast-forward; Kash mentioned the Whitmer case, and Jan. 6, and whether or not federal agents were involved in that, so you just stair-step, and then ultimately, this leads to what? This leads to something never done in American history before; you had a president's home ransacked by the same goons that were involved in all of this…"

Bartiromo asked if the individuals to whom Nunes was referring are Deputy Attorney General Lisa Monaco; National Security Adviser Jake Sullivan, who worked for Clinton when she was secretary of state; and National Security Adviser Susan Rice, who worked in the Bill Clinton and Obama administrations, to which Nunes replied, "If you don't believe that those people were involved, you're living under a rock somewhere."

"The very same people that are now in charge of the DOJ and are at the White House" are "making these calls," Nunes said. "You can just look at how they produce their narratives…the raid happened on Monday." After Trump related the events on TruthSocial, Nunes said, "…they immediately say, 'The White House didn't know anything about this.'"

Nunes recounted that Garland claimed in his short presser on Thursday that, "The White House knew nothing about this." "That tells you the White House knew everything about this," Nunes said.

On his show Sunday night, Mark Levin made a similar case that high-level DOJ operatives are behind the Mar-a-Lago raid and that the law has been turned against political enemies of the Biden regime.

Later in the interview, Patel revealed that Trump "named me his representative to the National Archives months ago, and we've been in a bureaucratic battle…"

"We found whole sets of documents we needed out to the American public from Russiagate," Patel said. "We got out about 60%. That's why President Trump made it his mission to declassify and be transparent. In October of 2020 he issued a sweeping declassification order for every Russiagate document and every single Hillary Clinton document. Then on the way out of the White House he issued further declassification orders, declassifying whole sets of documents…President Trump, as a sitting president, is a unilateral authority for declassification. He can literally stand over a set of documents and say, 'These are now declassified.'"

However, he added, as a result of the latest "ongoing FBI counterintelligence investigation," the DOJ will claim to the public, "You will never be allowed to see the Russiagate docs or any other docs that President Trump lawfully declassified."

Nunes added that a grand jury has been asked to evaluate charges of "treason" against Trump. "This is the second time; this never stops…They went to a grand jury" with the Russia collusion allegations as well, Nunes said. "So once again, this is a continued investigation of Trump and the Republican Party; it's basically an investigation in search of a crime, and then conveniently, they brought back the Mueller witch hunt argument that, 'He's obstructing justice' — obstructing justice on what, you jerks? On stuff that you had planted on an investigation that you basically created out of whole cloth…"

Title 18 793 2071

Why the Trump search warrant is nothing like Clinton's emails

The president has decried the FBI's search of his home. But legal experts say the agency is likely on firm ground. They note Trump could clear a lot of the mystery up himself.

Donald Trump — after a fierce campaign against Hillary Clinton in which he called for her to be jailed for her handling of classified material — signed a law in 2018 that stiffened the penalty for the unauthorized removal and retention of classified documents.

By **Kyle Cheney**
08/09/2022 05:11 PM EDT

The Justice Department official who oversaw the investigation of Hillary Clinton's handling of classified records says there's simply no comparing the search of Donald Trump's Mar-a-Lago residence to the case against the former secretary of State.

"People sling these cases around to suit their political agenda but every case has to stand on its own circumstances," said David Laufman, who led the Justice Department's counterintelligence section until 2018 and is now a partner at the firm Wiggin and Dana.

Laufman has the credentials to judge the severity of these matters. In addition to the Clinton case, he managed the investigation of David Petraeus, the former general and CIA director who pleaded guilty to a misdemeanor for mishandling classified material. CNN reported that one of the DOJ officials involved in the Trump investigation is his immediate successor.

"For the department to pursue a search warrant at Mar-a-Lago tells me that the quantum and quality of the evidence they were reciting — in a search warrant and affidavit that an FBI agent swore to — was likely so pulverizing in its force as to eviscerate any notion that the search warrant and this investigation is politically motivated," he said.

Twenty-four hours after it transpired, there remain few details about why the FBI raided Trump's private estate beyond months-old questions about the former president's handling of records that appear to have been relocated to Mar-a-Lago as he departed the Oval Office.

In the absence of more concrete details, Trump's defenders have clamored to bear hug the former president more fiercely than ever, deriding the FBI and Justice Department as weapons of partisan Democrats. But Laufman's take echoes the consensus of other experts who operate in the corner of the legal world that deals with the handling of classified material. It's highly unlikely the DOJ would have pursued — and a judge would have granted — such a politically explosive search warrant without extraordinary evidence.

"As far as I can tell, the FBI is not prone to the kind of — to what members of Congress have called a banana republic-like invasion. That doesn't happen, especially with a court order."

Steven Aftergood, Federation of American Scientists

"Sooner or later, the Justice Department and Mr. Trump will have to clarify the substance of what has happened," said Steven Aftergood, a longtime Federation of American Scientists advocate against government secrecy. "Then we will know, was there a real violation of the law or was this some kind of speculative adventure. As far as I can tell, the FBI is not prone to the kind of — to what members of Congress have called a banana republic-like invasion. That doesn't happen, especially with a court order."

In the absence of more detailed information about the investigation, it's unclear what potential crimes DOJ is probing. Notably, Trump — after a fierce campaign against Clinton in which he called for her to be jailed for her handling of classified material — signed a law in 2018 that stiffened the penalty for the unauthorized removal and retention of classified documents from one year to five years, turning it into a felony offense.

That was the same statute that just three years earlier Petraeus pleaded guilty to in order to avoid a felony conviction.

While both the DOJ and FBI have been silent amid calls they further explain the context of the Mar-a-Lago search, they are not the only ones in possession of relevant information.

Trump is in perhaps the best position to reveal more details about what transpired on Monday. The former president has access to the full inventory of items that federal investigators were seeking as well as what was taken from his estate during the search. He or his lawyers were almost certainly presented with a copy of the search warrant executed at Mar-a-Lago — though not the underlying affidavit or other supplemental materials, which are usually kept confidential until charges are issued or a case is closed. In addition, Trump can speak to the nature of any potentially classified material that may have been the basis for the search and whether he took steps to declassify any of it as he left office.

"If people are calling for it to be made public, I believe that is within the power of Mr. Trump to do," Aftergood said. "He could describe what was at stake and what the point of disagreement was. He doesn't need to speculate."

Laufman and Aftergood emphasized that the potential culpability for Trump or his allies depends entirely on potential aggravating circumstances — from the volume of classified material in his possession to the level of classification of the information, whether he or any allies misled the National Archives or Justice Department about the inventory at Mar-a-Lago and whether there were efforts to conceal it or resist turning it over.

Court-authorized FBI search, like the one that occurred Monday, would be warranted, Aftergood said, if "the material is of such extraordinary national security sensitivity that it absolutely must be within government custody."

"That's not something you write letters about," he added. "That's something you need to take custody of now and argue about later."

Though the grand jury investigation of efforts by Trump and his allies to disrupt the transfer of power on Jan. 6, 2021, has drawn more intense public scrutiny, it's the investigation of his handling of presidential records that poses its own legal threat. In fact, some of the very Trump allies who cooperated with the House's Jan. 6 probe were among those charged by Trump with managing his presidential records after leaving office.

A day before Joe Biden's inauguration, Trump named seven administration officials as his representatives to the National Archives. Among them were his chief of staff, Mark Meadows; White House counsel Pat Cipollone; his deputies Patrick Philbin, Scott Gast and Michael Purpura;

national security attorney John Eisenberg; and Justice Department Office of Legal Counsel chief Steven Engel.

Engel has testified to the Jan. 6 select committee about his resistance to Trump's plan to remove Justice Department leaders and replace them with compliant officials who would support his effort to remain in power. Cipollone also testified about his concerns with the legality of some of Trump allies' attempts to overturn the results of the election.

It's unclear whether all seven of the officials remain authorized representatives for Trump, but the former president has also recently added at least two additional representatives: reporter John Solomon and former Pentagon official Kash Patel.

Patel told Breitbart in May that Trump had declassified the materials he removed to Mar-a-Lago, even though the documents still had classified markings on them. As president, Trump had total power to declassify any classified material in the government's possession.

Josh Gerstein contributed to this report.

Justice Department files notice to appeal special master decision in Trump documents case

Caitlin Dickson

September 8, 2022, 4:51 PM

A guide to the Mar-a-Lago search fallout: Yahoo News Explains

In early August, the FBI executed a search warrant at Mar-a-Lago, the Florida country club owned by former President Donald Trump and his primary residence since leaving the White House. In the weeks since, we've learned a lot about what happened and why. As the search for a third-party special master to review the potentially sensitive materials seized at Mar-a-Lago begins and new reporting points to alleged nuclear secrets contained in them, Yahoo News explains where things stand and what to expect next.

The Justice Department on Thursday filed a notice that it will appeal a judge's recent controversial decision to appoint a special master to review documents seized from former President Donald Trump's Mar-a-Lago estate.

Trump had requested to have an independent arbiter oversee the review of evidence recovered by the FBI during its search of his Palm Beach, Fla., residence last month, to determine if any of the seized materials might be protected under attorney-client privilege or executive privilege, which shields internal executive branch deliberations.

U.S. District Judge Aileen Cannon, of Florida's Southern District, ruled in favor of the former president in an order earlier this week. She also temporarily blocked the Justice Department from using the records for investigative purposes. Cannon, a Trump appointee, had set a Friday deadline for both sides to submit a list of proposed candidates for the special master.

In a motion filed in the Southern District of Florida on Thursday afternoon, the Justice Department asked that, pending its appeal of the special master decision, the judge grant a partial stay of her earlier ruling with regard to classified documents recovered from Mar-a-Lago, writing that "those aspects of the Order will cause the most immediate and serious harms to the government and the public."

An aerial view of former President Donald Trump's Mar-a-Lago resort after Trump said that FBI agents searched it, in Palm Beach, Fla., on August 15. (Marco Bello/Reuters/File Photo)

The 21-page motion makes the case that the Justice Department should be allowed to continue its review of classified documents seized from Mar-a-Lago, which it describes as "a discrete set of just over 100 documents," arguing that Trump "does not and could not assert that he owns or has any possessory interest in classified records; that he has any right to have those government records returned to him; or that he can advance any plausible claims of attorney-client privilege as to such records that would bar the government from reviewing or using them."

"Among other things," the motion states, "the classified records are the very subject of the government's ongoing investigation."

Justice Department attorneys had previously urged Cannon to deny Trump's request, arguing that he did not have the legal standing to demand independent review of government documents. The government also argued that the request would impede its ongoing criminal investigation and pose a risk to national security interests.

Federal prosecutors had outlined their position on the matter in a lengthy court filing submitted late Tuesday night. In it, they noted that if Cannon did agree to appoint a special master — which she had said she was inclined to do — such a person would need to have the security clearance necessary to view materials marked Top Secret and "sensitive compartmented information," or SCI.

Part Sixteen

FBI Special Agents -FBI Whistleblowers

FBI agent Timothy Thibault hid Intel from whistleblower on Hunter and the 'Big Guy' Joe Biden

By **Miranda Devine**

September 4, 2022 11:08pm

Updated

- Tyrannical old Joe's secret police state
- FBI put the Hunter Biden story right in Facebook's lap
- Warning signs for the GOP abound
- The left's mask slips on brazen Trump bias
- Liberals' FBI trust is a real gut buster

Timothy Thibault, the FBI agent alleged to have interfered with an investigation into Hunter Biden, was assigned by the Washington Field Office as "point man" to manage whistleblower Tony Bobulinski, the first son's former business partner, before the 2020 election — but he suppressed his damning revelations, sources say.

Bobulinski spent over five hours secretly being interviewed by the FBI on Oct. 23, 2020, about his inside knowledge of then-presidential candidate Joe Biden's involvement in his son's business deals with China.

The previous day, he had revealed in a press conference that Joe Biden was the "Big Guy" due to get a 10% cut of a lucrative joint venture with Chinese energy firm CEFC, according to an email found on Hunter's abandoned laptop.

Bobulinski gave the FBI the contents of three cellphones containing encrypted messages between Hunter and his business partners, along with emails and financial documents detailing the Biden family's corrupt influence-peddling operation in foreign countries during Joe's vice presidency.

But his evidence appears to have fallen into the same black hole at the FBI as Hunter's laptop, never to be seen again.

Bobulinski's FBI interview came the week after The Post published material from the laptop, including the "Big Guy" message and an email from a Ukrainian energy company executive thanking Hunter for organizing a 2015 meeting in Washington with then-VP Biden.

Hunter's ex-partner Tony Bobulinski: Joe Biden's a liar and here's the proof

On the day Bobulinski went to the FBI's Washington Field Office, 11 days before the 2020 presidential election, he was told not to walk in the front door, but to drive into an underground parking garage at the back of the nondescript, eight-story building in northwest DC, one mile from FBI headquarters.

He was met by James Dawson, then-special agent in charge of the Criminal and Cyber Division, and FBI Supervisory Special Agent Giulio Arseni.

They turned him over to two younger agents, William Novak and Garrett Churchill, who conducted the videotaped interview and provided a receipt for Bobulinski's digital data.

He told them about the work Hunter, his uncle Jim Biden, and partners James Gilliar and Rob Walker did during Joe's vice presidency, in 2015 and 2016, using the Biden name to help CEFC expand into Oman, Romania, Georgia, Kazakhstan and beyond. He told them about Hunter's lucrative personal relationship with CEFC chairman Ye Jianming at the time the company was brokering China's $9 billion acquisition of the Russian state oil giant Rosneft. Ye was arrested in China in 2018 after the deal fell apart.

CEFC was the capitalist arm of China's Belt and Road initiative to extend the Communist regime's influence around the globe.

Bobulinski also told the FBI about Hunter's associations with oligarch Mykola Zlochevsky, owner of corrupt Ukrainian energy company Burisma, with Romanian billionaire Gabriel Popoviciu, and with retired FBI Director Louis Freeh, who was brought in by Hunter as a consultant to help Popoviciu escape corruption charges in Romania.

New York Post cover for Wednesday, October 28, 2020.

Novak and Churchill paused the interview to consult with Dawson a number of times, according to one insider.

Arseni came into the room occasionally and an FBI forensic team visited.

Top FBI agent resigns amid claims he shielded Hunter Biden from probe: report

Bobulinski and his lawyer were given Thibault's cellphone number and told that he would be their "point man" at the FBI thereafter.

That night, Bobulinski's lawyer phoned Thibault, who said he would soon advise on next steps and whether Bobulinski should do a follow-up interview.

But neither Bobulinski nor his lawyer was contacted again. Nor was Bobulinski brought before a Delaware grand jury investigating Hunter.

Dawson moved to the field office in Little Rock, Ark., last July.

Thibault retired from the FBI last week, amid an investigation by the Office of Special Counsel into his anti-Trump social media posts, and after Republican senators made public allegations that he buried Hunter Biden material that would have damaged Joe's candidacy.

'Improperly discredited'

Whistleblowers alleged to Sen. Chuck Grassley that, in the same month as Bobulinski's FBI interview, then-Assistant Special Agent in Charge Thibault ordered that an investigation into Hunter Biden's alleged "criminal financial and related activity" be closed.

"In October 2020, an avenue of additional derogatory Hunter Biden reporting was ordered closed at the direction of ASAC Thibault," Grassley wrote six weeks ago in a letter to FBI Director Christopher Wray and Attorney General Merrick Garland.

"It's been alleged that the FBI HQ team suggested to the FBI agents that the information was at risk of disinformation; however, according to allegations, [it] was either verified or verifiable via criminal search warrants ... Thibault allegedly ordered the matter closed without providing a valid reason, as required by FBI guidelines [and] it's alleged that FBI officials, including ASAC Thibault, subsequently attempted to improperly mark the matter in FBI systems so that it could not be opened in the future."

President Joe Biden with his son Hunter Biden waves as they leave Holy Spirit Catholic Church.Manuel Balce Ceneta/AP

Timothy Thibault recently retired.FEDERAL BUREAU OF INVESTIGATION

Grassley also alleged that FBI Supervisory Intelligence Analyst Brian Auten had opened an assessment in August 2020, which was used by an FBI headquarters team to "improperly discredit negative Hunter Biden information as disinformation and caused investigative activity to cease ... Verified and verifiable derogatory information on Hunter Biden was falsely labeled as disinformation."

Thibault denied Grassley's allegations last week. A statement from his pro-bono lawyer said he "did not supervise the investigation of Hunter Biden which ... is being handled by the Baltimore Field Office.

"In particular, Mr. Thibault was not involved in any decisions related to any laptop that may be at issue in that investigation and he did not seek to close the investigation."

But Thibault's statement omits any explanation of what he did with Bobulinski's information.

Did he give it to the FBI's Baltimore field office, which was assisting Delaware US Attorney David Weiss' four-year probe of Hunter for alleged tax evasion, money laundering and foreign agent violations?

If he did, then why has Bobulinski never testified before the grand jury convened by Weiss last year?

Other business partners of Hunter testified and at least one was asked the identity of "the Big Guy," according to a source.

It seems inexplicable that Bobuļinski — who met twice with Joe Biden in 2017 over the CEFC deal, and provided information that corroborates damning material on Hunter's laptop — is not a star witness, especially since the FBI has been in possession of the laptop since December 2019, and knows it is authentic.

It is not as if Bobulinski is not highly credible. He is a decorated former US Navy officer with top secret security clearances from the National Security Agency and the Department of Energy. A successful businessman, he has donated to both sides of the political aisle.

In the interests of national security, it was the FBI's duty to investigate credible evidence suggesting the future president may have been compromised by China via millions of dollars paid to his family.

Even if the FBI was reluctant, after its 2016 Hillary email debacle, to take action that could be deemed political during an election campaign, there is no excuse for not following up with Bobulinski afterward.

The FBI's failure to do so amounts to interference-by-omission in the 2020 election.

Wray: Allegations 'troubling' about FBI agent covering up Hunter Biden information

Timothy Thibault is accused of partisan social media activity and efforts to suppress information in the probe into the president's son's business activities.

A former FBI agent allegedly downplayed or discredited negative information obtained about Hunter Biden during the 2020 election, according to accounts Sen. Chuck Grassley received from a "highly credible" whistleblower. | Susan Walsh/AP Photo

By **Kelly Hooper** and **Josh Gerstein**
08/04/2022 04:11 PM EDT

FBI Director Christopher Wray said on Thursday that allegations of an FBI agent's partisan social media posts and efforts to suppress information in the investigation into Hunter Biden's business activities were "deeply troubling."

Speaking at a Senate Judiciary Committee oversight hearing, Wray appeared to condemn the alleged actions of Timothy Thibault, who he said was an FBI assistant special agent in charge at the Washington field office until "relatively recently."

Sen. John Kennedy (R-La.), who pursued the line of questioning with Wray, said that Thibault — who had been at the FBI for more than 25 years — is now on leave.

Kennedy grilled Wray on Thibault's alleged partisan actions on social media over the past few years, such as "liking" a Washington Post article titled "William Barr has gone rogue" and tweeting to Rep. Liz Cheney (R-Wyo.) that her father — former Vice President Dick Cheney — was a "disgrace." Kennedy also mentioned Thibault's retweet of a Lincoln Project post saying that "Donald Trump is a psychologically broken, embittered, and deeply unhappy man."

Kennedy then pressed Wray on allegations that Thibault — who Kennedy said worked on both the investigation of links between Trump and Russia and the ongoing Hunter Biden probe — had "covered up derogatory info about Mr. Biden while working at the FBI."

Wray gave similar answers to Kennedy's questioning on both the social media posts and covering up of information, saying that he'd seen "descriptions to that effect" but wanted to be "careful" of not interfering with any ongoing personnel matters. But he did concede to finding the allegations about the social media posts "troubling."

"I should say that when I read the letter that describes the kinds of things that you're talking about, I found it deeply troubling," he told Kennedy.

Senate Judiciary Chair Chuck Grassley (R-Iowa) first raised alarms about Thibault's alleged partisan actions in May, demanding that the Justice Department and the FBI investigate whether the agent violated department guidelines with his social media posts. Grassley sent a second letter to the Justice Department and the FBI in late July saying that he had received "highly credible" whistleblower accounts alleging that Thibault had downplayed or discredited negative information obtained about Joe Biden's son during the 2020 election.

Wray on Thursday didn't definitively confirm or deny the allegations against Thibault and seemed to be trying to preserve his ability to act as an impartial decision-maker on potential discipline against the agent. However, the FBI director stressed that the actions Kennedy was describing were "not representative of the FBI."

"I feel very strongly, and I have communicated consistently since I started as director, that our folks need to make sure that they're not just doing the right thing, that they're doing it in the right way and that they avoid even the appearance of bias or lack of objectivity," Wray said.

Kennedy said he agreed with Wray's statement that the majority of FBI employees have "tremendous integrity and objectivity," but stressed that the situation with Thibault is only hurting the FBI's image and needs to be addressed with the public.

"You're killing yourselves with this stuff," Kennedy said. "And this investigation needs to be completed on this gentleman and the results need to be reported to the American people."

Wray seemed to raise doubts that Thibault was working at any recent time on issues related to Hunter Biden. The FBI chief said that investigation, reportedly focused on tax issues and potential foreign influence related to Hunter Biden's business ties, is being run by the Bureau's Baltimore Field Office, which handles matters related to Delaware.

The Biden administration has permitted Trump's appointee as U.S. attorney for Delaware, David Weiss, to stay on to complete the probe of the president's son.

Hunter Biden in a December 2020 statement denied any wrongdoing in his tax affairs. Biden's lawyer did not immediately respond to a request for comment on the allegations.

"I take this matter very seriously but I am confident that a professional and objective review of these matters will demonstrate that I handled my affairs legally and appropriately, including with the benefit of professional tax advisors," he said.

Earlier in the hearing, Wray seemed to address indirectly the claims that during the 2020 election season the FBI helped downplay or suppress information about Hunter Biden's business ties by categorizing that as Russian disinformation.

The FBI director suggested it wasn't his agency's job in such situations to try to validate or verify the claims, only to alert U.S. officials, businesses or individuals that foreign powers are trying to exploit the situation.

"Sometimes this gets lost in a lot of public commentary. We are not investigating whether or not information we see is truthful or false," Wray said. "Our focus in the malign foreign influence space is whether or not there is a foreign adversary pushing the information."

Top FBI agent resigns amid claims he shielded Hunter Biden from probe: report

By **Emily Crane**

August 29, 2022 7:43pm

Updated

A top FBI agent at the Washington field office reportedly resigned from his post last week after facing intense scrutiny over allegations he helped shield Hunter Biden from criminal investigations into his laptop and business dealings.

Timothy Thibault, an FBI assistant special agent in charge, was allegedly forced out after he was accused of political bias in his handling of probes involving President Biden's son, sources told the Washington Times on Monday.

The agent was escorted out of the field office by at least two "headquarters-looking types" last Friday, the sources said.

Thibault and the FBI didn't immediately respond to The Post's request for comment on Monday.

Thibault, a 25-year-veteran, had already been on leave for a month after the top Republican on the Senate Judiciary Committee, Chuck Grassley (R-Iowa), started raising concerns about whistleblower claims the FBI had obstructed its own investigations into the first son.

Timothy Thibault, an FBI assistant special agent in charge, was reportedly forced out after being accused of political bias in the handling of Hunter Biden probes.

In a letter to FBI Director Christopher Wray in July, Grassley said Thibault and FBI supervisory intelligence analyst Brian Auten were allegedly involved in "a scheme" to "undermine derogatory information connected to Hunter Biden by falsely suggesting it was disinformation."

Bottom of Form

Thibault also allegedly tried to kill off a valid avenue of investigation of possible Hunter Biden criminality up until at least one month before the Nov. 2020 election, according to Grassley.

"Thibault allegedly ordered the matter closed without providing a valid reason as required by FBI guidelines…. [and] subsequently attempted to improperly mark the matter in FBI systems so that it could not be opened in the future," Grassley wrote.

It was the same month The Post first started reporting on Hunter Biden's abandoned laptop, which included troves of emails related to his shady overseas business dealings.

Facebook founder Mark Zuckerberg revealed last week that the social media giant suppressed The Post's bombshell Hunter Biden report following a vague FBI warning about possible "Russian propaganda" tied to the 2020 presidential election.

The agent was reportedly escorted out of the bureau by at least two "headquarters-looking types" last Friday, sources said.Bloomberg via Getty ImagesChuck Grassley (R-Iowa) has been raising concerns about whistleblower claims the FBI had obstructed its own investigations into the first son.Bloomberg via Getty Images

"Basically, the background here is the FBI, I think, basically came to us — some folks on our team — and was like, 'Hey, just so you know, like, you should be on high alert,'" Zuckerberg told "The Joe Rogan Experience" podcast.

Zuckerberg said the FBI added, "'We thought that there was a lot of Russian propaganda in the 2016 election. We have it on notice that, basically, there's about to be some kind of dump that's similar to that. So just be vigilant.'"

Meanwhile, Republican senators have also publicly scrutinized Thibault's alleged anti-Trump social media activity ahead of the 2020 election, including a retweet of a Lincoln Project message that called Donald Trump a "psychologically broken, embittered and deeply unhappy man."

He also allegedly tweeted that he wanted to "give Kentucky to the Russian Federation."

Wray admitted under grilling from GOP senators earlier this month that allegations of political bias at the hands of FBI agents, including Thibault, was "deeply troubling."

FBI Agents Association vouches for Wray, disputes reports of resignation calls within bureau

FBI Director Christopher Wray speaks during a news conference, Wednesday, Aug. 10, 2022, in Omaha, Neb. (AP Photo/Charlie Neibergall)

By Kerry Picket - *The Washington Times - Thursday, September 1, 2022*

Supporters of embattled FBI Director Christopher A. Wray are circling the wagons following The Washington Times' exclusive report that the bureau's rank-and-file agents want him to resign.

Brian O'Hare, president of the FBI Agents Association, insisted Mr. Wray still has the support throughout the bureau.

"Attempts to politicize FBI Agents' work and divide our team should be rejected. While some claim to speak on behalf of FBI Agents, only the FBI Agents Association, representing more than 90 percent of active duty Special Agents, serves as the voice for these Agents," he said in a statement to The Times.

"It is with this voice that FBIAA acknowledges the important partnerships that field Agents have with Director Wray and Bureau leadership, prosecutors making charging decisions, state and local law enforcement, and the private sector. FBI Agents work hard every day to protect the public and our Constitution. With a clear eye on our mission, we remain confident in Director Wray, his leadership team, and our Agents," he said.

The Times recently reported Kurt Siuzdak, a lawyer and former FBI agent who represents whistleblowers at the bureau, said agents tell him that Mr. Wray has lost control of the agency and should resign.

Whistleblowers describe 'out of control' culture of corruption at FBI field offices

By Kerry Picket - *The Washington Times - Monday, August 22, 2022*

FBI whistleblowers accused bureau management in different field offices of corruption, cover-ups and retaliation against rank-and-file agents who attempted to expose it, The Washington Times has learned.

Current and former FBI leaders at the bureau's offices in Miami, Salt Lake City, Buffalo, New York, and Newark, New Jersey, are facing whistleblower complaints that the supervisors:

• Forced or coerced agents to sign false affidavits.

• Fabricated terrorism cases to pump up performance statistics.

• Sexually harassed and stalked a female agent.

• Engaged in sexual acts with a subordinate in a government vehicle and crashed the vehicle.

Report — FBI Agents Have 'Lost Confidence' in Director Wray: 'He's Got to Leave'

about an hour ago

A number of FBI agents say they have "lost confidence" in Director Christopher Wray and are now calling for his resignation, according to a report.

Former FBI agent Kurt Siuzdak, an attorney who represents whistleblowers, said agents have told him they "feel like the director has lost control of the bureau," the Washington Times reported.

"They're saying, 'How does this guy survive? He's leaving. He's got to leave," Siuzdak added.

The report of Wray's suffering reputation among rank-and-file agents comes just after senior FBI official Timothy Thibault left the bureau last week.

Thibault, who says he retired on his own accord, was facing numerous allegations, including from FBI whistleblowers, about displaying political bias on his social media, suppressing a line of investigation into Hunter Biden, inconsistently pursuing investigations, mishandling election-related matters, and inflating domestic violent extremism cases.

Sen. Chuck Grassley (R-IA), the lead Republican on the Senate Judiciary Committee, has fielded several FBI whistleblower allegations and was the first to shed light this year on some of those leveled against Thibault.

Upon Thibault's exit from the FBI, Grassley said in a statement provided to Breitbart News that Thibault's alleged bias "casts a shadow over all of the bureau's work that he was involved in," much of which was high-profile and carried national impact.

"Political bias should have no place at the FBI, and the effort to revive the FBI's credibility can't stop with his exit," Grassley said.

The Times noted calls for Wray's resignation have occurred in the past, including in 2018, when then-Florida Gov. Rick Scott called for Wray to step down over allegedly not following a tip about the Parkland shooter, and in 2020, when then-Rep. Doug Collins (R-GA) called for Wray's resignation over his handling of the now-debunked Russia collusion charges.

FBI agents "are telling me they have lost confidence in Wray. All Wray does is go in and say we need more training and we're doing stuff about it or we will not tolerate it," Siuzdak said, per the Times.

In addition to Thibault's seemingly abrupt departure from the FBI, Rep. Jim Jordan (R-OH), the top Republican on the House Judiciary Committee, has made headlines for the numerous whistleblowers who have approached his office.

Jordan recently estimated that 14 FBI whistleblowers with useful information have spoken with his office in the past year, a number he told Breitbart News "underscores how political that place has become."

In addition to the array of whistleblower allegations, the FBI raided former President Donald Trump's Mar-a-Lago residence this month in search of classified documents. The stunning move prompted top Republicans such as Trump, House Minority Leader Kevin McCarthy (R-CA), House Republican Conference chair Rep. Elise Stefanik (R-NY), and others to blast the FBI's raid as politically motivated rather than fair.

In response to the reported calls for Wray to resign, the FBI told the Times in a statement, "The men and women of the FBI work hard every day to protect the American people and uphold the Constitution."

"All employees are held to the highest standards of professional and ethical conduct, and we expect them to focus on process, rigor, and objectivity in performance of their duties," the statement read. "Allegations of misconduct are taken seriously and referred to the Inspection Division or appropriate investigative body."

After 20 Whistleblowers Crack Open the FBI – Now Internal Agents Are Calling for Resignation of FBI Director

By Adam Casalino| *August 31, 2022*

What's Happening:

Not that long ago, Donald Trump called on the FBI agents to stand up to their politicized leaders. That includes President Biden, who claims he knows nothing about what's been going on at the FBI.

Already, we saw dozens of "rank-and-file" agents approaching Republican lawmakers. They exposed a number of top brass who undermined investigations to seemingly help Democrats.

One official has been forced out. Now, a growing number of agents want the top dog gone.

From The Washington Times:

Kurt Siuzdak, a lawyer and former FBI agent who represents whistleblowers at the bureau, said agents tell him that Mr. Wray has lost control of the agency and should resign…

FBI whistleblowers talking to Congress about corruption and retaliation say in disclosures that Mr. Wray was often notified of the problems within the bureau but never took action to resolve them.

This is pretty big. Numerous FBI agents are pushing back against the agency.

They are demanding that Christopher Wray, the current director, step down.

There doesn't seem to be evidence that Wray has done wrong. However, whistleblowers revealed that the many problems within the FBI have long been reported to the director.

But he's done nothing about it.

Recent reports revealed that top officials have coerced agents into signing false affidavits, accusations of sexual harassment, and even fabricated terrorism claims.

This comes just after bombshell reports that "top brass" suppressed the Hunter Biden laptop investigation intentionally to avoid influencing the 2020 Election. That is to say, actively influence the election.

One top agent was forced to resign after a claim that he suppressed the partisan nature of evidence to get an investigation opened on Trump.

Now all of this is blowing back on Director Wray. Agents are saying the director has ignored these growing problems, only saying they need more training, etc.

Some are saying Wray has lost control of the bureau and that "chaos" is reining.

Hmm… sounds about right for a Biden-led agency!

At least 20 whistleblowers have approached Republican congressmen with information. The pressure is mounting for something to change.

If we had a real president, Wray would already be gone. But it's up to Republicans to do the hard work, once they retake the majority.

Adam Casalino is a freelance writer, author, and blogger. He is a regular contributor for the Patriot Journal. Find his other work: www.talesofmaora.com

Bizarre arrest of FBI agent spotlights accusations of bureau corruption

By **Dana Kennedy**

July 24, 2021 6:09pm

Updated

Angry, and armed, the militiamen in Michigan were gearing up, getting ready to unleash their fury over an unjust government and zeroing in on a target who they believed upended their lives with pandemic restrictions: Gov. Gretchen Whitmer.

They trained with live assault weapons; skulked around Whitmer's summer mansion in the dark as they allegedly plotted a wild scheme to kidnap her, even relying on an Iraq war veteran among them for his tactical experience.

The June 2020 plot by the Wolverine Watchmen — which authorities claim included the possible use of a stun gun on Whitmer and talk of blowing up a bridge to prevent cops from giving chase — never came to pass, broken up by the Federal Bureau of Investigation in a celebrated bust in which 14 people have been arrested so far.

But as it was revealed that the FBI had at least a dozen informants heavily involved in the Watchmen — including that Iraq veteran — critics say the G-Men did as much to prod the plot as they did to prevent it from happening in the first place.

Michigan Gov. Gretchen Whitmer was the target of a militia group's kidnapping plot last year.Carolyn Kaster/AP

The agents took an active part in the scheme from its inception, according to court filings, evidence and dozens of interviews examined by BuzzFeed. Some members of the Wolverine Watchmen are accusing the feds of entrapment.

One FBI informant from Wisconsin allegedly helped organize meetings where the first inklings of the Whitmer plot surfaced, even paying for hotel rooms and food to entice people to attend, BuzzFeed reported. The Iraq veteran, identified as "Dan" by BuzzFeed, allegedly shelled out for transportation costs to militia meetings and apparently goaded members to advance the plot.

Members of the militia group accused of plotting to kidnap Michigan Gov. Gretchen Whitmer claim they were set up by the FBI. Kent County Sheriff via AP

Kareem Johnson, a black, left-wing attorney representing Pete Musico, one of the 14 arrested, told The Post the FBI played an outsize — and, at the very least, inappropriate — part in the incident. Before the bureau was involved, Johnson and other attorneys said, the Watchmen weren't even considered a violent threat.

"The FBI knew these people had some beliefs and were egging them on and providing help and ammunition," Johnson said. "They encouraged, helped instigate and escalated the criminal conduct of those individuals. At the end of the day, there were almost as many FBI agents leading the group as the other people in the group."

FBI agents took an active part in the scheme to kidnap Michigan Gov. Gretchen Whitmer from its inception, according to court filings.Alamy

It's not the first time the FBI's use of informants has come under fire.

Since the 9/11 attacks, the FBI has reportedly recruited thousands of informants. Some, according to a recent investigation in The New York Times that centered on the dubious arrest and conviction of the so-called "Herald Square Bomber" by the use of an informant, said they were retaliated against if they refused.

Shahawar Matin Siraj, was sentenced to 30 years in prison for trying to blow up Herald Square during a 2004 plot. The lonely 21-year-old, who had just moved to New York from Pakistan, ultimately decided he couldn't go forward with the plan, and apparently backed out of the scheme despite pressure from a pal, Osama Eldawoody, who turned out to be an FBI informant. Siraj was arrested anyway.

Notorious Boston mobster Whitey Bulger always denied it, but the FBI admitted he'd been an informant for several years, beginning in 1975. While dishing out intel about various Boston and Providence, Rhode Island, crime families, Bulger was moved with impunity and without fear of prosecution when running his Winter Hill Gang out of Southie.

The FBI's use of informants has come under fire in the past.Jim Lo Scalzo/EPA

And questions still linger about the FBI's relationship with Tamerlan Tsarnaev and his brother, Dzhokhar, who carried out the deadly bombings at the Boston Marathon in 2013. The Tsarnaevs, however, didn't make the bombs, and cops in Boston told Newsweek in 2018 they believe the FBI is protecting whoever did.

"It appears to me that there are allegations, with evidentiary support, that the FBI may have or currently is infiltrating, inciting or spawning alleged fringe group operations in this country," attorney Darren Richie told The Post. "The citizens of this country deserve to know if any of the stories permeating this subject are valid."

Richie represents ex-DEA special agent Mark Sami Ibrahim, who was arrested Tuesday for allegedly trespassing at the Capitol with a gun during the Jan. 6 riot. Ibrahim allegedly claimed to investigators he was at the Capitol to help a friend who was documenting the event for the FBI.

At least one veteran FBI agent dismissed allegations of "entrapment" against the agency in the Michigan case.

Danny Coulson, a former deputy assistant director of the FBI who led the 1995 search for and arrest of Oklahoma City bomber Timothy McVeigh, told The Post cries of entrapment have long been used by perps and he doesn't believe the FBI acted improperly in Michigan.

But he said that he and other FBI agents, both past and present, have "very grave concerns" about today's bureau.

Coulson said he was shocked at the FBI's tweet last week urging citizens to monitor "family members and peers" for signs of extremism. "The bureau's job is to collect evidence, not to develop informants," Coulson said. "That was inappropriate."

Coulson said he and others are "very upset" the FBI hasn't arrested anti-government and anti-fascist protesters who have been leading violent demonstrations in Portland and Seattle for more than a year — yet are bearing down so hard on those arrested for the insurrection at the Capitol.

Coulson used to run the Portland, Ore. FBI office and said the FBI has the jurisdiction under racketeering statutes to go after the activists who set fire and vandalized federal office buildings and threatened police.

"I am not demeaning what happened that day," Coulson said of Jan. 6. "But I'm asking why [those] people are being punished at this level and others aren't. In Portland and Seattle you clearly have federal laws being violated in plain sight and nothing done."

Asked for comment, the FBI's Portland office referred The Post to the bureau's Washington, DC office, who pointed to FBI Director Chris Wray's overall statement on FBI Oversight at the House Judiciary Committee last month.

"We do not investigate groups or individuals based on the exercise of First Amendment protected activity alone. But, when we encounter violence and threats to public safety, the FBI will not hesitate to take appropriate action," Wray said at the time.

Renewed criticism of the FBI's use of informants comes amid a set of embarrassing episodes for the G-men, starting last week with the arrest of Richard Trask, the lead agent in the attempted kidnapping case involving Whitmer.

STrask, 39, allegedly slammed his wife's head into a nightstand and choked her with both hands after the pair had attended a swinger's party, according to a report. The wife, who was covered in blood and had "severe" bruises around her neck, according to court documents, managed to stop the attack by grabbing his crotch, authorities said in court documents.

Last week, Special Agent Karen Veltri in Las Vegas claimed she was sexually harassed by a supervisor, who texted her a photo of a rainbow-colored dildo near his crotch, and spoke to her about his "ground balls," the woman claimed in a lawsuit.

And in the latest black eye for the agency, a top FBI official was accused of having a fling with an underling, then participating in a personnel decision involving her lover. The Thursday report from the U.S. Department of Justice's inspector general accused Jill Tyson, the assistant director of the bureau's Office of Congressional Affairs, of misconduct and failing to disclose the relationship.

Men accused in plot to kidnap Michigan Gov. Whitmer claim FBI set them up

The missteps and criticisms come as the Biden administration announced that white supremacists and militias inside the US are the biggest threat to national security.

Wayne Manis, a former FBI agent who took on the Ku Klux Klan, the Aryan Nations, and the Weather Underground before retiring in 1994, said the bureau today bears little resemblance to the place he worked for years. Manis, author of the 2017 book "Street Agent: He took on the mob, the Klan and the terrorists-The true story," said the new FBI has an agenda he doesn't understand.

"I and many of my friends from the old FBI are completely astounded about seeing things that we would have moved on being totally ignored over the past year," he said. "Burning a police station? Where are the arrests? There've been multiple incidents of violence by Antifa and BLM activists that fall under FBI statutes. The majority of domestic terrorism is on the left, but we're being told it's coming from the right."

Kurt Siuzdak left his job as an FBI agent — after almost 25 years — in March because, he told The Post, bureau management does not hold bosses accountable. He blames that on politicization at the top.

Former agent Kurt Siuzdak said FBI management does not hold bosses accountable. Provided by Kurt Siuzdak, who is also a lawyer and wrote an upcoming book on whistleblowers, has been in touch with Veltri. Washington, DC, attorney David Shaffer filed a sex harassment suit on Veltri's behalf last week.

"She got threatened with being investigated for misconduct, and they gave the guy who sent her the dick pic an award for professionalism," Siuzdak said. "That's today's real FBI."

Special Agent Roth

Assuming that Americans had access to all relevant information to cast their ballots in the 2020 Presidential Election and all of the ballots were
accurately counted, then Joe Biden won the Election legally.
However, virtually all of his policies have been a disaster. Donald Trump
had a successful term.
Therefore, the only explanations are that Americans did not have all the
relevant information and/or ballots for Biden were fraudulent.

BIDEN POLICIES

Biden sells oil from strategic reserves to China. Hunter Biden involved in UKRAINE WAR-Trump warned NATO countries not to buy Russian gas

STOCK MARKET
The stock market has dropped 7 Trillion Dollars since Biden has taken office.

Thousands of migrants join new caravan through Mexico, call for Title 42 repeal

By **Callie Patteson**
June 6, 2022, 3:19 pm
 Updated

- Mexico prez to skip Biden's Summit of Americas over Cuba, Venezuela snub

- Will the secret New York migrant flights ever stop?
- Security concerns leave Afghan evacuees stuck in Balkan camp
- Japan and Brazil are linked by soccer, baseball, and immigration

Up to 15,000 migrants — many of them from Central America, Venezuela, and Cuba — may soon join a massive caravan that set off from southern Mexico toward the US border Monday, with its members calling on President Biden to repeal the Title 42 health policy by the time they reach the frontier.

"[Biden] promised the Haitian community he will help them," one migrant from the Caribbean nation told Fox News. "He will recall Title 42. He will help us have real asylum."

The caravan began its journey from Tapachula, less than 10 miles from Mexico's border with Guatemala, a departure timed to coincide with the start of the Summit of the Americas in Los Angeles.

Reuters, citing witnesses, reported that at least 6,000 people had set off from Tapachula. Organizer Luis Villigran told Fox News that the caravan stretched more than 32 miles and estimated that 9,500 people were taking part.

INFLATION

Federal Reserve Chairman Dismantles Biden's Narrative on Inflation Crisis

Posted on June 22, 2022, by Constitutional Nobody

On Wednesday, Federal Reserve Chairman Jerome Powell pushed back against the narrative being spread by the Biden Administration, stating that the massive rise in inflation has not been caused by the invasion of Ukraine.

As recently as Monday, The White House has claimed that "the biggest single driver of inflation [is] Putin's war against Ukraine." However, when Powell testified before the Senate Banking Committee, he was asked by Senator Bill Hagerty, R-Tenn, if Biden's claims were true.

"I realize there are a number of factors that play a role in the historic inflation that we're experiencing: supply chain disruptions, regulations that constrain supply, we've got rising inflation expectations and excessive fiscal spending, But the problem hasn't sprung out of nowhere," Hagerty said. "In January of 2021, inflation was at 1.4%. By December 2021, it had risen to 7% — a fivefold increase. Now, since the war in Ukraine began in late February, the rate of inflation has risen incrementally from another 1.6% to a current level of 8.6%. So again, from 7% to 8.6%."

Hagerty then asked, "Given how inflation has escalated over the past 18 months, would you say that the war in Ukraine is the primary driver of inflation in America?"

Powell's response was blunt and damaging to Biden's claims. "No, inflation was high before, certainly before the war in Ukraine broke out," he said.

Powell also told Congress that the actions taken by the Federal Reserve in order to combat rising inflation might trigger a recession.

Others, however, believe that a recession is all but guaranteed.

"Look, nothing is certain, and all economic forecasts have uncertainty," Larry Summers, former Treasury Secretary, said Sunday on NBC. "My best guess is that a recession is ahead."

Summers explained, "I base that on the fact that we haven't had a situation like the present with inflation above 4% and unemployment beyond 4% without a recession following within a year or two. And so I think the likelihood is that in order to do what's necessary to stop inflation, the Fed is going to raise interest rates enough that the economy will slip into a recession."

The post-Federal Reserve Chairman Dismantles Biden's Narrative on Inflation Crisis appeared first on Resist the Mainstream.

Treasury Secretary Janet Yellen says she was wrong about the risks of inflation

June 1, 2022 12:18 PM ET

Ximena Bustillo

Treasury Secretary Janet Yellen said she was wrong a year ago when she said she anticipated inflation would be "a small risk," "manageable," and "not a problem."

In an interview with CNN's Wolf Blitzer on Tuesday, she admitted she had misjudged the threat inflation posed.

"There have been unanticipated and large shocks to the economy that have boosted energy and food prices," Yellen told Blitzer. "And supply bottlenecks that affected our economy badly that I didn't, at the time, fully understand."

Yellen said looking ahead, "core inflation" is moving down, but prices remain high, adding that the war in Ukraine is to blame for increasing oil and gas prices.

The comments came just after a White House meeting with Yellen, President Biden, and Federal Reserve Chair Jerome Powell to talk about inflation.

"Respect the Fed's independence," Biden said. "I am not going to interfere with their critically important work. ... Chair Powell and other leaders of the Fed have noted that at this moment they have a laser focus on addressing inflation, just like I am," he said. "And with a larger complement of board members now confirmed, I know we'll use those tools and monetary policy to address the rising prices for the American people."

Yellen's concession also comes on a week when the Biden administration is touting its approach to tackling rising prices ahead of the November midterms.

In a Wall Street Journal Op-ed published on Tuesday, the president said he would let the Fed take the lead in fighting inflation, urged Congress to pass clean energy tax credits, and discussed tackling foreign ocean freight companies' export and transport fees.

But when asked questions about whether or not the administration misjudged inflation as "transitory," White House National Economic Council Director Brian Deese told reporters, "that falls squarely into the category of things that we will leave to the independent judgment of the Fed" and that the president understands prices are a top issue.

As NPR reported, Powell has admitted inflation has been "more persistent" than he first expected.

CONSIDER THIS FROM NPR

Why Americans Feel The Toll Of High Inflation Beyond Gas Pumps & Grocery Stores

The most recent Commerce Department data showed that consumer prices were up 6.3 percent in April compared to a year ago. The Fed has begun raising interest rates aggressively in an effort to bring prices under control.

New inflation data is expected to be released next week.

A Treasury spokesperson told NPR in an email that the comments made by Yellen were aimed at "pointing out that there have been shocks to the economy that have exacerbated inflationary pressures which couldn't have been foreseen 18 months ago, including Russia's decision to invade Ukraine, multiple successive variants of COVID, and lockdowns in China."

The **Consumer Price Index (CPI)** is a measure of the average change over time in the prices paid by urban consumers for a market basket of consumer goods and services. Indexes are available for the U.S. and various geographic areas. Average price data for select utility, automotive fuel, and food items are also available.

NEWS RELEASES

CPI for all items rises 0.3% in April; shelter, food, and airfare indexes rise
05/11/2022
In April, the Consumer Price Index for All Urban Consumers rose 0.3 percent, seasonally adjusted, and rose 8.3 percent over the last 12 months, not seasonally adjusted. The index for all items less food and energy increased 0.6 percent in April (SA), up 6.2 percent over the year (NSA).

NEXT RELEASE

May 2022 CPI data are scheduled to be released on June 10, 2022, at 8:30 A.M. Eastern Time.
The annual rate of inflation worldwide, as measured By the consumer price index (CPI), accelerated to 9.2 percent in March 2022, up from 7.5 percent in February 2022, 6.8 percent in January 2022, and 6.4 percent in December 2021.
Food prices, in particular, are now soaring. In March 2022, they were 9.1 percent higher than in March 2021.

SUPPLY CHAIN
No BaBy Formula
BIG CITY CRIME
'It's just crazy': 12 major cities hit all-time homicide records
"It's worse than a war zone around here lately," a police official said.
Video by **Jessie DiMartino**
By **Bill Hutchinson**
December 08, 2021, 6:08 AM

How George Soros funded progressive 'legal arsonist' DAs behind US crime surge

By **Isabel Vincent**
December 16, 2021, 4:03pm
 Updated
Billionaire George Soros (center) funnels cash through a complicated web of federal and state political action committees as well as non-profits to support soft-on-crime DAs across the country.NY Post photo composite

- Boudin's recall shows voters are fed up with the chaos fueled by soft-on-crime DAs — like those backed by Soros
- How George Soros' billions are remaking America's justice system
- Soros-backed Spanish radio stations out to 'disinform' Miami residents: DeSantis
- George Soros says 'civilization may not survive' Russia-Ukraine war

For the last several years, billionaire philanthropist George Soros has been quietly financing a revolution in criminal justice reform, doling out tens of millions of dollars to progressive candidates in district attorney races throughout the country amid movements to abolish bail and defund the police.

Working with an activist attorney, Soros, 91, mainly funnels cash through a complicated web of federal and state political action committees as well as non-profits from coast to coast, public records show.

Last year, the Foundation to Promote Open Society, a nonprofit in Soros' orbit, gave $3 million to the Community Resource Hub for Safety and Accountability, according to a recent report. The group provides resources to "local advocates and organizations working to address the harm of policing in the US."

Hungarian-born philanthropist Soros and his Open Society group of non-profits have mainly doled out cash to political action campaigns controlled by attorney and criminal justice reform activist Whitney Tymas, 60. She is the treasurer of the Justice and Safety PAC as well as 20 other similarly named groups at both the state and federal levels, according to public filings.

The goal of the myriad PACs is focused on electing progressives to end tough policing and mass incarceration, according to Tymas. "If we are to reach a place of true progress, it will take the sustained efforts of local elected prosecutors across the country to rectify and reimagine their role in the criminal legal system — not just as gatekeepers, but as active catalysts for change," wrote Tymas in an opinion article last year.

Chicago's Kim Foxx was Soros' first success, contributing $300,000 to her first campaign in 2016 and another $2 million for her successful re-election run last month.

Her efforts, coupled with Soros' largesse, have played an outsize role in some of the most controversial district attorney campaigns in the US, including George Gascon in Los Angeles as well as Larry Krasner in Philadelphia and Kim Foxx in Chicago, among others. Soros also donated $1 million to Alvin Bragg's successful DA campaign in Manhattan, funneling the cash through the Color of Change political action committee, according to public filings.

"George Soros has quietly orchestrated the dark money political equivalent of 'shock and awe' on local attorney races through the country, shattering records, flipping races, and essentially making a mockery of our entire campaign finance system," said Tom Anderson, director of the Government Integrity Project at the National Legal and Policy Center in Virginia. (Calls to Soros' camp went unreturned on Thursday.)

Between 2015 and 2019, Soros and his affiliated political action committees spent more than $17 million on local DA races in support of left-wing candidates, according to the Capital Research Center, a non-profit that tracks lobbying and charitable giving. That number is expected to top $20 million in the last two years, according to estimates from the NLPC.

San Francisco District Attorney Chesa Boudin, whose parents were members of the Weather Underground domestic terrorist group, wants to end mass incarceration and cash bail, earning Soros' campaign dollars.

"I don't think we've ever seen anything like this where federal election level money and resources are brought to bear and coordinated to effectively flip local level races where campaign finance restrictions make it almost impossible to counter," said Anderson, adding that conservative opponents are hamstrung by local campaign finance laws that Soros doesn't have to abide by because he is using independent expenditures and not directly coordinating with the campaigns.

Critics say the policies of Soros-funded DAs, which have included abolishing bail and, in the case of Chicago, placing hundreds of violent criminals on electronic tracking systems, have led to a spike in crime throughout the country. According to the FBI's annual Uniform Crime Report released in September, the country saw a 30 percent increase in homicides in 2020 — the largest single-year spike since they began recording crime statistics 60 years ago. The report also saw a 24 percent decrease in arrests across the country.

This year, Philadelphia, a city of 1.5 million, had more homicides than New York and Los Angeles, the country's two largest cities. The city recorded 521 homicides — the highest since 1990 — compared to 443 in New York and 352 in Los Angeles. Chicago, the country's third largest city, registered the highest number of homicides at 739, up three percent from the previous year.

Los Angeles County District Attorney George Gascon, also backed by Soros, has presided over a crime spike since he was inaugurated in December 2020.AFP via Getty Images

"Everywhere Soros-backed prosecutors go, crime follows," said Arkansas Republican Senator Tom Cotton in a statement to The Post. "These legal arsonists have abandoned their duty to public safety by pursuing leniency even for the most heinous crime, and they often flat-out refuse to charge criminals for shoplifting, vagrancy, and entire categories of misdemeanors."

In Los Angeles, where critics say that criminal justice reforms have recently led to a wave of looting and violent crimes, Soros funneled more than $2.5 million into a California political action committee to support Gascon, who left the San Francisco District Attorney's office to run against incumbent Jackie Lacey in 2020. The Cuban-born Gascon, who moved with his family to the US in 1967, said in his December 2020 inauguration speech that the rush to "incarcerate generations of kids of color" had torn the "social fabric of our communities. The status quo hasn't made us safe."

Boudin, whose parents were members of the Weather Underground domestic terrorist group, echoed similar sentiments during his campaign in San Francisco. A former public defender and translator for former Venezuelan president Hugo Chavez, Boudin has promised to end mass incarceration and cash bail. Former San Francisco homicide prosecutors Brooke Jenkins and Don Du Bain recently quit their jobs, two of 59 attorneys to resign since Boudin took office in January 2020.

Philadelphia District Attorney Larry Krasner has seen crime in his city skyrocket, with more homicides than New York and Los Angeles, the country's two largest cities.

Earlier this week, San Francisco mayor London Breed announced an emergency crackdown on crime after a spike in gun violence and lethal fentanyl overdoses in the city's Tenderloin neighborhood. "It's time for the reign of criminals who are destroying our city; it is time for it to come to an end," she said. "And it comes to an end when we take steps to be more aggressive with law enforcement. More aggressive with the changes in our policies and less tolerant of all the b–ls–t that has destroyed our city."

The problem begins with lax law enforcement at the DA level, according to critics.

"The only good Soros prosecutor is a defeated Soros prosecutor," Cotton told The Post.

But that's becoming increasingly rare as Soros and other progressive groups step up their funding. Chicago's Kim Foxx was Soros' first success. He contributed $300,000 to her first campaign in 2016 and a further $2 million for her successful re-election run last year. The Cook County State's Attorney came under fire when her office dismissed all the charges in the original 16-count indictment against "Empire" actor Jussie Smollett in 2019, three weeks after a grand jury had issued it. Last week, Smollett was convicted of staging a false hate crime.

And Soros' funding doesn't end with electing progressive prosecutors. In October, Soros' Open Society Policy Center donated $500,000 to Equity PAC, a Texas-based group that funds progressive causes and was working to oppose a ballot proposition that would have seen the capital city of Austin hire hundreds of new police officers amid a spike in violent crime. Although the city has seen a 10 percent rise in aggravated assaults over 2020, Proposition A was overwhelmingly defeated last month — apparently thanks to Soros' cash injection, which funded ad campaigns throughout Austin.

Soros' donation came a year after his non-profit funneled $652,000 to the Texas Justice and Public Safety PAC group that backed the election of Jose Garza, who assumed office as Travis County DA based in Austin.

AFGHANISTAN

American troop withdrawal.

POLLS

"Meet the Press" moderator Chuck Todd joins Sunday TODAY's Willie Geist to discuss a new NBC News poll indicating that 71% of Americans believe the U.S. is headed in the wrong direction. He says it's the economy that's driving that feeling. Chuck says, "That's not just Republicans; a majority of Democrats think we're headed in the wrong direction."

Appearing: Savannah GuthrieHoda Kotb

Poll: Biden disapproval hits new high as more Americans say they would vote for Trump

Andrew Romano

June 17, 2022, 5:00 AM

As inflation keeps rising and recession fears loom, a new Yahoo News/YouGov poll shows that Joe Biden is currently in the worst shape of his presidency.

The survey of 1,541 U.S. adults, which was conducted from June 10-13, found that if another presidential election were held today, more registered voters say they would cast ballots for Donald Trump (44%) than for Biden (42%) — even though the House Jan. 6 committee has spent the last week linking Trump to what it called a "seditious conspiracy" to overturn the 2020 election and laying the groundwork for possible criminal prosecution.

President Biden outside the White House on Tuesday. (Stefani Reynolds/AFP via Getty Images)

Since Biden took office, no previous Yahoo News/YouGov poll has shown him trailing Trump (though Biden's most recent leads have been within the margin of error, like this one is for Trump).

312

One year ago, Biden led Trump by 9 percentage points. In 2020, Biden won the White House by more than 7 million votes.

Yet Biden's job approval rating has been atrophying for much of the last year, and the new survey shows that it has never been weaker. A full 56% of Americans now disapprove of the president's performance — the highest share to date — while just 39% approve. Three weeks ago, those numbers were 53% and 42%, respectively.

On average, Biden's job approval scores are now a few points worse than Trump's were at the parallel stage of his presidency.

Among all Americans, Trump (43%) now has a higher personal favorability rating than Biden (40%) as well. Meanwhile, nearly two-thirds of independents (64%) have an unfavorable opinion of Biden, and just 28% say they would vote for him over Trump.

The bad news for Biden comes as prices continue to increase at the fastest pace in 40 years, upending expectations and overshadowing other concerns. According to the poll, 40% of registered voters (up from 33% last month) now say inflation is "the most important issue to you when thinking about this year's election" — more than four times the number for any other issue. Former President Donald Trump in Casper, Wyo., last month.

Politically, this is crippling for Biden. A full 61% of voters disapprove of the president's handling of the economy (up from 58% last month), and Republicans now hold a 15-point advantage among voters on the question of which party would do a better job handling the economy (up from 11 points last month).

In recent days, a series of stories questioning whether Biden will run for reelection in 2024 — and quoting concerned Democratic sources — have surfaced in the press. The concern isn't limited to party officials. Just 21% of Americans — down from 25% three weeks ago and the lowest number to date — say Biden should run again. But perhaps more strikingly, a greater share of 2020 Biden voters now say he shouldn't run again (40%) than say he should (37%). Last month, those numbers were reversed.

In contrast, a clear majority of Trump voters (57%) say Trump should mount another bid. Just 21% say he shouldn't. And while 57% of independents say Trump shouldn't try to make a comeback in 2024, far more — a full 76% — say the same about Biden.

The Yahoo News survey was conducted by YouGov using a nationally representative sample of 1,541 U.S. adults interviewed online from June 10 to 13, 2022. This sample was weighted according to gender, age, race, and education based on the American Community Survey, conducted by the U.S. Bureau of the Census, as well as the 2020 presidential vote (or nonvote) and voter registration status. Respondents were selected from YouGov's opt-in panel to be representative of all U.S. adults. The margin of error is approximately 2.9%.

Poll: Half of Americans now predict the U.S. may 'cease to be a democracy' someday

Andrew Romano

June 15, 2022, 5:00 AM

Trump supporters clashed with police outside the U.S. Capitol on Jan. 6, 2021. (Roberto Schmidt/AFP via Getty Images)

A new Yahoo News/YouGov poll shows that most Democrats (55%) and Republicans (53%) now believe it is "likely" that America will "cease to be a democracy in the future" — a stunning expression of bipartisan despair about the direction of the country.

Half of all Americans (49%) express the same sentiment when independents and those who do not declare any political affiliation are factored in, while just a quarter (25%) consider the end of U.S. democracy unlikely, and another quarter (25%) say they're unsure.

At the same time, however, a large number of Americans seem indifferent to the high-profile hearings by the House committee investigating the Jan. 6, 2021, attack on the Capitol — an effort to get to the bottom of one of the most dramatic assaults on the democratic process in U.S. history. In fact, the new survey of 1,541 U.S. adults — which was conducted from June 10 (the day after the committee's first hearing) to June 13 (the day of its second) — found that fewer than 1 in 4 (24%) say they watched last Thursday's initial primetime broadcast live. Only slightly more (27%) say they caught news coverage later. Nearly half (49%) say they did not follow the hearings at all. Donald Trump is pictured during the second hearing of the Jan. 6 committee on Monday. (Tom Williams/CQ-Roll Call via Getty Images)

So while the data indicates that many Americans seem to be losing faith in the future of U.S. democracy, relatively few seem interested in reckoning with a real-life attempt to undermine it. That raises a disturbing question: Have Americans simply given up on democracy?

The poll doesn't go quite that far. But it does suggest that Americans have largely given up on each other.

As usual, partisanship is key to understanding what's happening here. Live viewership of the hearings was lowest among Donald Trump voters (9%), Republicans (13%), and Fox News viewers (22%); it was highest among Joe Biden voters (47%), Democrats (44%), and viewers of MSNBC (52%). Nearly three-quarters (72%) of those who watched identified as Democrats or Democratic-leaning independents.

In part, as a result, less than half of Americans (45%) say they believe the Democrat-led committee's central claim: that the Jan. 6 attack "was part of a conspiracy to overturn the election." The rest either say it was not (35%) or that they're unsure (20%).

Likewise, just 37% of Americans believe there was a conspiracy and that "Donald Trump was at the center of [it]" — the committee's other major argument.

Again, partisan affiliation defines these views: 84% of Biden voters and 77% of Democrats believe the attack was part of a conspiracy to overturn the election; 71% of Trump voters and 59% of Republicans believe the attack was not part of such a conspiracy. Independents are evenly split — 39% yes versus 41% no — on the question.

But if Republicans and Republican-leaning independents are largely dismissive of the Jan. 6 riot at the Capitol, then why are most of them pessimistic about the future of democracy? For the same reason, most refused to watch the hearings in the first place: because they see Democrats — not the Trump supporters who invaded the Capitol — as the real problem.

And Democrats largely feel the same way about Republicans.

When asked to choose the phrase that best "describes most people on the other side of the political aisle from you," a majority of Republicans pick extreme negatives such as "out of touch with reality" (30%), a "threat to America" (25%), "immoral" (8%) and a "threat to me personally" (4%).

A tiny fraction selected more sympathetic phrases such as "well-meaning" (4%) or "not that different from me" (6%).

The results among Democrats are nearly identical, with negatives such as "out of touch with reality" (27%), a "threat to America" (23%), "immoral" (7%), and a "threat to me personally" (4%) vastly outnumbering positives such as "well-meaning" (7%) or "not that different from me" (5%).

Meanwhile, the number of Trump and Biden voters who say the other side is primarily a threat to America (28% and 25%, respectively) is double the number who say the other side is primarily "wrong about policy" (14% and 13%).

This explains why 43% of Republicans continue to say that "left-wing protesters trying to make Trump look bad" deserve "the most blame" for Jan. 6, versus just 7% who blame Trump himself, 10% for "Trump supporters who gathered at the Capitol" and 12% for "right-wing groups like the Proud Boys" — even though there is zero evidence that liberals were involved.

It also helps explain why members of the Jan. 6 committee have their work cut out for them if they hope to move public opinion. The new Yahoo News/YouGov survey suggests that outrage toward the targets of the House investigation has only eroded over the last seven months.

- While still confined to a small minority, the belief that the attack on the Capitol was "justified" (17%) has risen 5 percentage points since December (12%); it is now the highest it has ever been.
- The number of Americans who describe Jan. 6 participants as "primarily peaceful and law-abiding" (30%) has also gone up 6 points (from 24%) since December.
- At the same time, the number of Americans assigning "a great deal" of blame to Trump for the Jan. 6 attack has fallen 6 points (from 45% to 39%), as have the numbers saying the same about "Republicans who claimed the election had been stolen" (down from 42% to 36%) and "Trump supporters who gathered at the U.S. Capitol" (down from 50% to 43%).
- And while 60% of Americans said in December that they believed "another attack like January 6 could happen in the future," fewer (53%) say that now.

The survey does contain one small kernel of hope for the House committee. In December, 72% of Republicans predicted the committee *would not* "tell the truth" about Jan. 6. But today, the number of Republicans who say the committee *is not* telling the truth is 12 points lower (60%), while the number who say they're not sure is 10 points higher (28%). That could suggest some openness to persuasion.

Yet even such uncertainty is likely to be consumed by partisan animosity in the end. A full 60% of Democrats and 61% of Republicans now believe America is becoming a "less democratic country"; just 23% say the country is becoming "more democratic."

Republicans, in particular, are far more inclined to agree that America treated "people like them" fairly "in the past" (71%) than "today" (36%) — though more Democrats also say the former (50%) than the latter (46%).

A majority of Republicans (52%) also say it's likely that "there will be a civil war in the United States in [their] lifetime"; half of the independents (50%) and a plurality of Democrats (46%) agree. In each group, fewer than 4 in 10 say another civil war is unlikely.

A Trump supporter with a Confederate flag outside the Senate chamber during the Capitol assault. (Saul Loeb/AFP via Getty Images)

And perhaps most unsettling of all, only about half of Americans are willing to rule out "physical violence" (50%) and "to take up arms against the government" (47%) when asked if there are times when such measures "would be justified in order to protect the country from radical extremists." About a quarter of Americans say that violence (26%) and taking up arms (23%) could be justified. These tendencies, it's worth noting, are particularly pronounced on the right — as Jan. 6 itself demonstrated. Nearly 8 in 10 Trump voters (79%) say "limiting free speech" is off-limits as a method to protect the country from radical extremists; 65% say the same about "protesting outside personal residences of government officials." Yet only 39% reject taking up arms against the government in such situations — and nearly as many (31%) say it could be justified.
Just 15% of Biden voters agree.

NY Times: Polls May Give Dems False Hope

A voter sits alone at a poll kiosk to cast his vote at a Mississippi Second Congressional District Primary election precinct, in Jackson, Mississippi, on June 7. (Rogelio V. Solis/AP)

By Charlie McCarthy | *Monday, 12 September 2022, 09:02 AM EDT*

e left-leaning New York Times expressed skepticism over Democrats' improved showing in recent polls for November's midterms.

Although recent surveys indicate, Democrats are expected to retain control of the Senate and lose control of the House – both narrowly – the Times suggested that polling might not give a true picture of the current landscape.

The newspaper based its concern on the 2020 election final polls, which overstated President Joe Biden's strength, especially in places such as North Carolina, Wisconsin, and Ohio – states with key Senate races this year.

"One factor seems to be that Republican voters are more skeptical of mainstream institutions and are less willing to respond to a survey," Times senior writer David Leonhardt said Monday. "If that's true, polls will often understate Republican support until pollsters figure out how to fix the problem."

The outlet said there's also uncertainty about how polls are affected by former President Donald Trump not being on the ballot, as he was in 2016 and 2020. YouGov's chief scientist Douglas Rivers, told the Times that "there is something particular about Trump that complicates polling."

The Times, noting pollsters' challenge to find likely voters willing to respond to surveys, said, "there are still some big mysteries about the polls' recent tendency to underestimate Republican support."

Times' chief political analyst Nate Cohn even suggested this year's surveys could be off due to pollsters "understating Democratic support this year by searching too hard for Republican voters in an effort to avoid repeating recent mistakes."

One issue in trying to assure survey accuracy nationwide is that not all states have produced questionable polling results.

For example, polls in states such as Georgia, Nevada, and Pennsylvania have been fairly accurate in recent years.

The Times said the 2020 election "does have two dynamics" that might help Democrats – the Supreme Court overturning Roe v. Wade and Trump's continued influence on Republican supporters.

"As a result, this year's election may feel less like a referendum on the current president and more like a choice between two parties," the Times said.

Still, midterms usually hurt the party — especially in the House — of the sitting president.

Emphasizing that every election cycle is unique, the Times said, "there's always a way to spin up a rationale for why old rules won't apply."

"In the end, history usually prevails," Leonhardt said. "That's a good thing to keep in mind right now as Democrats show the strength that seems entirely at odds with the long history of the struggles of the president's party in midterm elections.

"But this cycle, there really is something different — or at the very least, there is something different about the reasons this cycle might be different."

Poll: Biden's approval rating hits an all-time low of 33 percent

Joe Biden
Grayson Quay, Weekend editor
Wed, April 13, 2022, 4:17 PM·1 min read
In this article:
Joe Biden
46th and current president of the United States
President Biden's approval rating is at an all-time low, according to a new Quinnipiac poll released Wednesday.
When asked if they "approve or disapprove of the way Joe Biden is handling his job as president," 33 percent of respondents said they approved, 54 percent expressed disapproval, and 13 percent said they didn't know or had no opinion.
Biden's approval rating previously hit 33 percent on Jan. 12, 2022, though his disapproval rating at the time was only 53 percent.
At the same point in his presidency, former President Donald Trump's approval/disapproval spread was 39-55, according to Gallup. In April 2010, former President Barack Obama stood at 48-45. George W. Bush, still riding the wave of post-9/11 unity, had an approval rating of 75 percent, while only 20 percent of respondents disapproved of his job performance.
As of Wednesday afternoon, Gallup had not yet released April job approval numbers for Biden. Gallup polling puts his lowest approval rating at 40 percent in the first half of Jan. 2022. According to Gallup, Trump hit his low point of 34 percent in the aftermath of the Jan. 6 Capitol riot.
The Quinnipiac poll surveyed 1,412 U.S. adults from April 7–11 with an error margin of 2.6 percent.

Biden's approval rating drops to a new low of 41%, Reuters/Ipsos poll finds

Jason Lange

February 3, 2022, 4:27 PM

WASHINGTON (Reuters) - President Joe Biden's public approval rating fell to the lowest level of his presidency this week, a dangerous sign for his Democratic Party, which risks losing control of Congress in the Nov. 8 elections, according to a Reuters/Ipsos opinion poll.

The national poll, conducted Feb. 2-3, found that 41% of U.S. adults approved of Biden's performance in office, while 56% disapproved, and the rest were not sure. The prior week's poll had put Biden at a 45% approval rating and 50% disapproval.

Americans appear increasingly exhausted by the COVID-19 pandemic and its economic toll. About six in ten think the country is heading in the wrong direction, with the economy and public health most often cited as top concerns, the poll showed.

After holding above 50% in his first months in office, Biden's popularity began dropping in mid-August as COVID-19 deaths surged across the country and the U.S.-backed Afghan government collapsed.

Democrats are increasingly worried that dissatisfaction with Biden's presidency could cost them their congressional majorities. If Republicans take control of either the U.S. House of Representatives or Senate, Biden's legislative agenda could be doomed.

Biden's popularity remains above the lowest levels seen by his predecessor, Donald Trump, whose approval rating sank to as low as 33% in December 2017.

The Reuters/Ipsos poll is conducted online in English throughout the United States. The latest poll gathered responses from a total of 1,005 adults, including 443 Democrats and 377 Republicans. It has a credibility interval - a measure of precision - of 4 percentage points.

(Reporting by Jason Lange; Editing by Scott Malone and Alistair Bell)

By *Allan Smith*

Prime Minister Macron of France advised President Biden that Saudi Arabia and the United Arab Emirates have no oil no sell to the United States.

Section 2

Part Seventeen

Assassination of President John F. Kennedy

SPECIAL AGENTS SHELTON AND ROTH- The purpose of this section of this book is to compare the Trump-Russian Collusion case to the Assassination of President Kennedy case. The purpose is not to solve the Kennedy case. It most likely will never be solved. The focus of this section is on the investigation of the Kennedy case by the Central Intelligence Agency and the Federal Bureau of Investigation and to compare these agencies' investigations to their investigations of the Trump-Russian Collusion case. There are some startling similarities, if not identical, aspects to both cases. There are some startling differences in both cases.

There are hundreds, if not thousands, of rumors, hypotheses, etc., in the public domain regarding bits and pieces of information possibly connected to the JFK Assassination. The information may not be completely corroborated or developed. **However, if only a small number of these rumors and hypotheses are true, they would confirm that there was a conspiracy to assassinate President John F. Kennedy.**

BACKGROUND

President John F Kennedy was in Dallas, Texas, on November 22, 1963. He was traveling through downtown Dallas at 12:30 P.M. The President was accompanied by his wife, Jackie, and they were traveling by car in a motorcade along with other vehicles and dignitaries. Texas Governor John Connolly was sitting in the front seat of the vehicle, and a Secret Service Agent was driving the vehicle. The President was seated in the back seat behind the driver. First Lady Jackie Kennedy was seated in the back seat next to the President.

All of a sudden, gunshots were heard. President Kennedy was shot. The driver drove to Parkland Hospital, and President Kennedy was admitted directly to the emergency room. What unfolded is one of the biggest murder cases in United States history. To this day, the Federal Bureau of Investigation has not provided all the evidence that it has obtained. All that is known to the American public is that Lee Harvey Oswald, a mysterious man who is connected to other mysterious men, was pronounced by J. Edgar Hoover, Director of the Federal Bureau of Investigation, to be the lone shooter and a "nut". Director Hoover sent a communication to the Dallas FBI Field Office on November 23, 1963, that the shooter was in custody and no further investigation was required.

However, on November 24, 1963, Oswald was shot by Jack Ruby, a strip joint owner with alleged contacts with organized crime.

INITIAL INDICATIONS OF A COVERUP BY GOVERNMENT OFFICIALS

The Warren Commission's treatment of Jack Ruby followed its attitude toward the assassination as a whole. Within hours of Oswald's death, insiders in Washington were aware of the need for what became the Warren Commission and had determined its purpose.

A memo by the deputy Attorney General, Nicholas Katzenbach, summarized the issue:

The public must be satisfied that Oswald was the assassin, that he did not have confederates who are still at large, and that the evidence was such that he would have been convicted at trial. …

We need something to head off public speculation or Congressional hearings of the wrong sort. (*FBI HQ JFK Assassination File, 62–109060–18*)

The lone nut explanation was a political imperative and came about as a direct consequence of Oswald's impersonation in Mexico City about seven weeks before the JFK assassination; see "A Little Incident in Mexico City."

J. Edgar Hoover, the director of the FBI, also emphasized the need for a public relations initiative: The thing I am concerned about, and so is Mr. Katzenbach, is having something issued so that we can convince the public that Oswald is the real assassin. Mr. Katzenbach thinks that the President might appoint a Presidential Commission of three outstanding citizens to make a determination.

The Warren Commission's conclusion was in place before the Commission had even been established: Oswald was guilty and had acted alone. To counteract suspicions of conspiracy, it was necessary for the Warren Commission to show that Jack Ruby also had acted alone.

FBI had a conclusion in place before all the evidence was gathered.
FBI failed to conduct interviews with multiple people who most likely had knowledge of the case.

The Warren Commission's conclusion was in place before the Commission had even been established: Oswald was guilty and had acted alone. To counteract suspicions of conspiracy, it was necessary for the Warren Commission to show that Jack Ruby also had acted alone.

All that is known to the American public is that Lee Harvey Oswald, a mysterious man who is connected to other mysterious cases, was pronounced by J. Edgar Hoover, Director of the Federal Bureau of Investigation, to be the lone shooter and a "nut". Director Hoover sent a communication to Dallas Field Office that the shooter was in custody and no further investigation was required.

FBI – assassination of the President was not a federal crime.
FBI cannot open a case without permission of The Depart of Justice.

The *HSCA Report* found that the FBI's investigation was "seriously flawed":
The committee concluded from its lengthy study of the roles of the FBI, Secret Service, CIA, and other Federal agencies that assisted the Warren Commission that the final determinations of who was responsible for President Kennedy's murder and whether there had been a conspiracy were based largely on the work of the FBI. With an acute awareness of the significance of its finding, the committee concluded that the FBI's investigation of whether there had been a conspiracy in President Kennedy's assassination was seriously flawed. The conspiracy aspects of the investigation were characterized by a limited approach and an inadequate application and use of available resources.

The committee concluded that the FBI's investigation into a conspiracy was deficient in the areas that the committee decided were most worthy of suspicion — organized crime, pro- and anti–Castro Cubans, and the possible associations of individuals from these areas with Lee Harvey Oswald and Jack Ruby. In those areas, in particular, the committee found that the FBI's investigation was, in all likelihood, insufficient to have uncovered a conspiracy.

Special Agents Shelton and Roth- The Media approach to the Trump-Russia Collusion Case and the JFK Assassination case is most likely the major factor in the outcome of these two cases. The Media took a "hands-off" approach to the JFK Assassination, with the result being the case was never solved. The Media chose to amplify the false statements of Hillary Clinton, the campaign staff, and her lawyers regarding Trump- the Russia Collusion, with the result being Republicans and conservative media began to defend President Trump. The conservative and Republican media were simply overwhelmed.

Documents made public many years later reveal the extent to which senior figures in the print and broadcast media were involved in shaping the official response to the assassination. One such figure was the syndicated newspaper columnist Joe Alsop.

MEDIA - Major news outlets failed to report any information concerning the JFK Assassination other than the "Oswald Lone Nut."

Major reporters George Wil and Walter Cronkite

WELCOME SKEPTICISM

I'm no expert on the JFK assassination, but it seems to me that Oliver Stone has done us all a valuable service and does not deserve the pillorying he has received in the media what George Will {"'JFK': Paranoid History," op-ed, Dec. 26} and other critics fail to appreciate is that Stone has reminded us of what our Founding Fathers knew 200 years ago when they set out a Bill of Rights: that we should be vigilant in seeing that government does not become too powerful. A sure way for the government to gain such power is if its citizens do not question its actions and pronouncements.

Why, then, has Stone been so roundly criticized for challenging the "official" version of the Kennedy assassination? The truth of Stone's version of history is not the issue. Rather, Stone's point is that we should not take at face value the official assertions that Lee Harvey Oswald acted as a crazed lone gunman in assassinating President Kennedy. I believe that Stone would agree that his version of history should not be swallowed as incontrovertible fact as well.

Stone's contribution is in reminding us that complacency is a threat to democracy just as much as, if not more than, we thought communism was. The Pentagon Papers, the Gulf of Tonkin Resolution, Watergate, and Iran-contra should be proof enough that we need no reminder. But apparently, our blind acceptance of the invasion of Grenada and lack of outrage at Pentagon censorship throughout the gulf war indicate that we have not fully learned our lesson. The stone should be applauded for continuing what has been and should continue to be one of our wisest traditions: raising a healthy dose of skepticism at the words and deeds of our government.
-- Roger Kosson

With his vitriolic diatribe against Oliver Stone, George Will joins the avalanche of Stone-bashing that seems all the rage and all out of proportion to the release of what is, after all, just a movie. Like others, Will seems to deliberately ignore the fact that Garrison's and Stone's theory about a conspiracy to kill Kennedy is just that -- a theory. It is a theory that attempts to explain some of the more troubling aspects of the assassination that point to at least some element of participation by some person or persons working within the government.

But just as Clay Shaw's not-guilty verdict neither proved his innocence nor validated the Warren Commission Report, the various "flaws" in Stone's movie similarly do not somehow eliminate the hundreds of as yet unexplained pieces of evidence and testimony that contradict the lone-assassin theory. One does not have to agree with Stone's conclusion to believe that a conspiracy existed. Moreover, even if Stone's theory is wrong, that does not make the movie, as Will put it, "an act of execrable history and contemptible citizenship."

It is ironic that the movie "JFK," which Stone has never claimed to be the conclusive answer to this mystery, is being subjected to much more nitpicking scrutiny by the mainstream press than the Warren Commission Report ever has been. I would have more confidence in Will's and others' objectivity if, along with their criticism of Stone, they also supported the opening of evidence sealed by the Warren Commission and House Select Committee on Assassinations. Or would asking for that evidence also be an act of "contemptible citizenship?"

-- Donald Squires

As a 24-year-old second-year law student at Catholic University, I have just recently entertained the notion that John F. Kennedy was assassinated through a conspiracy perpetrated by the CIA or other government officials. I and friends of my age owe much gratitude to Oliver Stone for his eye-opening motion picture, "JFK". After seeing the movie, I was not content to limit my exposure to the subject, so I read some of the leading literature on the matter.

Recently your paper has published columns concerning "JFK" by David Belin and Gerald Ford, George Will, Stephen S. Rosenfeld, and Stone himself. Stone's movie is attacked on the basis that it is unpatriotic, fallacious, and stirs up unwarranted and harmful sentiment against the government for something that occurred 28 years ago and should be left alone. As someone who was born after Nov. 22, 1963, I find the attacks on "JFK" exhibit the obvious biases and protection of vested interests in Washington circles and the value of truth in the democratic process.

The days are over when Walter Cronkite can tell the nation that it is in its best interest to believe the "official" version of a national disaster because it will promote national security. Watergate and Iran-contra have dispelled any myths about the credibility of the CIA or other government actors.

The answer to who shot John F. Kennedy is important because our government should be held accountable for its actions. But more importantly, the answer carries much value in framing the mood and manner in which the American people will scrutinize future actions by their government. As someone of the post-Kennedy generation with no illusions about government excesses, I believe I speak for most when I say that an objective analysis of the weight of the evidence on both sides clearly shows that "JFK" is an accurate representation of history. **No more convincing evidence of this can be asked than Lyndon Johnson's statement in 1975 that he never believed that Oswald acted alone and the House Select Committee on Assassinations' determination that a conspiracy was "probable" in the murder of John F. Kennedy.**

GEORGE WILL-

In a small section of his most recent column, *Washington Post* conservative columnist George Will demonstrates the deference to authority that has come to characterize the mainstream media with respect to the JFK assassination. Will writes:

For many years, some people insisted that a vast conspiracy, not a lone gunman, masterminded the 1963 assassination of President John F. Kennedy near the grassy knoll in Dallas's Dealey Plaza. To these people, the complete absence of evidence proved the conspiracy's sophistication. They were demented.

Now, it stands to reason that mainstream journalists at the time of the Kennedy assassination would make that type of statement. That was a time when almost everyone placed undaunted faith in the U.S. national-security establishment and any official narrative it issued. This was especially true for conservative columnists, almost all of whom bought into the extreme anti-communist animus that was used to justify the Cold War and the conversion of the U.S. government to a national-security state. Of course, there was also Operation Mockingbird to consider. That was the CIA's successful secret operation to acquire assets within the U.S. mainstream press that could be relied upon to publish articles reflecting the views and narratives of the national-security establishment. Thus, when a mainstream journalist in 1963 or even 1964, immediately after the issuance of the Warren Report, made a statement similar to that made by Will, it was somewhat understandable. At that time, while there were people who suspected that something was amiss in the assassination, most of the evidence pointing to a U.S. national-security regime-change operation was hidden from view because of the shroud of national-security secrecy that was immediately placed over the assassination.

But that was 1963. Today things are entirely different. Over the decades, the national-security state secrecy surrounding the assassination has been pierced, which has brought forth a large body of incriminating evidence pointing to a joint Pentagon-CIA operation to protect "national security" from a president whose policies, they believed, were leading to a communist victory in the Cold War and, ultimately, a communist takeover of the United States.

This is what mainstream journalists like Will just don't get. Owing to a large amount of evidence that has surfaced pointing toward a domestic regime-change operation, it is no longer sufficient for a mainstream journalist to mouth the standard mantras about the Kennedy assassination that were being mouthed in 1963 or to simply label people who challenge the official lone-nut narrative in the Kennedy assassination "conspiracy theorists." Now, it is incumbent on mainstream journalists who wish to maintain the official narrative to confront and deal with the actual evidence that has surfaced since then, especially after the JFK Records Act in 1993, which was enacted in the wake of Oliver Stone's movie *JFK*. That law forced the Pentagon, the CIA, and other federal agencies to disclose many, but certainly not all, of their long-secret records relating to the assassination.

Let me give you an example. In the late 1960s, New Orleans District Attorney Jim Garrison brought a criminal prosecution against a man named Clay Shaw. In the trial, Garrison alleged that the JFK assassination was a highly sophisticated domestic regime-change operation carried out by the Pentagon and the CIA, no different in principle from those carried out both before and after the Kennedy assassination, most of which were supported and are still supported by conservatives — e.g., Iran 1953, Guatemala 1954, Congo 1961, Cuba 1960s, Chile 1973.

The mainstream press criticized and derided Garrison. Their mindset was one of complete deference to the authority of the national-security establishment and its official theory that a lone nut with no apparent motive had killed the president.

In the process, the mainstream press failed to note some extremely important aspects of the Shaw trial, especially those relating to the testimony of one of the military pathologists who had helped carry out the official autopsy on President Kennedy's body, Lt. Col. Pierre Finck.

Finck testified that he received a call at 8 p.m. on the night of the assassination from one of the other two pathologists for the autopsy, Commander James Humes, asking Finck to come over and help with the autopsy. In that 8 p.m. telephone call, Humes told Finck that they already had x-rays of the president's head.

A big problem arises, though: The president's body was being carried into the Bethesda morgue at precisely 8 p.m. by a military color guard.

Do you see the problem? How could Humes already have x-rays of the president's head if the president's body had not yet been brought into the morgue?

To my knowledge, that testimony didn't bother any mainstream journalist at the time. They were all so deferential to the national-security establishment that that problem didn't seem to get their attention. But wouldn't you think that any self-respecting investigative journalist would say, "I need to get to the bottom of this"?

How about you, George? How do you explain this problem? I would love to hear your explanation.

Another interesting aspect of Finck's testimony was when he was asked by the prosecutor why the pathologists had failed to "dissect" Kennedy's neck wound, which would ordinarily have been standard autopsy procedure. At first, Finck repeatedly refused to answer the question. When the judge finally required Finck to answer, he said that he had been ordered by someone in authority to refrain from doing so. Finck then maintained that he couldn't remember the identity of the person in authority who issued that order to him.

Now, wouldn't you think that any self-respecting investigative journalist would say, "I need to get to the bottom of this"? After all, the three autopsy pathologists were supposed to be in charge of the autopsy. Finck's testimony established that there was obviously a secret super-force that had ultimate control over the autopsy and the autopsy physicians.

How about you, George? Aren't you at least a bit curious as to who composed that force and how, when, where, and why it came into existence?

After the House Select Committee on Assassinations hearings in the 1970s, a group of enlisted men who were released from vows of secrecy that the military had forced them to sign immediately after the autopsy began telling a remarkable story. They said that they had secretly carried the president's body into the Bethesda morgue in a cheap, military-style shipping casket rather than the expensive, ornate casket into which the president's body had been placed in Dallas; they maintained that they secretly brought the body into the morgue at 6:35 p.m., almost 1 1/2 hours before the official entry time of 8 p.m.

What's up with that? How about it, George? You can't say that witness statements don't constitute evidence, can you? What's your explanation for this phenomenon? I would love to hear it.

In the 1990s, the Assassination Records Review Board secured a written report from a Marine sergeant named Roger Boyajian, which was prepared soon after the November 22, 1963, weekend. In the report, Boyajian stated that his team did, in fact, carry the president's body into the morgue at 6:35 p.m.

How about it, George? You can't really maintain that Boyajian's statement and his written report don't constitute evidence, can you? How do you deal with that? What's your explanation for it? I would love to hear what you have to say about it.

The ARRB also secured the testimony of Saundra Spencer, who worked in the military's photography lab in Washington, D.C. She told the ARRB a remarkable story. She said that on the weekend of the assassination, she was asked to develop the official autopsy photographs of Kennedy's body on a top-secret basis. She had kept her secret for some 30 years. When shown the official photographs of the autopsy in the records today, she said that those weren't the photographs she had developed. The ones she developed showed a massive-sized exit wound in the back of Kennedy's head, which would imply a shot having been fired from the front. The official autopsy photographs show the back of the president's head to be intact.

How about it, George? How about giving us your take on Spencer's testimony? You can't really say that sworn testimony doesn't constitute evidence, can you? I would love to hear your explanation for Spencer's sworn testimony.

Spencer's testimony, of course, matched the statements of the Dallas treating physicians immediately after the assassination, in which they described a massive exit-sized wound in the back of Kennedy's head.

How about it, George? How do you deal with the steadfast statements from Dr. Robert McClelland, Dr. Charles Crenshaw, and the other treating physicians describing the big exit-sized wound in the back of the president's head, which matched up with what Saundra Spencer testified to 30 years later?

The ARRB also discovered that there were two separate examinations of President Kennedy's brain. At the first examination, the brain was "sectioned" or cut up like a loaf of bread, which is standard procedure in gunshot wounds to the head. At the second brain exam, the brain was damaged but intact — i.e., not sectioned. There is no way that a sectioned brain can reconstitute itself, which means that the brain at the second exam could not possibly have been Kennedy's; how about it, George? How do you deal with that one? I would love to know.

Dr. David Mantik, a radiation oncologist in Rancho Mirage, California, has spent nine complete days closely examining the x-rays in the JFK autopsy. He has concluded that they are fraudulent. How about it, George? How do you deal with Mantik's detailed analysis? I would love to know.

Why is all this autopsy evidence important? Because there is no way to come up with an innocent explanation for a fraudulent autopsy. But George, if you can do so, please let us know what that explanation is. I don't think you can. Certainly, no one else has. And one thing is for sure: It was the national-security establishment that was solely responsible for carrying out the fraudulent autopsy on President Kennedy's body just a few hours after the assassination.

In fact, George, maybe you wouldn't mind providing your theory as to why the military, rather than the civilian authorities in Dallas, were even charged with carrying out the autopsy on President Kennedy's body. After all, while conservatives love the national-security state form of governmental structure, the United States isn't a military nation like the Soviet Union was, or at le.

The Role of the Media

Documents made public many years later reveal the extent to which senior figures in the print and broadcast media were involved in shaping the official response to the assassination. One such figure was the syndicated newspaper columnist Joe Alsop.

SINGLE BULLET THEORY

It was necessary for the Warren Commission to show that Jack Ruby also had acted alone.

The **single-bullet theory**, also called the **magic-bullet theory** by its critics, was introduced by the Warren Commission in its investigation of the assassination of U.S. President John F. Kennedy to explain what happened to the bullet that struck Kennedy in the back and exited through his throat. Given the lack of damage to the presidential limousine consistent with it having been struck by a high-velocity bullet, and the fact that Texas Governor John Connally was wounded and was seated on a jumper seat 1 ½ feet (0.5 meters) in front of and slightly to the left of the president, the Commission concluded they were likely struck by the same bullet.

Generally credited to Warren Commission staffer Arlen Specter (later a United States Senator from Pennsylvania), this theory posits that a single bullet, known as "Warren Commission Exhibit 399" (or "CE 399"), caused all the wounds to the governor and the non-fatal wounds to the president, which totals up to seven entry/exit wounds in both men.

The theory says that a three-centimeter-long (1.2") copper-jacketed lead-core 6.5×52mm Mannlicher–Carcano rifle bullet fired from the sixth floor of the Texas School Book Depository passed through President Kennedy's neck and went into Governor Connally's chest, went through his wrist, and embedded itself in the Governor's thigh. If so, this bullet traversed 15 layers of clothing, seven layers of skin, and approximately 15 inches of muscle tissue, struck a necktie knot, removed 4 inches of rib, and shattered a radius bone. The bullet was found on a gurney in the corridor at Parkland Memorial Hospital after the assassination. The Warren Commission found that this gurney was the one that had borne Governor Connally. This bullet became a key exhibit for the Commission. Its copper jacket was completely intact. While the bullet's nose appeared normal, the tail was compressed laterally on one side.

In its conclusion, the Warren Commission found "persuasive evidence from the experts" that a single bullet caused the President's neck wound and all the wounds found in Governor Connally. It acknowledged that there was a "difference of opinion" among members of the Commission "as to this probability" but stated that the theory was not essential to its conclusions and that all members had no doubt that all shots were fired from the sixth-floor window of the Depository building.

Most pro- and anti-conspiracy theorists believe that the single-bullet theory is essential to the Warren Commission's conclusion that Lee Harvey Oswald acted alone. The reason for this is timing: if, as the Warren Commission found, President Kennedy was wounded sometime between frames 210 and 225 of the Zapruder film, and Governor Connally was wounded in the back/chest no later than frame 240, there would not have been enough time between the wounding of the two men for Oswald to have fired two shots from his bolt-action rifle. FBI marksmen, who test-fired the rifle for the Warren Commission, concluded that the "minimum time for getting off two successive well-aimed shots on the rifle is approximately 2 and a quarter seconds" or 41 to 42 Zapruder frames.

The United States House Select Committee on Assassinations published their report in 1979 stating that their "forensic pathology panel's conclusions were consistent with the so-called single bullet theory advanced by the Warren Commission".

The first preliminary report on the assassination, issued By the FBI on December 9, 1963, said: "Three shots rang out. Two bullets struck President Kennedy, and one wounded Governor Connally." After the report was written, the FBI received the official autopsy report, which indicated that the bullet that struck the president in the back had exited through his throat. The FBI had written their report partly based on an initial autopsy report written By their agents, which reflected the early presumption that that bullet had only penetrated several inches into the president's back and had likely fallen out. The FBI concluded, therefore, that the governor had been struck By a separate bullet.

The Warren Commission commenced the study of the Zapruder film, the only known film to capture the entire assassination sequence, on January 27, 1964. By then, the FBI had determined that the running speed of Abraham Zapruder's camera was 18.3 frames per second and that the Mannlicher–Carcano rifle found at the Texas School Book Depository, the presumed murder weapon, could not be fired twice in less than 2.3 seconds or 42 frames of the Zapruder film.

When the Commission requested and received after February 25 higher-resolution images of the Zapruder film from *Life* magazine (who had purchased the film from Zapruder), it was immediately apparent that there was a timing problem with the FBI's conclusion that three bullets had found their mark. Kennedy was observed by the Commission to be waving to the crowd in frame 205 of the Zapruder film as he disappears behind the Stemmons Freeway sign and seems to be reacting to a shot as he emerges from behind the sign in frames 225-226, a little more than a second later. In their initial viewing of the film, Connally seemed to be reacting to being struck between frames 235 and 240.

Given the earliest possible frame at which Kennedy could have been struck (frame 205) and the minimum 42 frames (2.3 seconds) required between shots, there seemed to be insufficient time for separate bullets to be fired from the rifle. Several assistant counsels, upon viewing the film for the first time, concluded there had to be two assassins.

On April 14 and 21, two conferences were held at the Commission to determine when, exactly, the president and governor were struck. Assistant counsel Melvin Eisenberg wrote in a memorandum dated April 22 on the first conference that the consensus of those attending was, among other issues, that Kennedy was struck by frames 225–6 and that "the velocity of the first bullet [which struck Kennedy] would have been little diminished by its passage through the President. Therefore, if Governor Connally was in the path of the bullet, it would have struck him and caused the wounds he sustained in his chest cavity... Strong indications that this occurred are provided by the facts that... if the first bullet did not strike Governor Connally, it should have ripped up the car, but it apparently did not." However, the memorandum stated, given the relatively undamaged condition of the bullet presumed to have done this, CE 399, the consensus was a separate bullet probably struck his wrist and thigh. While not specifying a precise frame for when it was thought Connally was struck by the same bullet which struck Kennedy, the consensus was "by Z235," as afterward, his body position would not have allowed his back to be struck the way it was.

By the end of April 1964, the Commission had its working theory, the single-bullet theory, to account for the apparent timing discrepancies found in the Zapruder film and the lack of any damage to the limousine from a high-velocity bullet exiting the president's throat. (Impact damage was observed in the limousine but was indicative of lower-velocity bullets or bullet fragments. For example, a nick on the limousine's chrome was not from a high-velocity bullet as such a bullet would have pierced the chrome, not merely dented it.)

On May 24, the FBI and Secret Service reenacted the shooting in Dallas, and the Commission tested its theory. Agents acting as the president and the governor sat in a car of approximately the same dimensions as the presidential limousine, which was unavailable for re-creation. Adjustments to measurements were made to account for the differences in the vehicles.[26] Positions were recreated by matching them to particular frames of the Zapruder film, calibrated with other films and photographs taken that day. With the agents in position, photographs were taken from the sniper's nest of the Texas School Book Depository. It was from this re-creation, and the testimony of the agent in the sniper's nest, that the Commission verified the theory to its satisfaction, as the governor was in a direct line to be struck by any bullet fired between frames 207 and 235 to 240, which exited the president's throat, though the agent, in fact, testified that from frame 226 onward the governor was "too much towards the front" and his wounds were therefore misaligned from that point. An oak tree partially obscured the line of sight until frame 210, so the Commission concluded that "the President was not hit until at least frame 210 and that he was probably hit by frame 225."

Further evidence gathered suggested to the Commission that the initial April consensus that a separate bullet caused the governor's wrist and thigh injuries were incorrect, as the Army Wound Ballistics experts concluded that those wounds were "not caused by a pristine bullet," and therefore bullet CE 399 "could have caused all his wounds." Other evidence, such as the nature of Connally's back wound (see below), was also cited by the Commission as corroborating the theory. The Commission, however, did not conclude the single-bullet theory had been proven, as three members of the body, Representative Hale Boggs, Senators Richard Russell, and John Cooper, thought the theory improbable. Russell requested that his opposition to the theory be stated in a footnote in the report. In the end, the Commission changed the word "compelling" to "persuasive" and stated: "Although it is not necessary to any essential findings of the Commission to determine just which shot hit Governor Connally, there is very persuasive evidence to indicate that the same bullet which pierced the President's throat also caused Governor Connally's wounds." Nevertheless, all seven members of the Commission signed off on the statement: "There was no question in the mind of any member of the Commission that all the shots which caused the President's and Governor Connally's wounds were fired from the sixth-floor window of the Texas School Book Depository."

Number and sequence of the shots

Within minutes after the shots rang out in Dealey Plaza in downtown Dallas, Texas, at 12:30 p.m. on November 22, 1963, sources began reporting that three shots had been fired at the President's motorcade. At 12:34 p.m., approximately four minutes after the shots were fired, the first wire story flashed around the world:

DALLAS NOV. 22 (UPI) -- THREE SHOTS WERE FIRED AT PRESIDENT KENNEDY'S MOTORCADE TODAY IN DOWNTOWN DALLAS. JT1234PCS

This report had been transmitted by United Press International (UPI) reporter Merriman Smith from a radio telephone located in the front seat of the press car in the Presidential

motorcade, six cars behind the President's limousine. Smith's communication with the Dallas UPI office was made less than a minute after the shots were heard as his car entered the Stemmons freeway en route to Dallas' Parkland Hospital.

Merriman Smith's dispatch was the first of many reports. There were dozens of journalists riding in the motorcade in three open press cars and a press bus, none of whom reported hearing a number of shots other than three. Photographers Robert Jackson and Tom Dillard riding in a car in the motorcade, heard three shots. *The Dallas Morning News* reporter Mary Woodward described hearing three shots as she stood in front of the Texas School Book Depository.

There has been some controversy regarding the number of shots fired during the assassination. The Warren Commission concluded that three shots were fired. The vast majority of witnesses claim to have heard three, but there are some witnesses who could recall only one or two shots. A few witnesses thought there were four or more shots. Of 178 witnesses whose evidence was compiled by the House Select Committee on Assassinations (HSCA), 132 reported hearing exactly three shots, 17 recalled hearing two, and 7 said they heard two or three shots (Total: 88%). A total of 6 people said they thought they heard four shots, and 9 said they were not sure how many shots they heard. Another 7 people said they thought they heard 1, 5, 6, or 8 shots.

Governor Connally, riding in the middle jump seat of the President's limousine in front of the President, recalled hearing the first shot, which he immediately recognized as a rifle shot. He said he immediately feared an assassination attempt and turned to his right to look back to see the President. He looked over his right shoulder but did not catch the President out of the corner of his eye, so he said he began to turn back to look to his left when he felt a forceful impact on his back. He stated to the Warren Commission: "I immediately, when I was hit, I said, "Oh, no, no, no." And then I said, "My God, they are going to kill us all." He looked down and saw that his chest was covered with blood and thought he had been fatally shot. Then he heard the third and final shot, which sprayed blood and brain tissue.

United States House of Representatives Select Committee on Assassinations (HSCA)

The **United States House of Representatives Select Committee on Assassinations (HSCA)** was established in 1976 to investigate the assassinations of John F. Kennedy and Martin Luther King, Jr. in 1963 and 1968, respectively. The HSCA completed its investigation in 1978 and issued its final report the following year, which concluded that Kennedy was probably assassinated as a result of a conspiracy. In addition to acoustic analysis of a police channel dictabelt recording, the HSCA also commissioned numerous other scientific studies of assassination-related evidence that corroborate the Warren Commission's controversial findings.

The HSCA found that although the Commission and the different agencies and departments examining Kennedy's assassination performed in good faith and were thorough in their investigation of Lee Harvey Oswald, they performed with "varying degrees of competency," and the search for possible conspiracy was inadequate. The HSCA determined, based on available evidence, that the probable conspiracy did not involve the governments of Cuba or the Soviet Union. The committee also stated that the conspiracy did not involve any organized crime group, anti-Castro group, or the FBI, CIA, or Secret Service. The committee found that it could not exclude the possibility that individual members of the national syndicate of organized crime or anti-Castro Cubans were involved in a probable conspiracy to assassinate President Kennedy. However, some members of the committee would later state their personal belief that one of those groups was involved in the assassination, with Representative Floyd Fithian believing that the Kennedy assassination was orchestrated by members of organized crime.

In a Justice Department memo to the House Judiciary Committee in 1988, the Assistant Attorney General formally reviewed the recommendations of the HSCA report and reported a conclusion of active investigations. In light of investigative reports from the FBI's Technical Services Division and the National Academy of Science Committee determining that "reliable acoustic data do not support a conclusion that there was a second gunman", the Justice Department concluded "that no persuasive evidence can be identified to support the theory of a conspiracy in ... the assassination of President Kennedy".

The HSCA investigated the assassinations of John F. Kennedy (left) and Martin Luther King Jr. Several forces contributed to the formation of the HSCA. With the growing body of assassination conspiracy material, public trust in the findings of the Warren Commission report was declining. The Hart-Schweiker and Church Committee hearings had recently revealed CIA ties to other assassinations and assassination attempts. There was also significant public interest after a video segment of the Zapruder film was first shown on TV in March 1975, after having been stored by *Life* magazine out of view for almost twelve years.

In September 1976, the United States House of Representatives voted 280-65 to establish the Select Committee on Assassinations (HSCA) in order to investigate the assassinations of John F. Kennedy and Martin Luther King Jr. The committee was both controversial and divided among itself. The first chairman, Thomas N. Downing of Virginia, retired in January 1977 and was replaced by Henry B. Gonzalez on February 2, 1977. Gonzalez and Chief Counsel Richard A. Sprague had irreconcilable disagreements over control of the committee, budget, and investigative techniques, ending with Gonzalez's resignation. Sprague also resigned, in part to increase the chances of Congress voting to reconstitute the HSCA for the new two-year congressional term. Sprague's like-minded deputy Robert K. Tanenbaum also resigned shortly thereafter. Louis Stokes replaced Gonzalez as chairman, and G. Robert Blakey was appointed as Chief Counsel and Staff Director to replace Sprague.

Investigation

The HSCA commissioned a number of expert scientific studies to re-investigate the physical evidence of the JFK assassination. In comparison to witnessing testimony and government documents, the committee felt that such investigations would particularly benefit from the scientific advances of the fifteen years since the Warren Commission. Several lines of inquiry were followed to both reaffirm the single shooter/single-bullet theory as well as to disprove specific conspiracy theory allegations. **The HSCA concluded that these scientific studies of assassination-related evidence do "not preclude the possibility of two gunmen firing at the President."**

Ballistic analysis

Forensic analysis confirmed that the mostly-intact stretcher bullet, bullet fragments from the presidential limo, and the three cartridge casings from the sniper's nest were all fired from Oswald's rifle to the exclusion of all others. A technique using Neutron activation analysis (NAA), a form of what has become known as comparative bullet-lead analysis (CBLA), was used to analyze the bullet lead from the JFK assassination. It revealed that it was highly likely that only two lead bullets were the source of all the following pieces of evidence: the mostly-intact stretcher bullet, fragments found in the presidential limousine's front seat and rug, fragments recovered from JFK's brain autopsy, and fragments recovered from Governor Connally's wrist. Whether CBLA data can be used to actually exclude the possibility that there were fragments from more than two bullets in the wounds and the car has been the subject of controversy.

Additionally, the location of the shooter (at the 6th-floor Texas School Book Depository window) was determined using trajectory analysis. The origin of the rifle bullets was calculated using the location of the presidential limousine and its occupants combined with the bullet wounds found on the president and governor.

Photographic analysis

A team of photographic experts was used to answer several questions related to the photographic evidence of the case. Forensic anthropologists, as well as photographic and radiographic experts, based on unique anatomical details, verified that JFK's autopsy photos and x-rays were only of the late president. Forensic anthropologists were also used to verify that all relevant photographs of Lee Harvey Oswald were of only one person. They verified that the backyard photos (showing Oswald holding the rifle used to kill the president) depicted the same rifle found in the Texas school book depository building after the crime. The panel of photographic experts was also used to verify the authenticity of the assassination-related photos and to analyze for any tampering or fakery; none was detected.

Forensic Pathology Panel

The HSCA's Forensic Pathology Panel included Michael Baden, John I. Coe, Joseph H. Davis, George S. Loquvam, Charles S. Petty, Earl Rose, Werner Spitz, Cyril Wecht, and James T. Weston.

With the benefit of authenticated photographs, x-rays, and notes from the Kennedy autopsy, a nine-doctor panel of expert pathologists reviewed and corroborated the Warren Commission's medical findings. Although the HSCA medical panel was critical of the thoroughness and methodology of the original autopsy, they concurred, although Cyril Wecht dissented, with the Warren Commission's conclusion that two and only two bullet wounds entered from above and behind (the direction of Oswald in the Book Depository). Their conclusion that the President was struck by a bullet that entered in the right rear of the head near the cowlick area and exited from the right front side of the head differed from a diagram in the Warren Commission's report showing this entrance wound low in the back of the head.

Fingerprint and handwriting analysis

The authenticity of several fingerprints and a palm print found on assassination-related materials was reaffirmed by a fingerprint expert. Lee Harvey Oswald's prints were found on the trigger guard and underside of the Mannlicher–Carcano rifle used to shoot the president, the brown paper container used to transport the rifle, several cardboard boxes in the sniper's nest, and on the magazine order form to purchase the rifle.

In addition, dozens of documents were analyzed by a panel of three handwriting experts who verified that "the signatures and handwriting purported to be by Oswald are consistently that of one person." These include such incriminating items as the envelope and order form used to purchase the rifle, the application forms to rent the PO Box that the rifle was delivered to, and the notated backyard photo depicting Oswald holding the rifle.

Dictabelt audio recording

Main article: Dictabelt evidence relating to the assassination of John F. Kennedy

Although the HSCA had prepared a draft report confirming the Warren Commission's single shooter theory and finding no evidence of conspiracy, at the eleventh hour, the committee was swayed by a since-disputed acoustic analysis of a dictabelt police channel recording. This acoustic analysis of the dictabelt recording by the firm Bolt, Beranek, and Newman Inc. concluded that four shots were fired at the president, thus causing the HSCA to reverse its earlier position and report "that Kennedy was probably assassinated as a result of a conspiracy." In terms of scientific evidence, the HSCA acknowledged that the existence of a second shooter was only supported by this acoustic analysis.

As recommended by the HSCA, the Justice Department reviewed those findings through the FBI's Technical Services Division and by contracting the National Academy of Science, which specially appointed the Committee on Ballistic Acoustics (CBA). Both the FBI and CBA analyzed the acoustic data and BBN's scientific methodology and concluded that their findings were mistaken.[15][16] Although there has been some recent back and forth between different researchers, the HSCA's acoustic analysis is widely considered to be discredited.

Conclusions

General conclusions

In particular, the various investigations performed By the U.S. government were faulted for insufficient consideration of the possibility of a conspiracy in each case. The Committee, in its report, also made recommendations for legislative and administrative improvements, including making some assassinations Federal crimes.

Conclusions regarding the Kennedy assassination

On the Kennedy assassination, the HSCA concluded in its 1979 report that:

1. Lee Harvey Oswald fired three shots at Kennedy. The second and third shots Oswald fired struck the President. The third shot he fired killed the President.
2. Scientific acoustical evidence establishes a high probability that at least two gunmen fired at the President. Other scientific evidence does not preclude the possibility of two gunmen firing at the President. Scientific evidence negates some specific conspiracy allegations.
3. The committee believes, on the basis of the evidence available to it, that Kennedy was probably assassinated as a result of a conspiracy. The committee was unable to identify the other gunmen or the extent of the conspiracy.
   - The committee believes, on the basis of the evidence available to it, that the Soviet Government was not involved in the assassination of Kennedy.
   - The committee believes, on the basis of the evidence available to it, that the Cuban Government was not involved in the assassination of Kennedy.

- The committee believes, on the basis of the evidence available to it, that anti-Castro Cuban groups, as groups, were not involved in the assassination of Kennedy, but that the available evidence does not preclude the possibility that individual members may have been involved.
- The committee believes, on the basis of the evidence available to it, that the national syndicate of organized crime, as a group, was not involved in the assassination of Kennedy but that the available evidence does not preclude the possibility that individual members may have been involved.
- The Secret Service, Federal Bureau of Investigation, and Central Intelligence Agency were not involved in the assassination of Kennedy.

4. Agencies and departments of the U.S. Government performed with varying degrees of competency in the fulfillment of their duties. President Kennedy did not receive adequate protection. A thorough and reliable investigation into the responsibility of Lee Harvey Oswald for the assassination was conducted. The investigation into the possibility of conspiracy in the assassination was inadequate. The conclusions of the investigations were arrived at in good faith but presented in a fashion that was too definitive.

The Committee further concluded that it was probable that:
- four shots were fired
- The fourth shot came from a second assassin located on the grassy knoll but missed. The HSCA concluded the existence and location of this alleged fourth shot based on the later discredited Dallas Police Department Dictabelt recording analysis.

The HSCA agreed with the single bullet theory but concluded that it occurred at a time point during the assassination that differed from any of the several time points the Warren Commission theorized it occurred.

The Department of Justice, FBI, CIA, and the Warren Commission were all criticized for not revealing to the Warren Commission information available in 1964, and the Secret Service was deemed deficient in their protection of the President.

The HSCA made several accusations of deficiency against the FBI and CIA. The accusations encompassed organizational failures, miscommunication, and a desire to keep certain parts of their operations secret. Furthermore, the Warren Commission expected these agencies to be forthcoming with any information that would aid their investigation. **But the FBI and CIA only saw it as their duty to respond to specific requests for information from the commission. However, the HSCA found the FBI and CIA were deficient in performing even that limited role.**

Criticisms

Although the HSCA publicly released its findings in 12 volumes and a single-volume summary report, the majority of primary documents were sealed for 50 years under congressional rules. In 1992, Congress passed legislation to collect and open up all the evidence relating to Kennedy's death and created the Assassination Records Review Board to further that goal. No materials have been uncovered that significantly change the conclusions or opinion of the HSCA.

The ARRB reported: "Because the HSCA investigation was marked by internal squabbling and disillusioned staffers, the Committee's records were the subject of ongoing controversy. Some ex-staffers claimed the HSCA report did not reflect their investigative work, and that information that did not conform with the Committee leadership's preconceived conclusions was ignored or left out of the report and supporting volumes."

In 1992, author Bonar Menninger dismissed the committee report as *Blakey's $5 Million Folly*.

Robert Blakey, the Chief Counsel of the committee, later changed his views that the CIA was being cooperative and forthcoming with the investigation when he learned that the CIA's special liaison to the Committee researchers, George Joannides, was actually involved with some of the organizations that Lee Harvey Oswald was involved with in the months leading up to the assassination, including an anti-Castro group, the Directorio Revolucionario Estudiantil, which was linked to the CIA, where the liaison, Joannides, worked in 1963. Chief Counsel Blakey later stated that Joannides, instead, should have been interviewed by the Committee rather than serving as a gatekeeper to the CIA's evidence and files regarding the assassination. He further disregarded and suspected all the CIA's statements and representations to the Committee, accusing it of obstruction of justice.

In the same 2003 interview, Robert Blakey issued a statement on the Central Intelligence Agency:

...I no longer believe that we were able to conduct an appropriate investigation of the [Central Intelligence] Agency and its relationship to Oswald... We now know that the Agency withheld from the Warren Commission the CIA–Mafia plots to kill Castro. Had the commission known of the plots, it would have followed a different path in its investigation. The Agency unilaterally deprived the commission of a chance to obtain the full truth, which will now never be known. Significantly, the Warren Commission's conclusion that the agencies of government co-operated with it is, in retrospect, not the truth. We also now know that the Agency set up a process that could only have been designed to frustrate the ability of the committee in 1976–79 to obtain any information that might adversely affect the Agency. Many have told me that the culture of the Agency is one of prevarication and dissimulation and that you cannot trust it or its people. Period. End of story. I am now in that camp.

According to a 2015 Politico report, newly declassified documents show that CIA director John A. McCone hid evidence from the Warren Commission, set up by Governor Connolly to investigate JFK's assassination. According to a once-secret report[33] written in 2013 by the CIA's top in-house historian, David Robarge, the CIA admits McCone and other senior CIA officials withheld 'incendiary' information from the Warren Commission, thereby perverting the course of justice.

Jack RuBy and 'Chicago's Criminal Element'

The *Warren Report* admitted that Ruby's upbringing in one of the rougher districts of Chicago had led to some youthful indiscretions but went on to claim that he was no more than a minor criminal: According to his brother Hyman, Jack Ruby's only legal difficulty as a youth resulted from an altercation with a policeman about ticket scalping. ... Ruby has indicated that during the depression, he served a short jail sentence for the unauthorized sale of copyrighted sheet music. ...

Some of Ruby's childhood friends eventually became criminals; however, Hyman Rubenstein and his sister Mrs. Eva Grant and virtually all of Ruby's friends and acquaintances who were questioned reported that he was not involved with Chicago's criminal element.

(*Warren Report*, p.785)

[T]he Commission believes that the evidence does not establish a significant link between Ruby and organized crime. Both State and Federal officials have indicated that Ruby was not affiliated with organized criminal activity. And numerous persons have reported that Ruby was not connected with such activity.

(*ibid.*, p.801)

Jack Ruby and the Dallas Police Headquarters

The *Warren Report* admitted that Ruby had maintained extensive contacts with the Dallas police but claimed that he had not used those contacts to obtain access to Oswald:

Jesse Curry, chief of the Dallas Police Department, testified that no more than 25 to 50 of Dallas' almost 1,200 policemen were acquainted with Ruby. However, the reports of present and past members of the Dallas Police Department, as well as Ruby's employees and acquaintances, indicate that Ruby's police friendships were far more widespread than those of the average citizen.

(*ibid.*, p.801)

[T]he Commission has found no evidence that Ruby received assistance from any person in entering the basement ....

After considering all the evidence, the Commission has concluded that Ruby entered the basement unaided, probably via the Main Street ramp, and no more than 3 minutes before the shooting of Oswald.

(*ibid.*, p.219)

HSCA: Warren Commission Was Wrong

The House Select Committee on Assassinations was critical of the Warren Commission's conclusions about Jack Ruby. It produced a report of more than 1,000 pages containing details of Ruby's criminal associations: *HSCA Report*, appendix vol.9, pp.125ff.

Jack Ruby's "Contacts with Underworld Figures"

The HSCA refuted the Warren Commission's main conclusion about Jack Ruby's criminal associations:

The committee, as did the Warren Commission, recognized that a primary reason to suspect organized crime of possible involvement in the assassination was Ruby's killing of Oswald. For this reason, the committee undertook an extensive investigation of Ruby and his relatives, friends, and associates to determine if there was evidence that Ruby was involved in crime, organized or otherwise, such as gambling and vice, and if such involvement might have been related to the murder of Oswald.

The evidence available to the committee indicated that Ruby was not a "member" of organized crime in Dallas or elsewhere, although it showed that he had a significant number of associations and direct and indirect contacts with underworld figures, a number of whom were connected to the most powerful La Cosa Nostra leaders. Additionally, Ruby had numerous associations with the Dallas criminal element.

(*HSCA Report*, p.149)

THE CIA CONNECTION

Rudolph Hecht - An owner of the CIA-linked Standard Fruit concern, Hecht was a prominent figure in the New Orleans Jewish community and, as chairman of the board of directors of the International Trade Mart, was Permindex board member Clay Shaw's primary sponsor.

James Jesus Angleton - Angleton, the CIA's long-time chief of counterintelligence, was the CIA's primary high-level conspirator in the murder of President Kennedy and the subsequent cover-up. Angleton, who had been co-opted by and was totally loyal to the Israeli Mossad, played a major role in the effort to frame Lee Harvey Oswald. Final Judgment is the first JFK assassination study to delve into Angleton's role in the conspiracy.

David Atlee Phillips - A long-time high-level CIA official, Phillips was the CIA station chief in Mexico City at the time; a strange effort was underway to implicate Lee Harvey Oswald as a Soviet KGB collaborator. If anyone in the CIA knew the truth about Oswald, it was Phillips. He confessed publicly that the story about Oswald being in Mexico City was not precisely what the CIA had long claimed.

E. Howard Hunt - Long-time CIA officer and liaison to the anti-Castro Cuban exiles. Testimony by ex-CIA contract operative Marita Lorenz placed Hunt in Dallas, Texas, the day before the president's assassination. The full truth about Hunt's actual involvement in the affair may never be known, but there is no question that Hunt was deeply involved in the intrigue surrounding the president's murder. Evidence does indeed indicate that there was a conscious effort to frame Hunt for involvement in the crime. **(E. Howard Hunt was Involved in the Watergate case and President Richard Nixon.)**

Guy Banister -The former FBI agent-turned-CIA contract operative whose New Orleans office was a central point for international intrigue involving the CIA, the anti-Castro Cuban exiles, and the anti-DeGaulle forces in the French Secret Army Organization (OAS). Under Banister's direction, Lee Harvey Oswald established a public profile for himself as a "pro-Castro" agitator in the streets of New Orleans.

David Ferrie - An enigmatic adventurer and CIA contract operative, Ferrie was closely involved with Lee Harvey Oswald during Oswald's stay in New Orleans in the summer of 1963, working alongside Oswald out of Banister's headquarters. The investigation of Ferrie by New Orleans District Attorney Jim Garrison ultimately led to Garrison's discovery of Permindex board member Clay Shaw's ties to both Ferrie and Oswald.

Marita Lorenz - A former CIA contract operative, she testified under oath that one day prior to the assassination of President Kennedy, she arrived in Dallas in an armed caravan of CIA-backed Cuban exiles who were met by not only Jack Ruby, who later killed Lee Harvey Oswald, but also CIA official E. Howard Hunt.

Guillermo & Ignacio Novo - Two brothers, veterans of the CIA-backed Cuban exile wars against Fidel Castro. According to Marita Lorenz, the Novo brothers were part of the armed caravan that arrived in Dallas one day before the assassination of President Kennedy. Many years after Dallas, the Novos were later convicted of participating in the murder of a Chilean dissident in collaboration with international adventurer Michael Townley whom himself had ties to high-level figures implicated in the JFK conspiracy.

John Tower - In 1963, Tower was a newly-elected Republican U.S. Senator from Texas with close ties to the CIA. Shortly after the assassination, he told associates of his own inside knowledge of the bizarre story of what really happened in Dealey Plaza. The story told by Tower strongly suggests that there were many unseen forces at work, manipulating many of the key players in the JFK assassination conspiracy. It was not until the release of Final Judgment that Tower's name was ever connected to the mystery surrounding the JFK assassination.

Victor Marchetti - A high-ranking CIA official who left the agency in disgust, Marchetti later made a career writing about the CIA. In a 1978 article, he charged that the CIA was about to frame its long-time operative, E. Howard Hunt, with involvement in the JFK assassination. A libel suit resulting as a consequence of Marchetti's article resulted in a climactic finding by a jury that the CIA had been involved in the assassination of the president.

Robin Moore - A journalist with long-standing close ties to the CIA, Moore co-authored former CIA man Hugh McDonald's book, LBJ and the JFK Conspiracy, which promoted James Jesus Angleton's false claim that the KGB was behind the president's murder-another of disinformation stories that emerged following the assassination.

THE LANSKY SYNDICATE

Meyer Lansky - Chief executive officer and de facto "treasurer" of the international crime syndicate; active in gun-running on behalf of the Israeli underground; collaborated closely with American intelligence on a number of fronts; later settled in Israel. Researchers who have claimed that "the Mafia Killed JFK" have pointedly refused to acknowledge Lansky's preeminent positioning in the underworld.

Carlos Marcello - The head of the Mafia in New Orleans, Marcello owed his status to Meyer Lansky, who was his chief sponsor in the crime syndicate. Marcello could not have orchestrated the JFK assassination-as some suggest-without Lansky's explicit approval.

Seymour Weiss - Meyer Lansky's chief bagman and liaison with the political establishment in Louisiana, he later served as a director of the CIA-linked Standard Fruit company and may actually have been a high-ranking CIA contract operative in New Orleans at the time of the JFK assassination.

Sam Giancana - The Mafia boss of Chicago, Giancana was a player in the CIA-Mafia plots against Castro; later murdered, probably at the behest of Santo Trafficante, Jr. His family says that Giancana admitted having been involved in the planning of the JFK assassination.

Santo Trafficante, Jr. - Although best known as the head of the Mafia in Tampa, Trafficante actually functioned as Meyer Lansky's chief lieutenant in the crime syndicate and as Lansky's liaison with the CIA in the Castro assassination plots.

Johnny Rosselli - A roving "ambassador" for the Mafia, Rosselli was the primary conduit between the CIA and the mob in the plots against Fidel Castro; he may have arranged the murder of Sam Giancana for Trafficante and was later murdered himself.

Mickey Cohen - Meyer Lansky's West Coast henchman; Jack Ruby's role model and a gun-runner for the Israeli underground, Cohen collaborated closely with Israeli diplomat Menachem Begin prior to the JFK assassination; Cohen arranged for John F. Kennedy to meet actress Marilyn Monroe who was assigned the task of finding out JFK's private views and intentions toward Israel.

Jack Ruby - A long-time functionary for the Lansky syndicate, Ruby was the Lansky connection man in Dallas and also engaged in CIA-linked gunrunning to the anti-Castro Cuban exiles. Evidence suggests there is more to Ruby's sudden "death" than meets the eye.

Jim Braden - A veteran personal courier for Meyer Lansky, Braden was almost assuredly in contact in Dallas with Jack Ruby prior to the JFK assassination. He was briefly detained in Dealey Plaza minutes after the president's murder, but those JFK assassination researchers who have mentioned Braden prefer to cast him as a "Mafia" figure rather than as Lansky's man on the scene in Dallas.

Al Gruber - A henchman of Meyer Lansky's West Coast operative, Mickey Cohen, Gruber, and Ruby spoke by telephone just shortly before Ruby killed Lee Harvey Oswald. It is believed that Gruber gave Ruby the contract on Oswald on behalf of his superiors.

Jack RuBy 's Access to the Police Basement

The HSCA also found fault with the Warren Commission's treatment of the evidence concerning Ruby's entry to the basement of the Dallas police headquarters, which indicated that his killing of Oswald had been premeditated:

The committee also investigated the relationship between Ruby and the Dallas Police Department to determine whether members of the department might have helped Ruby get access to Oswald for the purpose of shooting him. Ruby had a friendly and somewhat unusual relationship with the Dallas Police Department, both collectively and with individual officers …. Ruby's close relationship with one or more members of the police force may have been a factor in his entry to the police basement on November 24, 1963.

The conclusion reached by the Warren Commission that Ruby entered the police basement via the ramp was refuted by the eyewitness testimony of every witness in the relevant area; only Ruby himself excepted. … Even though the Warren Commission and the Dallas police investigative unit were aware of substantial testimony contradicting the ramp theory, they arrived at their respective conclusions by relying heavily on Ruby's own assertions and what they perceived to be the absence of a plausible alternative route. …

Based on a review of the evidence, albeit circumstantial, the committee believed that Ruby's shooting of Oswald was not a spontaneous act in that it involved at least some premeditation. Similarly, the committee believed that it was less likely that Ruby entered the police basement without assistance, even though the assistance may have been provided with no knowledge of Ruby's intentions. The assistance may have been in the form of information about plans for Oswald's transfer or aid in entering the building, or both.

(*ibid.*, pp.156f)

Jack Ruby and the Dallas Police

Ruby's connections to the Dallas Police Department appear to have been more than social:

- Jack Revill had been part of the Dallas police narcotics unit and had known Ruby since 1953. He implied that Ruby had supplied information: Revill had "a professional relationship of a police officer to an individual such as Jack Ruby." Revill stated that in later years Ruby "was not used as an informant by the intelligence unit. Whether or not Jack Ruby was used as a source of information, and there is a difference, this I don't know" (*HSCA Report*, appendix vol.4, pp.570f).
- Richard Clark, a detective in the narcotics and vice units, claimed that he had regularly used Ruby as an informant (*Warren Commission Document 85*, p.64).

340

- According to the FBI, Ruby had been "influential with Dallas Police Department" as long ago as 1948 (FBI HQ JFK File, 62–109060–10).

Why the Warren Commission Was Wrong

The Warren Commission had no investigative staff of its own. It relied almost entirely on information supplied By the FBI, which had its own institutional reasons to withhold information that contradicted the notion of Jack RuBy as a lone nut.

Jack Ruby and the FBI

The Commission was aware of rumors linking the FBI and Lee Harvey Oswald but was unaware of solid evidence that connected Jack Ruby with the FBI. About four years before the JFK assassination, Ruby had been casually employed as a provisional criminal informant. For the FBI's 1959 report on Ruby as an informant, see *HSCA Report*, appendix vol.5, pp.205–220.

J. Edgar Hoover, the director of the FBI, also emphasized the need for a public relations initiative:
The thing I am concerned about, and so is Mr. Katzenbach, is having something issued so that we can convince the public that Oswald is the real assassin. Mr. Katzenbach thinks that the President might appoint a Presidential Commission of three outstanding citizens to make a determination. (*HSCA Report*, appendix vol.3, p.472)

The Warren Commission's conclusion was in place before the Commission had even been established: Oswald was guilty and had acted alone. To counteract suspicions of conspiracy, it was necessary for the Warren Commission to show that Jack Ruby also had acted alone.

FEDERAL BUREAU OF INVESTIGATION INVOLVEMENT

"The FBI's Investigation Was Deficient"

The *HSCA Report* found that the FBI's investigation was "seriously flawed":

The committee concluded from its lengthy study of the roles of the FBI, Secret Service, CIA, and other Federal agencies that assisted the Warren Commission that the final determinations of who was responsible for President Kennedy's murder and whether there had been a conspiracy were based largely on the work of the FBI. With an acute awareness of the significance of its finding, the committee concluded that the FBI's investigation of whether there had been a conspiracy in President Kennedy's assassination was seriously flawed. The conspiracy aspects of the investigation were characterized by a limited approach and an inadequate application and use of available resources.

The committee concluded that the FBI's investigation into a conspiracy was deficient in the areas that the committee decided were most worthy of suspicion — organized crime, pro– and anti–Castro Cubans, and the possible associations of individuals from these areas with Lee Harvey Oswald and Jack Ruby. In those areas, in particular, the committee found that the FBI's investigation was in all likelihood insufficient to have uncovered a conspiracy. (*HSCA Report*, pp.241f)

CENTRAL INTELLIGENCE AGENCY INVOLVEMENT

The CIA Withheld Information
The FBI was not

the only organization that had withheld pertinent information from the Warren Commission. The HSCA also found fault with the CIA, whose associations with elements of the mafia had been made public by the Church Committee's Schweiker–Hart Report in 1975:

The committee found that the Commission acted in good faith, and the mistakes it made were those of men doing their best under difficult circumstances. **That being said, on the subject that should have received the Commission's most probing analysis — whether Oswald acted in concert with or on behalf of unidentified co-conspirators — the Commission's performance, in the view of the committee, was, in fact, flawed.**

Virtually all former Warren Commission members and staff contacted By the committee said they regarded the CIA–Mafia plots against Fidel Castro to be the most important information withheld from the Commission. They all agreed that an awareness of the plots would have led to significant new areas of investigation and would have altered the general approach of the investigation. J. Lee Rankin, who was the Commission's General Counsel, said he was outraged on learning in 1975 of the CIA's use of underworld figures for Castro assassination plots.

(*HSCA Report*, p.258)

What the Warren Commission Got Wrong

The HSCA listed the main problems with the Warren Commission's approach not only to Jack Ruby but to the assassination as a whole:

Particular areas where the committee determined the performance of the Commission was less than complete include the following:

- Oswald's activities and associations during the periods he lived in New Orleans;
- The circumstances surrounding the 2½ years Oswald spent in the Soviet Union;
- The background, activities, and associations of Jack Ruby, particularly with regard to organized crime;
- The conspiratorial and potentially violent climate created by the Cuban issue in the early 1960s, in particular the possible consequences of the CIA–Mafia assassination plots against Castro and their concealment from officials of the Kennedy administration;
- The potential significance of specific threats identified by the Secret Service during 1963 and their possible relationship to the ultimate assassination of the President;
- The possible effect of the FBI's investigation from Director Hoover's disciplining agents for their conduct in the Oswald security case;
- The full nature and extent of Oswald's visit to Mexico City 2 months prior to the assassination, including not only his contact with the Soviet and Cuban diplomatic offices there and the CIA's monitoring of his activities there but also his possible associations and activities outside of those offices;
- The violent attitude of powerful organized crime figures toward the President and Attorney General Robert Kennedy, their capacity to commit murder, including assassination, and their possible access to Oswald through his associates or relatives; and
- Analysis of all available scientific evidence to determine the number of shots fired at the President.

(*ibid.*, pp.260f)

The Mafia's Role in the JFK Assassination

The Need for a Safe Conspiracy Theory

The Warren Commission claimed that both Lee Harvey Oswald and Jack Ruby were lone nuts. By the time of the HSCA in the late 1970s, the notion that Oswald had acted alone was losing credibility with the general public:

- The essential elements of the Warren Commission's case against Oswald had been dismantled by the early critics.
- The showing of the Zapruder film on national television in 1975 had cast further doubt on the single–bullet theory and had turned the lone–nut hypothesis into a laughing stock.

The HSCA grudgingly acknowledged the possibility that the JFK assassination had been the result of a conspiracy. It noted Jack Ruby's obvious connections to the mafia and concluded that although "organized crime, as a group, was not involved in the assassination … individual members may have been involved." (*HSCA Report*, p.147).

The 'Mafia Killed JFK' Theory

The 'mafia killed President Kennedy' theory was stated more forcefully by two prominent members of the HSCA, its chief counsel, Robert Blakey, and the editor of the *HSCA Report*, Richard Billings:

[Ruby's] business activities were an integral part of a system of criminal operations, even if they were not illegal as such. At least on his trip to Cuba, Ruby played an important, if minor, role in a sophisticated syndicate operation that involved one of the most powerful underworld leaders. Ruby's associates in Dallas for the years and months prior to the assassination included a number of prominent organized–crime figures. He was in serious financial difficulty in the period leading up to the assassination, and a number of organized–crime figures were aware of it. Those same figures, under heavy pressure from the Kennedy organized–crime program, had a strong motive to assassinate the President. …

The murder of Oswald by Jack Ruby had all the hallmarks of an organized crime hit, an action to silence the assassin, so he could not reveal the conspiracy.

(Robert Blakey and Richard Billings, *The Plot to Kill the President*, NYT Books, 1981, pp.338f)

Leaving aside the unfounded assumption that Oswald had been aware of the conspiracy, the notion fails for a more substantial reason. Like most JFK assassination conspiracy theories, the 'mafia did it' theory fails to account for the central event that preceded the assassination. No plausible case has yet been made to explain how the mafia could have organized the impersonation of Lee Harvey Oswald in Mexico City.

The Function of the 'Mafia Did It' Theory

Peter Dale Scott pointed out that the House Select Committee on Assassinations, and Blakey and Billings, concentrated on Jack Ruby's mafia connections but neglected to consider Ruby's political connections. He concluded that the HSCA, just like the Warren Commission, was involved in a cover-up:

The Committee studiously avoided the following important propositions:

- From as early as 1946–47, Ruby was involved in major narcotics dealings, and yet he was protected from arrest, most probably because he was also a US government informant.
- Ruby was, as reported, involved in payoffs to the Dallas police, for whom he was unquestionably a narcotics informant.
- Ruby was on good, but probably illicit, terms with judges and other high members of the Dallas political establishment.
- According to his lawyer, Ruby was an informant for the Kefauver Committee; and in exchange for this service, the Kefauver Committee agreed to ignore contemporary organized crime and police corruption in Dallas, specifically with respect to the 1946 takeover by organized crime of the national racing wire service.
- The wire–service operation was a key organizing force for criminal activity in that era, including narcotics. Profits from the resulting system of protected crime (in which Ruby was somehow implicated) were invested in legitimate businesses (such as international hotels and defense industries like General Dynamics), which formed part of the expansive postwar US military-industrial establishment.

344

To sum up, the Warren Commission ... suppressed Ruby's links to organized crime and the political establishment. The House Committee rectified the first half of this suppression but not the second.
(Peter Dale Scott, *Deep Politics and the Death of JFK*, University of California Press, 1993, p.70)

AUTOPSY OF JFK

No autopsy was done at Parkland Hospital. JFK's Body was put in a casket for Transportation to Bethesda Naval Hospital. 2 Secret Service Agents Dr. Robert McLlellan.

The autopsy of President John Fitzgerald Kennedy was performed at the Bethesda Naval Hospital in Bethesda, Maryland. The autopsy began at about 8 p.m. EST on November 22, 1963 (on the day of his assassination) and ended at about 12:30 a.m. EST on November 23, 1963. The choice of autopsy hospital in the Washington, D.C. area was made by his widow, Jacqueline Kennedy. She chose the Bethesda Naval Hospital because President Kennedy had been a naval officer.

Ground

Following the assassination of President Kennedy, the Secret Service was concerned about the possibility of a larger plot and urged the new President Lyndon B. Johnson to leave Parkland Memorial Hospital for Love Field so that he could return to the White House; however, Johnson refused to do so without any proof of Kennedy's death. Johnson returned to Air Force One around 1:30 p.m., and shortly thereafter, he received telephone calls from McGeorge Bundy and Walter Jenkins advising him to return to Washington, D.C., immediately. He replied that he would not leave Dallas without Jacqueline Kennedy and that she would not leave without Kennedy's body. According to *Esquire*, Johnson did "not want to be remembered as an abandoner of beautiful widows."

Dallas County medical examiner

Dallas County medical examiner Earl Rose was in his office at Parkland Hospital across the corridor from Trauma Room 1 when he received the word that President Kennedy had been pronounced dead. He walked across the corridor to the trauma room occupied by Jacqueline Kennedy and a priest who had been called in to administer the last rites to the president. There, Rose was met by Secret Service agent Roy Kellerman and Kennedy's personal physician George Burkley who told him that there wasn't any time to perform an autopsy because Jacqueline Kennedy would not leave Dallas without her husband's body which was to be delivered promptly to the airport At the time of President Kennedy's assassination, the murder of any United States President was not under the jurisdiction of any federal organization. Rose objected, insisting that the Texas state law required him to perform a post-mortem examination before the body could be removed. A heated exchange ensued as he argued with Kennedy's aides. Kennedy's body was placed in a coffin and, accompanied by Jacqueline Kennedy, rolled down the corridor on a gurney. Rose was reported to have stood in a hospital doorway, backed by a local policeman, in an attempt to prevent anybody from removing the coffin. According to Robert Caro's *The Years of Lyndon Johnson: The Passage of Power*, the President's aides "had literally shoved [Rose] and the policeman aside to get out of the building." In an interview with the *Journal of the American*

Medical Association, Rose stated that he had stepped aside, feeling that it was unwise to exacerbate the tension.

Death certificates

Kennedy's personal physician, Rear Admiral George Gregory Burkley, signed a death certificate on November 23 and noted that the cause of death was a gunshot wound to the skull.[6][7] He described the fatal head wound as something "shattering in type causing a fragmentation of the skull and evulsion of three particles of the skull at the time of the impact, with resulting maceration of the right hemisphere of the brain." He also noted that "a second wound occurred in the posterior back at about the level of the third thoracic vertebra." The second certificate of death, signed on December 6 by Theron Ward, a Justice of the Peace in Dallas County, stated that Kennedy died "as a result of two gunshot wounds (1) near the center of the body and just above the right shoulder, and (2) 1 inch to the right center of the back of the head."

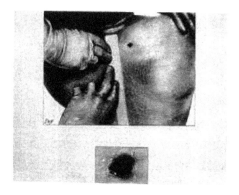

Official findings of the autopsy

Drawing depicting the back wound of President Kennedy. Made from an autopsy photograph. The gunshot wound in the back.

1. The Bethesda autopsy physicians attempted to probe the bullet hole in the base of Kennedy's neck above the scapula but failed as it had passed through the neck strap muscle. They did not perform a full dissection or persist in tracking, as throughout the autopsy, they were unaware of the exit wound at the front of the throat. Emergency room physicians had obscured it while performing the tracheotomy.

2. At Bethesda, the autopsy report of the president, Warren Exhibit CE 387, described the back wound as being oval-shaped, 6 by 4 millimeters (0.24 in × 0.16 in), and located "above the upper border of the scapula" (shoulder blade) at a location 14 centimeters (5.5 in) from the tip of the right acromion process, and 14 centimeters (5.5 in) below the right mastoid process (the bony prominence behind the ear).

3. The concluding page of the Bethesda autopsy report[9] states that "[t]he another missile [the bullet to the back] entered the right superior posterior thorax above the scapula, and traversed the soft tissues of the supra-scapular and the supra-clavicular portions of the base of the right side of the neck."

4. The report also said that there was contusion (i.e., a bruise) of the apex (top tip) of the right lung in the region where it rose above the clavicle and noted that although the apex of the right lung and the parietal pleural membrane over it had been bruised, they were not

346

penetrated. This indicated the passage of a missile close to them but above them. The report pointed out that the thoracic cavity was not penetrated.

5. This bullet produced contusions both of the right apical parietal pleura and of the apical portion of the right upper lobe of the lung. The bullet contused the strap muscles of the right side of the neck, damaged the trachea, and exited through the anterior surface of the neck.

6. The single bullet theory of the Warren Commission Report places a bullet wound at the sixth cervical vertebra (C6) of the vertebral column, which is consistent with 5.5 inches (14 cm) below the ear. The Warren Report itself does not conclude bullet entry at the sixth cervical vertebra, but this conclusion was made in a 1979 report on the assassination by the HSCA, which noted a defect in the C6 vertebra in the Bethesda X-rays, which the Bethesda autopsy physicians had missed and did not note. The X-rays were taken by US Navy Medical Corps Commander John H. Ebersole.

Even without any of this information, the original Bethesda autopsy report, included in the Warren Commission report, concluded that this bullet had passed entirely through the President's neck, from a level over the top of the scapula and lung (and the parietal pleura over the top of the lung) and through the lower throat.

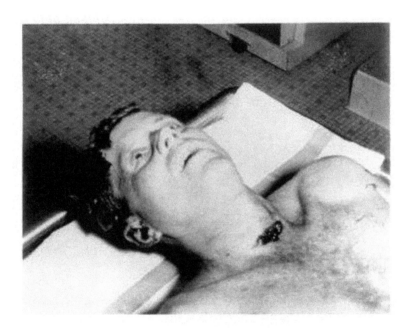

The gunshot wound to the head

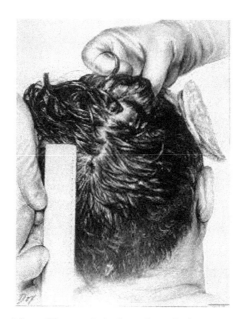

A photograph of President Kennedy's head and shoulders taken at the autopsy

A drawing depicting the posterior head wound of President Kennedy was made from an autopsy photograph. The small, nearly circular posterior scalp wound is at the end of the hair part, near the end of the ruler, and immediately to the right of it.

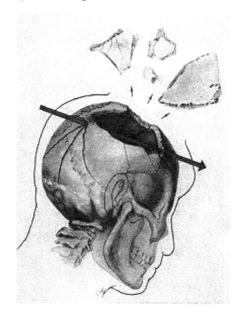

A diagram made for the House Committee showed the trajectory of the bullet through President Kennedy's skull. The rear wound corresponds with the small entry wound above. The skull fragments are shown exploded for illustrative purposes; most stayed attached to the skull by skin flaps, which are being pulled forward by the gloved hand in the drawing made from an autopsy illustration.

1. The gunshot wound to the back of the president's head was described by the Bethesda autopsy as a laceration measuring 15 by 6 millimeters (0.59 in × 0.24 in), situated to the right and slightly above the external occipital protuberance. In the underlying bone is a corresponding wound through the skull showing beveling (a cone-shaped widening) of the margins of the bone as viewed from the inside of the skull.

2. The large and irregularly-shaped wound on the right side of the head (chiefly to the parietal bone but also involving the temporal and occipital bone) is described as being about 13 centimeters (5.1 in) wide at the largest diameter.

3. Three skull bone fragments were received as separate specimens, roughly corresponding to the dimensions of the large defect. In the largest of the fragments is a portion of the perimeter of a roughly circular wound, presumably of exit, exhibiting beveling of the exterior of the bone and measuring about 2.5 to 3.0 centimeters (0.98 to 1.18 in). X-rays revealed minute particles of metal in the bone at this margin.

4. Minute fragments of the projectile were found by X-ray along a path from the rear wound to the parietal area defect.

Later government investigations

Ramsey Clark Panel analysis

U.S. Attorney General Ramsey Clark appointed a panel of four medical experts in 1968 to examine photographs and X-rays from the autopsy. The panel confirmed findings that the Warren Commission had published: the President was shot from behind and was hit by only two bullets. The summary by the panel stated: "Examination of the clothing and of the photographs and X-rays taken at [the] autopsy reveal that President Kennedy was struck by two bullets fired from above and behind him, one of which traversed the base of the neck on the right side without striking bone and the other of which entered the skull from behind and exploded its right side."

Rockefeller Commission analysis (1975)

The five-member Rockefeller Commission, which included three pathologists, a radiologist, and a wound ballistics expert, did not address the back and throat wounds, writing in its report that "[t]he investigation was limited to determining whether there was any credible evidence pointing to CIA involvement in the assassination of President Kennedy," and that "[t]he witnesses who [had] presented evidence believed sufficient to implicate the CIA in the assassination of President Kennedy placed [too] much stress upon the movements of the President's body associated with the head wound that killed the President."

The Commission examined the Zapruder, Muchmore, and Nix films, the 1963 autopsy report, the autopsy photographs, and X-rays, President Kennedy's clothing and back brace, the bullet and bullet fragments recovered, the 1968 Clark Panel report, and other materials. The five-panel members came to the unanimous conclusion that President Kennedy had been hit by only two bullets, both of which were fired from the rear, including one that hit the back of the head. Three of the physicians reported that the backward and leftward motion of the President's upper body following the head shot was caused by a "violent straightening and stiffening of the entire body as a result of a seizure-like neuromuscular reaction; to major damage inflicted to nerve centers in the brain."

The report added that there was "no evidence to support the claim that President Kennedy was struck by a bullet fired from either the grassy knoll or any other position to his front, right front, or right side … No witness who urged the view [before the Rockefeller Commission] that the Zapruder film and other motion picture films proved that President Kennedy was struck by a bullet fired from his right front was shown to possess any professional or other special qualifications on the subject."

HSCA analysis (1979)

Main article: United States House Select Committee on Assassinations

Medical drawing of a cross-section of President Kennedy's neck and chest, showing the trajectory of the projectile from back to the throat

The **United States House Select Committee on Assassinations** (HSCA) contained a forensic panel that undertook the unique task of reviewing original autopsy photographs and X-rays and interviewing autopsy personnel as to their authenticity. The Panel and HSCA then went on to make some medical conclusions based on this evidence.

The HSCA's major medical-forensic conclusion was that "President Kennedy was struck by two rifle shots fired from behind him." The committee found acoustic evidence of a second shooter but concluded that this shooter did not contribute to the president's wounds and therefore was irrelevant to the autopsy results.

The committee's forensic pathology panel included nine members, eight of whom were chief medical examiners in major local jurisdictions in the United States. As a group, they were responsible for over 100,000 autopsies, an accumulation of experience that the committee deemed invaluable in the medical evidence evaluation — including the autopsy X-rays and photographs — to determine the cause of the President's death as well as the nature and locations of his wounds. The committee also employed experts to authenticate the autopsy materials. Neither the Clark Panel nor the Rockefeller Commission undertook to determine if the X-rays and photographs were, in fact, authentic. Considering the numerous issues that have arisen over the years with respect to autopsy X-rays and photographs, the committee believed that authentication was a crucial step in the investigation. The authentication of the autopsy X-rays and photographs was accomplished by the committee assisting its photographic evidence panel as well as forensic dentists, forensic anthropologists, and radiologists working for the committee. Two questions were put to these experts:

1. Could the photographs and X-rays stored in the National Archives be positively identified as being of President Kennedy?
2. Was there any evidence that any of these photographs or X-rays had been altered in any manner?

To determine if the photographs of the autopsy subject were actually of the President, forensic anthropologists compared the autopsy photographs with antemortem pictures of him. This comparison was made based on both metric and morphological features. The metric analysis relied on various facial measurements taken from the photographs. The morphological analysis dealt with the consistency of physical features, particularly those that could be considered distinctive, such as the shape of the nose and patterns of facial lines (i.e., once unique characteristics were identified, posterior and anterior autopsy photographs were compared to verify that they depicted the same person).

The anthropologists studied the autopsy X-rays together with premortem X-rays of the President. A sufficient number of unique anatomic characteristics were present in X-rays taken before and after the President's death to conclude that the autopsy X-rays were of President Kennedy. This conclusion was consistent with the findings of a forensic dentist employed by the committee. Since many of the X-rays taken during the course of the autopsy included Kennedy's teeth, it was possible to determine, using his dental records, that the X-rays were of the President.

As soon as the forensic dentist and anthropologists had determined that the autopsy photographs and X-rays were of the President, photographic scientists and radiologists examined the original autopsy photographs, negatives, transparencies, and X-rays for signs of alteration. They concluded that there was no evidence of the photographic or radiographic materials having been altered, so the committee determined that the autopsy X-rays and photographs were a valid basis for the conclusions of the committee's forensic pathology panel.

While the examination of the autopsy X-rays and photographs was mainly based on its analysis, the forensic pathology panel also had access to all relevant witness testimony. Furthermore, all tests and evidence analyses requested by the panel were performed. It was only after considering all of this evidence that the panel reached its conclusions.

The pathology panel concluded that President Kennedy was struck by only two bullets, each of which had been shot from behind. The panel also concluded that the President was struck by "one bullet that entered in the upper right of the back and exited from the front of [his] throat, and one bullet that entered in the right rear of [his] head near the cowlick area and exited from the right side of the head, toward the front" saying that "this second bullet caused a massive wound to the President's head upon exit." The panel concluded that there was no medical evidence that the President was struck by a bullet entering the front of the head, and the possibility of such a bullet had struck him and yet leaving no physical evidence was extremely remote.

Because this conclusion appeared to be inconsistent with the backward motion of the President's head in the Zapruder film, the committee consulted a wound ballistics expert to determine what relationship, if any, exists between the direction from which a bullet strikes the head and the subsequent head movement. The expert concluded that nerve damage caused by a bullet entering the President's head could have caused his back muscles to tighten, which, in turn, could have forced his head to move toward the rear. He demonstrated the phenomenon in a filmed experiment involving the shootings of goats. Therefore, the committee determined that the rearward movement of the President's head would not have been fundamentally inconsistent with a bullet striking from the rear.[16]

The HSCA also voiced certain criticisms of the original Bethesda autopsy and the handling of evidence from it. These included:

1. The "entrance head wound location was incorrectly described."
2. The autopsy report was "incomplete", prepared without reference to the photographs, and was "inaccurate" in a number of areas, including the entry in Kennedy's back.
3. The "entrance and exit wounds on the back and front neck were *not localized with reference to fixed body landmarks and to each other*".

The Sibert and O'Neill Report

Two FBI agents, James Sibert and Francis O'Neill, attended the autopsy of President Kennedy. Their report is presented below, along with a memorandum in which they confirmed several of their observations.

The Sibert and O'Neill Report is significant to the study of President Kennedy's assassination in several ways:

- it is the only contemporaneous eye–witness account of events at the autopsy;
- it strongly contradicted certain elements of the case against Lee Harvey Oswald;
- it illustrated the treatment of evidence by the Warren Commission and various investigative agencies;
- And it helped to generate an influential, though highly implausible, conspiracy theory involving the surgical alteration of President Kennedy's body.

The Single–Bullet Theory

The FBI agents' account contains several observations about the location, angle, and depth of President Kennedy's back wound, which, if accurate, would invalidate the Warren Commission's single–bullet theory:

- The bullet wound "was below the shoulders and two inches to the right of the middle line of the spinal column," a location consistent with the bullet holes in the president's shirt and jacket but too low to be consistent with the single–bullet theory.
- "This opening was probed by Dr. HUMES with the finger, at which time it was determined that the trajectory of the missile entering at this point had entered at a downward position of 45 to 60 degrees." A bullet entering at a downward angle could not have come out through the throat, as the single–bullet theory demanded.
- "Further probing determined that the distance traveled by this missile was a short distance inasmuch as the end of the opening could be felt with the finger." It became known several years later that the pathologists had been forbidden, presumably by one or more of their military superiors, to dissect the back and throat wounds (see *Clay Shaw Trial Transcript*, pp.115–8). Such dissection would almost certainly have confirmed or denied the possibility that a single bullet had passed through President Kennedy's body and had caused both wounds.

Evidence that Two Types of Bullet Were Used

Sibert and O'Neill stated that "inasmuch as no complete bullet of any size could be located in the brain area and likewise no bullet could be located in the back or any other area of the body as determined by total body X–Rays and inspection revealing there was no point of exit, the individuals performing the autopsy were at a loss to explain why they could find no bullets."

The chief pathologist, Dr. James Humes, was told by the FBI agents during the autopsy that an intact bullet had been discovered on a stretcher at Parkland Hospital. Humes concluded that this bullet must have worked its way out of President Kennedy's back during his treatment.

The presence of dozens of tiny bullet fragments in the president's skull and brain indicated that the wound to his head had been caused by one or more soft-nosed bullets and not by metal–jacketed bullets such as those associated with the shells that had been discovered on the sixth floor of the Texas School Book Depository.

The FBI and the Warren Commission

Sibert and O'Neill's observations became the basis of the FBI's report on the assassination, which remains the Bureau's official verdict on the crime. It contradicts several important aspects of the final version of the autopsy report, which was rewritten after Oswald's murder. In particular, the pathologists claim in their report that during the autopsy, they had deduced a link between President Kennedy's back and throat wounds. The agents make it clear in their memorandum that this was not the case.

In common with other important documents that contradicted the Commission's conclusions, such as the Parkland Hospital press conference transcript, the Sibert and O'Neill Report was deliberately ignored and was neither quoted in the *Warren Report* nor published in the 26 volumes of *Hearings and Exhibits*. The document was placed in the National Archives, where it was discovered in 1966 by Harold Weisberg.

Neither Sibert nor O'Neill was interviewed By the Warren Commission. Both agents gave interviews to the House Select Committee on Assassinations in the late 1970s and to the Assassination Records Review Board in the early 1990s, in which they again contradicted important elements of the lone–assassin argument.

Body Alteration Theory

The Sibert and O'Neill Report's use of the phrase "it was also apparent that a tracheotomy had been performed, as well as surgery of the head area, namely, in the top of the skull," led to the theory, elaborated By David Lifton in his book, *Best Evidence*, **that President Kennedy's body had been surgically altered before the autopsy in order to conceal evidence of shots from in front. For an alternative interpretation, see Roger Feinman,** *Between the Signal and the Noise*, **chapter 1.**

In an affidavit submitted to the House Select Committee on Assassinations in 1978, James Sibert explained that the pathologists revised their initial suspicions of "surgery of the head area":

When the body was first observed on the autopsy table, it was thought By the doctors that surgery had possibly been performed in the head area, and such was reflected in my notes made at the time. However, this was determined not to be correct following detailed inspection and when the piece of bone found in the limousine was brought to the autopsy room during the latter stages of the autopsy.

Sibert and O'Neill dictated their report on Tuesday, 26 November 1963, four days after the assassination. A summary of their observations was contained in a teletype to FBI headquarters a few hours after the autopsy: Assassination Records Review Board Medical Document 149. Their memorandum was written on 29 June 1966.

At approximately 3 p.m. on November 22, 1963, following the President's announced assassination, it was ascertained that Air Force One, the President's jet, was returning from Love Field, Dallas, Texas, flying the body back to Andrews Air Force Base, Camp Springs, Maryland. SAS FRANCIS X. O'NEILL, JR., and JAMES W. SIBERT proceeded to Andrews Air Force Base to handle any matters which would fall within the jurisdiction of the Federal Bureau of Investigation, inasmuch as it was anticipated that a large group of both military and civilian personnel assigned to the Base would congregate at Base Operations to witness the landing of this flight.

Lt. Col. ROBERT T. BEST, Director of Law Enforcement and Security, advised the President's plane would arrive at 5:25 p.m. Subsequently, Col. BEST advised that the plane would arrive at 6:05 p.m.

At approximately 5:55 p.m., agents were advised through the Hyattsville Resident Agency that the Bureau had instructed that the agents accompany the body to the National Naval Medical Center, Bethesda, Maryland, to stay with the body and to obtain bullets reportedly in the President's body. Immediately agents contacted Mr. JAMES ROWLEY, the Director of the U.S. Secret Service, identified themselves, and made Mr. ROWLEY aware of our aforementioned instruction. Immediately following the plane's landing, Mr. ROWLEY arranged seating for Bureau agents in the third car of the White House motorcade, which followed that ambulance containing the President's body to the Naval Medical Center, Bethesda, Maryland.

President Kennedy's Body Arrives at Bethesda

On arrival at the Medical Center, the ambulance stopped in front of the main entrance, at which time Mrs. JACQUELINE KENNEDY and Attorney General ROBERT KENNEDY embarked from the ambulance and entered the building. The ambulance was thereafter driven around to the rear entrance, where the President's body was removed and taken into an autopsy room. Bureau agents assisted in the moving of the casket to the autopsy room. Tight security was immediately placed around the autopsy room by the Naval facility and the U.S. Secret Service. Bureau agents made contact with Mr. ROY KELLERMAN, the Assistant Secret Service Agent in Charge of the White House Detail, and advised him of the Bureau's interest in this matter.

People Present at President Kennedy's Autopsy

He advised that he had already received instructions from Director ROWLEY as to the presence of Bureau agents. It will be noted that the aforementioned Bureau agents, Mr. ROY KELLERMAN, Mr. WILLIAM GREER, and Mr. WILLIAM O'LEARY, Secret Service agents, were the only personnel other than medical personnel present during the autopsy.

The following individuals attended the autopsy:

- Adm. C.B. HOLLOWAY, U.S. Navy, Commanding Officer of the U.S. Naval Medical Center, Bethesda;
- Adm. BERKLEY, U.S. Navy, the President's personal physician;
- Commander JAMES J. HUMES, Chief Pathologist, Bethesda Naval Hospital, who conducted the autopsy;

- Capt. JAMES H. STONER, JR., Commanding Officer, U.S. Naval Medical School, Bethesda;
- Mr. JOHN T. STRINGER, JR., Medical photographer;
- JAMES H. EBERSOLE;
- LLOYD E. RAINES;
- J.T. BOZWELL;
- J.G. RUDNICKI;
- PAUL K. O'CONNOR;
- J.C. JENKINS;
- JERROL R. CRESTER;
- EDWARD F. REED;
- JAMES METZLER.

During the course of the autopsy, Lt. Col. P. FINCK, U.S. Army Armed Forces Institute of Pathology, arrived to assist Commander HUMES in the autopsy. In addition, Lt. Cmdr. GREGG CROSS and Captain DAVID OSBORNE, Chief of Surgery, entered the autopsy room.

Major General WEHLE, Commanding Officer of the U.S. Military District, Washington, D.C., entered the autopsy room to ascertain from the Secret Service arrangements concerning the transportation of the President's body back to the White House. AMC CHESTER H. BOWERS, U.S. Navy, visited the autopsy room during the final stages of such to type receipts given by the FBI and Secret Service for items obtained.

At the termination of the autopsy, the following personnel from Gawler's Funeral Home entered the autopsy room to prepare the President's body for burial:
- JOHN VAN HAESEN
- EDWIN STROBLE
- THOMAS ROBINSON
- Mr. HAGEN

Brigadier General GODFREY McHUGH, Air Force Military Aide to the President, was also present, as was Dr. GEORGE BAKEMAN, U.S. Navy.

Preparing for President Kennedy's Autopsy

Arrangements were made for the performance of the autopsy by the U.S. Navy and Secret Service. The President's body was removed from the casket in which it had been transported and was placed on the autopsy table, at which time the complete body was wrapped in a sheet, and the head area contained an additional wrapping that was saturated with blood. Following the removal of the wrapping, it was ascertained that the President's clothing had been removed, and it was also apparent that a tracheotomy had been performed, as well as surgery of the head area, namely, in the top of the skull. All personnel, with the exception of medical officers needed in the taking of photographs and X–Rays, were requested to leave the autopsy room and remain in an adjacent room.

Bullet Damage to President Kennedy's Brain

Upon completion of X–Rays and photographs, the first incision was made at 8:15 p.m. X–Rays of the brain area, which were developed and returned to the autopsy room, disclosed a path of a missile that appeared to enter the back of the skull and the path of the disintegrated fragments could be observed along the right side of the skull. The largest section of this missile, as portrayed by X-Ray, appeared to be behind the right frontal sinus. The next largest fragment appeared to be at the rear of the skull at the juncture of the skull bone.

The Chief Pathologist advised approximately 40 particles of disintegrated bullets and smudges, indicating that the projectile had fragmentized while passing through the skull region.

During the autopsy inspection of the area of the brain, two fragments of metal were removed by Dr. HUMES, namely, one fragment measuring 7 x 2 millimeters, which was removed from the right side of the brain. An additional fragment of metal measuring 1 x 3 millimeters was also removed from this area, both of which were placed in a glass jar containing a black metal top which was thereafter marked for identification and, following the signing of a proper receipt, were transported by Bureau agents to the FBI laboratory.

The Bullet Wound in President Kennedy's Back

During the latter stages of this autopsy, Dr. HUMES located an opening that appeared to be a bullet hole that was below the shoulders and two inches to the right of the middle line of the spinal column.

This opening was probed by Dr. HUMES with the finger, at which time it was determined that the trajectory of the missile entering at this point had entered at a downward position of 45 to 60 degrees. Further probing determined that the distance traveled by this missile was a short distance inasmuch as the end of the opening could be felt with the finger.

Inasmuch as no complete bullet of any size could be located in the brain area and likewise, no bullet could be located in the back or any other area of the body as determined by total body X–Rays and inspection revealing there was no point of exit, the individuals performing the autopsy were at a loss to explain why they could find no bullets.

The Bullet Found at Parkland Hospital

A call was made by Bureau agents to the Firearms Section of the FBI Laboratory, at which time SA CHARLES L. KILLION advised that the Laboratory had received through Secret Service Agent RICHARD JOHNSON a bullet that had reportedly been found on a stretcher in the emergency room of Parkland Hospital, Dallas, Texas. This stretcher also contained a stethoscope [*sic*] and pair of rubber gloves. Agent JOHNSON had advised the Laboratory that it had not been ascertained whether or not this was the stretcher that had been used to transport the body of President Kennedy. Agent KILLION further described this bullet as pertaining to a 6.5-millimeter rifle which would be approximately a 25-caliber rifle, and that this bullet consisted of a copper alloy full jacket.

Immediately following receipt of this information, this was made available to Dr. HUMES, who advised that, in his opinion, this accounted for no bullet being located which had entered the back region and that since external cardiac massage had been performed at Parkland Hospital, it was entirely possible that through such movement the bullet had worked its way back out of the point of entry and had fallen on the stretcher.

A Piece of President Kennedy's Skull

Also, during the latter stages of the autopsy, a piece of the skull measuring 10 x 6.5 centimeters was brought to Dr. HUMES, who was instructed that this had been removed from the President's skull. Immediately this section of the skull was X–Rayed, at which time it was determined by Dr. HUMES that one corner of this section revealed minute metal particles, and inspection of this same area disclosed chipping of the top portion of this piece, both of which indicated that this had been the point of exit of the bullet entering the skull region.

Two Bullets Hit President Kennedy from Behind

On the basis of the latter two developments, Dr. HUMES stated that the pattern was clear — that the one bullet had entered the President's back and had worked its way out of the body during the external cardiac massage and that a second high-velocity bullet had entered the rear of the skull and had fragmentized prior to exit through the top of the skull. He further pointed out that X–Rays had disclosed numerous fractures in the cranial area, which he attributed to the force generated by the impact of the bullet in its passage through the brain area. He attributed the death of the President to a gunshot wound in the head.

President Kennedy's Autopsy Photographs and X–Rays

The following is a complete listing of photographs and X–Rays taken by the medical authorities of the President's body. They were turned over to Mr. ROY KELLERMAN of the Secret Service. X–Rays were developed by the hospital; however, the photographs were delivered to Secret Service undeveloped:

- 11 X–Rays
- 22 4 x 5 color photographs
- 18 4 x 5 black and white photographs
- 1 roll of 120 films containing five exposures

Mr. KELLERMAN stated these items could be made available to the FBI upon request. The portion of the skull measuring 10 x 6.5 centimeters was maintained in the custody of Dr. HUMES, who stated that it also could be made available for further examination. The two metal fragments removed from the brain area were hand carried by SAs SIBERT and O'Neill to the FBI Laboratory immediately following the autopsy and were turned over to SA KURT FRAZIER.

Sibert and O'Neill: Memorandum

Date: 6/29/66

From: SAs FRANCIS X. O'NEILL, JR. and JAMES W. SIBERT

Subject: ASSASSINATION OF PRESIDENT JOHN F. KENNEDY, 11/22/63 DALLAS, TEXAS MISCELLANEOUS — INFORMATION CONCERNING

The following information is being submitted to the file as a matter of record.

During of [sic] 5/30/66–6/3/66, Bureau supervisor KENNETH RAUPACH telephonically contacted SA JAMES SIBERT at the Hyattsville Resident Agency advising that a "Special" was being conducted at the Bureau in connection with an article that appeared in the newspapers relating to events that took place during the autopsy on 11/22/63 at the Navy Medical Training Center, Bethesda, Maryland.

Confidentiality of the Autopsy's Findings

Mr. RAUPACH asked if any member of the KENNEDY family had appeared in the autopsy room during the time that the autopsy was in progress, making a request that the findings of such autopsy be kept confidential. He was advised that at no time during the autopsy did either ROBERT F. KENNEDY or the President's wife appear at the autopsy room and that it was understood that these two individuals were in the tower at the Medical Center. **RAUPACH was advised that one of the Senior Medical Officers had made the statement prior to the termination of the** autopsy that "what had gone on in this room tonight should remain confidential and should not be discussed outside of that room".

Measurements By the Pathologist

RAUPACH also questioned whether or not the measurements as set forth in FD 302s submitted by SAs SIBERT and O'NEILL had actually been measurements furnished by the Pathologist or had been represented conclusions [*sic*] reached by the Agents. He was informed that all figures set forth in such FD 302 had been obtained from the Pathologist performing the autopsy.

FBI Agents' Presence at the Autopsy

Later in the week, a telephone call was received from the Bureau supervisor FLETCHER THOMPSON, who advised that he had additional questions pertaining to the captioned matter and stated that he desired to know whether or not at least one agent was present in the autopsy room during the time that the autopsy was in progress and until it was completed. He was advised that such was the case and that if one agent was out of the room, it was understood and followed that the other agent was present at all times and that at no time were both agents out of this room from the time that the autopsy began until it was terminated.

No Mention of a Bullet Exiting the Throat

Mr. THOMPSON also asked if the Pathologist conducting the autopsy had made any mention of a bullet passing out of the neck at the point that the tracheotomy had been preformed [*sic*] at Parkland Hospital in Dallas, Texas. He was advised that no such statement was made and that, in fact, the Pathologist was quite concerned concerning injury in the back and could not find a point of exit for this bullet, nor could he find the projectile. Mr. THOMPSON was further advised that at that time, Agent SIBERT had telephonically contacted SA CHARLES L. KILLIAN in the Firearms Section at the Bureau, at which time it had been ascertained that a bullet had been found on a stretcher in the Parkland Hospital, and this information was relayed to the Pathologist conducting the autopsy who stated that in all probability this accounted for no bullet being found in the body in the back region and that such had probably been worked out by cardiac massage which had been performed when the President was on a stretcher at Parkland Hospital.

Duplicated Questions

Mr. THOMPSON again asked if any member of the KENNEDY family had requested that the results of the autopsy be maintained confidential and was informed that no mention had been made by any members of the Military or other personnel attending the autopsy that the KENNEDY family had requested that the results of the autopsy be held in confidence, however, one o

Katzenbach: Memo to Moyers

The assassination of President Kennedy not only removed the head of state but also incapacitated the head of the Justice Department, Robert Kennedy. Nicholas Katzenbach, the Deputy Attorney General, was to play an important role in the early development of official responses to the assassination.

Katzenbach wrote this memo by hand on the evening of Sunday, 24 November, a few hours after Lee Harvey Oswald had been shot dead by Jack Ruby. A typed version was prepared the following morning and sent to Bill Moyers, an assistant to President Johnson.

The Road to the Warren Commission

Katzenbach set down ideas that had been discussed within the White House over the previous two and a half days. He pointed out that:

- **Conspiracy theories about the assassination had already started to circulate.**
- **Some sort of official report should be issued to counteract these theories.**

JFK Assassination Conspiracy Theories

Some of Oswald's activities in Mexico City a few weeks before the assassination had generated two opposing conspiracy theories:

- either the Soviet or Cuban regimes were behind the assassination,
- or elements within the US had manipulated events to blame those regimes.

There were suspicions that Oswald had been working for one side or the other. Many aspects of Oswald's career were to remain hidden for years, but enough information had already come to light to cast doubt on the sincerity of his pro-communist public persona.

The Need for the Lone–Nut Theory

Although Oswald had been proclaimed the lone assassin, there was substantial disbelief among both domestic and foreign observers. This disbelief was quickly recognized to be harmful to established US political institutions.

Whatever the real story behind the assassination, the only acceptable political solution was that Oswald had acted alone and with no political or ideological motive. The question of Oswald's guilt or innocence was not a consideration.

Official Promotion of the Lone–Nut Theory

Katzenbach hoped that a report By the FBI into the assassination would be sufficient to contain public skepticism. <u>Even before the entirely inadequate FBI report </u>(Warren Commission Document 1<u>) was complete, the </u>news media<u> felt that it needed a stronger, more objective source of information if it was to perform its task of convincing the public that Oswald had acted alone</u> (see, e.g., Alsop to Johnson, White House Telephone Transcripts, 25 November 1963, 10:40 am, LBJ Library, Austin, Texas). A few days after this memo was written, Katzenbach's suggestion was adopted, and the Warren Commission was established.

Memorandum for Mr. Moyers

It is important that all of the facts surrounding President Kennedy's Assassination be made public in a way which will satisfy people in the United States and abroad that all the facts have been told and that a statement to this effect be made now.

1. The public must be satisfied that Oswald was the assassin, that he did not have confederates who are still at large, and that the evidence was such that he would have been convicted at trial.
2. Speculation about Oswald's motivation ought to be cut off, and we should have some basis for rebutting the thought that this was a Communist conspiracy or (as the Iron Curtain press is saying) a right-wing conspiracy to blame it on the Communists. Unfortunately, the facts on Oswald seem too pat — too obvious (Marxist, Cuba, Russian wife, etc.). The Dallas police have put out statements on the Communist conspiracy theory, and it was they who were in charge when he was shot and thus silenced.
3. The matter has been handled thus far with neither dignity nor conviction. Facts have been mixed with rumor and speculation. We can scarcely let the world see us totally in the image of the Dallas police when our President is murdered.

I

think this objective may be satisfied By making public as soon as possible a complete and thorough FBI report on Oswald and the assassination. This may run into the difficulty of pointing to inconsistencies between this report and statements By Dallas police officials. But the reputation of the Bureau is such that it may do the whole job.

The only other step would be the appointment of a Presidential Commission of unimpeachable personnel to review and examine the evidence and announce its conclusions. This has both advantages and disadvantages. It [*sic*] think it can await the publication of the FBI report and public reaction to it here and abroad.

I think, however, that a statement that all the facts will be made public property in an orderly and responsible way should be made now. We need something to head off public speculation or Congressional hearings of the wrong sort.

Nicholas deB. Katzenbach

Direct Interference

It is often assumed that the media coverage of the JFK assassination is the result of direct interference by organizations such as the CIA. There is some evidence for this.

An internal CIA memo lamented the extent of public disbelief in the Warren Commission's conclusions and pointed out that such distrust in government institutions affected the CIA directly and indirectly:

This trend of opinion is a matter of concern to the U.S. government, including our organization. The members of the Warren Commission ... represented both major parties ... efforts to impugn their rectitude and wisdom tend to cast doubt on the whole leadership of American society. ... Innuendo of such seriousness affects ... the whole reputation of the American government. Our organization itself is directly involved: among other facts, we contributed information to the investigation. Conspiracy theories have frequently thrown suspicion on our organization, for example, by falsely alleging that Lee Harvey Oswald worked for us. The aim of this dispatch is to provide material countering and discrediting the claims of the conspiracy theorists.

(*NARA RIF no. 104–10009–10022*)

The memo suggested several courses of action, including:

To discuss the publicity problem with liaison and friendly elite contacts (especially politicians and editors) ... To employ propaganda assets to answer and refute the attacks of the critics. Book reviews and feature articles are particularly appropriate for this purpose.

(*ibid.*)

Nine years after the memo was written, the Church Committee pointed out that criticism of the CIA's provision of information to the Warren Commission was justified (see Church Committee, Book V). The Committee also disclosed the CIA's extensive links with foreign journalists and media outlets (see Church Committee, Book I, p.455). For more about the influence of the CIA on the media both in the US and abroad, see Carl Bernstein, 'CIA and the Media,' *Rolling Stone*, 20 October 1977.

For Release 11:00 P.H., E.D.T., Sunday. September 11th, 1977

CIA NEW YORK TIMES CARL BERNSTEIN

Rolling Stone Magazine
745 Fifth Avenue
New York, New York 10022
(212) Plaza 8-3800
(212) 350-1283 (office)
989-7106 (home)

In a copyrighted story that will appear in a forthcoming issue of Rolling | Stone magazine (going to press next Monday), reporter Carl Bernstein details far more extensive CIA-use of the American news media than previously acknowledged By Agency officials publicly or in closed sessions with members of Congress.

Bernstein reports that during the past 25 years more than 400 American journalists secretly carried out assignments for the Central Intelligence Agency, according to documents on file at CIA headquarters. In many instances the journalists performed tasks for the CIA with the consent of the management of America's leading news-gathering organizations.

Carl Bernstein, 33, formerly a reporter for the Washington Post, is the co-author of "All the President's Men" and "The Final Days. He began his inquiry into this subject over one year ago.

Bernstein says journalists involved in the CIA program provided a full range of services to the Agency, from simple intelligence collection to helping recruit and direct spies in foreign countries. Some of the reporters involved were Pulitzer Prize winners and household names. Some received partial CIA payment for their work, almost always in cash.

In addition, at least 25 news organizations provided jobs and credentials ("journalistic cover") for full-time CIA employees masquerading as journalists abroad.

Among those major media whose top executives lent cooperation to the CIA were CBS, ABC, NBC, the Associated Press, United Press International, Newsweek, Time Inc., The New York Times, Mutual Broadcasting System, Reuters, Copley News Service, and the Hearst Newspapers, among others.

The Agency's relationship with the New York Times was by far its most valuable among newspapers, according to CIA officials. Bernstein reports that the Times provided press credentials to approximately 10 undercover CIA employees, with the full approval of the late Publisher Arthur Hays Sulzberger.

In the field, journalists were used to helping recruit foreign agents, conveying instructions and dollars to foreign officials bought and controlled by the CIA, acquiring and evaluating information, and planting false information with officials of foreign governments. Many signed secrecy agreements with the Agency, pledging never to discuss their involvement.

Although some details of CIA-press relationships have trickled out in recent years, neither media accounts nor congressional hearings have hinted at their extensive scale, Bernstein reports in Rolling Stone.

During the 1976 CIA investigation by the Senate Intelligence Committee, the true extent of the Agency's involvement with the media became apparent to several members of the committee but was deliberately concealed from its full membership, the Senate, and the public. The decision to misrepresent the dimensions of the situation was made after intensive lobbying from CIA officials. Bernstein reports on one such CIA-Senate meeting — an extraordinary dinner session at the Agency's headquarters in Langley, Virginia, in late March 1976. Those present included Senators Frank Church and John Tower, members of the committee staff, CIA Director George Bush, and two other Agency officials.

A Senator who was the object of the Agency's lobbying effort said later;

"From the CIA point of view, this was the highest, most sensitive covert program of all." "There is quite an incredible spread of relationships, " reported Senate committee investigator William B. Bader. "You don't need to manipulate Time magazine, for example, because there are Agency people at the management level."

PALEY. SULZBERGER. ALSQP BROTHERS AND OTHERS NAMED

The origins of the Agency's intimate dealings with the press, Bernstein writes, are traceable to CIA director Allen Dulles, who saw that journalistic cover would give CIA operatives abroad a degree of access unobtainable under almost any other means. In the words of one high-level CIA official, "one journalist is worth 20 agents — he has access and can ask questions without arousing suspicion."

In addition to numerous accredited correspondents and freelancers, there were perhaps a dozen well-known columnists and broadcast commentators whose relationship with the CIA went far beyond those normally maintained between reporters and their sources, according to Bernstein.

These are referred to by the Agency as "known assets" and are considered receptive to the Agency's point of view. These included C*L. Sulzberger at the New York Times, **Joseph Alsop,** and the late Stewart Alsop.

In preparing his article for Rolling Stone, Carl Bernstein interviewed more than 35 former and present CIA officials, plus Senators and staff members of the Senate Intelligence Committee. He traces the close working relationship between former CIA Directors, beginning with Allen Dulles and John McCone, and news executives, including CBS's William Paley, Newsweek's Publisher, the late Phillip Graham, The New York Times' Publisher, the late Arthur Hays Sulzberger, the late Henry Luce of Time Inc., and James Copley of the Copley News Service.

CIA USE OF JOURNALISTS CONTINUES

As for the possible continuing relationship between the CIA and these major media, Bernstein reports that the Agency maintained ties with 75 to 90 journalists at least until 1976, according to high-level CIA sources. He also cites an unpublished report by the House Select Committee on Intelligence, chaired by Rep. Otis Pike, showing that at least fifteen news organizations were still providing cover for CIA operatives as of 1976. The Agency - press relationship, Bernstein writes, "continues to be shrouded by an official policy of obfuscation and deception," according to CIA sources.

I said I didn't want to get entangled and told them, 'Go to my uncle (Arthur Hays Sulzberger, then publisher of the New York Times ^, and if he says to sign it, I will. '" His uncle subsequently signed such an agreement, Sulzberger said, and he thinks he did too, though he is unsure. "I don't know, twenty-sane years is a long time." He described the tool question as "a bubble in a bathtub." Stewart Alsop's relationship with the Agency was even more extensive than Sulzberger's. One official who served at the highest levels in the CIA said flatly: "Stew Alsop was a CIA agent." An equally senior official refused to define Alsop's relationship with the Agency except to say it was a formal one. Other sources said that Alsop was particularly helpful to the Agency in discussions with officials of foreign governments — asking questions to which the CIA was editing answers, planting misinformation advantageous to American policy, and assessing opportunities for CIA recruitment of well-placed foreigners.

"Absolute nonsense," said Joseph Alsop of the notion that his brother was a CIA agent. "I was closer to the Agency than Stew was, though Stew was very close. I daresay he did perform some service — he just did the correct thing as an American ...The Founding Fathers of the CIA were close personal friends of ours. Dick Bissell, ^former CIA deputy director," was my oldest friend from childhood. It was a social thing, my dear fellow. I never received a dollar; I never signed a secrecy agreement. I didn't have to .... I've done things for them when I thought they were the right thing to do; I call it doing my duty.

There is little reason to doubt that, in particular instances, the CIA does act as an ideological enforcer, using its network of paid and freelance collaborators to influence newspaper and television coverage of sensitive topics such as the JFK assassination. In general, however, it is likely that simple institutional factors have more effect.

Institutional Reasons for Media Bias

The coverage of the JFK assassination By the print and broadcast media is bad for the same institutional reason that coverage of many serious issues By the print and broadcast media is bad.

Large corporate and state media organizations are not democracies. The editorial policy is not generated from below; it is dictated from above. Nor do these organizations function as bulletin boards. Access to print and airtime is not open to all; it is almost always available only to those sanctioned By the needs of the institutions.

Objectivity and Power

There are certain topics and news events that are, for the most part, reported accurately and fairly. The reporting of natural disasters, for example, usually reflects the available facts. Sporting and cultural events can be expected to be reported honestly.

Earthquakes and football matches, however, do not often give rise to ideas critical of established power. The more closely a topic relates to political power, the less likely it is that the topic will be treated objectively.

Individuals and Institutions

Institutions are made up of individuals. Some journalists sincerely believe that they are free to express whatever views they want:

The fact that BBC journalists perform as they do without overt external interference is offered as proof of their independence. In 2007, Justin Webb, then the BBC's North America editor, rejected the charge that he is a propagandist for US power, saying: "Nobody ever tells me what to say about America or the attitude to take towards the United States. And that is the case right across the board in television as well."

It is no doubt true that reporters and editors are not often instructed in what to write and say. Direct interference is rarely necessary for obvious reasons.

Social selection ensures that institutions that undermine themselves do not survive for long. Established social institutions generate filtering mechanisms that tend to identify and weed out individuals who threaten to undermine those institutions. Someone, for example, who advocates democratic control over the economy is unlikely to be appointed to the board of directors of a large company. Someone who resists the electronic surveillance of peaceful dissidents is unlikely to rise high within the NSA, the FSB, or GCHQ.

A career in the media, as elsewhere, usually requires an employee to demonstrate that he or she can be trusted to toe the institutional line. A dependable journalist rarely needs to be told what position to take on issues that affect established power. As the famous phrase goes: 'you write what you like — because they like what you write.'

How Bad Is the Media Coverage?

There are exceptions, of course. The control mechanism is not absolute, and not all journalists are unthinking drones.

In the case of the JFK assassination, anomalous facts do occasionally get reported, although they rarely affect the dominant narrative. So the Zapruder film may indicate at least one shot from the front, but Oswald was still on the sixth floor, firing the rest of the shots, and the Warren Commission did an honest job.

An enterprising journalist will occasionally get a critical story into a mainstream newspaper. On the other hand, the tracking down and publication of previously secret documents, which one might naively imagine is the task of the fearless professional journalist, has almost always come about as the result of action by members of the public. One notable exception is the attempt by the former *Washington Post* reporter, Jefferson Morley, to secure the release of CIA files that should have been made public years ago.

The JFK assassination does much better than many other topics that might be considered subversive, a fact which no doubt reflects the level of danger that it is now considered to pose to established power. Anyone who is attuned to corporate or state propaganda will be aware that many topics of more fundamental relevance to contemporary lives than the killing of a politician half a century ago are given little or no critical coverage. The assassination may be covered badly, but at least it gets covered.

The Future of the JFK Assassination

The proportion of the US population who doubt the official lone–nut interpretation has been kept down to roughly three out of four by the media's consistently one-sided coverage of the assassination. With the declining influence of traditional media and easier access to more objective sources of information, that proportion is likely to increase. Although search engines will probably take on some of the filtering roles that news organizations have performed, it is difficult to imagine that they will be as effective as newspapers and television have been.

Famed CBS TV Newsman Dan Rather Zapruder Film Gaffe Gave Birth to JFK Assassination 'Lone Nutters'

by Dave O'Brien

He didn't know it at the time, but when CBS newsman Dan Rather became one of the first people to see the Zapruder film of President John F. Kennedy's assassination, his live TV reporting of what he saw created controversy that endures decades later.

CBS newsman Dan Rather reached international fame even though, at his biggest moment, on his biggest stage in American history, his misreporting of what the Zapruder film showed helped to misshape history for a dozen years.

After Rather's CBS news lost a bidding war to Life Magazine, which bought the Zapruder film on the night of the assassination for $150,000, the then little-known Dallas CBS TV reporter went on national television and gave the first-ever report of what the film showed.

In giving the very first account of what happened at the critical moment that a bullet struck President Kennedy's head, this is what Rather told his horrified nationwide American audience:

"His head went FORWARD with considerable violence!"

Rather than not only saying those misguiding words on national television, he said them, he visually affirmed that description by moving the upper half of his body significantly forward to denote what he said happened to President Kennedy.

Not to give him too much credit, but what Rather reported to the American people soon became the official government version of how President Kennedy died on November 22, 1963, namely:

John F. Kennedy died from a gunshot to the back of his head fired by Lee Harvey Oswald from the 6th-floor southeast corner window of the Texas School Book Depository Building, which was above and behind the President's limousine.

There's only one problem – That's not what happened when the fatal shot impacted JFK's skull. President Kennedy's head was actually driven violently '*backward!*'

'**Backward**' is the complete opposite of what Dan Rather says he saw on the Zap ruder film as a result of the fatal head shot striking JFK.

The sequence of still frames from the Zapruder film shown here demonstrate what actually happened:

Frame 312 is just 1/18th of a second before the fatal head shot. Note Mrs. Kennedy's position in relation to her husband.

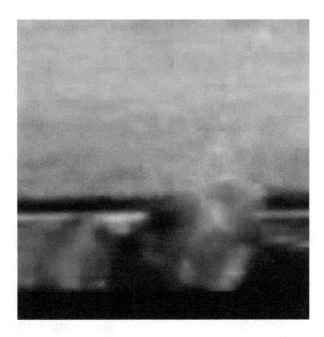

Frame 313 is the moment the fatal head shot struck President Kennedy. His natural, uncontrolled reaction in relation to this shot created controversy that endures to this day.

***Frame 321 is a little less than 1/2 second** after the head impact. Note how Mrs. Kennedy's position has not changed, but President Kennedy is thrust 'backward' against his car seat. Dan Rather of CBS News told a nationwide TV audience he saw JFK's head move* "forward with considerable violence. "

With the government's essential finding that the kill shot came from above and behind the President, first planted in the minds of the American people by Dan Rather's reporting of the Zapruder film, the Warren Report in 1964 went on to conclude:

Dan Rather's erroneous account of what he saw on the Zapruder film paved the way for Lee Harvey Oswald being declared the 'lone nut' assassin of President John F. Kennedy.

A) **One Assassin** – Lee Harvey Oswald was the lone assassin. There was no conspiracy, foreign or domestic. Oswald was branded a 'lone nut' who was a misfit in society and sought a place in the history books.

B) **A Second Lone Assassin** – Oswald was himself assassinated before public trial by Jack Ruby, who also acted completely alone.

BIRTH OF THE 'LONE NUTTERS'

Gerald Posner has become the literary hero of the 'Lone Nutters' with his book claiming that Oswald was the sole killer of JFK.

Like any good issue of controversy, there is the 'official version' of events countered by one or more alternate theories purporting to be what 'truly' happened.

As it relates to the JFK assassination, due in part to Dan Rather's early and mistaken interpretation of the Zapruder film, 'lone nut' believers (Lone Nutters) had their way in the court of public opinion until three events helped cause the emergence of JFK 'conspiracy theorists.'

1. **Our Right to Know** – The work of pioneer JFK assassination researchers and critics such as Mark Lane, Penn Jones Jr., Mary Ferrell, Harold Weisberg, Edward Jay Epstein and Josiah Thompson were given a boost when the Freedom of Information Act was passed into law in 1967. Researchers could now petition the courts for the release of 'classified files' on the Kennedy assassination. Slowly, over time, documents and evidence were released that contravened the official findings of the Warren Report.

2. **Watergate** – The 1972 bungled burglary of the Democratic National Headquarters led to Richard Nixon's resignation as POTUS. More tragically, the Watergate incident shamed America by demonstrating that the U.S. government, at its highest levels, could act criminally, disregard the public's trust with blatant lies and then attempt to cover it all up.

3. **Public Viewing of the Zapruder Film** – On March 6, 1975, the Zapruder film was shown for the first time to the American people by Geraldo Rivera on ABC's Good Night America.

Geraldo Rivera of ABC's Good Night America changed a nation's perception of the JFK assassination when he showed the Zapruder film for the first time to a nationwide TV audience.

While Watergate served to erode peoples' trust in government, the first ever public viewing of the Zapruder film nearly 12 years after the event shocked Americans because it showed, in the eyes of many, the complete opposite of what Dan Rather and the Warren Commission reported as fact. Millions of Americans watched in horror as President Kennedy's head exploded in a pink hazy mist and propelled him 'backward' against his car seat as a result of the lethal head shot.

For 12 years, Dan Rather's reported "***forward with considerable violence***" description of the President's head swayed the public's opinion that one assassin murdered the nation's 46-year-old President.

But with you and I finally able to see on TV what Dan Rather saw soon after the assassination, our belief system was shocked into disbelief.

Not only did we see history occur completely opposite to what we were told by trusted reporters and our own government, but for the second time in three years, we had to face the possibility that the U.S. government once again lied to us and tried to cover it up.

Once the Zapruder film was in the public domain, a new era of JFK assassination researchers emerged. Film expert Robert Groden, in concert with Penn Jones Jr., dissected the film for the American public to graphically show the 'rearward' result of the terrible kill shot.

Public perception of the JFK assassination would never be the same. Lone Nutters now had official opposition in vast numbers.

'LONE NUTTERS' VERSUS 'CONSPIRACY THEORISTS'

We can't be sure when the birth of JFK 'conspiracy theorists' occurred, but with the seed of mistrust in government now part of the human psyche thanks to Watergate, the first public viewing of the Zapruder film in 1975 may be the defining moment.

For sure, words such as lies, deception, conspiracy, and cover-up became associated with the Warren Commission and its report.

While the 1960's pioneer researchers mentioned above brought doubt to the Warren Report findings, the public airing of the 22-second Zapruder film changed everything.

A collective gasp could be heard across the country in 1975 upon seeing the gruesome result of the fatal head shot for the first time.

Then, when the shock of what we saw subsided, a new shock enveloped us.

You don't have to be a scholar of physics like Sir Isaac Newton to realize that the President's violent '*backward*' head movement following the bullet's impact is NOT consistent with a shot fired from behind Mr. Kennedy.

When you visit the link below and click on the play button on Rather's image, at 2:15 into Dan Rather's grim description of the Zapruder film, his verbal account would misinform the American people for more than a decade.

To put this to a harmless test, gently tap your forehead with the palm of your hand and take note of what happens to your head. Your head moves in the same direction of the incoming impact.

When we see JFK slammed '**rearward**' against the backrest of his car seat, this is consistent with a shot striking him from the front and slightly to the right, which is where the infamous grassy knoll is situated.

The Warren Commission, operating under assurances from President Lyndon Johnson that a 75-year ban on thousands of classified documents would hide the truth until 2038, decided there was no grassy knoll sniper and that Lee Harvey Oswald was a 'lone nut' assassin who wanted a place in the history books.

Oddly, when Dan Rather published his memoir, it was titled The Camera Never Blinks.

In his own words in his memoir, Dan Rather reflects back on getting history wrong when he had the very first opportunity to report the truth as a CBS news reporter:

"At the risk of sounding too defensive, I challenge anyone to watch for the first time a twenty-two second film of devastating impact, then describe what they had seen in its entirety, without notes."

 Unfortunately for historical truth, Dan Rather's excuse is as flawed as his incorrect observations of Zapruder's short film.

In fairness, today we can look at the Zapruder film at regular speed, slow speed, and frame-by-frame and enlarged frames as often as we want and the film still engenders controversy.

Although we all look at the same film, 'lone nutters' see the film one way to fit their narrative and 'conspiracy theorists' see the film entirely differently to support their narrative.

So, can we blame Dan Rather for not seeing the obvious and setting history on a wrong course for more than a decade?

THE MISREPORTED 'SINGLE SECOND' OF TIME THAT STILL DENIES HISTORY THE TRUTH!

The biggest mistake Dan Rather made on national TV was his attempt to provide play-by-play commentary for the entire 22 seconds of the Zapruder film. It's not as easy as it sounds, given Rather's limited one-time viewing of the shocking home movie.

Clearly, one of the most stunningly awful moments in recorded film history was the point of impact of the kill shot and the horrific result it caused.

Lost in the discussion of Rather's description of JFK's head moving violently forward is that by the time Rather gave his exclusive account on live TV of what happened to the President, he was already aware that:

A) Lee Harvey Oswald had been arrested and formally declared and charged as the 'lone' assassin.

B) Oswald worked in the building where he allegedly fired the shots, which was above and behind JFK in Dealey Plaza.

Accordingly, we must wonder if:

• **Skewed Viewing** – Rather subconsciously saw what 'must' have happened to the President based on the information about Oswald instead of what actually happened.

• **Rookie Mistake** – The young TV reporter, for whatever reason, didn't want to challenge the historical record as it was taking shape because he wasn't experienced enough or confident enough or…

• **Not His Fault** – It was an honest mistake due to the pressure and time constraint he faced at the viewing of the film.

Over these past 55 years, Rather has offered little more than an excuse for his misrepresentation of the shot that killed President Kennedy (see his quote above).

He has consistently stopped short of admitting to being wrong, a similar strategy undertaken by almost all mainstream media that has refused to acknowledge that they unquestionably reported the Warren Report findings as fact in the aftermath of its release.

HISTORICAL WHAT IF

Sir Isaac Newton's Laws of Motion, when applied to the Zapruder film, would make him a 'Conspiracy Theorist' instead of a 'Lone Nutter.'

We can only imagine how history might be different if Rather, with the weight of CBS news behind him, had become the first reporter to question the illogical '***backward***' movement of the President's head when the shot is said to have come from 'behind' the victim.

Science simply does not support the instinctive, natural reaction of the President's head and upper body to a bullet reportedly fired from above and behind.

It is hard to believe that the President, seen on film violently thrust '***rearward***' upon impact of the head shot, did not befuddle Rather because of the physics involved.

Remarkably, not only did Rather miss this obvious defiance of physics at the moment of Kennedy's death, he inexplicably reported the exact opposite of what happened.

Had Rather focused on that one critical second of time when a bullet tore into JFK's skull, instead of the full 22 seconds of footage, he may have noticed (and accurately reported) the President's reaction.

This is demonstrated every time I do a seminar for my book through The 'Oswald' Window and show the Zapruder film.

At the moment of impact to the President's skull, the audience always emits a collective gasp of horror. When the film ends, I ask the audience where the fatal shot came from based on what they observed.

Without exception, the audience agrees that the kill shot came from the front, not from behind Mr. Kennedy even though, like Dan Rather, they viewed the disturbing film in its entirety.

Why couldn't Dan Rather see what everyone else sees and make the same deduction that everyone else does?

If Rather had gotten it right on November 25, 1963, we have to wonder if the government could have proceeded with its assertion of Oswald as the lone shooter firing from above and behind.

If Dan Rather had seen the President's true and instinctive reaction to the lethal head shot that drove him violently '***backward***' against his car seat, he would not be known today as the father of the Oswald 'Lone Nutters.'

Instead, Dan Rather would be heralded as the iconic journalist who forced the truth to prevail and foiled the U.S. government's plan to suppress the conspiracy to assassinate the nation's 35th President until the year 2038.

James Earl Files (born January 24, 1942), also known as **James Sutton**,[a] is a former American prisoner. In 1994, while serving a 50-year sentence for the 1991 attempted murders of two police officers, Files gave interviews stating that he was the "grassy knoll shooter" in the 1963 assassination of United States President John F. Kennedy. Files has subsequently been interviewed by others and discussed in multiple books pertaining to the assassination and related theories. In 1994, the Federal Bureau of Investigation was quoted as having investigated Files' allegation and found it "not to be credible".

In 2010, *Playboy* magazine published an article by Hillel Levin in which Files also implicated Charles Nicoletti and John Roselli in the assassination of Kennedy.

Contents

Critical analysis

Notes

References

Background

The wooden fence on the grassy knoll, where Files claims to have made his shot.

Files have stated that he was born in Alabama, moved to California with his family shortly thereafter, then to an Italian neighborhood in Chicago...On May 7, 1991, Files and his friend, David Morley, were involved in a roadside shootout in Round Lake Beach, Illinois, with two police officers, Detective David Ostertag, and his partner, Gary Bitler. Ostertag and Bitler tried to apprehend the two for driving a stolen vehicle. During the shootout, Morley shot Detective Ostertag in the chest. Both Files and Morley shot at Detective Bitler but missed. Files and Morley then fled on foot but were arrested a few hours later. Files was charged with two counts of attempted murder and one count each of discharge of a firearm, aggravated battery with a firearm and armed violence. In August 1991, a jury found Files guilty of two counts of attempted murder. He was sentenced to 30 years for the shooting of Detective Ostertag and 20 years for attempting to shoot Detective Bitler. Files was initially imprisoned at Stateville Correctional Center in Crest Hill, Illinois, before being transferred to Danville Correctional Center in Danville, Illinois. Files was paroled in May 2016.

An "anonymous FBI source", later identified as Zack Shelton, has been reported By some researchers as having told Joe West, a private investigator in Houston, in the early 1990s about an inmate in an Illinois penitentiary who might have information about the Kennedy assassination. On August 17, 1992, West interviewed Files at Stateville Correctional Center in Crest Hill, Illinois.After West's death in 1993, his family requested that his friend, Houston television producer Bob Vernon, take over the records concerning the story. Vernon is the owner of a bullet casing with teeth marks on it, even though it was not found until 1987.However, the bullet casing's markings (head stamp) indicate it was manufactured before the year 1972 so it could have belonged to James Files.

Critical analysis

Vincent Bugliosi, author of *Reclaiming History: The Assassination of President John F. Kennedy*, has characterized Files as "the Rodney Dangerfield of Kennedy assassins." According to Bugliosi, very few within the majority of Americans (75%) who believe there was a conspiracy to kill Kennedy respect him or his story. However, psychology professor Jerome Kroth described Files as "surprisingly credible" and said his story "is the most believable and persuasive" about the assassination.

22 November 1963

RIP: Dr. Robert McClelland, the most important JFK witness

Assassination, Best of, Experts, They Talked / By Jefferson Morley

Dr. Robert McClelland, the surgeon who oversaw the effort to save President Kennedy's life in 1963, died earlier this month at age 89. In his interviews, you sense a man of considerable dignity, humility, and integrity. It comes as no surprise that he self-published an anthology of writings on surgery to which thousands of doctors subscribed. He was both a teacher and doctor, an instructor and a healer. And it is those qualities that make McClelland one of the most important witnesses to JFK's assassination.

In 1963, McClelland was 34 years old. He had just become the chief of surgery at Dallas's Parkland Hospital. When the mortally wounded JFK was brought to Trauma Room One, McClelland stood over the dying president and participated in the efforts to save him. He observed the president's fatal head wound for about 10 minutes from a distance of less than two feet.

"My God," he recalled saying to his colleagues. "Have you seen the back of his head. There's a wound in the back of his head that's about five inches in diameter."

After about ten minutes, Kennedy's breathing and heartbeat ceased. The Secret Service came and took the body away.

Jackie had a piece of JFK brain

No autopsy

Bullet came from Front o car not from behind

'From the grassy knoll'

McClelland concluded, on the basis of what he saw that day, and what he saw in a home movie of the assassination taken by a bystander, that Kennedy had been struck by a gunshot fired from in front, not behind.

"That bullet came from the grassy knoll, the picket fence," McClelland said of the fatal shot, referring to the area in front of the presidential motorcade at the moment the shots rang out.

How the New York Times handled McClelland's eye-witness testimony is a textbook case of the journalism profession's strange approach to the JFK assassination story. McClelland was a superb witness. Only one trained medical professional (his friend and colleague Dr. Kemp Clark) had a close a view of Kennedy's head wound so soon after he was shot. McClelland went on to a distinguished career.

Yet the Times did not report what he saw and what he said about JFK's head wound until he was dead. For some reason, McClelland's testimony, contradicting the Warren Commission, was not regarded as news. The Times obituary gingerly avoids any suggestion that McClelland might have been right or that his testimony was unique. In the headline, the Times reported that McClelland saw the "gravity" of the President's wound, not that he expressed a judgment about the shot from the front. In fact, he was a credible eyewitness whose well-informed account undermined the government's much-disputed version of events

McClelland didn't believe in "wild conspiracy theories," the Times assures us. The rather more relevant point, of course, is that he did not believe in the equally implausible anti-conspiracy theories of the Warren Commission, the CIA, the FBI, and Dallas Police Department, which hold that Lee Harvey Oswald–whose travels, politics and foreign contacts were known to certain senior CIA officers— shot JFK for no discernible reason.

McClelland's account is consistent with the accounts of 21 police officers at the crime scene who also thought gunfire had come from in front of JFK's limousine.

[Here is a 2013 video of McClelland explaining the nature of JKF's wounds. to another doctor. He describes the wound at 5:50. He talks about the effect of treating JFK on his life at 15:50. He talks about the wound in JFK's neck at 17:00. He talks about the meaning of Abraham Zapruder's film at 19:30.]

Was he right?

A cop runs toward the area known as "the grassy knoll" moments after President Kennedy was shot. Dr. McClelland concluded the fatal shot had come from that area.

McClelland was mistaken, say defenders of the official theory. Pay him no mind, they say. Just look at the JFK autopsy photos in the National Archives. But the autopsy photos cannot disprove McClelland's account if they do not depict the wounds that he saw. And there is sworn testimony that they do not.

Navy doctors conducted an autopsy on JFK about eight hours after Dr. McClelland saw him. The Secret Service had transported the president's body from Parkland to Air Force One, which then flew from Dallas to Washington where the body was taken to Bethesda Medical Center. The autopsy was conducted around 8 pm Eastern time in the evening.

One of the pathologists who conducted the autopsy, Dr. Pierre Finck, came to very different conclusion than McClelland. "It was very obvious that it [the fatal shot] came from the back and exited the front," Finck told a reporter in 1992.

Do the autopsy photographs resolve the two doctor's differences? Do they prove Finck right?

Not really. Photographs of the autopsy were developed on Sunday, November 24, 1963, by Sandra Spencer, the chief petty officer in the U.S. Navy's photography lab in Washington. Spencer was interviewed under oath by the JFK Assassination Records Review Board in June 1997. With the crisp, detail-oriented style of a career military officer, she described in detail how the photographs were made, what they showed, and how they were developed.

When shown the JFK autopsy photos now held in the National Archives, Spencer said, flatly and unequivocally, they were not the photographs she developed after JFK's death. The head wound she saw on the photographs she developed was much larger than the National Archives photo, she said. The photographic paper was different too.

Then she said this:

"Between those photographs and the ones we did, there had to be some massive cosmetic things done to the President's body."

If Spencer is right–and she was testifying under oath–the autopsy photos don't refute McClelland because they show "massive cosmetic things done to the President's body" after it was removed from Dallas.

The accounts of McClelland and Sandra Spencer tell a disturbing story that cannot be wished away. Their accounts undermine the official story and demonstrate that we still do not have the full story of JFK's death 56 years after the fact.

McClelland believed his eyes, not the theories of people who were not there, and he wasn't afraid to state the truth as saw it. No doubt there will be posthumous efforts by critics to discredit him, which are doomed to failure given his experience and integrity. He is one of the most important and credible JFK witnesses. Anyone who wants to know the truth about JFK's assassination is indebted to him.

RIP Dr. Robert McClelland.

ARRB-declassified documents hint at a possible explanation: evidence destruction. All three of JFK's pathologists, both autopsy photographers, a White House photographer Robert Knudsen, and, as Jeff mentioned, National Photographic Center employee Sandra Spencer, have all testified that photographs taken at JFK's autopsy are missing.

McClelland spent a good part of his retirement telling anyone who would listen what he saw. Again, the mainstream media doesn't report even the simplest of truths around the JFK assassination, starting with Dan Rather and his "mistake" about JFK being thrown violently forward from the head shot.

It's just incredible. Who or what do they think they are protecting? It ain't democracy or free speech, I guarantee you that.

JOSEPH DEE
DECEMBER 5, 2019 AT 9:57 AM
James Files killed JFK from the grassy knoll read his book and all the evidence ,, James Files was just doing his job conducted By the CIA the FBI the mafia and others ,,, we are living in a totally controlled environment ,,, (corrupt evil power The ruling elite) .. The gun that killed the president was a fireball XP 100 made By Remington arms ,to think that the president was killed with a varmint gun... shout out from many angles Oswald is a Patsy and I announce his innocence ... God bless America and may the truth heal all of us and set us free ,,,rest in peace Mr. President .....

HIDEJI OKINA
JANUARY 29, 2020 AT 7:48 PM
His interviewer Late Jim Marrs insist he is a liar. You not read "Cross Fire" 2013 ver?

DOUGLAS P HORNE
SEPTEMBER 26, 2019 AT 9:37 AM

Overall this is a great obituary of Dr. McClelland, but I need to correct a misstatement in the article. In reference to Navy Photographer's Mate Saundra Spencer (a Navy E-6 non-commissioned officer, or NCO), the article makes a misstatement about Saundra Spencer's work, as follows: "…they were not the photographs she took the day after JFK's death."

I'm going to offer a friendly correction below to Jeff Morley, someone whose work in service to the cause of truth in the JFK assassination I respect: Saundra Spencer did not TAKE any post mortem photos of JFK's body; instead, she DEVELOPED post mortem photos of JFK's body taken by someone else. She was not present at the autopsy.

But this correction aside, the importance of what she developed on Sunday, November 24th, 1963 is undeniable, and is important for two reasons: (1) they were post-embalming photos, taken after restorative work and reconstruction of his cranium and his body, which showed the President's body "cleaned-up," with no blood visible anymore and no longer with any open body cavities; and (2) the fact that she developed a key photo of the back of JFK's head—after cranial reconstruction—nevertheless showing a 2-2.5 inch open cavity in the occipital bone in the skull (what she called a "blown-out chunk"), blatantly contradicts the so-called "intact" back-of-the-head photos presently in the official autopsy collection.

Summarizing, Saundra Spencer provided testimony to the ARRB about the post mortem photos of JFK she developed, following reconstruction of JFK's cranium by Gawler's Funeral Home personnel, stating that there was STILL a defect in the back of his skull entirely consistent with an exit wound, i.e., evidence of a shot from the front. This not only contradicts the Warren Commission's conclusions, but contradicts the so-called "official autopsy photos" showing the back of JFK's head to apparently be intact at the autopsy.

Thus, Spencer's initial telephone interview with the ARRB late in 1996 and her sworn testimony to the ARRB in 1997 both corroborated Dr. McClelland's clear recollection, under oath in 1964, of what could only have been a large wound of exit in the back of JFK's head. Put simply, even after reconstruction of JFK's cranium by the embalmers, there was still a significant hole in the back of his head—unambiguous evidence of a fatal shot from the front (not from the rear, where the accused assassin was located in the TSBD).

The General Counsel at the ARRB, T. Jeremy Gunn—my boss on the ARRB staff—told me he considered Saundra Spencer the most credible of all of the ARRB's medical witnesses.

What Spencer's testimony provides is not only evidence of a fatal shot from the front, but it identifies a serious problem with some of the extant photos in the official autopsy collection that resides today in the National Archives. [The 6 to 8 color negatives developed by Spencer, and the two color prints made from each of the negatives Spencer developed, never made it into the official collection.]

I'm glad that Jeff Morley wrote about the importance of Dr. McClelland's observations in Trauma Room One at Parkland, and that he wrote about how Saundra Spencer's testimony before the ARRB in 1997 corroborated McClelland's testimony before the Warren Commission in 1964.

The key thing to understand here is that both Spencer and McClelland recalled a large wound (entirely consistent with a wound of exit and not with a wound of entry) in the back of JFK's skull. In fact, McClelland told Arlen Specter under oath in 1964 that he estimated that about one third of JFK's brain tissue was missing from the posterior portion of his brain—both cerebral and cerebellar tissue. This was overwhelming evidence of an exit wound in the back of JFK's skull which blatantly contradicted the Warren Commission's conclusions of a lone assassin shooting from behind. Instead of publishing McClelland's testimony in the Warren Commission Report itself, the Commission unsuccessfully tried to bury it in the 26 volumes of supporting evidence. That did not work, and throughout the remainder of his life, McClelland courageously stuck to his story: it was obvious to him that President Kennedy was shot from the front, and that the wound he observed in the back of President Kennedy's head was the exit wound from that shot. END

Douglas Horne, Former Chief Analyst for Military Records, ARRB

HIDEJI OKINA

OCTOBER 26, 2019 AT 12:27 PM

Dr.McClelland supported conspiracy version' "Magic Bullet Trajectory". He insisted JFK's head exit wound position is back of the right head. He insisted Grassy knoll shooter shot JFK. Knoll is not a JFK's right front, but between the front and right, slightly upward, almost right side. He questioned this point from Jacob Cater. "If knoll shooter shot JFK, why his head exit wound not a left position?" Dr.McClelland answer is "This is an unleaned opinion about wound ballistics".

And Mr.Horne, I read your books, you insisted JFK's back of head wound is not an exit wound, but parallel gunshot wound from Badgeman's position shot. Why you admire Dr's testimony? I read and analyzed "BEST EVIDENCE". This book is worst one. Lifton insisted official version wound ballistic is strange. Right! Lifton insisted conspiracy version wound ballistic is stranger. Right!

But he is not analyze this matter.

NORMAN SYKES

JANUARY 24, 2020 AT 2:33 AM

Where is the entry wound located exactly? Where the exit is wound exact location? I think everyone has argued and guessed for decades due to the reason there was no entry or exit because the brain had imploded from within and caused enough damage that it was almost impossible to tell where the bullet entered or had exited!

DAVID MANTIK

SEPTEMBER 26, 2019 AT 12:40 AM

Bravo, Jeff!

Even Humes told the ARRB that, even after embalming, JFK's scalp failed to cover 3-4 cm of the hole. Humes's statement is a near perfect match to Spencer's depiction—but you will never find this corroboration in the New York Times, so save your pennies.

Of course McClelland was accurate. His statement (and video) is nakedly unimpeachable eyewitness recollection. Who would know more than Mac?

David Mantik

GREG OTTERMAN

SEPTEMBER 25, 2019 AT 6:31 PM

He was truly an unimpeachable witness as you termed it years ago thanks Jeff

JIM DIEUGENIO

SEPTEMBER 25, 2019 AT 4:33 PM

Very nice Jeff, wonderful you quoted Spencer. Neither the WC nor the HSCA called her

HIDEJI OKINA

OCTOBER 26, 2019 AT 11:53 AM

Mr.DiEugenio, I recommended you read his interview with Jacob Cater'. He supported conspiracy version' "Magic Bullet Trajectory". His interview with D-magazine (2008 Nov), he insisted he remembered JFK's Back of head wound in 1975(ABC TV on-aired Zapruder Film). But JFK's big head wound position in this film is near the right ear, not back of the head? I think he is worst witness, his testimony is almost lie, fantasy, day dream.

The FBI's Investigation Was Deficient"

The *HSCA Report* found that the FBI's investigation was "seriously flawed":

The committee concluded from its lengthy study of the roles of the FBI, Secret Service, CIA, and other Federal agencies that assisted the Warren Commission that the final determinations of who was responsible for President Kennedy's murder and whether there had been a conspiracy were based largely on the work of the FBI. With an acute awareness of the significance of its finding, the committee concluded that the FBI's investigation of whether there had been a conspiracy in President Kennedy's assassination was seriously flawed. The conspiracy aspects of the investigation were characterized by a limited approach and an inadequate application and use of available resources.

The committee concluded that the FBI's investigation into a conspiracy was deficient in the areas that the committee decided were most worthy of suspicion — organized crime, pro– and anti–Castro Cubans, and the possible associations of individuals from these areas with Lee Harvey Oswald and Jack Ruby. In those areas in particular, the committee found that the FBI's investigation was in all likelihood insufficient to have uncovered a conspiracy.

As someone of the post-Kennedy generation with no illusions about government excesses, I believe I speak for most when I say that an objective analysis of the weight of the evidence on both sides clearly shows that "JFK" is an accurate representation of history. No more convincing evidence of this can be asked than Lyndon Johnson's statement in 1975 that he never believed that Oswald acted alone and the House Select Committee on Assassinations' determination that a conspiracy was "probable" in the murder of John F. Kennedy.

Section 3

Part Eighteen

Similarities and Differences between the

Assassination of JFK and the Coup of Trump

SIMILARITIES

FBI DIRECTORS TRY TO CLOSE THE CASES AND BEGIN COVERUPS

1) James Comey. Hillary Clinton e-mail case No reasonable prosecutor
2) James Comey It doesn't ring a bell. CIA noticed that Hillary was peddling Donald Trump's collusion with the Russians
3) FBI open case on Trump- McCabe said it was nonsense.
4) FBI had a conclusion in place before all the evidence was gathered.
5) FBI failed to conduct interviews of multiple people who most likely had knowledge of the case.

1) J. Edgar Hoover, the director of the FBI, also emphasized the need for a public relations initiative:
The thing I am concerned about, and so is Mr. Katzenbach is having something issued so that we can convince the public that Oswald is the real assassin. Mr. Katzenbach thinks that the President might appoint a Presidential Commission of three outstanding citizens to make a determination.

2) The Warren Commission's conclusion was in place before the Commission had even been established: Oswald was guilty and had acted alone. To counteract suspicions of conspiracy, it was necessary for the Warren Commission to show that Jack Ruby also had acted alone.

All that is known to the American public is that Lee Harvey Oswald, a mysterious man who is connected to other mysterious cases, was pronounced by J. Edgar Hoover, Director of the Federal Bureau of Investigation, to be the lone shooter and a "nut". Director Hoover sent a communication to all FBI Field Offices that the shooter was in custody and no further investigation was required.

FBI – assassination of the President, was not a federal crime.
FBI cannot open a case without DOJ Approval
FBI failed to conduct interviews of multiple people who most likely had knowledge of the case.

4) Review of FBI's investigations by Inspector General Michael Horowitz Foreign Intelligence Surveillance Act (FISA) report, DECEMBER 9, 2019 By Chrissy Clark.
The much-awaited Foreign Intelligence Surveillance Act (FISA) report, conducted by Inspector General Michael Horowitz, was released today. It finds that the FBI would not have had enough claimed evidence to secretly surveil former Trump aide Carter Page, and thus the Trump 2016 campaign, without using a "dossier" of opposition research funded by the Hillary Clinton campaign.
The *HSCA Report* found that the FBI's investigation was "seriously flawed":
The committee concluded from its lengthy study of the roles of the FBI, Secret Service, CIA, and other Federal agencies that assisted the Warren Commission that the final determinations of who was responsible for President Kennedy's murder and whether there had been a conspiracy were based largely on the work of the FBI. With an acute awareness of the significance of its finding, the committee concluded that the FBI's investigation of whether there had been a conspiracy in

President Kennedy's assassination was seriously flawed. The conspiracy aspects of the investigation were characterized by a limited approach and an inadequate application and use of available resources.

The committee concluded that the FBI's investigation into a conspiracy was deficient in the areas that the committee decided were most worthy of suspicion — organized crime, pro– and anti– Castro Cubans, and the possible associations of individuals from these areas with Lee Harvey Oswald and Jack Ruby. In those areas, in particular, the committee found that the FBI's investigation was in all likelihood insufficient to have uncovered a conspiracy.

FBI DIRECTORS J. EDGAR HOOVER AND JAMES COMEY TRY TO CLOSE THESE CASES AND BEGIN COVERUPS

SIMILARITY

James Comey closed the Hillary Clinton e-mail case. Comey failed to obtain the permission of the Attorney General, Loretta James, in violation of the Department of Justice and Federal Bureau of Investigation Guidelines. Comey announced that" No reasonable prosecutor would authorize prosecution." Both Comey and James were found by Michael Horowitz, the Department of Justice Inspector General to be in violation of Department of Justice guidelines.

DIFFERENCE

James Comey testified before the Senate Committee that he was asked by Senator if he recalled a notification from the Central Intelligence Agency that it didn't ring a bell. CIA noticed Hillary was peddling Donald Trump's collusion with the Russians. Comey replied that "it doesn't ring a bell."

Comey was again notified by CIA Director John Brennan Comey failed to open a case on Hillary Clinton. Instead, he did the exact opposite and opened a case on Donald Trump colluding with the Russians. Assistant Director Andrew McCabe testified before that the Trump-Russia case "was nonsense." McCabe also testified that "there would be no FISA warrant without the Steele Dossier. The FBI had a conclusion in place before all the evidence was gathered.

J. Edgar Hoover,

Neither Hoover nor any of the high-level staff of the FBI was ever ordered to testify before any Congressional Committees.

RESULT

The general public and even government officials obtained many false details TRUMP-RUSSIAN case.

The general public and even government officials were not provided with most of the details of the JFK Assassination.

SIMILARITY

The FBI failed to conduct interviews of multiple people who most likely had knowledge of the case. Most glaring is the non-interview of Hillary Clinton.

Also, the FBI failed to conduct interviews with multiple people who most likely had knowledge of the JFK Assassination.

DIFFERENCE
None
RESULT
The cases were not solved.

SIMILARITY
Fake Media
George Will
LBJ telephone call NY Times
Carl Bernstein
Dan Rather
DIFFERENCES
Communication advances-
Computers, Cellphones,
E-Mails, Texts
Twitter, Facebook
Retention of documents
Intense partisan re trump none e JFK

Newspaper and television

DIFFERENCE
RESULT
SIMILARITY
FBI knew collusion with Trump and Russia was false but kept on investigating the case.
FBI most likely knew there was a conspiracy but closed the case.
DIFFERENCE
None
RESULT
Americans were deprived of this information.
SIMILARITY
Hoover thought it was best that the American citizens did not know that there was some political or military reason for the JFK Assassination
Hoover, the director of the FBI, also emphasized the need for a public Relations initiative:
The thing I am concerned about, and so is Mr. Katzenbach is having something issued so that we can convince the public that Oswald is the real assassin. Mr. Katzenbach thinks that the President might appoint a Presidential Commission of three outstanding citizens to make a determination.
The Warren Commission's conclusion was in place before the Commission had even been established: Oswald was guilty and had acted alone. To counteract suspicions of conspiracy, it was necessary for the Warren Commission to show that Jack Ruby also had acted alone.

Comey wants Trump voted out of office, calls him 'morally unfit' Comey sat down with ABC's George Stephanopoulos for an interview that aired Sunday night. It came as part of the buildup for Comey's book, "A Higher Loyalty: Truth, Lies, and Leadership," set for release Tuesday.

"You write that President Trump is unethical, untethered to the truth," Stephanopoulos said. "Is Donald Trump unfit to be president?"

"Yes," Comey replied. "But not in the way I often hear people talk about it. I don't buy this stuff about him being mentally incompetent or early stages of dementia. He strikes me as a person of above-average intelligence who's tracking conversations and knows what's going on."

He added: "I don't think he's medically unfit to be president. I think he's morally unfit to be president."

Comey cited Trump's response to the white nationalist riots in Charlottesville, Virginia, his treatment of women, and what Comey called a tendency to lie "constantly about matters big and small."

15, 2018, 10:44 PM

"The big question in Comey's badly reviewed book aren't answered like, how come he gave up Classified Information (jail), why did he lie to Congress (jail), why did the DNC refuse to give Server to the FBI (why didn't they TAKE it), why the phony memos, McCabe's $700,000 & more?" Trump tweeted.

DIFFERENCE

None.

The Director of the FBI is supposed to be non-political. Their private thoughts are not supposed to enter into any of their decisions.

Neither Hoover nor Comey provided any specific and/or credible evidence why they made these statements.

Massive damage to the United States of America.

The Warren Commission's conclusion was in place before the Commission had even been established: Oswald was guilty and had acted alone. To counteract suspicions of conspiracy, it was necessary for the Warren Commission to show that Jack Ruby also had acted alone.

All that is known to the American public is that Lee Harvey Oswald, a mysterious man who is connected to other mysterious cases, was pronounced by J. Edgar Hoover, Director of the Federal Bureau of Investigation, to be the lone shooter and a "nut".

SIMILARITY

Review of FBI's investigations by Inspector General Michael Horowitz Foreign Intelligence Surveillance Act (FISA) report, *DECEMBER 9, 2019* By Chrissy Clark

The much-awaited Foreign Intelligence Surveillance Act (FISA) report, conducted by Inspector General Michael Horowitz, was released today. It finds that the FBI would not have had enough claimed evidence to secretly surveil former Trump aide Carter Page, and thus the Trump 2016 campaign, without using a "dossier" of opposition research funded by the Hillary Clinton campaign.

Foreign Intelligence Surveillance Act (FISA) report.

The *HSCA Report* found that the FBI's investigation was "seriously flawed":

384

The committee concluded from its lengthy study of the roles of the FBI, Secret Service, CIA, and other Federal agencies that assisted the Warren Commission that the final determinations of who was responsible for President Kennedy's murder and whether there had been a conspiracy were based largely on the work of the FBI. With an acute awareness of the significance of its finding, the committee concluded that the FBI's investigation of whether there had been a conspiracy in President Kennedy's assassination was seriously flawed. The conspiracy aspects of the investigation were characterized By a limited approach and an inadequate application and use of available resources.

The committee concluded that the FBI's investigation into a conspiracy was deficient in the areas that the committee decided were most worthy of suspicion — organized crime, pro– and anti–Castro Cubans, and the possible associations of individuals from these areas with Lee Harvey Oswald and Jack RuBy . In those areas, in particular, the committee found that the FBI's investigation was in all likelihood insufficient to have uncovered a conspiracy.

DIFFERENCE

RESULT

Special Agents Shelton and Roth- The Media approach to the Trump Russia Collusion Case and the JFK Assassination case is most likely the major factor in the outcome of these two cases. The Media took a "hands-off" approach to the JFK Assassination, with the result being the case was never solved. The Media chose to amplify the false statements of Hillary Clinton, her campaign staff, and her lawyers regarding Trump- the Russia Collusion, with the result being Republicans and conservative media began to defend President Trump. The conservative and Republican media were simply overwhelmed.

5) The Role of the Media
Documents made public many years later reveal the extent to which senior figures in the print and broadcast media were involved in shaping the official response to the assassination. One such figure was the syndicated newspaper columnist, Joe Alsop. A telephone conversation between Alsop and Johnson is reproduced below.

5) MEDIA - Liberal Democratic news outlets like Washington Post, New York Times, MSNBC, and CNN unleashed a deluge of Anti-Trump information, which has now been debunked as false information, for almost three years. Steele Dossier. Alfa Bank
 MEDIA - Major news outlets failed to report any information concerning the JFK Assassination other than the "Oswald Lone Nut.

Major reporters George Wil and Walter Cronkite

WELCOME SKEPTICISM

I'm no expert on the JFK assassination, but it seems to me that Oliver Stone has done us all a valuable service and does not deserve the pillorying he has received in the media. What George Will {"'JFK': Paranoid History," op-ed, Dec. 26} and other critics fail to appreciate is that Stone has reminded us of what our Founding Fathers knew 200 years ago when they set out a Bill of Rights: that we should be vigilant in seeing that government does not become too powerful. A sure way for the government to gain such power is if its citizens do not question its actions and pronouncements.

Why, then, has Stone been so roundly criticized for challenging the "official" version of the Kennedy assassination? The truth of Stone's version of history is not the issue. Rather, Stone's point is that we should not take at face value the official assertions that Lee Harvey Oswald acted as a crazed lone gunman in assassinating President Kennedy. I believe that Stone would agree that his version of history should not be swallowed as incontrovertible fact as well.

Stone's contribution is in reminding us that complacency is a threat to democracy just as much as, if not more than, we thought communism was. The Pentagon Papers, the Gulf of Tonkin Resolution, Watergate, and Iran-contra should be proof enough that we need no reminder. But apparently, our blind acceptance of the invasion of Grenada and lack of outrage at Pentagon censorship throughout the gulf war indicate that we have not fully learned our lesson. The stone should be applauded for continuing what has been, and should continue to be, one of our wisest traditions: raising a healthy dose of skepticism at the words and deeds of our government.

-- Roger Kosson

With his vitriolic diatribe against Oliver Stone, George Will joins the avalanche of Stone-bashing that seems all the rage and all out of proportion to the release of what is, after all, just a movie. Like others, Will seems to deliberately ignore the fact that Garrison's and Stone's theory about a conspiracy to kill Kennedy is just that -- a theory. It is a theory that attempts to explain some of the more troubling aspects of the assassination that point to at least some element of participation by some person or persons working within the government.

But just as Clay Shaw's not-guilty verdict neither proved his innocence nor validated the Warren Commission Report, the various "flaws" in Stone's movie similarly do not somehow eliminate the hundreds of as yet unexplained pieces of evidence and testimony that contradict the lone-assassin theory. One does not have to agree with Stone's conclusion to believe that a conspiracy existed. Moreover, even if Stone's theory is wrong, that does not make the movie, as Will put it, "an act of execrable history and contemptible citizenship."

It is ironic that the movie "JFK," which Stone has never claimed to be the conclusive answer to this mystery, is being subjected to much more nitpicking scrutiny by the mainstream press than the Warren Commission Report ever has been. I would have more confidence in Will's and others' objectivity if, along with their criticism of Stone, they also supported the opening of evidence sealed by the Warren Commission and House Select Committee on Assassinations. Or would asking for that evidence also be an act of "contemptible citizenship?"

-- Donald Squires

As a 24-year-old second-year law student at Catholic University, I have just recently entertained the notion that John F. Kennedy was assassinated through a conspiracy perpetrated by the CIA or other government officials. I and friends of my age owe much gratitude to Oliver Stone for his eye-opening motion picture, "JFK". After seeing the movie, I was not content to limit my exposure to the subject, so I read some of the leading literature on the matter.

Recently your paper has published columns concerning "JFK" by David Belin and Gerald Ford, George Will, Stephen S. Rosenfeld, and Stone himself. Stone's movie is attacked on the basis that it is unpatriotic, fallacious, and stirs up unwarranted and harmful sentiment against the government for something that occurred 28 years ago and should be left alone. As someone who was born after Nov. 22, 1963, I find the attacks on "JFK" exhibit the obvious biases and protection of vested interests in Washington circles and the value of truth in the democratic process.

The days are over when Walter Cronkite can tell the nation that it is in its best interest to believe the "official" version of a national disaster because it will promote national security. Watergate and Iran-contra have dispelled any myths about the credibility of the CIA or other government actors.

The answer to who shot John F. Kennedy is important because our government should be held accountable for its actions. But more importantly, the answer carries much value in framing the mood and manner in which the American people will scrutinize future actions by their government. As someone of the post-Kennedy generation with no illusions about government excesses, I believe I speak for most when I say that an objective analysis of the weight of the evidence on both sides clearly shows that "JFK" is an accurate representation of history.

GEORGE WILL-

In a small section of his most recent column, *Washington Post* conservative columnist George Will demonstrates the deference to authority that has come to characterize the mainstream media with respect to the JFK assassination. Will writes:

For many years, some people insisted that a vast conspiracy, not a lone gunman, masterminded the 1963 assassination of President John F. Kennedy near the grassy knoll in Dallas's Dealey Plaza. To these people, the complete absence of evidence proved the conspiracy's sophistication. They were demented.

Now, it stands to reason that mainstream journalists at the time of the Kennedy assassination would make that type of statement. That was a time when almost everyone placed undaunted faith in the U.S. national-security establishment and any official narrative it issued. This was especially true for conservative columnists, almost all of whom bought into the extreme anti-communist animus that was used to justify the Cold War and the conversion of the U.S. government to a national-security state. Of course, there was also Operation Mockingbird to consider. That was the CIA's successful secret operation to acquire assets within the U.S. mainstream press who could be relied upon to publish articles reflecting the views and narratives of the national-security establishment. Thus, when a mainstream journalist in 1963 or even 1964, immediately after the issuance of the Warren Report, made a statement similar to that made by Will, it was somewhat understandable. At that time, while there were people who suspected that something was amiss in the assassination, most of the evidence pointing to a U.S. national-security regime-change operation was hidden from view because of the shroud of national-security secrecy that was immediately placed over the assassination.

But that was 1963. Today things are entirely different. Over the decades, the national-security state secrecy surrounding the assassination has been pierced, which has brought forth a large body of incriminating evidence pointing to a joint Pentagon-CIA operation to protect "national security" from a president whose policies, they believed, were leading to a communist victory in the Cold War and, ultimately, a communist takeover of the United States.

This is what mainstream journalists like Will just don't get. Owing to a large amount of evidence that has surfaced pointing toward a domestic regime-change operation, it is no longer sufficient for a mainstream journalist to mouth the standard mantras about the Kennedy assassination that were being mouthed in 1963 or to simply label people who challenge the official lone-nut narrative in the Kennedy assassination "conspiracy theorists." Now, it is incumbent on mainstream journalists who wish to maintain the official narrative to confront and deal with the actual evidence that has surfaced since then, especially after the JFK Records Act in 1993, which was enacted in the wake of Oliver Stone's movie *JFK*. That law forced the Pentagon, the CIA, and other federal agencies to disclose many, but certainly not all, of their long-secret records relating to the assassination,

Let me give you an example. In the late 1960s, New Orleans District Attorney Jim Garrison brought a criminal prosecution against a man named Clay Shaw. In the trial, Garrison alleged that the JFK assassination was a highly sophisticated domestic regime-change operation carried out by the Pentagon and the CIA, no different in principle from those carried out both before and after the Kennedy assassination, most of which were supported and are still supported by conservatives — e.g., Iran 1953, Guatemala 1954, Congo 1961, Cuba 1960s, Chile 1973.

The mainstream press criticized and derided Garrison. Their mindset was one of complete deference to the authority of the national-security establishment and its official theory that a lone nut with no apparent motive had killed the president.

In the process, the mainstream press failed to note some extremely important aspects of the Shaw trial, especially those relating to the testimony of one of the military pathologists who had helped carry out the official autopsy on President Kennedy's body Lt. Col. Pierre Finck.

Finck testified that he received a call at 8 p.m. on the night of the assassination from one of the other two pathologists for the autopsy, Commander James Humes, asking Finck to come over and help with the autopsy. In that 8 p.m. telephone call, Humes told Finck that they already had x-rays of the president's head.

A big problem arises though: The president's body was being carried into the Bethesda morgue at precisely 8 p.m. by a military color guard.

Do you see the problem? How could Humes already have x-rays of the president's head if the president's body had not yet been brought into the morgue?

To my knowledge, that testimony didn't bother any mainstream journalist at the time. They were all so deferential to the national-security establishment that that problem didn't seem to get their attention. But wouldn't you think that any self-respecting investigative journalist would say, "I need to get to the bottom of this"?

How about you, George? How do you explain this problem? I would love to hear your explanation.

Another interesting aspect of Finck's testimony was when he was asked by the prosecutor why the pathologists had failed to "dissect" Kennedy's neck wound, which would ordinarily have been standard autopsy procedure. At first, Finck repeatedly refused to answerr the question. When the judge finally required Finck to answer, he said that he had been ordered by someone in authority to refrain from doing so. Finck then maintained that he couldn't remember the identity of the person in authority who issued that order to him.

Now, wouldn't you think that any self-respecting investigative journalist would say, "I need to get to the bottom of this"? After all, the three autopsy pathologists were supposed to be in charge of the autopsy. Finck's testimony established that there was obviously a secret super-force that had ultimate control over the autopsy and the autopsy physicians.

How about you, George? Aren't you at least a bit curious as to who composed that force and how, when, where, and why it came into existence?

After the House Select Committee on Assassinations hearings in the 1970s, a group of enlisted men who were released from vows of secrecy that the military had forced them to sign immediately after the autopsy began telling a remarkable story. They said that they had secretly carried the president's body into the Bethesda morgue in a cheap, military-style shipping casket rather than the expensive, ornate casket into which the president's body had been placed in Dallas; they maintained that they secretly brought the body into the morgue at 6:35 p.m., almost 1 1/2 hours before the official entry time of 8 p.m.

What's up with that? How about it, George? You can't say that witness statements don't constitute evidence, can you? What's your explanation for this phenomenon? I would love to hear it.

In the 1990s, the Assassination Records Review Board secured a written report from a Marine sergeant named Roger Boyajian, which was prepared soon after the November 22, 1963, weekend. In the report, Boyajian stated that his team did, in fact, carry the president's body into the morgue at 6:35 p.m.

How about it, George? You can't really maintain that Boyajian's statement and his written report don't constitute evidence, can you? How do you deal with that? What's your explanation for it? I would love to hear what you have to say about it.

The ARRB also secured the testimony of Saundra Spencer, who worked in the military's photography lab in Washington, D.C. She told the ARRB a remarkable story. She said that on the weekend of the assassination, she was asked to develop the official autopsy photographs of Kennedy's body on a top-secret basis. She had kept her secret for some 30 years. When shown the official photographs of the autopsy in the records today, she said that those weren't the photographs she developed. The ones she developed showed a massive-sized exit wound in the back of Kennedy's head, which would imply a shot having been fired from the front. The official autopsy photographs show the back of the president's head to be intact.

How about it, George? How about giving us your take on Spencer's testimony? You can't really say that sworn testimony doesn't constitute evidence, can you? I would love to hear your explanation for Spencer's sworn testimony.

Spencer's testimony, of course, matched the statements of the Dallas treating physicians immediately after the assassination, in which they described a massive exit-sized wound in the back of Kennedy's head.

How about it, George? How do you deal with the steadfast statements from Dr. Robert McClelland, Dr. Charles Crenshaw, and the other treating physicians describing the big exit-sized wound in the back of the president's head, which matched up with what Saundra Spencer testified to 30 years later?

The ARRB also discovered that there were two separate examinations of President Kennedy's brain. At the first examination, the brain was "sectioned" or cut up like a loaf of bread, which is standard procedure in gunshot wounds to the head. At the second brain exam, the brain was damaged but intact — i.e., not sectioned. There is no way that a sectioned brain can reconstitute itself, which means that the brain at the second exam could not possibly have been Kennedy's, How about it, George? How do you deal with that one? I would love to know.

Dr. David Mantik, a radiation oncologist in Rancho Mirage, California, has spent nine complete days closely examining the x-rays in the JFK autopsy. He has concluded that they are fraudulent. How about it, George? How do you deal with Mantik's detailed analysis? You can read it here. I would love to know.

Why is all this autopsy evidence important? Because there is no way to come up with an innocent explanation for a fraudulent autopsy. But George, if you can do so, please let us know what that explanation is. I don't think you can. Certainly, no one else has. And one thing is for sure: It was the national-security establishment that was solely responsible for carrying out the fraudulent autopsy on President Kennedy's body just a few hours after the assassination.

In fact, George, maybe you wouldn't mind providing your theory as to why the military, rather than the civilian authorities in Dallas, were even charged with carrying out the autopsy on President Kennedy's body. After all, while conservatives love the national-security state form of governmental structure, the United States isn't a military nation, like the Soviet Union was, or at le

The Role of the Media

Documents made public many years later reveal the extent to which senior figures in the print and broadcast media were involved in shaping the official response to the assassination. One such figure was the syndicated newspaper columnist, Joe Alsop. A telephone conversation between Alsop and Johnson is reproduced below.

SIMILARITIES
DIFFERENCES
RESULT
Communication advances-
Computers, Cellphones,
E-Mails, Texts
Twitter, Facebook
Retention of documents
Intense partisan re trump none e JFK